FREEDOM NOT YET

NEW SLANT:

RELIGION, POLITICS,

AND ONTOLOGY

A series edited by

Creston Davis,

Philip Goodchild,

and Kenneth Surin

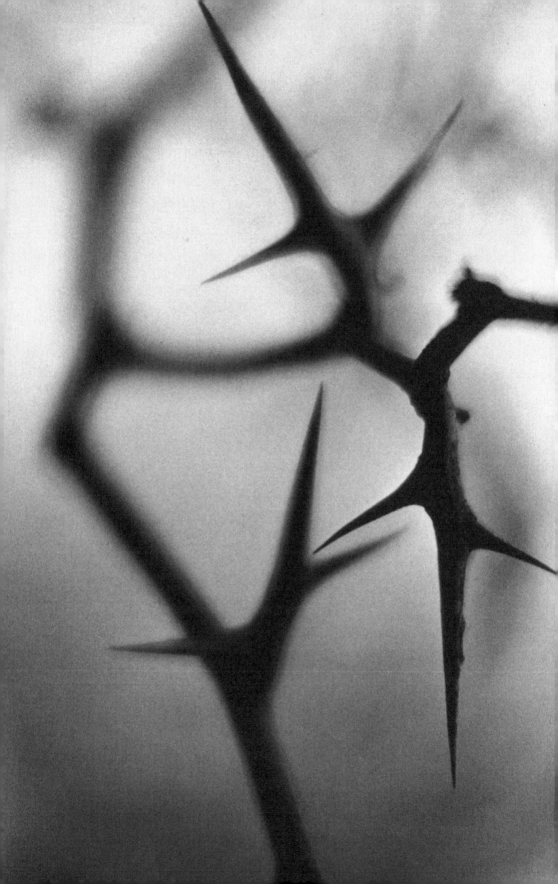

Kenneth Surin

FREEDOM NOT YET

Liberation and the Next World Order

DUKE UNIVERSITY PRESS

Durham and London

2009

© 2009 Duke University Press
All rights reserved
Printed in the United States
of America on acid-free paper ∞
Designed by Amy Ruth Buchanan
Typeset in Carter + Cone Galliard
by Tseng Information Systems, Inc.
Library of Congress Cataloging-in-
Publication data and republication
acknowledgments appear on the last
printed page of this book.

Frontispiece: James Baker Hall, *Thorns*.
Courtesy of the James Baker Hall Archive.

For Andrew Maclehose

CONTENTS

Acknowledgments

I am grateful to Janell Watson for much help given in countless ways while this book was written. Reynolds Smith, my editor at Duke University Press, was exemplary. Andrew Maclehose was my first teacher in economics and philosophy. He will not agree with many of my arguments, but my debt to him has been immense.

Dem an' dem economical plan
Still can't find solution
Borrowin' money fe lend
World Bank a nuh wi fr'en

Is life an' debt all wi a fret
Life an' debt freedom not yet

    MUTABARUKA, *Life and Debt*

We shed blood all these years in order to buy
land at market prices?

    USULUTÁN *campesino*, 1992,
    quoted in Elisabeth Jane Wood, *Forging*
    Democracy from Below

Men of good fortune often cause empires to fall.

    LOU REED, *Berlin*

Selbst in dem sagenhaften Atlantis
Brüllten doch in der Nacht, wo das Meer es verschlang,
Die Ersaufenden nach ihren Sklaven

(Even in fabled Atlantis
The night the ocean engulfed it
The drowning still screamed for their slaves)

    BERTOLT BRECHT, "Questions from a
    Worker Who Reads"

Introduction

Periodizations (not to be confused with chronologies, which merely indicate the dates of events), no matter how rough and ready, are indispensable for any understanding, at the systemic level, of the emergence and consolidation of political systems and institutions and their underlying structures of economic production and accumulation. Where periodization is concerned, the argument of this book is framed by two emblematic or symbolic dates, 1989 and 2001. At the time of writing it is possible that 2008 may be added to these symbolic dates at some future time, given the fact that there is a growing body of economically informed opinion coalescing around the view that the bank liquidity crisis which started in 2008 represents the most critical moment for modern capitalism since the great crash of 1929. It is, however, much too early to fasten ourselves to this judgment; suffice to say that the argument of this book, which has been in the process of formulation since the mid-1990s, is that the current financial crisis, like its predecessor economic crises, is broadly explicable in terms of a marxist (or neo-marxist) model of the inherently problematic structure of capitalist development. That is to say, the financial crisis which emerged in 2008 is the product of deep and postponed tensions and impasses in the capitalist system of accumulation, pressures, and deadlocks which are constitutive of the system itself, so that their removal will require a supersession of the system itself.[1]

1989

The year 1989, invariably associated with the fall of Soviet-style communism, coincides in the minds of many with the apogee of the political project associated with Ronald Reagan and Margaret Thatcher. This political project was trumpeted by its proponents as an American or British "renaissance" in the world order of that time. It was "morning again in America," said the ever-smiling Reagan (probably mindful of the need to create as much "media separation" between the now-famous images of his beaming optimism on America's behalf and the vote-losing sepulchral earnestness of his predecessor, Jimmy Carter). Thatcher in turn repeatedly invoked the reputed Victorian zenith of Britain's imperial supremacy in her pronouncements about her government's policies: "We must return to Victorian values," she brayed on such occasions. The Reagan-Thatcher project was of course premised on a staunch anti-Sovietism in particular, and a repudiation of any kind of "left" collective politics in general.

The Reagan-Thatcher project was in turn a response to the growing economic sclerosis which led to the downfall of the so-called Golden Age of postwar capitalist development, an era of relative overall prosperity which extended from 1945 to 1975 and which involved a protracted boom in mass production and mass consumption, to which the French gave the felicitous term *les trentes glorieuses*.[2] The economic complement of the political dimensions of the Reagan-Thatcher venture was neoliberalism, that is, the "free market" ideology which viewed the 1970s collapse of the long postwar economic expansion as the outcome of allegedly systemic, as opposed to inadvertent or merely contingent, impediments to the operation of markets and market forces. This neoliberal contention was in turn buttressed by declarations about so-called labor market rigidities (invariably attributed by Reagan and Thatcher to the "excessive" bargaining power of labor unions), "crippling" government regulation and intervention, "exorbitant" tax burdens placed by "big government" on heroic but somehow still hapless "entrepreneurs" (apparently some things never change; this, after all, was the overwhelming refrain of John McCain's 2008 presidential campaign, with its mindless and repeated salutations at campaign rallies of the tax-phobic "Joe the plumber"), as well as the allegedly paralyzing effects of a costly welfare system said to be laden with "disincentives" for the working force (one recalls here the moral panic generated by Reagan and his handlers around the fantasy figure of the "welfare queen," typically depicted as a black single mother who drove a Cadillac to pick up her welfare check).[3]

The 1970s economic disintegration associated with the demise of the Golden Age was therefore to be addressed by a simple policy prescription, according to the soon to be ascendant neoliberals: to make things better, said the followers of Reagan and Thatcher, governments should remove or ameliorate all these restrictive policies and their pointless rigidities in order to give markets and market forces a much freer hand. Governments, especially, had no business trying to control markets. *Deregulation* and *privatization* were thus adopted as key guiding principles, and monetarism and attention to the supply side became the favored governmental financial policy tools; this was the essence of the Reagan-Thatcher ideology (though as Jacques Mazier, Maurice Baslé, and Jean-François Vidal point out, the Organization for Economic Cooperation and Development [OECD] did temper this neoliberal approach with some elements of Keynesianism in its policy frameworks, and Reagan's overstuffed defense budgets, and his administration's willingness to run massive budget deficits, did amount to a kind of "military Keynesianism").[4]

This contrived evacuation of the political sphere in the somewhat disingenuous name of "small government" (Thatcher, after all, greatly augmented centralized government in Britain by virtually dissolving all of its subnational municipal structures, and George W. Bush dangerously, and some say unconstitutionally, advanced the prerogatives of the executive branch of government after September 11), along with the cod wisdom that "everything should be left to the market because the market knows best," helped create a political void, especially now that the collapse of the Eastern bloc has left the United States and its close allies in an uncontested globally hegemonic position.

With the gutting of the substantive political formations and their associated practices and strategies put in place by the regulated capitalism of the Euro-American postwar era, politics in the post-1970s West was increasingly degraded into the mere management of voter opinion, involving primarily the mass media–focused orchestration of "hot button" issues capable of mobilizing largely docile electorates. (Examples of such issues come easily to mind: the anxieties of American "security moms" after September 11; gay marriage and gun rights in the United States; the antisocial behavior of unruly inner-city youth, called "lager louts" and "racaille" [scum] by Tony Blair and Nicolas Sarkozy, respectively; campaigns to repatriate undocumented immigrants and radical Islamic clerics in London allegedly hell-bent on replacing British law with *sharia*; the frowned-upon but titillatingly publicized sexual practices of polygamist sects in the American West; and so on.)

In the course of such events, the traditional dividing lines between "left" and "right" came to be blurred or erased, as politics in the West became more and more a matter of occupying a palpably mythical "center," this being the presumed location where electoral majorities, no matter how ad hoc, could most easily be put together by the constant trumpeting of such hot-button issues, at least in theory or psephological fantasy.[5]

The nodal point of this by now epochal shift was subsequently located in the political movements associated with Bill Clinton and Tony Blair, whose basic though unstated function was to underwrite and consolidate the transformations brought about by Thatcher and Reagan and their acolytes. Blair's "Third Way" and the American president's "Clintonomics" involved the further "de-social democratization" (the term used by Gerassimos Moschonas) of society as the neoliberalism instituted by their predecessors, far from being tempered, came to be even more fully entrenched by Blair and Clinton.[6] The political void created by today's ubiquitous economic managerialism in the West (hence the mantra "What is good for Wall Street is good for all of us," admittedly not heard so much during the economic meltdown of 2008–9) and the accompanying deracination of civil society, have been compensated for ideologically by a spurious politics of human rights and the taking of the society of the spectacle to levels undreamed of by Guy Debord and his colleagues in the Situationist movement. "Human rights" interventions (of the kind undertaken in the past decade or so in Kosovo, Sierra Leone, East Timor, Liberia, and Darfur) were designed to show that the "new" politics espoused by Blair and Clinton (and it should be emphasized that such human rights interventions were not disavowed by the 2008 American presidential candidates, John McCain and Barack Obama) was premised on what gave the appearance of being a resolute and sincere ethical core. However, the vapidity of such appeals to human rights was quickly revealed by the West's failure to do anything during the terrible Rwandan genocide, its silence in the face of Russian atrocities in Chechnya (Russia, like Israel, said it was merely fighting "Islamic terrorism" in its own land), the well-documented abuses perpetrated by the pro-Western Sri Lankan government against its Tamil minority population, and the unending passivity of Europe and the United States in the face of Israel's brutal dispossession of the Palestinian people.[7]

Meanwhile political spectacles continue to proliferate. One recalls the British Conservative agriculture minister John Selwyn Gummer force-feeding beef burgers to his young daughters in front of television cameras at the peak of Britain's "mad cow" crisis in the 1980s in a piteous attempt to convince viewers that eating British beef at that time was safe, and Blair's artful manipulation of the Princess Diana effect at the time of her death. It is also hard not to notice the incessant pandering to second-rate film actors, elderly rock musicians, sports personalities, "celebrity" journalists, and media performers (hence the obligatory appearances on *Saturday Night Live* and the shows hosted by Oprah Winfrey and Jon Stewart in the United States and by Sir Michael Parkinson and Sir David Frost in the United Kingdom), evinced by Clinton, Blair, Sarkozy, and their followers, as well as the circus performances that now pass for summit meetings (the mandatory group photos of leaders clad in identical batik shirts or some other "native" costume of the host country). Many will recall George W. Bush's grotesquely staged "Mission Accomplished" aircraft-carrier landing, as well as his much publicized cycle ride with Lance Armstrong soon after the latter won the Tour de France for a record seventh time. There is also the seeming need at some stage during an election campaign for nearly every (white) American politician to be televised in a cowboy hat riding a horse or toting a rifle while wearing hunting camouflage.[8] The list can be extended nearly to infinity.

At the same time, the neoliberal economic agenda has been prosecuted with unremitting fervor by its sponsors in the advanced industrialized countries, and despite the back-slapping televised appearances that American and European government ministers make with co-opted celebrities such as Bono and Bob Geldof and the much trumpeted but largely cosmetic "initiatives" on global poverty announced every few years at G8 summits, the income gap between rich and poor countries continues to grow.[9] The neoliberal economic credo (emblematically associated here with 1989), while it has come under increasing criticism in recent years, especially after the spectacular collapses accompanying the 2000 dot-com and the 2008 U.S. credit market bubbles and the regionwide economic failure of the East Asian economies in the late 1990s, nonetheless shows no signs of running out of steam at the ideological level. Nor does it give any indication that those who manage the world economic system will alter its course to take this planet's dispossessed masses significantly into account.

In light of the spectacular economic failures just mentioned, all of which were initially publicized as neoliberal success stories, the advocates of the neoliberal prospectus have had to be much more judiciously understated in their support for it. But the ensuing subterfuges and disguises used by these advocates of neoliberalism do not diminish its underlying hold on the minds of those shaping public policy across the globe. Hence in the 2008 U.S. presidential election campaign, the same old strident advocacy of trickle-down tax cuts was made by the Republican Party candidate, John McCain, and the dogma that "only privatization can save the U.S. social security system" is voiced repeatedly, while the regulator of the United Kingdom's postal service (the Royal Mail) recently issued a call for its partial privatization.[10] It is one thing to discredit neoliberalism as an intellectual project (and this is increasingly being done); it is another to unfix its grip on the minds of decision-making elites in Europe and North America in ways that could bring about an epochal transformation of our current system of production and accumulation.

9/11/2001

While neoliberalism has held sway for over three decades as an economic and political ideology, it has to be acknowledged that the events now placed under the title "9/11/2001" have also had a very considerable impact on developed, developing, and nondeveloped countries alike, mainly because of the way these events have been used to mobilize American public opinion in an avowedly nationalist and exceptionalist direction. The political catechism identified with the American neoconservative movement—to wit, American exceptionalism, the adamant subordination of the rest of the world to America's interests, America's pursuit of unilateral and preemptive war in the name of "the struggle against terror" (as the former "war on terror" is now called in U.S. government circles during these more chastened, post-Iraq occupation, times)—has been given a free rein since the Al Qaeda attacks in New York and Washington.[11]

If neoliberalism is the *economic* regime unashamedly favored by America and its allies, then neoconservatism is the *political* complement strategically linked to this neoliberal popular religion. And if 1989 is the year marking the clear ascendancy of neoliberalism, then 9/11/2001 signifies the apotheosis of power for its neoconservative counterpart.[12]

There is of course no such thing as a "pure" politics existing only by and for itself. Every kind of politics is a politics motivated and driven by some regnant ideological notion of the nature and scope of the political. Hence for most of the seventeenth century the prevailing political framework in Europe was defined by the historic compromise between European aristocracies and a powerfully emergent mercantile bourgeoisie; as a result of this conciliation a politics marked by a deep and defining interest in questions of sovereignty and the rights of the (individual) citizen came to prevail. The political writings of Grotius, Hobbes, Pufendorf, Locke, and Spinoza are concerned overwhelmingly with such questions of individual rights and their connection with sovereignty, questions which could not have been posed by their predecessors in the Middle Ages.[13]

Similarly, in the eighteenth century a vision of politics highlighting the issue of the artificiality or mere conventionality of the political and social could begin to be addressed, now that Grotius, Hobbes, and others had already posed the key question of what came to be known as "constitutionality." Exemplary in this regard are Rousseau, Hume, and Kant, for whom the political is fundamentally a matter of contrivance or arrangement, so that constitutionality itself had an irreducibly factitious character. Perhaps the most radical acknowledgment of the sheer contingency that pervades social and political structures is Hume's statement (which is almost an uncanny prefiguration of later theories of ideology), "As Force is always on the side of the governed [for the many are governed by the few], the governors have nothing to support them but opinion. It is, therefore, on opinion only that government is founded; and this maxim extends to the most despotic and most military governments, as well as the most free and popular."[14]

This Humean appreciation of the artificiality that pervades all political and moral orders extends, with a number of significant differences, to Rousseau and Kant. Germane in this context is Rousseau's principle that civil society is the primary source of the evils that afflict its members, that people are what their government makes them into, and that the realm of the political therefore affords the only means that humans have of remedying these afflictions.[15] While it may seem implausible and even egregious to lump Kant with Hume and Rousseau, the commonality among these thinkers arises from Kant's insistence that all action can ultimately be reduced to the working of the human will and that the unconstrained capacity to exercise one's will (albeit in accordance with the law) is the basis of freedom, culminating in the insight that the ideal polity is one which enables the freedom (or "spontaneity") of one being to be reconciled with the freedom (or "spontaneities") of other beings according to a universal law.[16]

For Hume, Rousseau, and Kant, politics is thus essentially a set of institutional practices designed for the ordering of the human will, the primacy of the unimpeded will (except, where Kant is concerned, when the law is breached) reflecting the complete ascendancy and self-confidence of the bourgeoisie in eighteenth-century Europe. The problem of the political which preoccupied Grotius, Hobbes, Spinoza, and others—their primary goal being to produce a figure of the (early modern) citizen that could be reconciled with the ontology and explanatory schemas of the mechanist physical science of the time, as well as the outer limits of any prevailing Christian orthodoxy—was by the time of Hume, Rousseau, and Kant supplanted by a conception of the political in which the figures of the citizen and civil society could be taken for granted (at least philosophically). It was now possible, in this period of a by now fully anchored mercantile capitalism, to install the image of a "free" and entirely factitious civil society in which citizens could begin to be at home in the laissez-faire *mentalité* of the burgeoning capitalist markets.[17]

By the beginning of the nineteenth century, with the emergence of the main elements of what was to become the fully fledged modern European state system (as opposed to the early modern Westphalian dispensation of 1648), the several strands of Romantic nationalism began to permeate visions of the political. The Romantic repudiation of the legacy of the Enlightenment of the seventeenth and eighteenth centuries was manifested most directly in the linking of the state form to conceptions of ethnicity. Civil society itself was subsumed by the structures of the nation-state, as the notion of sovereignty was yet again transformed: where once sovereignty reposed in the people's assembly based on the active participation of citizens, now the people were disaggregated and only their representatives assembled. The people thus had to be unified by another principle, based this time on the nation-state defined, tribally, on the basis of ethnic and thus ultimately linguistic affiliation.[18] Martin Thom quotes Madame de Staël from her work *Des circonstances actuelles* on this powerful historical shift: according to Madame de Staël, while in bygone epochs liberty "consisted of whatever ensured the citizens the greatest possible share in the exercise of power[,] liberty in modern times consists of whatever guarantees the independence of citizens from governments."[19]

This paradigm of the political underwent a further transformation in the second half of the nineteenth century, when industrial capitalism superseded its mercantilist precursor, making it necessary for the paradigm's ethnically oriented nationalism to find ways of accommodating the industrial working classes of most Western European nations, as well as North America. In this period, electoral franchises were broadened, albeit grudgingly and unevenly (women were excluded even as the franchise was being extended; in most Western industrial nations women were denied the vote until after World War I). The altered paradigm managed to retain its laissez-faire economic orientation, though it was now adjusted for the ethnically bounded nation-state, with its growing population of proletarianized labor.[20]

After World War I the industrial capitalism of the previous period had to contend with the growing need to bring about a compromise between labor and capital, mainly as a consequence of the urgent requirement that the devastating economic consequences of the Great War of 1914–18 be addressed.

And so the first slow steps leading somewhat unevenly to the welfare capitalism of the Golden Age after World War II were taken. This compromise between labor and capital received a further and vital impetus from the Great Depression and World War II, and from these events came the enhanced institutionalization of the social democratic doctrines that occurred in most Western European countries during this period. (The New Deal was viewed as the American correlate of European social democracy, to the extent that it too required American capital to compromise with labor.)

The vision of the political that prevailed in this historical phase (the time from the Great Depression onward) still favored the nation-state as the primary locus of social and economic activity. But this notion was augmented by the principle that the individual political subject was entitled to a wide range of social rights: universal health care and education; subsidized housing, child care, and public transportation; employment and wage protections; state provision for old-age pensions; and a relatively capacious overall social safety net. The compromise between capital and labor notwithstanding, there still existed an effective dividing line between left and right; while in Europe during World War II the parties of the right tended to be Christian Democrat and mildly nationalist, their rival Social Democratic parties often had electorally viable communist parties to their left, which meant that redistributionist economic programs, no matter how cautious and mild, always had a viable political constituency. Hence the situation obtaining in Britain today, where the "new" Labour of Tony Blair and Gordon Brown is aligned with the Conservative Party as the two contending parties of the identifiable center-right, leaving the more or less centrist Liberal Democrats and the Welsh and Scottish nationalist parties to be the *more* radical parliamentary bloc, would have been simply unthinkable during the postwar Golden Age.[21]

As I mentioned earlier, this substantive political demarcation between left and right started to disappear when neoliberalism became hegemonic from the 1970s onward, and this loss became pervasive after the collapse of "actually existing communism" in 1989. A market zealotry which views politics solely in terms of positioning conformist citizens in front of the market, and which insists that economic equality can be presented to "realistic" voters only as an abstract "equality of opportunity" (as opposed to requiring even a minimal degree of actual income redistribution)—these convictions being this market fundamentalism's main propellant—had dovetailed with the wholesale incorporation of electoral politics into the society of the spectacle from the 1980s onward.

In the process, politics in Western Europe and North America has been put in the service of a sometimes bullying, sometimes cajoling populism (which is what the hugely revamped post-9/11 American nationalism really amounts to in domestic terms) that has effectively eviscerated the political by turning it into the mere business of manipulating and dragooning voters according to the largely fictitious rhythms of election cycles. In this "postpolitical" politics (not to be conflated with the "apolitical" annihilation of anything to do with politics), politicians and their attendant logos and slogans are advertised and marketed to their somewhat bemused and docile constituencies like the hard-to-differentiate fizzy beverages typically found in American and European vending machines. Politicians in America and Britain today have to possess a "brand" in order to succeed; hence in the 2008 U.S. presidential election, the McCain "Maverick" brand apparently flopped with the electorate, while Obama's "Mr. Cool" brand was deemed to have been a success. There is no other way to account for the influence wielded in the name of the prevailing market fundamentalism by such advisers as Karl Rove and Alistair Campbell on George W. Bush and Tony Blair, respectively. Indeed in the 2004 and 2008 U.S. presidential elections the category of the "low-information voter"—who knows almost nothing of a political platform or prospectus, but who can be relied on to be enticed by the media-conveyed "brand" of this or that politician with an appealing "personality," typically reflected in the ability to speak with a syrupy voice (Ronald Reagan), or having an alluring smile (Bill Clinton), or possessing a folksy demeanor (George W. Bush before his catastrophic decline in popularity helped expose this pretense for what it was), being blessed with "good hair" (John Edwards before his fall from grace), the ability to drop at will an upper-class accent for the more déclassé "Mockney" (Tony Blair), or having the ability to wink suggestively at an audience (Sarah Palin)—became crucial for the pollsters, focus groups, and public relations consultants of the major political parties.[22]

Hand in hand with this marketization of the liberal-democratic political sphere has been the full-scale conversion of political parties into post-ideological vote-harvesting machines run by professional cadres primarily attuned to the desires of corporate interests. Ross McKibbin describes this development thus:

> The typical politician today, whether minister, shadow minister or "adviser," proceeds from student politics (often with a politics degree), to political consultancy or a think-tank, to "research" or the staff of an active politician. He or she is "good at politics"—which means being good at

the mechanics of politics, not necessarily its ideas. The consequence is that the mechanics drives out the ideas, and the immediate expels the long-term. Politics is what the *Daily Mail* [a right-wing British tabloid] says today; the long-term is what the *Daily Mail* might say tomorrow. The crucial relationship now is between the politician, the journalist and the "adviser."[23]

Looking at this from another angle, it could be said that modern politics (that is, the politics of the West since 1776 or 1789), until the past couple of decades at least, has always been about the struggle to position or reposition sovereignty in some institutional formation or strategic mode of political agency (or both, more often than not). However, in today's "low-intensity democracy" sovereignty reposes mostly, if not entirely, in the market, and given the centrality of the self-serving internal apparatuses of the present-day political party (which, by being almost exclusively media-focused and driven by the systemically induced compulsion to garner votes for the sake of being at the top of the electoral count no matter what, ends up operating to the detriment of an adequately functioning public sphere), the "democratic citizen" of today has been left to dangle in the resultant void.[24] As McKibbin puts it, "The political élite is now probably more divorced from society, and from any wider organising principles or ideology, than at any other time in the last 150 years."[25]

What is desperately needed today, therefore, is a new sociopolitical settlement, at once practical and theoretical, that will reclaim the political for the project of a democracy that will always place the interests of the dispossessed at its heart. Given the present tarnished state of the political (to wit, the "media-theatricalized" politics referred to by Jacques Derrida) in Western Europe and the United States, this democratic project can advance itself only as a project of liberation, a liberation from the dispossession that is the fate of the overwhelming majority of children, women, and men on this planet. This book asks what, if anything, marxism has to say about this putative project of liberation.

The bank credit crisis of 2008 and 2009 has provided a massive impetus to commentary, some of it bordering on the imbecilic, even though the likely trajectories of this crisis have yet to reach a point of clear discernment. The aim of this book is not to deliver prognostications on events such as this, momentous though they may be, but to analyze the economic structure which provides enabling conditions for such economic crises as the Third World debt crisis of the 1980s (from which some developing economies have never truly recovered), the Mexican peso crisis of 1994, the Asian financial collapse in 1997, the dot-com failure in 2001, and now the credit market upheavals. As long as this capitalist structure continues to exist, it is likely that such crises will be chronically recurrent. My argument focuses on this capitalist structure, and while I advert to some of these crises for what they reveal about this underlying economic configuration, I proceed on the premise that the occurrence of an economic crisis is always contingent on the possibilities and capacities inherent in this structure. An analytic primacy thus has to be accorded to this structure, as opposed to the descriptions (however accurate and helpful they may be) of this or that specific crisis.

Marxism Today

For marxism it is a commonplace, enjoined by the mutual permeation of theory and practice, that things occur in specific and determinate ways, and possibilities in some situations are unavoidably conjoined with their absence in other circumstances, so that material limits invariably coexist with openings and opportunities. It is a truism also that liberation in the face of a massive dispossession must involve change. Marxism is first and foremost a theory and a practice of historical and political change, involving the following levels:

— A description and analysis of the cycles of capitalist accumulation and consumption
— A political theory and practice of liberation premised above all on the supersession of capitalist relations of production, it being understood that the space of the political is opened up by capitalist relations of production
— A reading of the history of philosophy, since philosophy is the science of the categories of the virtual, the possible, and the real, these categories being integral to any depiction and analysis of social being
— An analysis of sociocultural formations and subjects, since society and culture are the context in which such subjects act

Each of these levels develops in different and specific ways. However, the insight that breaks and continuities at one level are usually reflected at other levels is central to marxism. So, all else being equal, the existence or absence of an opportunity to engage in a quest for social and political liberation is likely to be accompanied by the existence or absence of a parallel crisis of production and accumulation at the economic level, and vice versa.

Any historical and political crisis is thus just as likely to be a crisis of categories, and the current crisis (the one that has existed since the demise of the Golden Age of postwar capitalist expansion in the 1970s) is also a crisis of the category of social class and the accompanying notion of a sociopolitical struggle. The material failure of a previous kind of institutional politics, something palpably evident after 1989 (our emblematic date), is reflected in the failure or problematization of these key categories, in particular the category of class struggle and its attendant political aspirations. With the collapse of a politics enjoining a substantive separation between right and left and the emergence of a "postpolitical" politics based on media-oriented populist spectacles, the categories of social class and class struggle, of militancy in the broadest sense, were jeopardized or pushed to one side, as politics and postpolitics—in late capitalism this is a politics that is one and the same time populist *and* authoritarian—have become more and more a matter of getting the right media-friendly façade for the hypocritical and gleaming-eyed professional politician.[26]

Innovation and change at the level of the political is therefore absolutely crucial, and so has an undoubted ontological primacy for marxism. But just as important for marxism is the innovation or renovation of its categories, especially those that bear on the notion of liberation. If this is a time when real political innovation has become more unexpected than ever, then this is also likely to be a time that is ripe for unexpected innovation at the level of (marxist) theory and philosophy. This book addresses the question of this categoreal innovation.

This book has three main sections. The first deals with the current regime of accumulation, where I argue that financialization on a largely global scale is now the chief instrument of subordination and dependency on the part of the poorer nations, and that our conceptions of a globalized political economy must be modified to take account of this momentous shift toward a highly mobile financial capital. Those, me included, who started to make this argument in the 1990s, and who were greeted with some skepticism then, now (at the end of 2008) invariably find ourselves talking to the converted when advancing this claim.

The second section deals with the constitution of subjectivity, since subjectivity is one of the key arenas in which the struggles against dispossession take place. Subjectivity, or the realm of culture more generally, is conceived here as the repository of the forces and drives that enable human beings to be produced and reproduced as social beings. It is a truism that without this production and reproduction of social and subjective being there can be no functioning economic order. The discussion in this section focuses on a number of key theorizations of subjectivity, and the emphasis here is philosophical, as opposed to the focus, inspired by social science, on international political economy in the first section.

The third section takes up the theme of liberation, and its key geopolitical proposition is the notion of an economic delinking on the part of the poorer nations. Where subjectivity is concerned, I argue that the precepts of a tired humanism need to be replaced by alternative conceptions of subjectivity and agency which do not require this jaded humanism as a premise; like liberal democracy, this concomitant humanism has failed in decisive ways to live up to what it promised, at least as a set of options materialized in a viable institutional politics. Is it possible to conceptualize (necessarily and unavoidably in theory but also necessarily for practice) something emancipatory that can potentially move the majority of human beings, disenfranchised and deprived as they are, beyond the reach of these increasingly evident systemic failures?

The following pages deal with the enabling conditions for these economic, political, and social failures. As I have indicated, my argument is avowedly marxist, and my motivating impulse is supplied by the conviction that the governing institutions and forces of our society are owned and managed by powerful elites, planetary in scale, paying lip service (if at all) to the veneer of accountability demanded by today's "thin" democracies. But the longing for something better, or less bad at any rate, cannot suffice by itself when it comes to launching an emancipatory project. Likewise the mere analysis of the fundamental structural impasses of "actually existing capitalism" is also not sufficient on its own. This analysis and the longing for a better world, indispensable though they are, need to be buttressed by a careful sense of where beyond "actually existing capitalism" the myriad forms of a creative and perhaps still to be imagined activism can take us. The failures of "actually existing socialism" associated here with the year 1989 mean that there can be no wholesale return to its previous forms and arrangements. The bureaucratically centralized state is dead, whether in its Soviet or milder corporatist forms. Which is not to say that there is no need for any kind of bureaucratic organization; after all, it is a commonplace that complex societies cannot function satisfactorily without at least a modicum of administrative scaffolding.

What we must aim for and at the same time experiment with, in my view, is something considerably to the political left of the nowadays skin-and-bone and barely living remnants of the previous social-democratic or New Deal consensus (some would say this consensus in fact expired some time ago), while eschewing any longing for the shapes of a Soviet-style state socialism. But simply arguing for this vision will not advance us toward its implementation unless we also scrutinize rigorously the possible ways of realizing this vision, and have as well an adequate grasp of the obstacles likely to stand in the way of any concerted attempt to institute such a project of liberation. Where do we begin to make a start on this undertaking?

There has to be a vigorous democratization of our economic and political institutions; it is imperative that we find ways to create vastly strengthened mechanisms of accountability that cannot be kicked to the side so effortlessly by those with the power and influence gained without too much difficulty in our society by just about anyone with a fat bank balance and bulky investment portfolio. As part of this process of redemocratization it will also be necessary to weaken the hold of the professionalized oligarchies who today run the major European and American political parties (the kind of "no ideology please, only the electoral count matters" oligarchy basically contemptuous of the electorate) and to replace it with a political system with parties once again committed to substantive ideological positions (and thus at least embodying a real difference between right and left), in this way becoming a little more reflective of the ramified and often contradictory wishes of the electorate. The situation prevalent in Britain and the United States today, where the mechanisms of political representation are in the hands of two virtually indistinguishable center-right parties, will therefore have to be rectified quite radically. Any form of democracy heedful of these imperatives would already be much less "thin" than the neutered versions being paraded today.

In addition, the amply documented weakening of the bonds of communal solidarity in the United States and in Western Europe (though let us not become enamored of romantic notions of the "organic communities" of bygone ages) has had as one of its concomitants a perceptible decline in the level of political engagement (the big turnout in the U.S. presidential election of 2008 notwithstanding).[27] The upshot is that a strengthening of these communal bonds is probably a necessary condition for enhancing participation in democratic arrangements potentially more substantive than those currently sanctioned by today's "thin" or "low-intensity" democracies. The reinvention of such forms of collective solidarity (involving what Raymond Williams aptly called "resources for a journey of hope") is thus a crucial task for those invested in the project of liberation. There can be no guarantee that this reinvention will actually take place or succeed in the longer term—there are no teleologically certified outcomes or "iron laws of history" here!—but that something like this reinvention is needed if the lives of the majority of human beings are to be bettered is a proposition that cannot really be gainsaid.

In some cases, these forms of collective solidarity and agency will have to be enacted at the national level (which is not to imply that they cannot also be ratified at a subnational or paranational level). In some countries there is also a vitally important place for a detribalized and popular civic nationalism, which may not be attainable in the immediate future or on a large enough initial scale, but which could nonetheless be indispensable for a project of liberation. (There are important lessons to be learned from the work of Tom Nairn on a civic as opposed to an ethnic nationalism.) This possibility will be discussed later, as will several other proposals concerning this project of liberation, once the conceptual scaffolding for them is set up in the subsequent chapters. The revolution I advert to should not be confused with something similar in the popular consciousness, namely, the stereotyped characterizations of "insurrection" or "rebellion." Insurrections and rebellions will occur as long as there are people who can no longer acquiesce in living conditions they find absolutely intolerable. There will certainly be times when such insurrections will help advance the course of liberation, and some when they will not. Only an abstract dogmatism will insist from the beginning that the lot of the downtrodden will never be improved by *any* recourse to an insurrectional violence. But by "revolution" I mean a fundamental and lasting transformation of the capitalist mode of production and accumulation and its accompanying structures of social relations, and a revolution of this kind may take many generations to bring to fruition (if indeed it were to succeed). Or a revolution may come about in a relatively short time, as was the case with the collapse of the former Eastern bloc in 1989–91. But the likelihood that this revolution will be long, involving as it does the fundamental supersession of the capitalist system, for now seems a less implausible scenario than that of a spectacular and rapid overturning of the present system.

The revolution may also be long because for the foreseeable future its eventual lineaments may be gleaned only indirectly, as opposed to being part of an explicit and quickly implementable political prospectus.[28] The exemplary militant in this situation will thus have to be not only active and engaged, but patient and persistent, and also alert to the possible emergence of hitherto undetectable modes of political and cultural expressivity.

As Raymond Williams put it, "Everything that I understand of the history of the long revolution leads me to the belief that we are still in its early stages."[29] Or maybe, just maybe, the movement toward revolution could be at a somewhat later stage? We have no way of knowing, but what cannot be gainsaid is that those massively disadvantaged by this system have little or no choice but to engage in an economic and social struggle in which the beneficiaries of this system will not surrender their positions of advantage willingly and quickly.

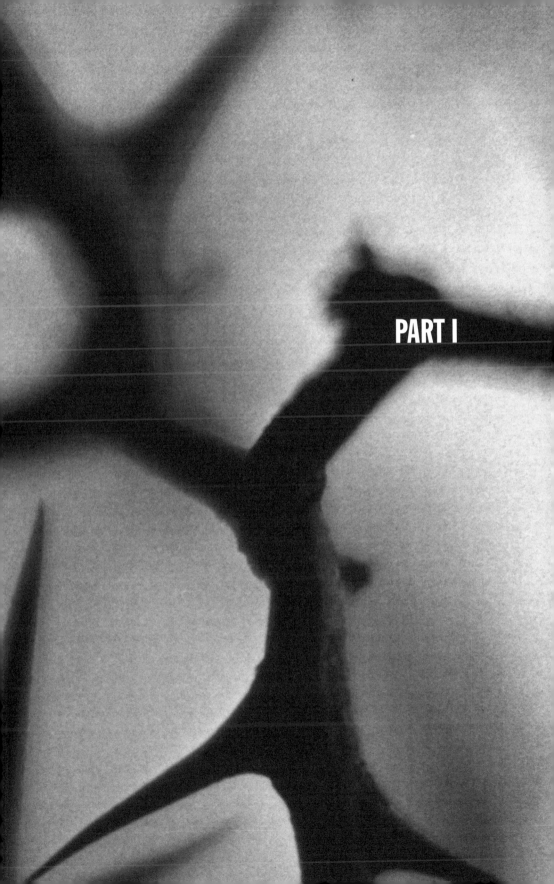

PART I

CHAPTER 1

The Complementary Deaths of the Thinking
Subject and of the Citizen Subject

The concept of the subject is one of philosophy's preeminent *topoi*, and like all philosophical concepts it operates in a field of thought defined by one or more internal variables. These internal variables are conjoined in diverse relationships with such external variables as historical epochs and political and economic processes and events, as well as functions which allow the concept and its associated variables to produce a more or less specific range of truth-effects.[1] The trajectory taken by the concept of the subject in the history of philosophy affords considerable insight into how this concept is produced, and as a result this philosophic-historical trajectory merits examination by anyone interested in this concept's creation.

The Classical Citizen Subject

There is a conventional wisdom in the history of philosophy regarding the more or less intrinsic connection between the metaphysical-epistemological project that seeks an absolute ground for thought or reason (What is it that enables reason to serve its legislative functions?) and the philosophico-political project of finding a ground in reason for the modus operandi of a moral and political subject (On what basis is reason able to legislate for the good life or right action?). According to the lineaments of what is by now a thoroughly well-seasoned narrative, the essential congruence between the rational subject of thought and the complementary subject of morality and politics was first posited by Plato and Aristotle. This unity between the two kinds of subject then found its suitably differentiated way into the thought of Hobbes, Locke, Spinoza, Leibniz, Hume, Kant, and Hegel (and a host of their successors). The core of this narrative is expressed by the somewhat Kantian proposition, characteristic of the Enlightenment in general, that reason provides the vital and indispensable criterion by which all judgments concerning belief, morality, politics, and art are to be appraised, so that reason is the faculty that regulates the thinking being's activity. This activity is in turn the essential means for reason's deployment in any legitimate thinking about the world, that is, for the thinking being's capacity to describe and explain the world in ways that accord fundamentally with reason's precepts. And this precisely because reason is the irreducibly prior and enabling condition of any use of this capacity on the part of the subject.[2] Reason, in other words, constitutes the thinking being, and the activity of this being in turn enables reason to unfold dynamically (to provide a somewhat Hegelian gloss on this initially Kantian proposition). In the topography of this unfolding of reason, both rational thought and politics and ethics are deemed to find their dovetailing foundation.

The philosophical tradition provides another way of delineating this connection between the rational subject of thought and the moral-political subject, one that also derives its focal point from Kant. Using the distinction between a *subjectum* (i.e., the thing that serves as the bearer *of* something, be it consciousness or some other property of the self) and a *subjectus* (i.e., the thing that is subjected *to* something else), the tradition has included among its repertoire of concepts a figure of thought taken from medieval philosophy that hinges on the relation between the subjectum and the subjectus. Etienne Balibar, in his fascinating essay "Citizen Subject," uses this distinction to urge that we not identify Descartes's thinking thing (*res cogitans*) with the transcendental subject of thought that very quickly became an ineliminable feature of Enlightenment epistemology. Nothing could be further from the truth, says Balibar, because the human being is for Descartes the unity of a soul and a body, and this unity, which marks the essence of the human being, cannot be represented in terms of the subjectum (presumably because the subjectum, qua intellectual simple nature, can exist logically without requiring the presupposition of a unity between soul and body).[3] As the unity of a soul and a body, the human individual is not a mere intellectual simple nature, a subjectum, but is, rather, a subject in another, quite different sense. In this very different sense, the human individual is a subject transitively related to an other, a "something else," and for Descartes this "something else" is precisely the divine sovereignty. In other words, for Descartes the human individual is really a subjectus and never the subjectum of modern epistemology, the latter in any case owing its discovery to Locke and not to Descartes. For Balibar, therefore, it is important to remember that Descartes, who is palpably a late scholastic philosopher, was profoundly engaged with a range of issues that had been central for his precursors in the medieval period, in particular the question of the relation of lesser beings to the supreme divine being. This was a question which both Descartes and the medieval philosophers broached, albeit in different ways, under the rubric of the divine sovereignty.

The Cartesian subject is thus a subjectus, one who submits, and this in at least two ways significant for both Descartes and medieval political theology: (1) the subject submits to the Sovereign who is the Lord God, and (2) the subject also yields to the earthly authority of the prince, who is God's representative on earth. As Descartes put it in his letter to Mersenne (15 April 1630), "Do not hesitate I tell you, to avow and proclaim everywhere, that it is God who has established the laws of nature, as a King establishes laws in his Kingdom."[4] From this passage, and from his other writings, it is clear that the notion of sovereignty was at once political *and* theological for Descartes, as it had been for the earlier scholastic philosophers.

This is not the place for a detailed discussion of Balibar's essay, or the magisterial work of Ernst Kantorowicz on this topic; the former, in addition to being a little brief (the section on Descartes is only intended to be an overview), is also not entirely new in what it proposes, since Leibniz, Arnauld, and Malebranche had long ago viewed Descartes, roughly their contemporary, as a follower of Augustine, who found philosophy's raison d'être in the soul's contemplation of its relation to God, and who therefore took the dependence of lesser beings on the divine eminence as philosophy's primary concern.[5]

But if Locke is the true inventor of the modern concept of the self, as Balibar maintains, who then is the real author of the fully fledged concept of the transcendental subject, if Balibar is indeed right to insist that it is not Descartes? The true culprit here, says Balibar, is not Descartes, but Kant, who needed the concept of the transcendental subject to account for the "synthetic unity" that provides the necessary conditions for objective experience. Kant in effect foisted onto Descartes a philosopheme that was really his own "discovery," with Heidegger as his more than willing subsequent accomplice in this dubious undertaking. The outcome of this grievous misattribution has been momentous for our understanding, or lack thereof, of the course taken by this branch of the history of philosophy.[6]

Kant, however, was about more than just the "discovery" of the transcendental subject. The Kantian subject also had to prescribe duties for itself in the name of the categorical imperative, and in so doing carve out a realm of freedom in nature that would enable this subject to free itself from a "self-inflicted tutelage" that arises when we can't make judgments without the supervision of an other; this of course includes the tutelage of the king. The condition for realizing any such ideal on the part of the enlightened subject is the ability to submit to nothing but the rule of reason in making judgments, and so freedom from the power of the despot when making one's judgments necessarily involves a critical repositioning of the place from which sovereignty is exercised. Kant declared that no more is the locus of sovereignty the body of the king, since this "tutelage" is stoppable only if the subject is able to owe its allegiance to a republican polity constituted by the rule of reason and nothing but the rule of reason. Whatever criticism Balibar levels at Kant for the (supposed) historical mistake he made with regard to Descartes, the philosopher from east Prussia nonetheless emerges as a very considerable figure in Balibar's account. For Kant also created the concept of a certain kind of practical subject, one who operates in the realm of freedom, and this practical subject, whose telos is the ultimate abolition of any kind of "self-inflicted tutelage," had to cease to be the "subject" of the king (i.e., the subjectus of Descartes and medieval political theology) in order to become a "self-legislating" rational being.[7]

Kant's great achievement therefore lay in his simultaneous creation of the transcendental subject (i.e., the subjectum of modern epistemology) and the philosophical discrediting of the subjectus of the previous theologico-philosophical and political dispensation. The concomitant of Kant's philosophical gutting of the "subject" who owed his fealty to the king was thus the political emergence of the republican citizen who from 1789 onward (though a good case can be made for including 1776 in this periodization) would supplant the subject/subjectus of the previous historical and philosophical epoch. In the process, Descartes's philosophical world of subjects who submit, albeit "irrationally" from the Kantian standpoint, to the laws of God and king was dislodged by Kant's world of "self-legislating" rational subjects who engage in this legislation precisely by adverting to the rational and non-theological notions of right and duty.

This new subject is the embodiment of right (*Recht*) and of the operation of practical reason (right being for Kant the outcome that can be guaranteed only by the proper use of practical reason). Furthermore the subject is considered a citizen to the extent that he or she embodies the general will, in which case the only laws worthy of the name are those which "come only from the general, united will of the people."[8] Sovereignty is thus glossed by Kant through a recasting of the Rousseauan social contract. Laws are rationally promulgated only when they exemplify the general will, and this exemplification of the general will is possible only if there is a perfectly just civil constitution. As Kant put it in his "Idea of a Universal History with a Cosmopolitan Purpose," "The highest task which nature has set for mankind must therefore be that of establishing a society in which *freedom under external laws* would be combined to the greatest possible extent with irresistible force, in other words, of establishing a perfectly *just civil* constitution."[9] The outcome, as the philosophy textbooks tell us, was a crucial separation of the earthly from the heavenly city, of earthly sovereignty from divine sovereignty. However, if Kant is the true inaugurator of the Citizen Subject, then for Balibar, Michel Foucault is the great theorist of the transition from the world of monarchical and divine sovereignty to the world of rights and duties determined by the state and its apparatuses. Balibar concludes his essay with the following observation: "As to whether this figure [the Citizen Subject,] like a face of sand at the edge of the sea, is about to be effaced with the next great sea change, that is another question. Perhaps it is nothing more than Foucault's own utopia, a necessary support for that utopia's facticity."[10] I would like now to address the Foucauldian question left by Balibar for future consideration and pose the question of the current destination or fate of the Citizen Subject. To do this we have to look again at Kant.

The reason that constitutes the subject is perforce a Transcendental Reason. The obvious Kantian inflection here is not accidental, because the reason that grounds the subject is not a reason that can be specified within the terms of the activity of the subject: this reason is the basis of this subject's very possibility qua subject, and by virtue of that, reason is necessarily exterior to the "activity" of the thinking subject. Reason in this kind of employment is thus the activity of a single and universal quintessence whose object is reason itself, so that reason has necessarily to seek its ground within itself, as Hegel noted.[11] Reason, by virtue of its self-grounding, is perforce the writing of the Absolute.[12] The subject's ground, which has to reside in Reason itself, is therefore entirely and properly metaphysical, and any crisis of Transcendental Reason unavoidably becomes a philosophical crisis of the thinking subject. Kant himself was the first to realize this, though it was left to his philosophical successors in the movement known as "early Romanticism" (*Frühromantik*) to make the acknowledgment of this crisis of Transcendental Reason into a starting point for philosophical reflection.[13]

With Nietzsche, however, the hitherto radical figure of the transcendental subject is propelled into a crisis, and with this ostensibly terminal crisis the fundamental convergence between the rational-epistemological subject and the moral-political subject is denied any plausibility. We know from the textbooks of the history of philosophy that reason, insofar as it operates on both the understanding and the will, is placed by Nietzsche entirely within the ambit of the *Wille zur Macht*, so that power or desire becomes the enabling basis of any epistemological or moral and political subject, thereby irretrievably undermining or dislocating both kinds of subject. The "will to knowledge" for this Nietzschean-Foucauldian school of thought depends on a logically and psychologically antecedent "will to power." As a result of the intervention represented by Nietzsche, truth, goodness, and beauty, that is, the guiding transcendental notions for the constitution of this epistemological and moral-political subject, are henceforth to be regarded merely as the functions and ciphers of this supervening will to power. The same conventional wisdom also assures us that Marx and Freud likewise "undid" the two kinds of subject and thus undermined even further any basis for their essential congruence. The constellation formed by Nietzsche, Marx, and Freud (and their successors) shows both the transcendental subject and the ethicopolitical subject of action to be mere conceptual functions, lacking any substantial being (Kant having already argued in the *Critique of Pure Reason* that the subject of thought is not a substance).

This hackneyed narrative about the collective impact of the great "masters of suspicion" is fine as far it goes; what is far more interesting, however, is the story of what had to come after Nietzsche, Marx, and Freud, of what it is that was going to be done with the ruins of the epistemological and moral and political subject who ostensibly had reigned from Plato to Hegel before being dethroned in the late nineteenth century.[14] It is interesting that Balibar, who is as resolute a marxist as anyone could be in these supposedly post-marxist days, appears not to take on board in "Citizen Subject" Marx's well-known critique of bourgeois democracy, but instead regards Foucault as the thinker who more than any other registered the crisis of this bourgeois Subject. Be that as it may, it is hard to deny that the transcendental subject of modern epistemology suffered calamitously at the hands of Nietzsche (and of Heidegger and Foucault after Nietzsche), and that political and philosophical developments in the twentieth century have cast the Citizen Subject adrift in a rickety lifeboat headed in the direction of the treacherous philosophical reefs mapped by Foucault.

But can the course of this stricken lifeboat be altered, and the functions and modes of expression typically associated with the Citizen Subject be reconstituted in some more productive way, so that this Subject, or its successor (but who would that putative successor be?), would be able to meet the political and philosophical demands generated by the presently emerging conjuncture? Here one senses a certain ambivalence at the end of Balibar's essay, a wish that Foucault was perhaps not going to be right when it came to a final reckoning of the fate of the Citizen Subject, and that new and better times would somehow come to await a radically transformed Citizen Subject. But what could be the shape and character of this new life for the Citizen Subject?

Balibar has an emphatic proposal: the Citizen Subject will live only by becoming a revolutionary actor. I want to take Balibar's proposal as the starting point for the discussion that will occupy the rest of this chapter. There is also the question of the theoretical "space" that was once occupied by the transcendental subject of epistemology. While we may not quarrel with Balibar's suggestion that the (modern) Citizen Subject supplanted the (medieval) subjectus who owed its fealty to the sovereign monarch and sovereign deity (this now being something of a philosophical commonplace), it has also to be acknowledged, and Balibar himself is certainly aware of this, that Kant placed under the category of *Right* not merely action, but also knowledge: the Kantian subject is both the Citizen Subject who acts *and* the epistemological subject who reflects in accordance with the principles of Reason. This subject may have been displaced or finally extinguished in the second half of the twentieth century, but the question of the "right use" of Reason remains, or at any rate, the question of the place of a hoped-for right use of Reason still poses itself. We cannot accept that Reason has "died" simply because its previous philosophic embodiments have been subjected to a concerted critique, no matter how devastating that critique may seem to be.

This issue is therefore one that demands to be addressed, as a prolepsis to dealing with the question that is this book's central concern, namely, that of a potentially enduring transformation of collective political practice, one capable of supporting a project of liberation adequate to the challenges posed by today's structural and conjunctural conditions. These conditions, as we saw in the introduction, are those of a globalizing neoliberalism that has been the dominant regime of accumulation since the end of the postwar boom in the 1970s (even if this economic neoliberalism appears to be on its knees as a result of the 2008 subprime lending crisis) and a neoconservatism that has bolstered the American political hegemony of the period since 1989. An adequate liberation would therefore be one that produced political subjects capable of surmounting the depredations associated with this globalizing neoliberalism and its complementary American neoconservatism.[15]

The Demise of the Classical Citizen Subject

Whatever Foucault may have said about the supersession of the postclassical *epistéme*, and the death of the Man-Citizen that accompanied this supersession (I take Foucault's Man-Citizen to be coextensive with Balibar's Citizen Subject), it is obvious that the subsequent political mutation of classical liberalism into a globalizing neoliberalism, as well as the disappearance of a viable socialism, have both served to form the basis of what is palpably a new conjuncture. This conjuncture, which some (including me) have called the "postpolitical" politics of the time after 1968, represents an added burden to the already harsh philosophical fate meted out to this Citizen Subject or Man-Citizen by the "masters of suspicion" in the late nineteenth century and early twentieth. The culmination of this trajectory in the postpolitical politics of the past few decades (as described in the introduction) seems to reduce the force of the critique embodied in the writings of Nietzsche, Marx, and Freud; the subject's apparent superfluity in this postpolitical dispensation undermines the very need for its critique. With the effacement of the focus (i.e., the Citizen Subject) of this critique, critique also finds itself fading into insignificance. At the same time, the apparent superfluity of the classical Citizen Subject makes more urgent the question of the ontological status of its putative successor, that is, the subject of this postpolitical politics. Is the subject of this postpolitical politics still some kind of vestigially effective subject, a barely breathing remnant of the Man-Citizen of Foucault's modern episteme or Balibar's Citizen Subject of the time after 1776 or 1789? And if this is truly so, there comes the question of what powers, if any, reside in this seemingly obsolescent remnant of the classical Citizen Subject. Have we been left with nothing for the metaphysical constitution of the possibility of politics but the sheer acknowledgment of the power of the body, the power of bare life (as proposed by the thinkers of the "inoperative" community and the community to come), or the appeal to some kind of undeconstructable justice (as proposed by Derrida and his epigoni)? We don't have to spend too much time thinking about such suggestions to recognize that the practices and orders of thought associated with the "societies of control" limned by Deleuze, and those of the domain of the biopolitical identified by Foucault but also developed by Agamben and Hardt and Negri, derive their saliency from this postpolitical conjuncture. The centrality of the problematic of the postpolitical, arising as it does from the effacement of the Citizen Subject, for any putative project of liberation can therefore hardly be gainsaid.

By the 1960s and 1970s it had become clear, or clear enough, that the politics of the past two hundred years was no longer able to manage the complex and uneven movements of force that had been unleashed by the newest regimes of capitalist accumulation. Although many periodizations take 1776 or 1789 to be the emblematic starting point for this politics of the "classical" Citizen Subject (a politics which by the 1970s and 1980s had become more and more clearly perceptible as a "previous politics"), by "classical" politics I mean both a politics based on a centrally planned economy of the party-state (i.e., the system of government that existed in the former Eastern bloc) and one predicated on the market-oriented liberal-democratic state (associated in a complementary way with what is still called "the West"). The citizens of the former Soviet bloc, and of the West adversarially situated in relation to the Soviet Union, were both members of dynamic political dispensations requiring visible and even intransigent distinctions between left and right, in ways that are becoming increasingly difficult to imagine in an epoch marked by such solecisms as "compassionate conservatism," "a socialism compatible with the requirements of the capitalist market," "we're all middle-class today," and so forth. No matter how one assesses this previous politics, with its somewhat rigid ideological demarcations between left and right, it was always, even in countries of the former Soviet bloc, the politics of a particular phase of capitalist development. As indicated, this classical politics lasted from 1776 or 1789 until the first unravelings of its supporting international system in the early 1970s.[16]

It has already been noted that the metaphysical heart of this classical politics was a particular conception of sovereignty and of the political subject ideally subsumed under the benison of this sovereignty through the principle of representation. Only those vested with sovereignty by those who qualify as members of the polity can truly represent those who qualify as members of the polity! Sovereignty is thus vested by a polity which in turn is deemed by the sovereign to be the body politic instituted to confer sovereignty, in an unending loop of mutual affirmation. Such is the defining, and circular (in the practical and not just the logical sense), formula of this model of liberal democracy.

With the new capitalist dispensation that came into being in the 1960s and early 1970s, a dispensation now described and analyzed under several familiar titles ("post-Fordism," "disorganized capitalism," "flexible accumulation," "worldwide integrated capitalism," "late capitalism," "empire after the age of imperial empires," "the domain of the biopolitical," and so forth), such notions of sovereignty were progressively eviscerated or circumvented. The unprecedented transformations in the capitalist order of the past four decades or so were accompanied by a deracination of the classical political subject, that is, the Citizen Subject who up to now had been at once enabled and constrained by the principles of sovereignty embodied in the previous political dispensation. To put it somewhat schematically, if Nietzsche, Marx, Freud, and Foucault undid this classical epistemological and political subject, and in the process undermined its philosophical rationales, then the move to a postpolitical politics associated with the latest stage of capitalist development has had, ostensibly, the effect of doing away with the very need for such a classical Citizen Subject as well as the accompanying philosophical rationales provided on its behalf.[17] The thing rendered equivocal and otiose by Nietzsche, Marx, Freud, and Foucault, but still needed by the politics that lasted from 1776 or 1789 up to the 1970s, had by the 1970s started to become something of a relic.

Today's regime of capitalist accumulation and the neoliberal and neoconservative ideologies identified with its current ascendancy simply have no need for the classical Citizen Subject, just as they have no need for the ideology of modernization that was an intrinsic component of the first or classical liberalism and the various socialisms and communisms which rivaled this liberalism in the period from 1870 until 1989.[18] The disciples of Milton Friedman and Leo Strauss who today control the U.S. government's elite do not give a hoot about substantive notions of an informed and involved citizenry (however mythicized these notions have tended to be in the self-exculpatory or self-congratulatory versions of America's special "destiny"). All that matters for Paul Wolfowitz, Richard Perle, Dick Cheney, Donald Rumsfeld, John McCain, and Sarah Palin (and Margaret Thatcher in the United Kingdom a couple of decades or so before, in her own version of English exceptionalism) is that you and I toe the line set down by those who wield power. One does not have to be Naomi Klein or George Monbiot to acknowledge that, however complex the processes are which led to the emergence of the current phase of capitalist development, it is virtually undeniable, especially in a time which is seeing the beginnings of an economic crisis whose scale is becoming comparable to the great crash of 1929, that corporations and markets have gained hugely in legitimacy and power at the expense of the now deracinated Citizen Subject. At the same time, the accompanying notion (however much pervaded by the several myths that buttress the ideology of liberal democracy) of a sovereignty lodged unconditionally in a state that, as a matter of principled necessity, placed its administrative functions at the disposal of its "people," has also succumbed completely to the dictates of corporations and the dogma of the market.[19]

The historical and social conditions that served to legitimize the liberal democratic state and its activities, as well as the figure of this now bygone Citizen Subject, were severely undermined in the episteme instituted by transnational late capitalism, whose influential proponents in the overdeveloped economies of the North see it as their right to administer everything in the name of capitalist (over)accumulation. Thus, for instance, anyone who is moderately well-informed is likely to know (albeit without necessarily being dismayed by such knowledge) that a coterie of energy company executives, including those of Enron until its demise, effectively policed the Bush administration's energy policy; that Italy's government is in the pocket of one of its richest men (who bought his way into the prime ministership of his country); that Tony Blair's entourage at the Johannesburg Earth Summit included the boss of one of Britain's biggest corporate polluters; that weapons manufacturers, as a result of brazen revolving-door hiring policies, are so completely in league with departments of defense in the advanced industrial countries that this is no longer reckoned a scandal; and so forth.

In the place of the Citizen Subject posited as an ideal by the liberal-democratic political systems of the past two centuries by and large now stands a new kind of ideal subject, to wit, a consumer subject cajoled and tutored in this country by Disney, Fox News, and USA Today. In place of the ideal of the sovereign state whose raison d'être was the representation of its "people" there now exists a state formation that has been transformed over the course of the past few decades into a much more loosely amalgamated bundle of functions and apparatuses (economic, political, ideological, military, and so forth), with some functions and apparatuses demanding very high concentrations of state power for their operation, and others little or none. Hence, to take an example very much in the news as I write, spying on American citizens without recourse to judicial warrants is deemed an absolutely necessary exercise of state power by President George W. Bush and his handlers, while the functions of the Internal Revenue Service and the government-run social security system are considered superfluous enough by some Republican politicians to warrant the wholesale privatization of

America's tax collection and social security systems.[20] The various components of this highly selective ideology of "market choice," "market flexibility and efficiency," and "the free mobility of capital" operate whenever the functions of the state can be abrogated in favor of the private interests that serve ruling elites, but are quickly suspended when they do not happen to advance the interests of these elites. Hence the pathos of the sentiment expressed in a bumper sticker sometimes seen on the vehicles of those likely to be typecast in the United States as "liberals": "It will be a great day when our schools get all the money and the air force has to hold a bake sale to buy a bomber." The cry behind this slogan is plaintive but truthful, insofar as it is true that for many, if not most, Americans it is simply inconceivable that privately organized sales of baked goods by schoolchildren and their parents be used to fund the production of air force bombers designed to create "shock and awe" in refractory Third World countries.[21]

The prevailing system of capitalist production and accumulation, and the state formations associated with it, constitute the external variables for the operation of the deboned political subject of today. Just as important for the argument of this book, the emergence or consolidation, at the level of the subject's activity, of political practices capable of overturning the regnant capitalist order will hinge crucially on the possibility of supplanting, at the systemic or structural level, this globalized system of production and accumulation.

The theoretical armature for a project of liberation capable of creating a postcapitalist society will therefore incorporate a critique of today's world-integrated capitalist system and its underlying conditions. To the extent that marxism (albeit one that is exploratory and not schematic and unilinear in the way that some previous versions were) has shown itself to be the only "theory" genuinely intended to furnish a comprehensive critique of this kind, the project of liberation can usefully employ marxism's distinctive practico-theoretical lexicon when approaching the question of this project's conditions of possibility. It is thus a truism for this undertaking that those who wish to be free first have to produce knowledge of the things that stand in the way of their freedom. This in fact is the acid test for such a project of liberation: Does it furnish such knowledge, or does it sweep it more or less gently to one side? Of course events can and do overtake those who form and steer public opinion. Thus even the most polished spin doctors were hard-pressed to serve up blandishments that could diminish what Hurricane Katrina revealed about the all too visibly racialized social and economic structures of New Orleans (in particular) and the United States (in general). The same state of affairs is also evident in the current financial crisis, when any campaigning American politician, of no matter what persuasion, has to join in the ritual condemnations of the "excesses" on Wall Street, while having done all he or she could to create a political framework that abetted these excesses.

CHAPTER 2

Producing a Marxist Concept of Liberation

The politico-historical and philosophical demise of the "classical" Citizen Subject, the primary features of which were sketched in chapter 1, was accompanied by a momentous modification of state sovereignty. The changes associated with this reconstitution of state sovereignty involved a powerful mutation of the capitalist system, and it will be possible to determine what is entailed by the shift from the Citizen Subject to his or her ostensible successor (i.e., the kind of subject sponsored by today's world-integrated capitalism and its complementary political formations) only by providing the rudiments of a description and analysis of this latest phase of capitalist development. Marxism has so far shown itself to be the only school of thought whose raison d'être is this overall critique of capitalism, and this chapter broaches the question of what precisely is involved in producing a marxist concept of liberation.[1]

The motivation for producing this concept of liberation is supplied by the conviction that liberated political and social subjects will emerge only when capitalism, which has failed comprehensively to improve the economic and social conditions of the majority of humankind, is supplanted, and that the critique of capitalism is therefore essential for any real insight into the conditions that will have to be remediated as a precondition for the emergence of such fully liberated subjects.

In the beginning was struggle. If there is, or has to be, something like a "postulate of reason" for the ensemble of theoretico-practical propositions that is marxism, it is perhaps this one. The struggles of countless women, children, and men for a better world have taken place over the ages in very diverse settings of theory and practice (and this is to state a commonplace!). This diversity is of such amplitude that it cannot be encompassed, theoretically or otherwise, within a single movement, even one as powerful and comprehensive as marxism. Many have engaged in different and not always necessarily congruent ways in such struggles. These struggles have never owed their "relevance" to marxism. Rather, it is marxism, in whatever form, that has owed its "relevance" to them. As long as people struggle for liberation—and this in the end is a collective and collaborative project inseparable from the quest for happiness—it will be possible for marxism to be, or to continue to be, "relevant."

Broaching the question of marxism's fundamental because constituting relation to the project of liberation, and acknowledging that marxism derives its saliency from the latter (and not vice versa), in turn poses the question of marxism's position in regard to the supersession of capitalism, since it is an axiom for all schools of marxism that liberation inextricably involves a countervailing action directed at the capitalist system of production and accumulation. But doesn't capitalism exercise its dominance in many modes and at many levels, not all of which give the appearance of being directed by the forces and agents of capitalism? Can't it plausibly be presumed, moreover, that specifically anticapitalist struggles are not the only ones germane for those seeking radical and permanent changes in their way of life? Attempts to address these questions can proceed on two fronts.

First, there are those who will argue that ascribing an overwhelming normativity of this kind to anticapitalist struggle inevitably de-emphasizes struggles in other contexts not usually associated with the forces and arrangements integral to capitalism, such as struggles for gender and racial equality and campaigns against discrimination based on sexual orientation. Second, there are those who will argue, in a way that seemingly parallels the argument about marxism in the previous paragraph, that mass movements with an emancipatory intent existed long before the emergence of the capitalist system. The implication is that marxism, whose raison d'être is overwhelmingly the critique of capitalist political economy, is not sufficiently encompassing as a result of this singular focus to do real justice to these precapitalist radical alternatives and the movements that were their vehicles.

The argument canvassed in this book does not require a detailed response to these hesitations over marxism's putative scope as a theory of liberation. Suffice it to say that the perspective espoused here on the emergence and development of capitalism departs from more standard marxist or marxisant accounts by proposing that marxism does not have to underwrite what is in essence a developmentalist conception of the growth and consolidation of capitalism.

According to this developmentalist conception, capitalism as a fully fledged mode of production was able to emerge only when it had supplanted its predecessor feudal mode of production, just as the feudal mode of production had in turn to displace a preceding slave-based mode of production in order to attain primacy. It is widely accepted, even in marxist circles, that this developmentalist scheme is unsatisfactory.[2] The position taken in this book eschews the conceptual underpinnings of this developmentalist scheme. Instead, it takes the core of any capitalist system to be constituted by practices and formations involving the employment of formally free labor by the owners of the means of production in order to enable the appropriation of surplus value through the operation of markets. In capitalism, labor and all other factors of production have the form of commodities, though it is of course not necessary for *all* social formations in an actually existing capitalist society to be subsumed under the commodity principle (after all, Trappist monasteries coexist with Goldman Sachs in contemporary America). Moreover, ownership of the means of production need not be confined to private individuals and companies, since owner-operators, consortia, banks, investment trusts, cooperatives, pension and mutual funds, and the state can all exercise the various forms of such ownership, even in a full-blown capitalist system.[3] In addition, formally free labor can exist alongside slavery, vassalage, debt-peonage, and family work in a capitalist system. All that matters in determining whether or not a mode of production is capitalist is for "free" wage labor to be the economy's primary means of realizing surplus value. The capitalist *mode of production* therefore has two components: (1) a production process that organizes the social relations of production and their patterns of interaction with the regnant technological paradigm, and (2) an accumulation regime which uses a range of macroeconomic instruments to promote capitalist production and consumption (figures 1 and 2).

In addition to comprising necessarily a mode of production, capitalism also requires for its proper functioning a system of regulation or domination with two constituent modes. The first is a *social mode of economic regulation*, which superintends the social conditions of possibility for the various processes of production and accumulation that in concert make up the capitalist system. The social mode of economic regulation, as its name implies, governs roles and functions inherent in manufacturing and other production processes, oversees labor practices, and manages the social basis of distribution networks. Hence, and this is just one example, in many European countries

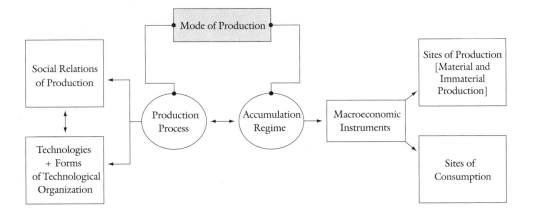

1. The mode of production

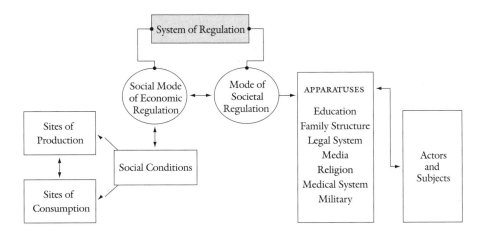

2. The system of regulation

a post office clerk often serves as a bank teller, since in these countries post offices are also commercial banks; this is a situation an American post office clerk does not have to deal with since the U.S. postal system is not a banking system in the way that the post office is in many European countries. The difference in job specification between a European post office clerk and his or her American counterpart is due to two quite different social modes of economic regulation (at least with regard to having the post office function as a bank).

The second element in the capitalist system of regulation is a *mode of societal regulation*, which, while not directly commanding the structures and formations that subtend capitalist production and accumulation (this being the task of the social mode of economic regulation), is nonetheless needed to mobilize an integrated system of apparatuses (education, the legal system, religious institutions, media and communications networks, and so forth) that create the agents and the structures of desire essential for continued capitalist production and consumption. A high school home economics class that teaches students to balance their checkbooks is making its contribution to maintaining this system of production and consumption, though more often than not teaching this skill is likely to be called "enabling students to deal with the real world." These apparatuses are harnessed to create a doxa or common sense in which any serious expectations regarding alternatives to capitalism are discounted from the outset, so that the accumulation of capital seems an entirely normal state of affairs for the overwhelming majority of citizens. In the parlance of the typical American local bar or pool hall habitué, or the effectively mythicized "Joe the plumber" or "Joe Sixpack" of the 2008 U.S. Republican election campaign, "Hey, what's wrong with making a buck (or two)?" or "Why the heck should I have to spread the wealth around?"

The two modes of the capitalist system of regulation therefore encompass a vast array of subsystems of control and regulation that enable this "regularization" of capitalism's modus operandi to take place. This doxa-forming assemblage includes organizations, general social rules and prescriptions, rituals, conventions, social roles, cultural dispositions with their attendant identities, collective outlooks, and modes of calculation, all of which coalesce to "regularize" or "normalize" (and not just to "regulate") the processes associated with capitalist accumulation.[4] The social processes which make possible the creation and distribution of surplus value operate through a class system (about which more will be said later) which is effectual in both the social mode of economic regulation and the mode of societalization.

It is important to note that the mode of regulation in its most basic form incorporates systemic constraints whose modus operandi is situationally defined. The circumscriptions embodied in this modus operandi are always specific to particular times and places, they encompass definable groups of agents, and their operation always involves a specific social strategy or set of social strategies. Especially helpful here is Bob Jessop's distinction between the "structural" and the "conjunctural" moments that are integral to the functioning of any field of social practices and collectively held beliefs. Structural moments are relatively invariant and cannot be changed merely by this or that agent or group of agents embarked on a given strategic course of action in that particular place and time. By contrast, conjunctural moments are those involving courses of action whose strategic basis is modifiable in principle. Jessop's distinction has the merit of acknowledging that what may be a constraint for a particular agent or group of agents can without any real or apparent change represent a "conjunctural opportunity" that can be used more or less productively by other agents. This account also suggests that a systemic constraint for a particular agent or set of agents can with the passage of time become a conjunctural opportunity for that individual or group of individuals should the latter have recourse to a different social strategy. By choosing different social strategies, provided of course that these happen to be available, agents can affect in varying ways and degrees the course and outcomes of the systemic constraints and opportunities inherent in the mode of regulation.[5]

It goes without saying that the structural constraints embodied in the mode of regulation are sometimes overwhelming, and that in such cases the ability of agents to obviate or bypass these strictures is inevitably going to be limited or nonexistent. But the possibility of change in regard to this or that component of the mode of regulation cannot be ruled out from the outset: constraints and opportunities are necessarily context-dependent, and any possibility of a change of social and political context carries with it the likelihood of social and political transformations that are potentially real and lasting.[6]

The overall logic of the mode of societal regulation need not be liberal-democratic, even if this has generally been the case historically where capitalism is concerned. As thinkers as diverse as those of the Ecole Régulation, Resnick and Wolff, and W. G. Runciman have indicated, the capitalist mode of production is also compatible with a quasi-feudal mode of societal regulation (as in latter-day Saudi Arabia and the Gulf Emirates), a communist social mode of economic regulation (as in the "state capitalism" of the former USSR), or even a putatively communist mode of societal regulation combined with a capitalist mode of economic regulation (as in China today).[7]

Hence, for instance, challenges to a quasi-feudal mode of societal regulation that happens to be coupled with a capitalist mode of production could still be salient for anticapitalist struggles even if the motivations of those contesting the quasi-feudal social formation in question in no way involve an animus directed toward capitalism per se. A case in point is the struggle for women's rights in the Gulf Emirates, which is clearly not anticapitalist in regard to its formative tendencies, but which, depending on the context, can nonetheless be encompassed, strategically, in an anticapitalist struggle which makes gender equality one of its primary concerns. A marxist or marxisant conception of liberation will therefore acknowledge that opposition movements which do not directly contest capitalism and its appurtenances are not by virtue of *that* fact necessarily tangential or epiphenomenal to ostensibly "real," because explicitly anticapitalist, struggles. Capitalism, as the nexus of a production process and an accumulation regime (these constituting the mode of production) and a social mode of economic regulation and a mode of societalization (these making up the mode of regulation), is after all a diverse ensemble of parts, each managed by a sublogic which need not correspond directly or immediately with the sublogics that control the functioning of other parts of the system.[8]

The various component parts of the capitalist system have an overdetermined relationship to each other, and challenges to capitalism can therefore occur potentially at many points (culture, legal institutions, etc.). As a result, there can be no preemption of a particular form of opposition simply because it does not possess the face of an overtly anticapitalist struggle. Revolutionary change in such a system, if it occurs, can involve a range of very diverse transformations, some of which may lack an immediate connection or congruence with movements whose raison d'être is the quest for an explicitly postcapitalist order. Challenges to the capitalist system therefore need not bear directly on the mode of production or the social mode of economic regulation, though it is much more likely that an unconcealed anticapitalist struggle will affect these two modes in directly visible ways. But struggles conducted at the level of the mode of social regulation can affect the prevailing form of capitalism even if they do not appear on the face of things to alter any existing arrangements in the mode of production and the mode of societalization.

It is politics, militancy, understood in the broadest terms, therefore, that makes it possible for marxism still to be germane, indeed central. But this is a politics which has to acknowledge that the dispositions of power in our current social and economic realities, and the irreducibly complex and uneven movements of force aligned with these dispositions, are too varied and unstable to be managed by a politics of the kind that has existed for the past two hundred years (the era of the Citizen Subject that prevailed from 1776 or 1789 to 1989, if not a decade or two earlier). As it has done for previous epochs, marxism provides a practical-theoretical armature for addressing some of the more decisive questions for a politics after 1989, that is, a politics that is inherently of the twenty-first century.

However, as we have seen, a marxism capable of encompassing this politics will have to be premised on the insight that the possible defeat of capitalism will necessarily involve a variety of struggles, not all of which will be manifestly anticapitalist. The mutations undergone by capitalism since the time of Marx and Engels, and the modes of resistance to which these mutations are a response, may have to be matched by parallel transformations of (marxist) theory itself.

As a political materialism, marxism has to register the import of these metamorphoses of capital in the very depth and scope of its conceptual operations where this happens to be appropriate. Consequently, the assertion made by some of its schools of marxism's character as a "science" is best understood not as an attempt to confer a stultifying incontrovertibility on its axioms (as happened in Stalinist Russia), but rather as the recognition of a "systemic" demand on the part of marxism for these principles to be revised in the light of changed historical circumstances. Capitalism's ceaseless dynamism is thus to be matched and complemented by the theoretico-practical dynamism of marxism itself. One recalls here that Lenin, when confronted with some new situation, used to say, "About this, Marx and Engels said not a word."[9]

The crucial question here is the one sometimes implied in the charge that the marxist paradigm is in crisis because capitalism is no longer (if indeed it ever was, as some diehard anti-marxists would insist) congruent with the axiomatic framework proposed for its analysis by what is basically an "outdated nineteenth-century ideology," as these critics of marxism allege it to be. In responding to such anti-marxist objections, I must note that this congruence between the field of capitalism and the axioms of marxist theory can be accounted for only by a principle, a second-order principle, that is not itself "marxist." This is necessarily so because the applicability of marxism to the field constituted by capitalism can be specified only metatheoretically.

This metatheoretical or "transcendental" specification, which, to repeat, is not something that marxism itself can furnish, will pinpoint the conditions and principles that enable *this* particular field (viz., capitalism) to be governed by *this* particular axiomatic (viz., marxism). The applicability of a theory or paradigm (any theory or paradigm, not just marxism) to a field cannot, on logical grounds, be certified by that theory itself, since the norms and axioms for the connection of the theory in question to its field cannot be determined intratheoretically. This is because the relation of the theory in question to its putative field, which has the typical logical form aRb (object a is in relation R

to object *b*), cannot be specified by *a* or *b*, since the relation *R* is external, logically, to both *a* and *b*, and its character can therefore be specified only by some other theory which has as its (own) object the entire logical frame of the relation between the two initial objects involved, in this case *[aRb]*.[10]

Marxist Metatheory

The project of a new and transformed human collectivity, essential to the realization of the emancipatory potentials that are a built-in requirement for a political materialism like marxism, is likely to have two primary components. The first is a politico-philosophical theory specifying the forms of, and the actual and potential practical trajectories taken by, this sought-for radical transformation of our current social and economic orders. The second is a critique of the circuits of economic and political power that impede those forces conducing to this radical transformation.

This marxist project has been pursued in recent years, albeit with a variety of crucial modifications, primarily by Althusser and the other thinkers who followed on from the Althusserian "moment," most notably Deleuze and Guattari, Antonio Negri (with his collaborators Guattari and Michael Hardt in *Communists Like Us* and *Empire*, respectively), Etienne Balibar, Jacques Rancière, Fredric Jameson, and Alain Badiou. Marx of course created the essential lexicon used by these and other thinkers to formulate the theoretical hub of this emancipatory project; some of the leading items featured in this Marxist glossary are "exploitation," "revolution," "accumulation," "commodity," "mode of production," "class," and other, somewhat more technical notions such as "surplus value," "commodity fetishism," "falling rate of profit," and "real subsumption."

This conceptual repertoire has been augmented in more recent times by these successors of Marx. Among a great many other things, for instance, Deleuze and Guattari added "desiring production" and a fascinating and expanded conceptual rendition of the "mode of production" to this lexicon; Badiou has theorized afresh the notion of revolutionary possibility from the standpoint of the "truth-event" and its ramifications for political subjectivity; Althusser provided a rigorous, yet in some ways imprecise expansion of the concept of "ideology" to designate the very thing that Foucault would later put at the heart of his disquisitions on "governmentality"; Negri has elaborated Marx's own somewhat underdeveloped concept of "real subsumption" in order to make it the cornerstone of a theory of globalized capitalism; in a brilliant and original way Negri also substituted Spinoza's notion of "the multitude" (*multitudio*) for notions of "masses" and "classes" that for some marxists have become less applicable to the realities of this current phase of capitalist expansion; Jameson has used marxist categories for an immensely creative exploration of the current conjuncture's symbolic and cultural forms; and Balibar has used this Marxian framework in his more recent work to produce some remarkable analyses of the politics of racism and ethnonationalism.

The elaborations provided by these writers cannot be regarded as a simple stretching of the marxian conceptual bungee cord to this or that limit. Marxism is perforce an "incomplete project" because capitalism has not yet reached a discernible point of total exhaustion or retreat. Each one of these representative thinkers has amplified the marxist project while acknowledging fully the hugely ramified and challenging task set by this incompletion. As I indicated earlier, at another, more ontological or logical level the incompleteness of the marxist enterprise is an incompleteness that is inherently constitutive, because marxism cannot deliver to itself its own metatheory; it cannot, that is, give us a logically required higher-order theory capacious enough to supply the overarching warrants for its own theory of the capitalist field.

The sought-for project of radical transformation, construed here as an application of the principles of an always exploratory political materialism, is the very heart of this metatheory. The logic or axioms that govern the notion of a collective human liberation therefore oversee any attempt to sketch the skeletal outlines of this metatheory. So what is the proper form of this metatheory heedful of the requirement of a collective liberation? How is a concept of the appropriateness of the marxist paradigm to be produced?

Producing the concept of the appropriateness of the marxist paradigm requires the producer of these concepts to begin by distinguishing adequately between the following:

1. Those concepts that constitute a *theory* of X or Y or Z.
2. Those concepts that belong to a particular *manifestation* of X or Y or Z and which constitute the "expressivity" of X or Y or Z, and which can become the objects described and analyzed by the aforementioned theory of X or Y or Z. These concepts can appropriately be designated X^* or Y^* or Z^* (the superscript asterisks indicate that X^* or Y^* or Z^* are manifestations of X or Y or Z).
3. The *state* or *condition* that is X or Y or Z as such, a condition which overdetermines the expressivities yielded by this state or condition (see figure 3).

Theory of X (X being an expressivity)

↕

Concepts belonging to a particular manifestation of X, and which constitute the *expressivity* of X. These conceptual manifestations are designated as X^*

↕

The state or *condition* of X as such (independently of any of its manifestations X^*)

3. Theory, expressivity, and condition per se

In the case of marxism, the application of 1–3 would yield the following results. The category (a) would be the marxist theory whose object could be a particular phase of capitalist development, a process within such a phase, a specific institution or set of institutions associated with the phase in question, the decisions of individuals and groups of individuals, and so on. Under (b) the objects in (a) receive expression through the words and texts of a very diverse range of agents and organizations (workers, immigrants, the unemployed, old-age pensioners, trade unionists, company managers, federations of bosses, local councils, members of the legislature, the output of think tanks (Heritage Foundation, Cato Institute, etc.), the news media, national governments, international organizations (UN, IMF, World Bank, EU, WTO, OECD, etc.), NGOs, the writings of academics, novelists, playwrights (Quesnay's *Tableau économique*, Adam Smith's *The Wealth of Nations*, Polanyi's *The Great Transformation*, the *Harvard Business Review*, Martin Amis's *Money*, Conrad's *Nostromo*, Arthur Miller's *Death of a Salesman*, etc.), films (Ken Loach's *Kes*, Sam Mendes's *American Beauty*, Elia Kazan's *On the Waterfront*, etc.), all these constituting the expressivities that are, or can be, "theorized" by this or that application of marxist theory (i.e., a). But (c) the expressivities in (b) have as their basis a diffuse array of material conditions whose overall effect is to overdetermine the expressivities in question. A currently existing conceptualization is always provisional and can therefore be superseded by a newer one; no conceptualization expresses or determines in a way that is completely exhaustive of the condition or situation that it brings to expression. An expressivity works by naming things, but the thing named is never the thing itself; it is instead the panoply of effects associated with the thing in question. (This is the basis for the famous Althusserian refrain "The concept of sugar is not sweet," "The concept of water is not wet," etc.) Spinoza was the first to turn this insight ("An expressivity is the effect of a thing") into a philosophical axiom, and Althusser and Deleuze (Deleuze admittedly somewhat later than Althusser) are to be credited with the systematization of this insight. The "thing," in this scheme, is a concrescence of its effects (it is the event of this concrescence), and the effects in question vary with the totality of interactions that have that particular thing as their point of focus.

It should be stressed that the process of experiencing an effect gives rise to an "affect," so that there is a close causal link between "effect" and "affect." For example, the horse that races is a very different "thing" (especially for its jockey and horse-racing fans) from the horse that drags a plow (especially for the peasant farmer using the horse for this purpose).[11] The "thing" being an assemblage of effects and affects, and there being in principle a huge variability in the way these assemblages can be organized, no expressivity (qua the title of the assemblage in question) can eliminate *ab initio* its competitor names and the assemblages designated by them. For instance, the collapse of the giant U.S. energy trading company Enron (with ties to three dozen or so senior officials in the Bush administration) has been placed by business commentators and analysts into a number of such assemblages. Enron's downfall has been characterized as "a resultant of an energy market collapse," "a classic run on the bank," "a hedging structure collapse causing a liquidity drop," "the American species of crony capitalism at work," "the bursting of the 1990s U.S. speculative bubble," "the result of inadequate business regulation," "the outcome of the greed and venality of top management," and more. A theory of capitalism, as marxism of course is, is not therefore about capitalism per se but about the concepts that are generated by capitalism and its denizens and even its critics, or indeed by anyone through which the effectivity of capitalism is bespoken. These concepts are in turn related in a variety of ways to other assemblages of practices. Hence the concepts generated by the conditions associated with capitalism can, in the relevant context, be related by an appropriate theory to the concepts or expressivities associated with the assemblage of practices named "Protestantism" (in the classic manner formulated by Max Weber in *The Protestant Ethic and the Spirit of Capitalism*) or "modernist art" (in the way understood by T. J. Clark and others). A theory of capitalism does not bear directly on capitalist formations as such, but rather on the *concepts* of this or that manifestation of capitalism and its associated agents and figures, and these concepts (what I have called "expressivities") are just as actual and effective as the condition or set of conditions that is capitalism itself.[12]

Theories operate on expressivities, and expressivities in turn are connected with the conditions that enable them. The correlations established between expressivities and their enabling conditions depend for their effectiveness on always specific, because contingently ordained, distributions and orderings of power. Theories are thus the outcome of a productive process, namely no more and no less than the putative object of this process, the expressivities that mediate the conditions which they express even as they are enabled by the conditions in question. A theory is a practice, just as the conditions mediated by an expressivity are always provisional multilinear assemblages of practices structured by arrangements of income, assets, status, power, and so on. A theory, in short, is a practice of concepts located in a macrosocial field with its own practical possibilities and outcomes from these possibilities.

Capitalism's concepts are not given in the ensembles of practices that constitute it, and yet they are capitalism's concepts, not theories about capitalism. Hence the formulations of a Rosa Luxemburg or Enrique Dussel constitute a theory "about" capitalism, while the concepts of capitalism are likely to include the notions (which may be inchoate or half-formed) of the ownership of private property, bank lending strategies, the place of the peasantry in rural social orders, GM crop technologies and their role in agribusiness, that actually are operative in, say, the thought and practice of a banker in pre–World War I Germany or a Mexican rural smallholder in the 1990s.

Every concrete rendering of capitalism generates for itself its own "thinkability" (and concurrently its own "unthinkability" as the obverse of this very thinkability), even if this or that capitalist condition is not taken to be such by those whose condition it happens in fact to be. Thus the Mexican smallholder (of today) or the German banker (in the time before World War I) in their respective historical and social conjunctures, the former (say) by owing deference to the rich landowner and the latter (say) by assuming that he is investing wisely on behalf of his customers by putting money in the pre–World War I German munitions industry, contribute to the thinkability of a particular instantiation of capitalism, even if the individuals in question are unable to acknowledge that this owing of deference (in the case of the Mexican smallholder) or blind thinking about the supposed virtues of investment in the pre–World War I German armaments industry (in the case of the German banker) are precisely the kind of conduct that enables a particular recension of capitalism to remain a viable system of production and accumulation, in the shorter term at any rate.

It is *this* smallholder's or *this* banker's concepts or expressivities that constitute the thinkability of the condition in which he or she is inserted, even though he or she may be unable to perform the requisite operation of transcoding that renders a particular piece of deferential behavior or routine thinking about the seeming benefits of certain investment strategies into an explicit marker or symptom (in something like the Lacanian sense) of a particular capitalist system of production and accumulation.

Another way of making this point would be to say that a particular capitalist dispensation, like each and every social and cultural condition, has to secrete its multiple expressivities precisely in order to be what it is, and that its concepts, in ways that are inescapably selective, confining, and even arbitrary, are thematizations or representations of these expressivities and their attendant conditions. Or more briefly, that the concepts of a particular capitalist order are its expressivities limned in the form of that order's thinkability.

Theories of capitalism, by contrast, are the outcome of a theoretical operation whose object is the natures and functions of these expressivities. Theories of capitalism operate on a particular capitalist order's thinkability and involve a kind of transcoding. It is possible to ask the question "What is the form of capitalism operating in this dispensation?," but there is another kind of question, involving quite another kind of theoretical operation, that can be asked as well, in this case: "What is (a) theory (of capitalism)?" Capitalism, qua order or dispensation, is a prodigiously varied and complex practice of signs and images with an accompanying orchestration of affectivity, whose theory thinkers such as Joan Robinson and Karl Polanyi and Samir Amin must produce, but produce precisely as conceptual practice, in this case a practice that generates, always in a metalanguage, concepts that reflect upon the concepts and expressivities of capitalism's denizens, expressivities which therefore constitute what is in effect a basal or first-order language that comes subsequently to be transcoded.

No theoretical intervention, no matter how refined or thoroughgoing it may be, can on its own constitute the concepts of this or that capitalist order; the concepts of the denizen of capitalism are expressed in advance and independently of the personage, invariably an academic, who reflects on the concepts of those whose situations are typically those of the peasant, banker, factory worker or manager, homemaker, retiree, refugee or asylum seeker, billionaire investor, and others. Theorists and intellectuals, qua theorists and intellectuals, can traffic only in theories of capitalism (or culture or collective fantasy or whatever).

The concepts that theorists produce can be operative in more than one field of thought, and even in a single field it is always possible for a concept to fulfill more than one function. An obvious example is the concept of "value," which features prominently in the discourses associated with economics, sociology, ethics, psychology, and aesthetics. Each domain of thought is defined by its own internal variables, variables that have a complex relation to their counterpart external variables, such as historical epochs, political and social conditions and processes, and even the brute physical character of things.[13] It is an implication of this account of conceptual practice that a concept comes into being or ceases to be operative only when there is a change of function or field. Functions for concepts must be created or invalidated for the concepts in question to be generated or abolished, and new fields must be brought into being in order for these concepts to be rendered inapplicable or illegitimate. To see this, we have only to consider the accounts of twentieth-century American capitalism provided in a well-known semipopular text like John Kenneth Galbraith's *The New Industrial State* or Michel Aglietta's now classic *Régulation et crises du capitalisme*.

Galbraith follows Thorsten Veblen's pioneering insights into the emergence of a technocratic class and uses the notion of a "technostructure" as a master concept to characterize the course taken by American capitalism in the twentieth century, basing his argument regarding the centrality of this technostructure for the dynamism of the American system of accumulation since World War I on an analysis of a number of textbooks on business organization and information provided by company executives (including Robert McNamara, then an executive at Ford), as well as more theoretical works in economics by Kenneth Arrow, Joseph Schumpeter, and others. These sources can be mined to provide a panoply of "stylized facts" that function as expressivities, which can then be used as the basis for theoretical formulation on the part of the economist, in this case the author of *The New Industrial State*.[14]

Likewise Michel Aglietta's more technical work uses detailed evidence drawn from key U.S. economic indicators to delineate Fordism's structure as a regime of accumulation and to show that falls in productivity and declining profitability, which had appeared first in the United States in the late 1960s, prior to spreading to other advanced industrial economies, were the harbinger of a more significant decline that marked the beginning of the end of this Fordist regime of accumulation. Under Fordism, according to Aglietta, production and consumption were both characterized by the use of mass standards. Production was based on large-scale, standardized conveyor-belt production of medium-size consumption goods (cars and the larger domestic appliances). Swift productivity gains ensued that were reflected in rising income and the emergence of mass markets. Aglietta highlights the wage relation as it impacted productivity and profit levels, as well as connecting production with the domain of consumption. He also emphasizes the labor process, and several sections of *Régulation et crises du capitalisme* deal with the tasks that workers characteristically undertake as well as the technologies employed in these undertakings. Fordism, in Aglietta's account, hinged crucially on the deployment of mass technologies by a trisectioned workforce of highly specialized, semiskilled, and unskilled workers who provided this regime of accumulation with its dynamism. *Régulation et crises du capitalisme* is therefore replete with "stylized facts" drawn from a welter of statistical sources: the National Bureau of Economic Research, the U.S. Department of Commerce, the U.S. Bureau of Labor Statistics, the Office of Business Economics, and the Federal Reserve Board. Aglietta also refers to histories of American labor and consults *Fortune* magazine and reports of congressional committees and subcommittees. These sources, which delineate the external field of a certain phase of capitalist development, constitute expressivities that Aglietta can then work into a theory of the Fordist regime of accumulation and the first stages of its demise.[15] Neither Aglietta nor Galbraith would be able to formulate their theories of capitalism without the expressivities that were lodged in such (nontheoretical) documents as *Fortune* or the recollections of Robert McNamara when he was president of the Ford Motor Company.

At a more general level, the concepts that are "expressive" of capitalism follow rules that govern their appearance and perpetuation. It may be the case, however, that capitalism is more plausibly viewed as an order of orders, that is, as an order that brings together and orchestrates rules for an amalgam or network of practices, practices having in more or less complex ways to do with everything from the establishment of the labor process and its reproduction, to the constitution of the production process (in some cases with a special emphasis on the role of technology), the distribution and redistribution of incomes, and the creation of patterns of consumption. The term "capitalism" is bestowed on the strategic logic that orchestrates these rules. However, focusing on the writings of economists such as Galbraith and Aglietta makes possible a depiction of this logic only at a relatively high level of abstraction, as much as these economists make recourse to more concrete expressivities that are perforce presented in the form of "stylized facts." To get to the more tangible dimensions of this logic's application one perhaps needs to resort to the irreducible specificity of historical or ethnographic description, that is, by turning to a form of characterization that studies expressivities in all their context-bound specificity. There are many well-known studies of one or more facets of capitalism by anthropologists writing as ethnographers; examples that come to mind are Michael Taussig's *The Devil and Commodity Fetishism in South America* and *Shamanism, Colonialism and the Wild Man: A Study in Terror and Healing*, and Aihwa Ong's *Spirits of Resistance and Capitalist Discipline: Factory Women in Malaysia*. It cannot be denied that works such as these involve descriptions of cultural and economic phenomena, and therefore involve willy-nilly an element of abstraction. But the task of description as undertaken by ethnographers involves a defining proximity to those who happen to confront the same phenomena in directly self-involving ways (these being the "participants" of the standard ethnographic schema). Ethnography's fundamental nearness to its putative object (of description) gives it a concreteness not typically possessed by other logics of description, though this in no way suggests that such ethnographic objects are raw data or brute facts which can then serve as the ground for subsequent (and proper) theoretical formulation.[16] For an ethnography is itself a species of description, and therefore operates at one remove on the expressivities of those who participate in the cultural or social formation being described by the ethnographer or local historian.

It is thus a truism worth repeating over and over again that marxism is a theory, one belonging to a domain of thought whose basic intellectual disposition is that of a political materialism (and in this sense marxism is therefore also a kind of practice), whose field is capitalism. This field is constituted by an immense range of expressivities, and these expressivities serve as an irremovable exteriority to the enterprise of theoretical formulation. The question of the nature of the field from which the concepts of marxism derive their saliency is obviously one that is especially crucial, since this field is the location of the external variables that are marxism's fundamental enabling condition. It follows from this that if the field that is capitalism did not exist, there would be no need for marxism. But before I discuss some of the primary external variables of the field in which the concepts belonging to a marxist theory are generated, something needs to be said about the mechanisms underlying the constitution of the lived world that is the context from which the perceptions, desires, thoughts, and actions of (capitalist) social and political agents are orchestrated.

The daily round of life for the social subject is complexly mediated by ensembles of images and affects; images and affects in turn are distributions of temporal and spatial relations.[17] Thus the lived world of, say, the newly unemployed Appalachian coal miner who leaves the town of Wheeling, West Virginia, to work as a loader in an air-cargo dispatching center in Newark, New Jersey, will be established by an ensemble of sign-images constituting the "new" world of the city of Newark, a similar ensemble constituting the "old" world of the Appalachian mining town, the sign-images prevalent in the new world that is Newark which designate the West Virginia mining town that used to be home for the ex-miner ("This is how the typical inhabitant of Newark thinks of the place I came from"), the sign-images designating Newark that prevailed in the old world of the small coal-mining town ("This is how the people of Wheeling typically view Newark"), and this because the semiotic registers of the movements between different life-worlds have themselves to be incorporated into the constitution of the worlds in question. The ex-miner's conceptual rendition of the Appalachian world left behind is now inflected by the ex-miner's insertion into the new semiotic ensemble that is Newark, just as the currently instantiated semiotic ensemble that is Newark is always itself constituted by the semiotic ensemble that is the ex-miner's previous lived world, in this case the Appalachian town in the mountains of West Virginia. The West Virginia mining town is always prehended in terms of the New Jersey city and vice versa, and the world I have left behind is prehended in terms of the world I have moved into, just as the world I have moved into is always prehended (if not entirely, then certainly partially) in terms of the world or worlds I previously inhabited. In this way a whole range of multiply linked sign-image assemblages underlies one's prehensions of the temporal and spatial relations embodied in the antecedents and proximities that enable a life-world (*that* ex-miner's world, but still a public world) to be constituted out of the flux that is composed of these antecedents and proximities.

These semiotic assemblages—designating Newark, the Appalachian town that the ex-miner has left behind, the ensemble regulating the transition from the one to the other, and so on and so forth—are crisscrossed by yet other assemblages (each with an associated affective component) that designate such formations as family, job, education, circle of friends and associates, race, regional accent and speech patterns, and of course class position. The notion of being a protagonist in any kind of social or political order, therefore, is an abstraction denoting a particular kind of relationship between these assemblages; the notion of being such a protagonist is inevitably mischaracterized when it is viewed as an object that is directly denoted by, for example, the concepts "capitalist subject," "Appalachian miner," "unemployed worker," and their various cognates. For the object itself is already an abstraction from this nexus of assemblages and the inherently unstable linkages between them. The expressivities of the capitalist subject have the subject's insertion into *this* matrix of assemblages as their condition of possibility; to not be embedded in them is perforce to be something other than a capitalist subject.[18]

At the same time, a considerable variation can exist in the kinds of assemblages that go into the constitution of the life-world of the capitalist subject. The assemblages that constitute the lived world of the London-based media tycoon who is a Russian citizen, or the Italian telephone operator working for a German multinational pharmaceutical company based in Milan, or the rice-growing peasant in rural Malaysia (so vividly depicted in the ethnography of James C. Scott's now classic *Weapons of the Weak: Everyday Forms of Peasant Resistance*)—these are just as much assemblages of capitalist subjects as is the life-world of the ex-miner from Appalachia. Marxism, as a theory of liberation, has no alternative but to present itself as a theory of the transformation of the life-world of capitalist subjects. It is not sufficient for marxists merely to posit a transformation of the mode of production and to regard this focus on the mode of production as the sole and exclusive rationale for those projects of liberation sanctioned by marxism. The transformation of the mode of production is of course an essential element of this sought-for liberation, but for marxism taking the project of liberation to its point of culmination will demand the transformation of the life-world (and its encompassing forms of subjectivity) of capitalism's denizens. Liberation, if it is to be effective, has to operate at the level of our subjectivity or life-world. Hence the need for a thorough description and analysis of these life-worlds, conducted at the ontological level in the manner just specified.[19]

The primary external variables of the field in which the concept of a capitalist subject is to be generated today will be identified through an account of the conditions of possibility for the emergence of the assemblages that create the personage of this subject and the expressivities that define this personage. It would take an extended and complex narrative to enumerate the full range of these external variables, and the account developed here is unavoidably schematic. To tell this story properly is, after all, to have to tell a fairly complete story about the course of modern capitalism. The theoretical and practical bedrock of the applicability and intelligibility of the concept of the capitalist subject is a particular structure of exploitation positioned in relation to specific historical and social structures and their associated conjunctures; the theoretical operation involved in producing the concept of the capitalist subject makes it axiomatic that he or she is *this* subject precisely because he or she happens to be exploited in some appreciable way, and this because he or she is subjected to the particularity of (capitalist) interests in ways that reflect fundamental asymmetries of power and the capabilities enabled by such power. The effect of these asymmetries of power is to place this subject in exactly *that* structure of exploitation.[20] There are many strands in the overall structure of exploitation, and it is a commonplace that the structure which subtends the lived world of the rice-growing peasant in Malaysia is perforce different from the lived world of the Milanese telephone operator.

In summary, the capitalist structure of exploitation at its highest level of generality has two axes: the mode of production and the regime of accumulation (with the latter always functioning under capitalism as a mode of domination). Struggles against capitalist exploitation, if they occur, have to occur along both these axes. Struggles regarding the mode of domination are primarily struggles for greater social visibility and more effective social agency; struggles regarding the mode of production have the reallocation of value as their primary (though not necessarily exclusive) focus. Abolishing the structure of exploitation is a necessary precondition for any pursuit of a project of liberation aspiring to be decisive and significant. Efforts directed at the abolition of the capitalist structure of exploitation can operate on one or both of these axes, and no effort expended along one axis is to be discounted in principle at the expense of the other. Struggle can involve innumerable paths, and the avenues to liberation are likewise uncountable. Since marxism is either a project of liberation or nothing, the surmounting of any component of capitalism's structures of exploitation is in absolute accord with marxism's raison d'être.

The Desire That Is the Ontological Ground
of Liberation and Truth

Liberation in its essence involves a strategic undertaking designed to overcome conditions enabling a structure of exploitation to hold onto its reach and effectiveness. The structure of exploitation therefore represents a critical impediment posed for the (marxist) project of liberation. The heart of any marxist project of liberation is the emancipation of subjects from some unacceptable state of the world or condition attendant upon their being in the (capitalist) world; this recognition is accompanied, for marxism, by the allied realization that capitalism is the primary (though not the only) causal factor responsible for the existence of this state or condition.

Liberation, then, is in its marxist manifestation a dynamism impelled by desire, in this case the desire to overcome, circumvent, or ameliorate an unacceptable state of being associated with a specific disposition of the capitalist system.[21] Liberation for marxism is thus a concept internally related to the desire for capitalism's abrogation. As such, liberation has to be approached through an analysis of the conditions and functions of this (for marxism) primal desire, and this desire's names, its situations, its outcomes, its productions. Desire has a role that is even more primary than this, however, since the production of the world begins with desire. The philosophical acknowledgment of this all-important proposition came from Spinoza, who said in his *Ethics*, "We do not endeavour, will, seek after, or desire something because we judge it to be good, but on the contrary we judge something to be good because we endeavour, will, seek after, or desire it."[22] Spinoza's proposition can be said to be an axiom for marxism, since the notion that the production of the world can begin only with desire requires marxism to acknowledge that the cornerstone of the project of liberation is a prior ontology of human constitutive power or desire.[23]

This ontology of constitutive power charts the various trajectories of human desire, and in so doing allows the project of liberation to have as its "knowledge" the theorems delivered by this ontological charting of the lineaments of desire (this in a nutshell being Spinoza's own program). The ontology of human constitutive power will delineate what it is that the ensembles of desire going by the name "human" are capable of, and what their aversions and attractions are. The ontology of human constitutive power is thus a necessary prolepsis to any specification of the theoretical core of the project of liberation.

This ontology has to be accorded priority in a marxist marking out of liberation as a concept, if only because a project of liberation is above all a system of truth-effects, and any truth-effect (or fusion of truth-effects) can, depending on historical and social circumstances (and the rudiments of these are always political), be prevented from displaying itself. A truth-effect does not produce automatically, and hence cannot guarantee, its own processes of actualization; it cannot of itself banish the material conditions, whatever they may be, that could in principle disrupt its realization as a truth-effect. (This is true of any system of thought, including the ontology of constitutive power being canvassed here; as a regime of truth-effects it too cannot institute by fiat its own modes of realization, and it too can always be prevented from realizing its truth-effects.)[24]

A truth-effect, on this account, is the resultant of active desire, often having the force and character of a "project," in this case a project motivated by a particular arrangement of this constitutive desire or striving. For instance, Nelson Mandela's desiring his freedom (and thus the abolition of apartheid) is a truth-effect because this desire functions as an enabling (though not in itself sufficient) condition for the removal of all that stands in the way of the realization of that desire. We could call this a "truism" of the logic of desire, inasmuch as to desire X is to aim, no matter how ambivalently, to make true what it is that conduces to the attainment of X. But what is it to desire X in ways that aim to make true what it is that conduces to the attainment of X?

The relation between truth and falsity becomes significant at this point. Falsity emerges when a fundamental undecidability is introduced between the real and the unreal. It is important to note here that falsity is not mere error or confusion, but the capacity, the sheer power that makes a potential event of truth succumb to the forces of nondecidability.[25] Truth is thus the force that counters the constitutive nondecidability lying at the heart of falsity, a falsity coextensive with the diminution of the possibilities for a real and sustainable liberation. If this nondecidability prevails on a decisive enough scale, those engaged in the pursuit of truth and liberation would not know which processes, constitutive of this pursuit, they would have to be involved in precisely as a condition of living liberated lives. As such, truth is the sine qua non of any materialization of the principles of liberation. To live in truth is to live under the name of liberation and all that conduces to it, and vice versa. In the case of the apartheid regime in South Africa, Nelson Mandela's quest for his country's liberation required him and his allies in this struggle to find ways of rendering decidable the questions of what had to be done in order to destroy apartheid: to fight against apartheid, Mandela and his associates had to place themselves in, and in the process create, specific truth-effects about the nature of white South African racism.[26] But liberation and its attainment are not the ever-so-visible physiognomy of an abstract ideal order.

To elaborate: bringing any principles of liberation to their point of realization requires—and this watchword bears frequent repeating—that attention always be given to concrete political circumstances, since the political is an insuperable condition for liberation's constitution as this or that specific event of liberation. For the truth of liberation, if it is to be achieved in material form, can be manifested only in a context indelibly marked by the particularities of power (including its abuse), and these particularities are perforce always political. The truth of liberation is therefore irreducibly the possible truth of a political standpoint.[27] It is unimaginable that Mandela, Aung San Suu Kyi, Albertina Sisulu, Steve Biko, Thomas Sankara, Martin Luther King Jr., Lenin, Emmeline Pankhurst, Bolívar, Garibaldi, and a host of others be the protagonists on behalf of liberation that they are without a protracted immersion in the political. Truth is inseparable from politics. However, when truth is applied to a political standpoint it must always be qualified by the word "possible." For truth is what breaks into and interrupts the seemingly undifferentiated continuity of life (a continuity permeated by the nondecidability that is falsity's defining mark, and which a fortiori conduces to the absence of liberation), just as it disrupts the fantasies that underlie and make possible the seamless continuity of everyday life ("God bless America," "It's great to be a Brummie [a native of Birmingham, England]," "Texas is one special place," "We live in a part of Virginia that is the real Virginia and the real America," and so on). An adequate politics always calls for decidability, regardless of whether this insight is purveyed by those on the right (Carl Schmitt comes to mind here) or the left (Badiou and Žižek) or in some more substantive versions of liberalism (Max Weber and Hannah Arendt).

The truth, as the event of this disruption of the (politically inaugurated) continuity of life's everyday course, as the power that counters life's (politically sustained) nondecidability, is always a "point of exception" (the phrase is Badiou's). Truth is an always specific series of operations on quotidian reality's fundamental propensity to nondecidability, or where the question of liberation is involved, on this reality's predisposition to render undecidable any basis for distinguishing adequately between liberation and those forces that militate against it.[28] The quality that defines truth—and this is a quality that eo ipso also characterizes justice—is thus the quality of a singularity or exception, a singularity that does not cohere with the (politically instituted) continuity of life.[29] This is the kind of singularity or exception in which a specific operation or amalgam of operations establishes the basis for an event of liberation by bringing to the point of absolute decidability a particular historical or political process that hitherto had eluded, or been bypassed by, the political forces that make effective the various structures of decidability. Politics thus establishes the "beingness" of truth and liberation, if one wants to put this in a Heideggerian idiom.

This operation or set of operations, whose name is truth, does not pro-

duce automatically, and hence cannot guarantee, its own mode of actualization; that is, it cannot of itself banish the historical and political conditions,
whatever they may be, that serve to preempt its realization as a truth operator. When this happens, and these preemptive political and historical conditions are active, nondecidability necessarily prevails. In this way untruth
holds sway and the possibility of liberation is diminished. The truth operator
and its encompassing regime therefore require a politics capable of activating
and sustaining them; quite simply, there is liberation only when there is a
politics able to banish the forces of nondecidability. Again, this is precisely
why liberation is inseparable from politics. Only political practice can annul
the nondecidability or untruth of all that counters liberation.

It is clear from this that any elaboration of liberation as a concept has to
place an inarguable centrality on the conditions underlying the production of
the truth-effects belonging to the system of liberation in question. No practice of liberation, nor any theoretical principles stemming from that practice,
can portray those actively seeking liberation as individuals or groups who
must "settle for life just as it is." Liberation's logic is irreducibly transformative. Even those conceptions of liberation that profess, or perhaps promote
in slightly more vigorous ways, an "acceptance" of the social and political
order or world as it is (as in some versions of stoicism) invariably affirm the
need, whether real or merely felt, for the protagonists involved actively to
come to the point of such an acceptance. This acceptance has to be worked
for. That is, inherent in these more quietistic conceptions of liberation is the
presumption that such individuals or collectivities have to change, practically
and in the end decisively, at least their dispositions toward the world (i.e.,
their own "subjectivity") even if not the world itself.

This is precisely the point at which the question of the conditions that
subtend the production (or the dissolution) of truth effects arises in all its
force, for the difference made to the life-world by any practice conducing
to liberation hinges crucially on the emergence of conditions that effectuate
truth by creating an event of truth. It goes virtually without saying that the
event of truth can also be forestalled by countervailing forces that obviate its
emergence, and that the project of liberation invariably takes the form of a
struggle with those countervailing forces directed against the surfacing of the
event of truth.

Also important for any "thematics" of liberation is the insight that there is
a perceived need for liberation only because something about the lived world
is distorted, because that world is for many of its subjects a place of misfor-
tune and even catastrophe. This basic distorted quality of the life-world, or

one's being in this world, which for this thematics is the driving force behind the quest for liberation, can have another consequence: for some of these subjects, the realities of a catastrophic world are the obvious starting point for battling the distortions and calamities that serve to underline the need for liberation. For these individuals or groups it may be the case that hope for the potential for change can survive or become effective only if the figures of liberation become figures of redemption rooted in some kind of transcendence—and these figures are hidden, or expressed indirectly by other means. This is especially true of many apocalyptic or messianic traditions. These concealed or partly shrouded figures can then be retrieved only through the use of rituals or interpretive resources that have been refined and attuned in suitably complex ways. The exemplary instance of this strand of messianic thinking is provided by Walter Benjamin, who in his "Theses on the History of Philosophy" used the code of a historical materialism to express, allegorically, utopian and messianic (and therefore "theological") impulses that for him were forced out of sight by a history that had succumbed to barbarism. For Benjamin the truth-effects of these hidden utopian propensities are marked by untimeliness and discontinuity, and thus can be registered only allegorically.[30]

A more complicated form of attention then needs to be paid to these characteristic discontinuities and their associated untimeliness, since a broken history discredits all conceptions of inexorable progress and teleology and ensures that any transcodings of potential images of liberation (and the truth-effects that go with these images) will be unfamiliar and hard to retrieve. The argument of this book does not require the support of these messianic or utopian traditions, though it acknowledges their saliency for the constitution of the life-worlds of many who are dispossessed or marginalized. A glance at the anthropological texts of Michael Taussig or Jean and John Comaroff will indicate the significance of messianic religious traditions and figures for such individuals and groups, and insofar as the ensuing convictions are powerful motivating forces for those seeking political change it is important for any theory of liberation to take these religious motivations into account.[31]

It is virtually axiomatic that the implementation of truth-effects depends crucially on the active presence of the conditions of possibility for a project of liberation. This is something of a conceptual requirement, since truth has value only because we first deem it valuable to become involved in the constitution of a particular truth-event, to continue to seek this event of truth, to avoid self-deception in regard to what is considered to be a truth-event, to heed those who are in the best position to discern this truth-event, and so forth. Thus, for instance, there may be someone who, contrary to the available evidence and contrary to the convictions of everyone else, happens to believe that her child survived the tsunami. She happens to be right, because it is true that her child survived the tsunami, and it is a good thing that this belief is true, that is, that her child's surviving has the character of a truth-event. But what makes it a good thing that this belief is true is simply that it is good that the child survived. Here the value of truth (its effects, in other words) is clearly dependent on the sheer value of material survival.[32] It is the reality of the child's survival that brings decidability to the event of the mother having the conviction that her child has survived the tsunami. If truth-effects, and indeed the value of truth as such, are inextricably bound up with the value attached to the relations that we have to the material conditions which underlie these effects, then the value of the truth-effects associated with any presumptive project of liberation will depend crucially on the conditions, always but not solely political, that subtend these projects. The truth-effects generated by this or that project of liberation depend for their decidability on the "making true" of this event of liberation by political practice; in the absence of such practice, the effects of truth are not likely to be compelling or far-reaching.

Identifying and characterizing these conditions of possibility for a particular quest of liberation will require the kind of dense specificity that only an ethnographic (or in some cases, microhistorical) description can aspire to provide; philosophy or theory (as we have seen) aims at something more general and in a sense more problematic, that is, conditions given in advance of their appearance in the realm of phenomena or material events. Nevertheless, it can be said that a "logic" of these conditions, of the kind being sought here, will contain a number of features intrinsic to the concept of liberation. These include the axiom that those engaged in a quest for liberation have to be possessed of at least a desire for the new or different, inasmuch as for these protagonists there is necessarily a contrast between a prevalent state of affairs (one held to be in need of liberation, i.e., "the old") and one which represents a supersession of this state (liberation itself, i.e., that which supplants "the old"). This "desire for the new" is thus the primary, though not the exclusive, defining characteristic of liberation. (It should be mentioned here that there are religious traditions which provide an apparent exception to this axiom, in that they posit the liberation or redemption of an entire people, an elect, or a community of the devout, even for those who are not in a position to evince any desire for the new, such as the unborn, infants who die, or the brain damaged. In such cases, this desire for the new clearly has to be predicated on the collectivity involved, and not on specific individuals belonging to it.)

The crux of this desire for the new comes when there is a situation in which this desire is confronted with the total absence of any conditions that conduce to its fulfillment. What happens to liberation when the desire for liberation is confronted with the stark impossibility of its realization? Liberation then necessarily has to become the desire or the thought of the new in the absence of all conditions.[33]

The absence of historical and political conditions for an adequate liberation can serve as a powerful intensification of the desire for liberation. Reflection may go beyond the boundary represented by these historical and political conditions, but it does so only as thought, as speculation, no matter how profound. The futility of any merely speculative practice having liberation as its object in the absence of its historical conditions of possibility means that liberation has to be lodged in nothing else but a countervailing power that is expressed bodily and only bodily, including of course bodily affects. Thought founders on this impossibility, but the body and its affects remain to confront what defeats thought. This prompts a turning to the directly lived, to zones of viscerality in the life-world as yet not permeated by the powers that destroy even the thought of liberation. Here is the core of a constitutive ontology of practice, one that furnishes the basis for resistance and the continued mobilization of the desire for the new.[34] This provides only a horizon, albeit one that is salutary and absolutely indispensable, for a resuscitation or sustaining of the desire for the new. Something more needs to be said about this ontological horizon and its relation to its precursors as horizons for the ontological constitution of practices of liberation.

The Conditions of Possibility for Liberation and the Future

Using the most general terms, it could be said that prior to the onset of modernity (bearing in mind that this is preeminently a category defined by and for Europeans and North Americans), infinity and perfection were the primary forces that shaped human beings. In this classical epoch that extended from antiquity until its demise in the European eighteenth century, liberation was understood as the quest for perfection and the transcending of finitude. In the modernity that succeeded this classical age, modernity being a relatively brief phase which reached its point of culmination in the European nineteenth century, finitude becomes the primary norm for envisioning the textures of human life, these textures extending across a space of contiguous domains that could be termed life, labor, and language.[35] The episteme whose name is modernity, and whose mark is finitude, marks a well-known crisis for religious sensibilities, perhaps most visibly reflected in the "works of suspicion" associated with Marx, Nietzsche, and Freud (as I pointed out in chapter 1). However, and this continues Foucault's periodization, this post-classical episteme itself went into crisis, and modernity was supplanted in turn by the current or postcontemporary episteme.

The onset of the current episteme was heralded by Nietzsche, but for Foucault it is still an episteme of the future. In it, finitude (understood typically as empirical constraint) is displaced by a ceaseless flux of forces and their mutations, a flux that Foucault's interpreter Deleuze calls an "unlimited finity" (*fini-illimité*).[36] In this new formation, beings do not approximate to or depart from perfect forms (as they did in the classical episteme), nor are they epistemically recalcitrant (as they were in the modern episteme, which viewed them as a problem for the constitution of knowledge, as witnessed by Kant's rigorous emphasis on the necessary "legislative" tasks of Reason). Instead, the current episteme views beings as ensembles of forces arranged algorithmically. The "unlimited finity" that marks these configurations of forces allows a "finite number of components [to yield] a practically unlimited diversity of combinations."[37] Recursiveness in the mode of an "unlimited finite" is thus, "emblematically," the modus operandi of the epoch that comes after modernity.

Foucault had a narrative that purported to account for the displacement or supersession of modernity along with its pivotal creation, the figure of Man. In Foucault's famous image, Man would be erased in the way that a wave washes away the drawing of a face at the edge of the sea.[38] Moreover, as Foucault saw it, of the three components of the so-called anthropological triad—life, labor, and language—it would be language that would pave the way for the episteme that superseded modernity and Man. Man would be undone or overcome by the "enigmatic and precarious being" of the word. Here, as Deleuze has argued, Foucault got it wrong, or at least he was somewhat off-track: as Foucault himself subsequently came to acknowledge, the practices and forms that are shaping the new episteme are arising not so much in the area of language as in the areas of life and labor (what subsequently came to be called "biopolitics" by Foucault). Deleuze's position on the practices of the emerging dispensation is clear from the following quotation: "The forces within man enter into a relation with forces from the outside, those of silicon which supersedes carbon, or genetic components which supersede the organism, or agrammaticialities which supersede the signifier. In each case we must study the operations of the superfold, of which the 'double helix' is the best known example. What is the superman? It is the formal compound of the forces within man and these new forces. It is the form that results from a new relation between forces. Man tends to free life, labour and language within himself."[39] It is important to be cautious about all such pronouncements on the character of epochal shifts and transformations, of the spirit of this or that age, even if they come from Foucault or Deleuze or Hegel. After all, even Foucault lived long enough to see that he did not get it right about language and its role in the emergence of the postcontemporary episteme. But with this cautionary note in mind let us assume that the new practices that have emerged, and are still emerging, in the domains of life and labor are clearly important for any understanding of postcontemporary knowledges and powers, and thus for the concept of liberation.

Deleuze makes a concluding comment about the superman, or the "parahuman," as one may prefer to call it, who comes to exist in our postcontemporary episteme and which forms a threshold for the next part of my account:

> The superman . . . is the man who is even in charge of the animals (a code that can capture fragments from other codes, as in the new schemata of lateral or retrograde). It is man in charge of the very rocks, or inorganic matter (the domain of silicon). It is man in charge of the being of language (that formless, "mute, unsignifying region where language can find its freedom" even from whatever it has to say). As Foucault would say, the superman is much less than the disappearance of living men, and much more than a change of concept: it is the advent of a new form that is neither God nor man and which, it is hoped, will not prove worse than its two previous forms.[40]

"The advent of a new form that is neither God nor Man": in other words, the dawning of times in which the desire for the new that prompts our search for liberation will take the form of a movement beyond the dialectic of perfection (God) and finitude (Man), these forms having been exhausted as modernity has been displaced by the postcontemporary, just as modernity itself once succeeded the episteme of the classical age. So, what is it to conceive of liberation, as desire but always as politics, without the forms of God and Man, or perhaps more precisely, God or Man? What happens to liberation as a category in this epoch of radically new practices of life and labor? (These questions will be taken up in chapter 9, when I deal with the model of liberation associated with Christian transcendence.)

The practices and the needs of the subjects of these very new worlds will be the practices and the needs of beings who take the aleatory and the material (Negri) as the basis of their self-constitution. Desire, or *conatus* in Spinoza's terms, is what constitutes human subjects, and desire exists only in exteriority, in the surpassing of itself in the always changing movement. That is the basis for a conception of liberation, one that can never find adequate figuration but that hopefully is likely to be satisfactory because it opens its subjects to the urgency and bareness of the never predictable event, "the new."

All this amounts to an outline "grammar" or "logic" of liberation, one that, qua logic or grammar, is unavoidably and maybe even problematically abstract. This abstraction may be especially troubling for those who are marxists, given marxism's customary injunction that abstraction be avoided because it is one step removed from idealism (if it is not already the very essence of idealism itself), and marxism is of course a self-professed materialism with a built-in propensity to view any idealism as a pernicious vice. An objection of this kind nonetheless overlooks marxism's reliance, as a political materialism, on some kind of reflection on the constitution of the political (or the historical, given the weight placed by Marx and his followers on its character as a historical materialism), and especially, given the context of the argument of this book, on an ontology of the political. This ontology of the political, and the human constitutive power that I view as the basis of the political, serves as the metatheory needed to connect marxism with its field, which is capitalism in all its ramified manifestations. Marxism, under the rubric of what its exponents term "historical materialism," has always had its own overarching theory of the processes, in both their practical and theoretical dimensions, involved in the material transformation of human life. In Ernest Mandel's words, "Historical materialism . . . provides a measuring stick for human progress."[41] The status of the theoretico-practical assemblage that is a historical or political materialism is profoundly contested even (or especially!) within the marxist tradition, but there is no need for us to enter here into the complex debates that surround the notion of a historical or political materialism; suffice it to say that what matters is precisely the principle identified by Mandel, namely, that any kind of social and political transformation, even marxism's own "theorization" of this transformation, needs some evaluative principle that makes possible the appropriate kinds of assessment of what transpired in the course of that particular shift in social and political conditions. A difference is necessarily enacted in the course of such transformations, and since a shift logically or conceptually implies a movement between two positions or conditions, it is the task of this overarching evaluative principle to account for the "difference" made by *that* difference (i.e., the movement between the positions and conditions and questions). What then does marxism register when dealing with the possibilities and realities of such transformations? To ascertain what marxism registers in such instances is perforce to have a theory of the analytical and practical difference made by marxism (the task of historical or political materialism), and this is precisely the metatheoretical task assigned to the conceptual cartography of liberation outlined in this chapter.

The question of the prospects and opportunities available for the kind of social and political transformation indicated by marxism can be answered only by a survey of the social, political, and economic developments brought about by capitalist expansion since the Second World War. These developments constitute the field of external variables underlying a concept of liberation congruent with a marxist elaboration of this project of liberation, and they are discussed in chapter 3.

CHAPTER 3

Postpolitical Politics and Global Capitalism

Some of the more significant external variables needing to be identified and characterized as part of our conceptualization of a marxist project of liberation are provided by a conspectus of the period of capitalist development that has been in existence since the Second World War. As I indicated in chapter 1, the demise of the classical Citizen Subject associated with the emergence of a postpolitical politics was accompanied by a momentous modification of state sovereignty, and the precise character of the changes associated with this reconstitution require in particular an account of the political and economic transformations that have taken place since the Second World War. These transformations involve a new mutation of the capitalist system, and they have to be depicted in some detail if the impact of this mutation on the form of the state is to be registered. Once this is done, and the shifts that have taken place in regard to the form of the state and the apparatuses it encompasses are clear, it will be possible to determine what is entailed in the move from the classical Citizen Subject to its ostensible successor, the subject sponsored by today's world-integrated capitalism and its accompanying postpolitical politics in the West.

After the Second World War

While there is considerable agreement (though not absolute unanimity) about the underlying causes for the demise of capitalism's so-called Golden Age (i.e., the prolonged expansion associated with high employment, growing wages and welfare expenditures, generally high consumption, and benign business cycles that lasted in the advanced industrial countries from 1945 to around 1973–74), there is no real consensus about the economic, political, and social transformations that have followed the end of the long age of prosperity.[1] Analysis of the transition from the Golden to the Leaden Age (to use a term of Joan Robinson's) is carried out under several familiar titles: "late capitalism," "advanced capitalism," "disorganized capitalism," "deregulatory capitalism," "integrated world capitalism," "postindustrialization," "post-Fordism," "flexible accumulation," "the information economy," "globalization," and others.[2]

The lack of agreement on what precisely is encompassed by these titles is compounded by the outright skepticism of those who maintain that it is not clear whether the major transformations associated with a putatively epochal movement to a less regulated, more "adaptive," and more "reflexive" system of capitalist accumulation have in fact taken place, and that these changes are not as full-blown as they are sometimes taken to be. Thus it is argued that the world prior to 1913 was just as economically integrated as the world after 1970, that domestic national markets have retained their primacy in the international economic system to this day, and that export markets, widely viewed as a key index of world trade integration, are still highly concentrated and unevenly spread.[3] The United Nations Development Programme's *Human Development Report 2005* is worth quoting here:

> One of the prevailing myths of globalization is that increased trade has been a catalyst for a new era of convergence. Expanded trade, so the argument runs, is narrowing the income gap between rich and poor countries, with the developing world gaining from access to new technologies and new markets. Like most myths, this one combines some elements of truth with a hefty dose of exaggeration. Some countries are catching up, albeit from a low base. But successful integration is the exception rather than the rule—and trade is a driver of global inequality as well as prosperity. For the majority of countries the globalization story is one of divergence and marginalization.[4]

Figures 4 and 5 indicate that a mere seven developing countries account for more than 70 percent of low-technology exports and 80 percent of high-technology exports. The *Human Development Report 2005* draws the inevitably stark conclusion from these figures: "Much of the developing world has little more than a toehold in manufacturing export markets. . . . Today, the share of world exports of Sub-Saharan Africa, with 689 million people, is less than one-half that of Belgium, with 10 million people."[5] With the transparent

High- and medium-technology exports
Share of world exports (%)

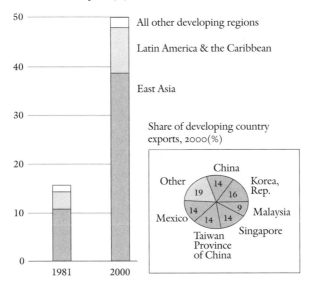

Low-technology exports
Share of world exports (%)

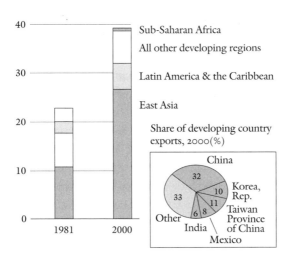

4. Export success is highly concentrated

Source: United Nations Development Programme, *Human Development Report 2005*, 116.

Share of world total (%)

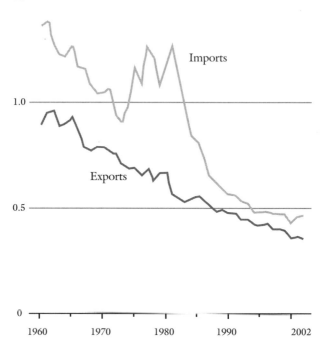

5. Sub-Saharan Africa's falling share of world trade

Source: United Nations Development Programme, *Human Development Report 2005*, 116.

failure to include the world's poorer (and poorest) countries in world trade, globalization in the form of world trade integration, despite its vaunted success in some quarters, has simply not advanced the economic and social interests of the hundreds of millions of people who live in these countries. There is doubtless a more complex story to be told about this and related developments, and though this is a very important area of debate, it is beyond the scope of this chapter to delve deeply into its extended implications and outcomes.[6] But the crucial point made here—that the world's poorer countries are not benefiting from world trade integration—is augmented in the rest of this book, and the conclusion drawn from it is reinforced in subsequent chapters.

What is significant for those who reflect on the role of the state in capitalist accumulation is the fact that from the late 1960s to the 1980s the prevalent phase of capitalist development started to encounter macroeconomic impasses with a resultant persistent stagflation, and that there ensued from this crisis political and economic conditions of a qualitatively new and different kind (those of a post-Fordism, etc., etc.) for the exercising of state capacities and functions.[7] Hence the suggestion was increasingly made that the processes associated with post-Fordism, globalization, flexible accumulation, and so forth have profoundly transformed the complexion of state apparatuses and strategies, and that these systemic transformations have cumulatively established the basis for a new kind of nation-state facing much greater (external) constraints on internally regulated economic development.

However, the debate over relative scales of world economic integration, when confined to the terms of the dichotomy "globalization today versus the pre-1913 internationalized economy," tends to overlook one absolutely crucial feature of capitalism, namely, that a global system of accumulation and class struggle has *always* been the basis of any form of modern capitalist accumulation. The segmentation of the world economy into the various national regimes of accumulation is a function of the constitutive polarization that pervades this global system, and the conflicts and antagonisms that exist between the different national regimes of accumulation are primarily, though by no means exclusively, the outcome of this worldwide polarization and its attendant processes of uneven development. To discuss worldwide economic integration within the confines of the rubric "globalization today versus the pre-1913 internationalized economy" is to consider integration only as a force that unifies to varying degrees the various already existing national components of an earlier (pre-1913) and a later (post-1960s) phase of capitalist expansion. It is to overlook the fact that a worldwide and constitutively polarized system of accumulation is precisely the prior condition for the emergence of all the phases of capitalist expansion and their associated national regimes of accumulation.[8] The various national regimes of accumulation and the structures devised to bridge them are at one and the same time expressions of this fundamental polarization and an attempt to manage the resulting uneven development that is this polarization's inevitable outcome. I shall return to the question of this worldwide capitalist polarization in chapter 4 since it is one of the pivotal arguments developed in this book.

The changes that were beginning to take place in the early to mid-1970s did of course have other significant modalities and implications. For instance, it became increasingly apparent that capitalism was attenuating its seemingly inextricable link with the project of modernity and modernization just as the crisis associated with the end of the Golden Age was entrenching itself. During the 1970s the increasingly fashionable neoliberal ideologies commended a form of capitalism detached from modernizing aspirations, and the received wisdom that industrialization and the possession of industrial capital are the engines par excellence of modernity, as well as being the decisive enablers of economic progress—so that an economy is said to be developed, developing, or undeveloped depending on whether or not it has traversed an appropriate path to industrialization, and thus to have taken the "right" steps toward modernization—would become increasingly discredited over subsequent decades. The state, according to the paradigm of economic development supported by this increasingly embattled received wisdom, was the primary instrument of industrialization and modernization, and with the abandonment of the notion that modernization *is* the royal road to economic advancement, the accompanying notion that the state was the dynamo powering any push toward modernity and development was also challenged, primarily by the popular supply-side ideology. For this neoliberal ideology, initially propelled by the Reagan and Thatcher administrations but soon taking root in the thinking of international organizations such as the IMF and the World Bank and in several European Social Democratic parties, adherence to the imperative of market expansion (i.e., liberalization, privatization, deregulation, etc.) was the "new" way forward. The state's function was to aid the expansion of the market by providing the appropriate macroeconomic and microeconomic environment, as well as an adequate institutional framework, for market activity. To do otherwise, said the neoliberal ideologues, would be to distort pricing mechanisms, and thus to hinder a country's economic development.[9] Although I won't consider this neoliberal de-emphasizing of the project of modernity and modernization (a project which posits, even if only as a collective aspiration, an inextricable link between economic advancement and social progress), the position developed here on the role of the state in the new regimes of international competition that have emerged since the end of the Golden Age will involve a critique of a number of aspects of this neoliberal ideology (especially the disjunction it posits between economic advancement and anything like a substantive notion of social progress and emancipation).

The "Hollowing Out" of the Nation-State?

There are several versions of the thesis that a qualitatively new kind of nation-state has emerged since the end of the so-called Golden Age of post–Second World War economic prosperity. Perhaps the best known of these in the literature is the thesis developed by Bob Jessop and others of a similar intellectual political-economic conviction (notably Joachim Hirsch).[10] This position—that of a "hollowing out" of the nation-state after the onset of the capitalist crisis of the 1970s—is embodied in the following theses:

1. Since the 1970s a post-Fordist regime of accumulation (which may not yet be fully realized) has provided the available contours for state formations or state projects.

2. Economic and political apparatuses and strategies whose previous basis was the nation-state are superseded or modified by systemic forces which exert themselves in two directions: (a) toward the transnational and global, and (b) toward the local and regional.

3. The resultant state, which does not emerge directly out of the crisis of Fordism, is the outcome of the complex interplay of two major transformations: (a) externally, it becomes a "competition state," adapted to the new international competitive environment created by the post-Fordist system of accumulation; and (b) as the internal complement of (a), the state becomes a post-Fordist "Schumpeterian workfare state," having abandoned the social and political consensual arrangements between capital and labor that provided the preceding Fordist "Keynesian welfare state" with its raison d'être.

To deal with each thesis in turn:

Thesis 1: The displacement of Fordism by its post-Fordist counterpart is taken by Jessop to involve a fundamental alteration: (a) to the character of the labor process and its means and methods of organization; (b) to the basic pattern of macroeconomic growth; and (c) to (what Jessop refers to as) "the social mode of economic regulation" and its associated social and political order.[11]

(a) Post-Fordism replaces the Taylorist mass-production labor process that typified Fordism with alternatives such as flexible specialization and Toyotism. Mass production is not eliminated in its entirety, but the move to flexibility is intended to overcome the blockages and structural weaknesses that undermine Taylorist mass-production systems.[12] In this way, says Jessop, capitalist entrepreneurs seek

to overcome the alienation and resistance of the mass worker, the relative stagnation of Taylorism and mass production, competitive threats from low-cost exporters in the Third World (or, indeed, from domestic or foreign competitors already using post-Fordist production techniques) and the relative saturation of markets for standardized mass production goods; and/or to meet the growing demand for more differentiated products, action to brake the rising costs of non-Fordist service sectors (notably in the public sector) and measures to boost productivity and profits in manufacturing.[13]

The structural limits and contradictions of the Fordist regime are a spur to innovation (to this extent Jessop is a follower of Schumpeter), and labor and production flexibility are intended by capitalist economic agents to provide a (post-Fordist) production environment attuned to the quest for innovation and responsive to the demand that more efficient ways of "operationalizing" the outcomes of innovation be found.

(b) Fordism rested on a macroeconomic framework that promoted full employment in the national economy primarily through the management of aggregate demand and the governance of collective bargaining and labor markets.[14] The aim of this concordat between capital and labor was to create a "virtuous spiral" of high employment, growing wages and welfare expenditures, mass consumption, and benign business cycles. For a variety of reasons, this macroeconomy became increasingly difficult to administer virtuously, and stagflation, productivity slowdowns, rising unemployment, a declining worldwide average profit rate, current account imbalances, and chronic debt (especially in the less-developed countries) became increasingly prevalent in the Fordist economic system. The reproduction of the capitalist means and relations of production was affected by the economic and political instabilities that accompanied this crisis, and key elements of the debilitated Fordist regime of accumulation were abandoned, albeit in piecemeal fashion and not always consistently (hence, for instance, Reagan's well-documented adherence to a "Keynesianism" based on military expenditures, as his administration incurred record deficits in order to ensure military supremacy over the USSR). From this decomposition of the Fordist regime there emerged, again somewhat unevenly and with significant national variations, the lineaments of a quite different macroeconomy.[15] The new macroeconomy aimed to cultivate flexibility and continual innovation through an array of supply-side instruments highlighting price and quality, with the goal of enhancing competitiveness through the "freeing" of market forces. The new macroeconomy would supplement the "lean" and "just-in-time" production methods that had arisen in response to the "production dilemmas" that appeared to beset Fordist-Taylorist mass production. With this new macroeconomy in place, a shakeout of the seemingly outdated Fordist industries could occur, and the new lean and just-in-time production systems introduced as their successor.[16]

(c) The "social mode of economic regulation" typical of post-Fordism reinforces the supply-side preference for flexibility that defines this new macroeconomic environment. The wage relation is manipulated to drive a bigger wedge between skilled and unskilled workers than was generally permitted under Fordist auspices, and labor market flexibility and fragmentation is actively promoted. Industrywide collective bargaining arrangements are replaced by individual enterprise or factory-level wage bargaining, and new forms of the social wage are devised and implemented as Schumpeterian "workfare" replaces Keynesian "welfare."[17] The same flexibility is sought after in the restructuring of corporations, who, now no longer constrained by state-sanctioned employer-worker compacts, can adopt policies based on the principle of "leanness" and the strategy of employee retrenchment. Markets have become more segmented as niche targeting becomes standard commercial practice. Bank credit systems have become internationalized, and the barriers between credit, insurance, and portfolio investment made more permeable as financial institutions combine previously compartmentalized activities in the name of "diversification," a deeply flawed process that reached its disastrous point of collapse in the 2008 financial crisis.[18] Jessop maintains that the post-Fordist "mode of societalization," which regulates the political and social order that buttresses the existing mode of economic regulation, is still in the process of being consolidated and that "it is too soon to anticipate what this would involve" beyond the claim that what exists at present is "unresolved competition which involves at least the Japanese, German, and American models—each of which is . . . encountering problems on its home ground," so that "a well-developed and relatively stable post-Fordist formation remains an as yet unrealized possibility."[19] Hirsch likewise makes a great deal of this new capitalist "triad."[20] This assertion of an "unresolved" triadic capitalist competition is deeply problematic, not least because it is at least ten years out of date. Jessop's and Hirsch's focus is evidently on productive capitals and their affiliated systems of accumulation, and their theoretical perspective, while it does acknowledge that an exponential growth in finance capital has occurred in the past two decades, does not really deal adequately with the full implications of this massive expansion of financial and currency markets. For this growth of finance capital has clearly made possible a reassertion of American hegemony, albeit in a somewhat different form from the one that prevailed in the heyday of Fordism. More will be said about this shortly.

Thesis 2: The Fordist regime had at its core economic and political apparatuses and strategies whose basis was the nation-state. With the onset of post-

Fordism, these state-oriented formations and principles came to be super-seded or modified by systemic constraints which extended themselves in two directions: (a) toward the transnational and global, and (b) toward the local and regional (though Jessop correctly indicates that the impetus toward the transnational and global which characteristically inflects post-Fordism was in fact inaugurated in the late phases of Fordism).[21] This trend was intensi-fied by the new convergence on flexible production and on the supply side, and was further galvanized by the freshly ascendant international competi-tive regimes which emerged from the crisis of the 1970s.[22] The upshot is that the capitalist state underwent a fundamental reorientation as its appara-tuses and governing axioms were reshaped by the pressures of international competitiveness, supply-side adaptation, and production method and labor market flexibility. This new environment compelled the state to adapt itself to a greatly expanded transnational economic and political domain, even as it had to find new opportunities for accumulation at the regional and local levels. Jessop provides a good description of this vertical and horizontal spa-tial expansion of the range of the state's activities, an outreach that constrains states while still providing strategically positioned countries (primarily those within the OECD) with opportunities to secure economic and political ad-vantages:

> While the national state remains politically important and even retains much of its national sovereignty (albeit as an ever more ineffective, primarily juridi-cal fiction reproduced through mutual recognition in the international com-munity of nations), its capacities to project its power even within its national borders are decisively weakened both by the shift towards internationalized, flexible (but also regionalized) production systems and by the growing chal-lenge posed by risks emanating from the global environment. This loss of autonomy creates in turn both the need for supranational coordination and the space for subnational resurgence. Some state capacities are transferred to a growing number of pan-regional, plurinational, or international bodies with a widening range of powers; others are devolved to restructured local or regional levels of governance in the national state; and yet others are being usurped by emerging horizontal networks of power—local and regional—which by-pass central states and connect localities or regions in several nations.[23]

For Jessop and Hirsch, a less autonomous state ensues from this "after-Fordist" state of affairs. But is this really the case? I shall contend later, fol-lowing Michael Mann, Linda Weiss, and others, that this is too sweeping (and simplifying) a view of the complex environment in which the contemporary nation-state operates (though to be fair, both Jessop and Hirsch grant that the nation-state retains its political importance despite being "hollowed out"), and that some state functions are actually enhanced by globalization, while others are attenuated.

Thesis 3: The resultant state (which, as Jessop and Hirsch point out, does not emerge directly out of the crisis of Fordism) is the outcome of the elaborate interplay of two major transformations: (a) externally, it becomes a "competition state," adapted to the new international competitive conditions created by the post-Fordist system of accumulation; and (b) as the internal complement of (a), the state becomes a post-Fordist "Schumpeterian workfare state," having abandoned the social and political rationales (premised above all on a corporatist "social contract" between capital and labor) that enabled the now receding Fordist "Keynesian welfare state" to function.

This Schumpeterian workfare state derives its enabling conditions from the surrounding emergent post-Fordist regime. Its telos is the consolidation of its (increasingly Schumpeterian) state apparatuses through an active promotion of this regime. This it does by developing state capacities whose raison d'être is the encouragement of innovation and new technologies, innovation and technological advancement being seen in the context of the workfare state as the best way to get the state to respond to the new international competitive environment.[24]

The upshot of this move to a Schumpeterian workfare state is a transformation of state apparatuses, as the activities and policies of supranational formations and systems, as well as international regimes and organizations, become more consequential in the after-Fordist political and economic setting. The various strategies of devolution favored by governments responding to this emergent regime of accumulation also foster the growth of regional or local states and translocal networks. But the nation-state continues to retain many of its political functions, especially those concerned with the reproduction of labor and the regulation of the wage form, even as it surrenders several of these to supranational and subnational levels of political organization. The state, suitably restructured or hollowed out to deal with this more "open" economic environment, is still required to manage the linkages across the various territorial demarcations established by the new geopolitical order that is aligned with post-Fordism, but as it does so its role is redefined by changes "in the balance of forces as globalization, triadization, regionalization and the resurgence of local governance proceed apace."[25]

The key political transformation involved in this hollowing out of the state is the transition from *government* to *governance*, that is, the movement from a form of political organization in which the official state apparatus employs its hegemony over its semi- and nonofficial counterparts to ensure the primacy of the state in the regulation of economic, political, social, and cultural life, to one in which the official state apparatus reduces or relinquishes its direct involvement in the regulation of these domains and concentrates instead on "meta-governance."[26] In metagovernance the state and its appurtenances provide the conditions and resources which enable nongovernmental and semigovernmental apparatuses to organize themselves, sometimes in tandem with governmental institutions and sometimes not. Governance in the Schumpeterian workfare state therefore involves an ensemble of state and nongovernmental partnerships, with no necessary or automatic presumption of the state's primacy in this configuration. The state and the other constituent elements in these partnerships are alike deemed to be constrained by market mechanisms and their intermediations.

The Rise of an Equity-Based Growth Regime

While Jessop and Hirsch recognize that the post-Fordist dispensation has seen a considerable expansion of the various forms of finance capital, this acknowledgment on their part nevertheless does not seem to encompass some of the more profound implications of the explosive growth that financial markets have undergone since the 1980s. Certainly this relative de-emphasizing of the role of finance-led regimes of accumulation in contemporary capitalist expansion has been a problematic feature of the thinking of the Ecole Régulation until very recently (when Michel Aglietta and Robert Boyer started to deal with the part played by deregulated financial markets in transforming the structures of competition that are a central feature of the Regulation School's account of post-Fordism). The increased primacy enjoyed by financial capital over industrial capital in the countries of the North and West in the past couple of decades is coterminous with the rise of an equity-based growth regime in most of the developed countries (and the Unites States in particular). This equity-based regime, which was perhaps still in the process of becoming fully fledged when the 2008 banking crisis started to bite, has made possible the reassertion of an American economic hegemony (which admittedly could turn out to be short-lived if a protracted and severe recession starts to embed itself at the end of 2008),[27] and this finance-led regime's current significance will greatly affect the state's role in the current and (in all likelihood) succeeding phases of capitalist development.

TABLE 1. Daily volume of global foreign exchange transactions (in US$ billion)

April 1986	188	April 1995	1,120	April 2001	1,380
April 1989	650	April 1998	1,590	April 2004	1,880
April 1992	840				

Source: Bank of International Settlements, *Triennial Central Bank Survey of Foreign Exchange and Derivatives Market Activity 2004*, March 2005.

Note: Turnover in this table is given at April 2004 exchange rates. The figure for April 1986 is taken from Elwell, "Global Capital Market Integration" (www.ncseonline.org/nle/crsreports) and is not given at 2004 exchange rates; Elwell takes his figures from the Bank of International Settlements. For a helpful analysis of global foreign exchange transactions, see Nissanke, "Revenue Potential of the Currency Transaction Tax for Development Finance: A Critical Appraisal," *World Institute for Development Economics Research*, December 2003 (www.currencytax.org).

Proponents of the view that the state is being hollowed out or is in retreat must therefore be willing to analyze this American-dominated equity-based growth regime; indeed, given that this regime is preeminent among current growth regimes, and bearing in mind also that financial markets are the most globally integrated of all the markets, the overall plausibility of the hollowing-out or retreat thesis will hinge on the outcome of this analysis. The rise of this equity-based growth regime has had a powerful impact on the economies of the less-developed countries (LDCs), and so any examination of this regime's impact on state formations and state capacities must take LDCs into account. Jessop and the members of the Ecole Régulation, while noting post-Fordism's considerable effects on the economies of the LDCs, nonetheless pay scant attention to LDC state formations and accumulation regimes.[28]

It is difficult to do full justice here to the many facets of the epochal transformations that have taken place in extraterritorial financial markets and institutions since the early 1970s. With the abolition of restrictions on international capital movements initiated in 1973, the volume of transactions in global foreign exchange markets rose from an average of $15 billion per day that year to $1,880 billion per day in 2004 (see table 1). In April 2004 overall turnover, including nontraditional foreign exchange derivatives and products traded on global foreign exchanges, averaged over $2 trillion a day. This was nearly fifteen times the size of the combined daily turnover on all the world's equity markets.[29]

Less than 2 percent of this sum is currently devoted to trade in goods

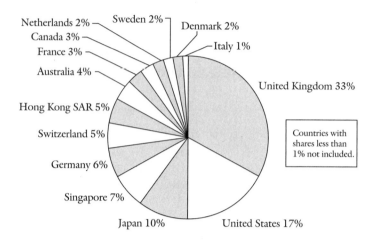

Netherlands 2%
Sweden 2%
Denmark 2%
Canada 3%
Italy 1%
France 3%
Australia 4%
United Kingdom 33%
Hong Kong SAR 5%
Switzerland 5%
Countries with shares less than 1% not included.
Germany 6%
Singapore 7%
Japan 10%
United States 17%

6. Country percentage of shares of the foreign exchange market, 2001

Source: Federal Reserve Bank of New York, *The Basics of Foreign Trade and Exchange,* "Foreign Currency Exchange," www.ny.frb.org/education.

and services (compared to 15 percent in 1973). The proportion for foreign direct investment (FDI) is just as small, though FDI flows to developing and emerging market countries have risen significantly since the 1990s. The rest, amounting to more than a trillion dollars a day (exceeding the aggregate gold and foreign exchange holdings of all the world's central banks), is devoted to transactions, mostly short term, by private individuals in currency and other financial markets.[30] But in noting some of the more distinctive features of these shifts, it can be seen that in addition to the stupendous growth in the overall daily volume of foreign exchange transactions between 1973 and 2004 there has been an equally marked change in the composition of the flows themselves, especially to the LDCs. Global foreign exchange transactions are very much dominated by three countries, the United Kingdom, the United States, and Japan, who between them have 60 percent of the foreign exchange market (figure 6).

Despite the primacy in regard to foreign exchange markets enjoyed by a mere three advanced industrial countries, the impact of capital flows to the markets of the emerging market countries has been considerable. Capital flows to emerging market countries amounted to $230 billion in 1996, nearly six times the level at the beginning of the 1990s and four times greater than in their previous high point, the commercial bank lending explosion of 1978–82. At that time the LDCs started to attract a greater share of these global capital flows, in spite of the setbacks represented by the Mexican peso crisis of 1994 and the Asian financial crisis of 1997–98. The share of developing and transition economies in global FDI rose from 15 percent in 1990 to nearly 40 percent in 1996. In addition, the rise in their share of global portfolio equity investment rose from less than 2 percent in 1990 to 30 percent in 1996.[31]

However, the Asian financial crisis of 1997–98 and the end of the American dot-com bubble in the first decade of the twenty-first century saw a decline in total net flows to emerging countries in the two years from 1999 to 2001. But there has been a steady revival since 2001, though as of 2003 these flows had still to reach their levels in 1997, and even while the steady rise of foreign direct investment has clearly been little affected by these crises, portfolio investment took a big tumble during these crises, from which it has not recovered (tables 2 and 3). Since the 1980s official flows have lost their previous centrality, and levels of bank lending have been low since the debt crisis of the 1980s. Portfolio investment grew significantly in the early 1990s but has remained a major cause of financial volatility, as witnessed by the Mexican peso and Asian crises, and its impact has been much reduced since the Asian crisis. Foreign direct investment, however, was the main component of private capital flows to the emerging market economies in the 1990s. This phase of development is well summed up in the Deutsches Bundesbank report on the role of foreign direct investment in the emerging economies:

> In the aftermath of the Asian crisis, according to the European Central Bank, net private capital flows to 45 Emerging Market Economies declined to 1% of GDP in 2002, after having stood at 3.7% of GDP in 1995. During this period FDI not only held up but actually increased. Striking is the shift that occurred simultaneously in the relative shares of net private capital flows for the different regions. While in 1996 the capital flows were evenly spread at around 4% of GDP, by 2002 the Asian share had fallen to 1% of GDP and that of Latin America to only 0.5% of GDP, while the European accession countries enjoyed an increase in their share to 7% of GDP.[32]

The global financial situation in the years since 2005 shows a basic continuity with the trends of the past two decades. Thus the Institute of International Finance said in a recent press release that "the net private capital flows to emerging markets rose to $782 billion in 2007 from the previous record level seen in 2006 of $568 billion."[33] The variability of some of their specific components notwithstanding, the available evidence therefore shows that there has been an exponential growth in overall capital flows to the emerging market economies in the two decades since the 1980s. (It is too early to tell what the longer term impact of the 2008 bank lending crisis will be.)

TABLE 2. Net private capital flows to emerging market economies, 1971–1989 (in US$ billions)

Countries/Position	Annual Average	
	1971–81	1982–89
All countries	11.4	16.6
FDI	5.3	12.0
Portfolio investment	0.6	6.2
Others	6.4	−1.7
Africa	n.a.	4.2
FDI	0.8	1.3
Portfolio investment	0.0	0.1
Others	n.a.	2.8
Asia	8.1	10.3
FDI	1.7	5.0
Portfolio investment	0.2	1.1
Others	6.2	4.2
*Middle East and Europe**	−14.6	1.1
FDI	−0.6	0.5
Portfolio Investment	−0.1	4.9
Others	−13.9	−4.4
Western Hemisphere	17.9	1.0
FDI	3.4	5.2
Portfolio investment	0.5	0.1
Others	14.1	−4.3
Memorandum items		
Total capital flows, net	n.a.	41.4
Net official flows	n.a.	27.3
Changes in reserves	−20.8	−2.5
Current account	−2.1	−30.0

Sources: Deutsche Bundesbank, *The Role of FDI in Emerging Market Economies Compared to Other Forms of Financing: Past Developments and Implications for Financial Stability of Emerging Market Economies* (Frankfurt, 2003), based on IMF, *World Economic Outlook*, September 2002; IMF database.

*Including the countries of the former USSR in transition.

This very substantial total private investment in the LDCs (albeit in only a few select ones, mainly in East Asia, though Brazil and Russia are beginning to see increased flows) has been made possible by important structural changes in the financial markets themselves and by the creation of several new instruments of international finance since the 1980s, largely because of liberalization and also because of the emergence of completely new international markets for securities, futures, options, swaps, international mutual funds, international bonds (these markets were opened to developing countries in the 1990s), and American and global depository receipts that gave American companies access to the stock markets of industrialized and industrializing countries.[34]

Part of this development was a new interest shown by investors in developing-country stock markets that led quickly to a boom in the East Asian bourses; in 1993 alone the share indexes in Hong Kong grew by 116 percent, in Jakarta by 115 percent, and in Manila (the best Asian performer in that year) by 154 percent.[35] The scale of this very rapid growth can be indicated by a comparison, made by Ajit Singh, between the relative times it took the United States and the LDCs to reach roughly the same capitalization ratios: "The speed of development of Third World stock markets in the recent period may be judged from the fact that it took eighty-five years (1810–1895) for the U.S. capitalization ratio (market capitalization as a proportion of GDP) to rise from 7 percent to 71 percent. In contrast, the corresponding Taiwanese ratio jumped from 11 percent to 74 percent in just 10 years between 1981 and 1991. Similarly, between 1983 and 1993 the Chilean ratio rose from 13.2 percent to 78 percent; the Korean from 5.4 percent to 36.2 percent and the Thai from 3.8 percent to 55.8."[36] The Asian financial crisis put a sudden brake on this exponential growth in Asian stock market capitalization, but by 2003 the Asian Development Bank, citing Institute of International Finance figures, reported:

> The outlook net private capital flows to emerging markets rose to a 3-year high of $194.1 billion in 2003, up from $128.3 billion in 2002. Net private flows to developing Asia accounted for $116.7 billion, nearly double the amount of $66.3 billion in 2002. Half of this total ($58.3 billion) was financed by direct investment, much of it flowing to the PRC [People's Republic of China]. An improving economic environment and rising corporate profitability led to a surge in portfolio inflows to developing Asia from $2.8 billion in 2002 to $29.4 billion in 2003. Bank and nonbank lending accounted for a further $29.0 billion, up from $6.7 billion in 2002.[37]

TABLE 3. Net private capital flows to emerging market economies, 1990–2003 (in US$ billions)

Countries/Position	Annual Average 1990–96	Annual Average 1997–2002	1996	1997	1998	1999	2000	2001	2002*	2003*
All countries	142.2	61.0	228.8	102.2	62.1	84.8	29.4	24.9	62.4	64.9
FDI	62.0	156.8	114.4	141.7	153.6	164.0	158.0	172.1	151.3	160.9
Portfolio investment	59.0	5.2	90.2	46.7	-0.1	34.3	-4.3	-42.6	-3.0	-4.0
Others	21.0	-101.0	24.1	-86.2	-91.5	-113.4	-124.3	-104.6	-85.9	-91.9
Africa	7.1	9.7	11.9	9.4	11.6	15.1	6.1	6.9	8.8	8.9
FDI	2.5	10.9	3.6	7.8	6.4	9.3	7.7	22.3	11.8	10.1
Portfolio investment	1.8	1.1	2.8	7.0	3.7	8.2	-2.2	-9.0	-1.0	-1.3
Others	2.9	-2.4	5.5	-5.4	1.5	-2.5	0.6	-6.4	-2.0	0.1
Asia	60.4	0.6	122.1	7.1	-45.9	6.8	-12.9	16.7	31.6	7.9
FDI	31.7	56.3	53.4	56.8	59.7	61.2	54.2	47.1	58.7	59.0
Portfolio investment	16.5	-0.8	32.8	7.3	-17.9	14.4	4.3	-13.5	0.7	-9.7
Others	12.2	-54.9	35.9	-56.9	-87.7	-68.8	-71.4	-16.8	-27.8	-41.3
Middle East and Turkey	22.5	-11.0	7.2	15.0	9.1	0.2	-22.4	-48.4	-19.6	-9.4
FDI	3.5	7.5	4.8	5.5	6.5	5.5	7.9	10.8	8.8	11.5
Portfolio investment	6.3	-10.5	1.8	-0.9	-13.2	-3.2	-13.7	-22.0	-9.8	-6.6
Others	12.7	-8.1	0.6	10.4	15.8	-2.1	-16.7	-37.1	-18.6	-14.4

Western Hemisphere	40.0	45.6	64.9	69.3	72.7	49.7	48.6	22.8	10.3	26.5
FDI	6.1	23.4	12.3	15.5	60.1	64.1	64.7	66.9	40.4	45.6
Portfolio investment	26.8	10.6	39.5	25.9	22.3	11.9	4.7	-2.2	1.0	7.6
Others	-5.0	-23.8	-14.9	-12.7	-9.8	-26.3	-20.8	-41.9	-31.1	-26.7
Countries in transition	11.8	16.2	22.6	1.3	14.6	13.0	10.0	26.8	31.2	31.1
FDI	6.1	23.4	12.3	15.5	20.9	23.9	23.4	25.1	31.5	34.7
Portfolio investment	7.5	4.7	13.3	7.5	5.0	2.9	2.6	4.2	6.1	6.0
Others	-1.8	-11.9	-3.0	-21.6	-11.3	-13.8	-16.0	-2.5	-6.4	-9.6
Memorandum items										
Total capital flows, net	165.0	92.1	226.5	170.5	132.0	97.0	29.6	40.3	83.0	83.1
Net official flows	23.1	31.1	-2.3	68.3	69.9	12.2	0.2	15.4	20.6	18.2
Changes in reserves	-69.9	-97.4	-108.1	-68.8	-48.2	-87.9	-113.2	-119.9	-146.6	-129.7
Current account	-80.8	32.9	-96.5	-69.1	-52.3	34.1	128.4	94.7	61.3	41.7

Sources: Deutsche Bundesbank, *The Role of* FDI *in Emerging Market Economies Compared to Other Forms of Financing: Past Developments and Implications for Financial Stability of Emerging Market Economies* (Frankfurt, 2003), based on IMF, *World Economic Outlook*, September 2002; IMF database.

*Estimate or projection.

Clearly, the Asian countries recovered well in the years after the crisis of 1997, and in the process portfolio inflows started to pick up as well.

The consequences of LDC reliance on external capital flows have been noted by students of international political economy in recent years; the growing dependence of LDCs on external capital flows has also been instrumental in creating the structural conditions responsible for a potentially chronic economic instability, especially when LDCs are confronted with large inflows that prove unsustainable for their economies or rapid outflows which quickly become unmanageable. Thus, in addition to the Mexican and Asian currency crises, there has been the Russian default of 1998, the Brazilian peso crisis in 1998 and 1999, and Argentina's financial crisis of 2001 (though financial market turbulence is certainly not the sole cause of these crises).[38]

To begin with, there is the sheer disparity of scale between the combined resources of the funds run by financial institutions in the wealthier countries and the market capital of low- to middle-income countries very new to this form of capitalism. In 1994 the combined pool of funds managed by financial institutions in the high-income countries ran to around $10 trillion to $15 trillion, whereas the total market capitalization of all lower-income countries was in the order of $1 trillion.[39] In 2000 the estimated total value of world stocks, bonds, securities, and other financial assets was $50 trillion.[40] Total global equity market capitalization in that year amounted to $37 trillion; of this, 40 percent was located in the United States and 20 percent in continental Europe, while a mere 10 percent went to developing countries. The United Nations High-Level Panel on Financing for Development reports that $7.5 trillion was saved or invested worldwide in 2000.[41] Of this, only $1.7 trillion was invested in developing countries in that year. Total world FDI inflows were $209 billion in 1990, $473 billion in 1997 ($178 billion, or 35 percent, was the developing countries' share), and $1,118 billion ($190 billion, or 17 percent, was the developing countries' share) in 2000. However, the share of the world's 48 least developed countries in 1999 total world FDI was a meager 0.5 percent. In fact, 70 percent of incoming FDI in the period 1993–1998 went to a mere 20 developing countries (out of 138). The ability of many LDCs to influence trends and developments in global financial markets is therefore extremely limited. The Morgan Stanley economist Stephen Roach made precisely this point in his testimony to the U.S. House of Representatives in May 1999:

> It may well be that the tiny emerging market economies of the world are literally awash in the turbulent seas of financial capital. For example, the equity

market capitalization of large emerging market countries such as Korea, Malaysia, Taiwan and Brazil each totaled about $150 to $200 billion in the pre-crisis period of the mid-1990s. By contrast, the capitalization of the U.S. equity market was about $6 to $7 trillion during that period (and is now closing in on $13 trillion). . . . At today's market levels just a 0.5% move out of U.S. equities into the emerging-market asset class—hardly an unreasonable asset allocation shift for performance-oriented institutional investors—would be worth around $60 billion. Such an increment would equate to fully 6% of the combined market capitalization of the major equity markets in the developing world.[42]

The effects of an imbalance of this kind during a rapid capital-movement episode are potentially catastrophic for an LDC, whose stock exchange is likely to be dominated by foreign-owned portfolios that can be pulled out very quickly. Portfolio investors are prone to make quick withdrawals of their funds if short-term performance targets are not met or if other economic indicators are thought to portend weakness (such as the high levels of nonperforming loans in East Asian banking systems that are said to have been instrumental in bringing about the financial crisis in 1997). This is especially true of U.S. mutual funds, which are inclined to jettison their holdings if quarterly performance standards are not reached or if a falling market is expected. A third feature of the new kinds of portfolio capital that promote instabilities of the kind seen in a number of LDCs in the 1990s (Mexico, the East Asian countries) has to do with the disposition of short-term investment capital not to reflect underlying economic "fundamentals" such as output or employment.[43] A rise in U.S. or European interest rates, say, with no change whatsoever in the macroeconomic conditions of the LDC involved, can nonetheless induce a change of perception on the part of foreign portfolio investors with holdings in that lower-income country. A swift reversal of investment flows results as funds are channeled elsewhere in a stock market stampede, with possibly devastating consequences for prices in the equity markets of the LDC thus affected. The behavior of this new form of short-term portfolio capital is quite different from that of financial and industrial capital as characterized by Marx, since the virtual autonomy it enjoys in relation to actual economic activity (this being the primary source of its volatility) makes it correspond more to what he calls "fictitious capital" in volume 3 of *Capital*, where it is used to designate a form of capital that creates money in ways completely detached from the productive process and the exploitation of labor.[44] Chapter 4 provides a more detailed description of this finance-led, equity-based accumulation regime.

The Impact of the Current Finance-Led, Equity-Based Growth Regime

The immense proliferation of pension, insurance, and mutual funds in the past two decades or so has changed radically the circuits of realization and accumulation that are currently at the disposal of the capitalist system. The LDCs, as we have seen, are in an even more vulnerable position than their wealthier counterparts when it comes to dealing with financial market volatility. This is not to suggest that LDC governments are entirely powerless when confronted with surges of external capital; there is considerable evidence that a number of viable policy instruments are available to governments seeking to control financial market turbulence.[45] In fact, the instances provided by Mexico and Vietnam provide interesting contrasts with regard to the issue of market openness and a country's ability to adhere to economic policies which eschew market liberalization. Larry Elliott, summarizing the views of Dani Rodrik and Ha-Joon Chang, notes the following differences between the economic strategies of these two countries, which have espoused diametrically opposed strategies with regard to "market openness":

> One has a long border with the richest country in the world and has had a free-trade agreement with its neighbour across the Rio Grande. It receives oodles of inward investment and sends its workers across the border in droves. It is fully plugged in to the global economy. The other was the subject of a U.S. trade embargo until 1994 and suffered from trade restrictions for years after that. Unlike Mexico, Vietnam is not even a member of the WTO. So which of the two has the better recent economic record? The question should be a no-brainer if all the free-trade theories are right—Mexico should be streets ahead of Vietnam. In fact, the opposite is true. Since Mexico signed the Nafta (North American Free Trade Agreement) deal with the U.S. and Canada in 1992, its annual per capita growth rate has barely been above 1%. Vietnam has grown by around 5% a year for the past two decades. Poverty in Vietnam has come down dramatically: real wages in Mexico have fallen.[46]

Acknowledging the fact that "market openness" is not a panacea for the LDCs cannot obscure the equally compelling fact that the important changes brought about during the two decades-long ascendancy of the finance-led, equity-based growth regime necessitate a revision in one of marxism's key positions on the genesis of capital, namely, that a precapitalist "space" has to adjoin the "space" of an existing capitalist accumulation to provide the latter with a source for the extraction of surplus value (this being the essence of what Marx called "primitive accumulation").[47] The problem with Marx's theory of primitive accumulation is that, as Rosa Luxemburg noted, the notion rests on a seeming incongruity, namely, that in capitalist accumulation the conditions of direct exploitation and the conditions for realizing surplus value are separated by space and time. The former are limited by the productive capacities of the society in question, while the latter depend, not on productive capabilities, but on the power to consume (and this in turn hinges on that society's "antagonistic conditions of distribution").[48] The upshot is that the mere presence of the conditions of direct exploitation is not sufficient to enable capitalist reproduction to take place. For Luxemburg, therefore, capitalism, if it is to reproduce itself and expand, must have available to it, even in its maturity, both the primordial capacity to consume *and* the allied resources of distribution needed to satisfy this capacity.

The problem with Luxemburg's resolution of Marx's conundrum regarding primitive accumulation is that the several and varied instruments of credit can intervene repeatedly to reactivate capacities to consume, thereby obviating the spatiotemporal gap between Luxemburg's conditions of direct exploitation and the conditions for realizing surplus value lodged in the capacity to consume.[49] For instance, the nub of the 2008 financial crisis was the set of economic and political circumstances which enabled housing to become the principal object of financial speculation in America and Britain. Shelter has from time immemorial been regarded as one of the primal human needs, and a rational society would deal with it in these terms, so there is no inevitability which necessitates that housing be the focal point of a financial market speculative frenzy. The speculative housing market unleashed for a short time a phase of "easy credit," which in turn fueled consumption, albeit with the disastrous economic consequences that are now becoming more and more apparent. Money is thus the essential bridge between the two sets of conditions required for the realization of capital's circuit of value, and credit (in this case, equity-derived wealth) forms a "surplus" fueling the power to consume. An equity-based, financialized growth regime of the kind that has existed in the past two decades or so is nowadays very much the synchronizing link between capital's production and consumption conditions. In fact, the wealth derived from equity that feeds consumption undertakes one of the key functions assigned by Marx and Luxemburg to a "primitive accumulation."

The finance-led and equity-based regime adverted to here has been characterized in a number of very recent works by members of the Ecole Régulation.[50] This regime, which is now dominant and is variably dispersed across the advanced economies, possesses the following distinguishing features, many of them associated with the phenomenon of "the new economy." For the pivotal role played by the wage-labor link in Fordism it substitutes a matrix of financial institutions and innovative instruments, and the stability of the system is entrusted to the Central Bank and not to state-mediated capital-labor collective wage arrangements (as was the case in the heyday of Fordism).[51] Firms become oriented toward capital markets and their logic of public valuation rather than meeting performance criteria based on increasingly outmoded principles of corporate organization and governance, so that "successful companies capture quasi-rents downstream in fast-expanding markets for final goods and services where the goodwill resides and at the same time pass the costs of making commodities on to others."[52] Its other characteristics have been described thus by Robert Boyer:

> Many giant mergers, capital mobility between countries, pressures on corporate governance, diffusion of equity among a larger fraction of population, all these transformations . . . lead to a totally novel regulation mode . . . [combining] labour market flexibility, price stability, developing high tech sectors, booming stock market and credit to sustain the rapid growth of consumption, and permanent optimism of expectations in firms. The capacity of each country to adapt and implement such a model would be a key factor in macroeconomic performance and would determine that country's place in a hierarchical world economy governed by the diffusion of a financialized growth regime.[53]

At the same time, the structure of consumer demand has been reconstituted as a response to unprecedented levels of product innovation and niche marketing. Since both demand and supply are generally regulated by asset price expectations, the possibility exists of a benign spiral in which heightened expectations of profits lead to an appreciation of asset prices, which in turn boosts incomes and consumer demand, and this is turn vindicates the initial heightened expectation of profits, thereby triggering (hopefully!) another round of self-fulfilling profit expectations. As is clear from the U.S. housing-loan crisis of 2008, it was the combination of loans to less creditworthy borrowers and the unwarranted expectation that housing prices would continue rising indefinitely (and thereby serving as a source of easy credit) which fueled the anticipation of an unending "virtuous spiral" in the U.S. housing market. The potential risk of making loans to "marginal" borrowers was presumed to be offset by the rising "value" of the assets purchased by these hazardous loans, and when the assets in question subsequently declined in value in a classic bubble collapse, the now unsafe loans became "toxic" (the favored term used by journalists working in the business and finance segments of U.S. media outlets).

This new profit-propelled system of accumulation enables the top echelon of salary earners to rely on more than fixed wages for incomes, since they now enjoy greater access to wealth derived from equity and pension fund holdings. The wealth originating from financial markets is able to galvanize consumption on an overall scale barely conceivable in previous regimes of accumulation. In this ostensibly benign spiral, therefore, "the whole macro-economic dynamic is . . . driven by the compatibility between the expectations emanating from financial markets, the reality of firms' profit growth and interest-rate dynamics, which the central bank is trying to direct."[54]

This finance-led system, though led by the United States, is of course globalized, and so other national economies must respond to the financial rate of return available in their counterpart economies: movements of capital affect exchange rates, and a country's exchange-rate policy affects its credibility as a protagonist in global financial markets. Even the perennial external trade deficits of the United States have to be financed by the savings of other countries (primarily China), giving the economically bankrupt United States an incentive (though there are others) to promote an open and "competitive" international financial system that will give it access to the savings of Asian and European countries.

The international system of financial markets has thus undergone a series of historic structural transformations since 1972, several of which are still taking place.[55] These include changes in the sources of international credit and a new capital-recycling mechanism; together they began a revolutionary transformation that has continuing effects. The changes in the sources of international credit are well known, but, says Randall Germain, the more important changes have taken place in the capital-recycling mechanism, that is, "the form of credit made available to the world economy, in the networks of monetary agents which control access to this credit, and in the relationship between public monetary agents and private monetary agents within the global financial system."[56] As a result, Germain goes on to say, a new era in international finance came to exist, one that can appropriately be called "decentralized globalization" and which is to be associated with the enfranchisement of a whole range of new and not always disciplined systemic creditors,[57] the rise generally of unstable institutional arrangements,[58] the diminished authority and effectiveness of state and public monetary institutions (except when it came to leading the way in deregulating financial markets),[59] the complementary growth in the authority and effectiveness of private monetary institutions (toward whom the balance of power has now gravitated), and the changing of the criteria used to govern access to flows of mobile capital (these having already moved in favor of the interests of largely unregulated private agents).[60]

While private institutions have grown hugely in importance, the state continues to have a role because capital mobility is not perfect, in at least two respects. One is that the state still possesses a degree of macroeconomic policy autonomy, though this room for maneuver is nonetheless circumscribed by the global integration of financial markets and by the propensity of states in this situation to allow private agents use of their policy instruments in ways which effectively make these agents proxies for state and public authority. The second is the preeminence enjoyed by the United States (and to a lesser extent the Western European nations and Japan) in determining the course and constitution of global financial markets; allied with this is the primacy enjoyed by the financial markets in New York, Tokyo, and London. A state-based hegemony is thus very much the continuing core of the international financial system. But this state capability notwithstanding, today no single state or public authority has effective control of the international financial system (even if the institutions of American hegemony and the OECD central banks have a pivotal place in this system). The result is a growing regionalization of interest rates and the declining importance of reserve requirements as financial institutions become more hybridized and their resources more interchangeable as a result.[61]

There is no unitary model of how this finance-led growth regime relates to other regimes whose raison d'être is less the accumulation of financial assets and more the production and exchange of commodities. Boyer identifies a number of alternative post-Fordist growth regimes: those led by Toyotism (Japan until 1990), services (the United States in the 1980s), information and communication technologies (Silicon Valley since the mid-1980s), knowledge-based sources (the United States since the 1990s), competition (most OECD countries since 1985), exports (the East Asian "tiger economies"), and finance (the United States and United Kingdom since the 1990s). It is evident from this typology that there can be hybrid post-Fordist formations (e.g., the U.S. economy's dependence on knowledge-based sources, information and communication technologies, and finances, with the last preponderating primarily because it is the strategic locus of the country's resources for macroeconomic management).[62]

At the same time, the weight of evidence, considered earlier in this chapter, indicates overwhelmingly that the poorer LDCs have virtually no place in this system from which they can hope realistically to influence its overall direction. Fundamental asymmetries permeate the international financial system, and the divorce between financial and productive capital, integral to the equity-based, finance-led growth regime, only reinforces the worldwide economic polarization that has been a feature of capitalist accumulation since its inception.

This time, however, a different kind of account must be given of the worldwide economic polarization from the account that prevails in the standard theories of uneven development and dependency. In the standard theories, unequal exchange exists because of an international division of labor which allows the advanced industrial countries to commandeer high-level industrial productive capacity while consigning LDCs to the production of "low value-added" commodities or the extraction of raw materials (this being the phenomenon of compulsory maldevelopment described by Samir Amin and others in the dependency and uneven development school), and because international trade on these terms can never be mutually advantageous. Figure 7 indicates that in 2001 35 percent of developing country exports were devoted to agriculture and food, as well as ores and minerals. Figure 8 shows, conversely, just how small the agricultural sector is in relation to industry and services where the developed countries are concerned.

However, in the finance-led growth regime, the main source of international economic polarization is precisely the autonomy of finance capital from productive capital. Finance capital, or "money," often in forms that are sometimes hard to recognize, so far have they departed from run-of-the-mill conceptions of "currency," synchronizes the production and consumption circuits identified by Rosa Luxemburg, and this synchronization speeds up the processes that realize surplus value by abbreviating the linkages between production and consumption. Command over the essential instrument of synchronization, that is, finance or money, therefore translates more or less immediately into the capacity to realize surplus value, and this in ways detached from the productive process itself and the direct exploitation of labor itself (which nonetheless takes place, especially in "low value-added" zones of production).[63]

This fundamental disconnection of finance (and "fictitious") capital from productive capital in the equity-based growth regime causes asymmetries between the high- and low-income countries that appear to be even more deeply entrenched than the parallel asymmetries in previous growth regimes, where political-economic power resided (largely) in a country's ability to

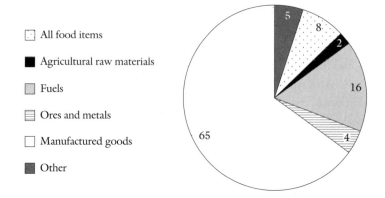

All food items

Agricultural raw materials

Fuels

Ores and metals

Manufactured goods

Other

5

8

2

16

4

65

7. Developing country exports by commodity group

Source: United Nations Conference on Trade and Development, *2004, Development and Globalization: Facts and Figures* (New York: United Nations, 2004), 5.

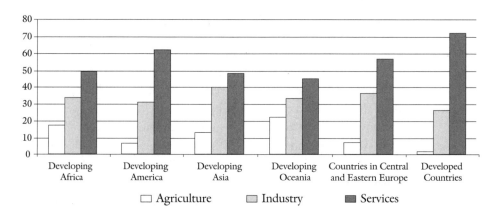

Developing Africa · Developing America · Developing Asia · Developing Oceania · Countries in Central and Eastern Europe · Developed Countries

☐ Agriculture ▨ Industry ▮ Services

8. Gross Domestic Product by expenditure and economic activity
(in percentages), 2001

Source: United Nations Conference on Trade and Development, *2004, Development and Globalization: Facts and Figures* (New York: United Nations, 2004), 21.

command industrial capacity (the ability of the USSR to keep up with the United States up to the 1970s being the paradigmatic case). Questions of the organizing of the power to command industrial capacity are undeniably complex, but this particular form of command is in principle less path-dependent than the power to command a financialized economy, where the structures of financial intermediation are so path-dependent (so far they seem quite specific to the United States and United Kingdom) that they are likely to defeat any attempt at replication.[64] A Singapore or Tokyo and, to a much lesser extent, a China (or rather Shanghai and Hong Kong) or India (or rather Mumbai) may benefit by performing selective functions in this equity-led regime, but a Mali or Ecuador or Fiji can do little or nothing to establish even a toehold in such a system. So the question remains whether the more damaging effects of the asymmetries generated by the finance-led, equity-based growth regime can be surmounted by an LDC such as Mali or Fiji or indeed any of the 150 or so LDCs.

CHAPTER 4

The Exacerbation of Uneven Development
Analysis of the Current Regime of Accumulation

Chapter 3 showed that powerful asymmetries exist between the economically advanced "metropolitan" countries and the countries of the less-developed periphery, so that capital flows between the metropolitan center and the LDC periphery accord fundamentally with the requirements of the economically advanced countries. For the poorer LDCs, it is very much a case of "If you play by our rules, you may perhaps hope that small rewards will come your way every now and then." Markets and governments in the LDCs are given little or no option but to tailor their strategies and policies to the requirements of markets and governments in the economically advanced countries. Anyone who thinks that Alan Greenspan (then) and Ben Bernanke (now) somehow lose one minute of sleep over economic trends in (say) Angola or Nepal during their respective tenures as chairmen of the U.S. Federal Reserve clearly does not live in the world taken for granted by *The Economist* and the *Wall Street Journal*, let alone *USA Today* and Fox News. (Certainly the world would be a better place for most of its inhabitants if more people refused to live in the world defined by *The Economist*, etc., but entertaining such fantasies about Greenspan's or Bernanke's possible nocturnal global economic anxieties is not even going to make us *think* that the world needs to be a different and better place for its most economically downtrodden citizens.)

On Retaining and Modifying the Dependency Paradigm

In this chapter I examine the claim, advanced in many quarters and in several versions, that the most recent forms of capitalist development have effectively discredited theories of uneven or dependent development, because these theories hinge crucially on conceptions that are no longer plausible theoretically and that have moreover been sidelined by recent historical events. Thus, as I mentioned in chapter 3, the end of the Golden Age of postwar economic prosperity in the West resulted in a radical restructuring of world capitalism that enabled the emergence of new regimes of international competition. These new regimes have caused many LDCs to lurch into protracted chronic debt and current account imbalances. At the same time these LDCs have had to face the foreclosure of any real alternative to complete assimilation into the capitalist system of production, especially since the only apparent alternative to capitalism, the "actually existing socialism" of the former Eastern bloc, fell into desuetude in 1989 (if not before).

However, while the majority of peripheral and semiperipheral countries have not benefited from the regime of accumulation superseding that of the Golden Age, the countries of East Asia (the so-called East Asian Tigers) have until recently been able to advance economically, thereby controverting a major tenet of the *dependencia* school. With the significant advance of the East Asian countries, it was no longer possible to maintain a hard and fast distinction between "core," "semiperipheral," and "peripheral" nations (if indeed this was ever really possible) and to insist that dependency is an ineluctable condition of nations not initially situated inside the capitalist core, and that moreover the very constitution of the core requires other national economies to exist in a systemic state of economic subordination to the metropolitan countries.

At a more purely theoretical level, critiques have also been made of the various "essentialisms" and false "universalisms" that are said to bedevil the underdevelopment and dependency paradigms. Examples of these include the presumption that industrialization and the possession of industrial capital are absolutely crucial requisites of economic progress (so that a country's economy is deemed to be developed, developing, or undeveloped depending on whether or not it has traversed an appropriate path to industrialization, hopefully reaching W. W. Rostow's mythical "takeoff" point, and thus to have amassed a commensurate kind and scale of industrial capital; the inability to think beyond the state as the primary and essential vehicle of economic development; the (often unacknowledged) importation of problematic assumptions regarding the role of foreign investment and foreign trade in the LDCs; a Eurocentric bias; an overlooking or de-emphasizing of production undertaken by women; and an underestimation of the implications of widespread and haphazard industrial development for the environment.

In the face of these and other challenges to their paradigm, proponents of theories of uneven development or dependency have, according to their critics, done little more than reiterate (1) their conviction that some form of socialism can still function as a potential countervailing force to capitalist depredation, and (2) their belief in the efficacy of some kind of strategic decoupling of the LDCs from the capitalist world-system, again with the hope that this can function as a protection against capitalist encroachment. But, say these critics, neither (1) nor (2) appears to be viable in the current capitalist dispensation. This dispensation is more staunchly and comprehensively inhospitable to socialist aspirations than it has ever been (thereby blocking off any "socialist path" to socialism). Moreover, the completely integrated character of actually existing world capitalism ostensibly makes any attempt at decoupling a surefire recipe for economic collapse or extinction.

In examining these charges leveled against the theory of uneven development, I suggest that there is a good case to be made for the retention of notions of uneven development and dependency, albeit framed in very different terms. After all, as the previous chapters indicate, persistent international economic inequalities remain, and if anything are becoming even more intractable, and the problems of chronic debt and pervasive international market instability are still around, as was apparent in the East Asian crisis, the collapse of the U.S. subprime loan market in 2008 (whose ramifications are still being registered), and the plight of nearly every sub-Saharan nation since the 1970s. Furthermore, at a theoretical level, the past decade or so has seen several compelling attempts on the part of dependency theorists to rid their formulations of essentialisms and false universalisms, and especially to think of the developmental state in other than purely mechanistic or monolithic terms.[1]

I won't engage specifically with any of these attempts at reformulation, however, convincing though many of them may be. Instead, my goal is to arrive at a version of dependency theory through the construction of an account of the impact, both economic and political, of transnational financial capital on the LDCs. The impact of global financial markets is a phenomenon not usually taken into consideration by proponents of the theory of uneven development. Underdevelopment has tended to be viewed primarily in terms of a country's flawed or incomplete negotiation of the processes of industrialization, and the large-scale effects of a whole range of new global financial markets on LDCs have been felt only fairly recently (and primarily within the past decade or so at that), thus making it difficult for them to be registered by all but the most current analyses of underdevelopment and dependency.

With this objective in mind, I take the dependency or uneven development paradigm essentially to involve accepting some version of each of the following related propositions:

1. Disparities in wealth between nations as a group are due fundamentally to asymmetries of economic and political power that are constitutive of the capitalist system of development, and indeed of world capitalism generally.

2. The asymmetries of economic and political power existing between groups of nations cannot be removed or significantly ameliorated within the structures and strategic possibilities that are integral to the prevailing system of capitalist accumulation.[2]

The Continuing Economic Polarization

The polarization between North and South is more pronounced than it has ever been. The United Nations *Human Development Report* for 1997 showed that the share of world trade for the forty-eight least developed nations, representing 10 percent of the world's population at that time, had halved in the previous two decades to just 0.3 percent, with over 50 percent of all developing countries not receiving any foreign direct investment (two-thirds of which went to just eight developing countries).[3] The 1997 *Human Development Report* indicated that around a hundred developing and transition countries experienced slow economic growth, stagnation, or outright decline, and the incomes of more than a billion people no longer reached levels attained ten or even thirty years before. The 1997 *Report* indicated that 1.3 billion people lived on a dollar a day or less, that there were 160 million malnourished children, that one-fifth of the world's population was not expected to live beyond forty (in some countries life expectancy has fallen by five years or more), and that 100 million people in the North lived below the poverty line (the North also has 37 million jobless people). Well over a billion human beings lacked access to safe water, nearly a billion were illiterate, and around 840 million experienced hunger or food insecurity. The same report also showed that the net wealth of ten billionaires was 1.5 times the combined national incomes of the forty-eight least developed nations.[4] The accomplishments of some nations in the face of such adversity are commendable and even heroic: during 1980–95 Burkina Faso, Gambia, Senegal, and Zimbabwe reduced child mortality by a third to a half in the face of declining incomes for much of this period, and Algeria, Jordan, Peru, Syria, and Trinidad and Tobago by a half to two-thirds (the latter nations despite reductions in per capita income of 20 percent or more over the previous decade). What was the situation nearly a decade later?

The United Nations *Human Development Report* of 2005 recorded some improvements in overall human well-being in the LDCs over the course of the 1990s, but also described a situation in which the world's poorest citizens continue to face a daunting struggle for survival. In some respects, their plight is even more dire now than it was in the 1990s: in 2003, the 460 million people of eighteen poor countries saw the human development indexes of these countries sink below their 1990 levels, a situation the 2005 *Report* describes as "an unprecedented reversal."[5] In addition, 10.7 million children a year die before their fifth birthday, and more than 1 billion people (20 percent of the earth's population) live on less than a dollar a day, while 2.5 billion live on less than two dollars a day (3–4).[6] The human cost of the HIV/AIDS epidemic has been staggering: in 2003, 3 million sufferers died and a further 5 million individuals were infected, with millions of children left behind as orphans and life expectancy levels in African countries being greatly reduced (in Botswana, for example, HIV/AIDS has caused a decline in life expectancy of thirty-one years; 3–4). The growth in the number of countries undergoing an HDI reversal (i.e., a significant decline in living standards, based on the Human Development Index) is shown in table 4. The latest *Human Development Report*, published in 2007, shows that sixteen countries have suffered HDI reversal since 1990, that is, a decline of only one country since the *Report* published in 2005.

It is therefore undeniable that the disparities between North and South have increased in the era of globalization as economic stagnation has become the lot of many LDCs during this period. According to the *Human Development Report* of 2005, "During the 1990s, 25 countries in Sub-Saharan Africa and 10 in Latin America experienced a sustained period of economic stagnation" (35).[7] The *Report* adds that in "the two years after Russia was engulfed by a financial crisis in 1998, 30 million people were forced below the poverty line. In Argentina the population living below the extreme poverty line more than tripled from 2000 to 2003" (36). The 2005 *Report* goes on to say that this "underlin[ed] yet again a lesson delivered by the 1997 East Asian financial

TABLE 4. Countries experiencing HDI reversal

1980–90	1990–2003
Democratic Republic of the Congo	Botswana
Guyana	Cameroon
Haiti	Central African Republic
Niger	Democratic Republic of the Congo
Rwanda	Côte d'Ivoire
Zambia	Kazakhstan*
	Lesotho
	Republic of Moldova*
	Russian Federation*
	South Africa
	Swaziland
	Tajikistan*
	Ukraine*
	United Republic of Tanzania*
	Zambia
	Zimbabwe

Source: United Nations, *Human Development Report 2005*, 21.

*Country does not have HDI data for 1980–90, so drop may have begun before 1990.

crisis: integration into global capital markets comes with high human development risks attached" (36).

The share in global income of the poorest 20 percent of the world's people has fallen from 2.3 percent in 1960 and 1.4 percent in 1991 to 1.1 percent in 1994, while the ratio of the income of the top 20 percent to that of the poorest 20 percent rose from 30:1 in 1960 to 61:1 in 1991 and grew still further to 78:1 in 1994.[8] One way of rectifying this income disparity would be for poor countries to achieve the international equivalent of upward mobility, that is, to begin to acquire a greater share of world income in relation to their better-off neighbors. But here too the prospects are disheartening for the world's poorer countries. Distinguishing between "rich," "contender," "Third World," and "Fourth World" countries, Branko Milanovic, then lead economist in the World Bank's research department, shows that where country mobility is concerned, the trend is for stability in the Fourth World (or

TABLE 5. Country mobility matrices 1960–78 and 1978–2000 (in percentages)

	Rich	Contenders	Third World	Fourth World	Total
1960–78					
Rich	73	20	7	0	100
Contenders	14	32	36	18	100
Third World	0	5	59	36	100
Fourth World	0	0	0	100	100
1978–2000					
Rich	82	12	6	0	100
Contenders	13	6	69	13	100
Third World	3	6	28	64	100
Fourth World	0	0	5	95	100

Source: Milanovic, *Worlds Apart*, 69, table 7.3.

poorest) echelon, combined with downward mobility for the contender and Third World groupings (tables 5 and 6 and figure 9).[9]

These figures point to two fairly inescapable conclusions: (1) there has been more immovability at the extremes, that is, among the countries grouped as "rich" and "very poor" (all the poorest countries were in the bottom in the 1960–78 period, and 95 percent were in the same position during 1979–2000), and (2) any movement among the "contender" nations was largely downward. Thus, among the contender countries, twelve were downwardly mobile and three upwardly mobile in 1960–78, and thirteen were downwardly mobile and two upwardly mobile in 1979–2000. Almost two-thirds of Third World countries slid into the Fourth World category in 1979–2000. Taken as a whole, upward mobility was a mere 4 percent and 3 percent in the two periods, respectively; downward mobility as a whole was 24 percent and 29 percent for the same periods.[10]

These figures suggest that prospects are less than rosy for the nations of the South, many of which have been on a path of downward income mobility since the 1960s. It is estimated that the nations of the South need to expand economically at a rate of around 6 percent annually for several years if they are to provide employment opportunities for their expanding labor forces (growing at about 3.5 percent a year in countries such as Brazil and Mexico) and if they are to hope to meet their citizens' basic needs for food,

TABLE 6. Country mobility matrices 1960–78 and 1978–2000
(number of countries)

	Rich	Contenders	Third World	Fourth World	Total
1960–78					
Rich	30	8	3	0	41
Contenders	3	7	8	4	22
Third World	0	2	23	14	39
Fourth World	0	0	0	25	25
1978–2000					
Rich	28	4	2	0	34
Contenders	2	1	11	2	16
Third World	1	2	10	23	36
Fourth World	0	0	2	42	44

Source: Milanovic, *Worlds Apart*, 69, table 7.4.

shelter, clothing, health, and education over a twenty-year period.[11] This is in addition to the fact, noted in chapter 3 and confirmed in figures 9 and 10, that the wealthy countries are the overwhelming beneficiaries of the investment flows needed for economic advancement. Where all inward flows (i.e., both FDI and portfolio equity) are concerned, from 1995 to 2000 the rich countries received five times as much investment as the poor countries. It is also noteworthy that in 2002 the developed countries received 64.5 percent of FDI stocks. Given such figures, which indicate that the world's poorest countries are nowhere near meeting the growth targets required for their advancement, prospects for the countries of the Third and Fourth Worlds appear to be ominous, if not already dreadful, for large numbers of their inhabitants.

At the same time it needs to be said that in the two decades between 1985 and 2005 in the twenty-four OECD (i.e., high-income) countries where data were available, the cumulative rise in inequality in these countries was 7 percent.[12] Therefore, even the world's high-income countries have experienced a significant internal rise in income disparity in the past two decades. This phenomenon has thus to be coupled with the widening income gap between rich and poor countries.

Worse is that these trends show no sign of slowing down, let alone re-

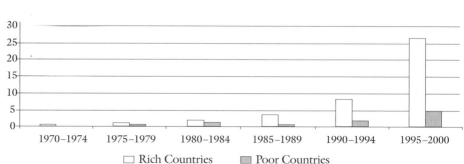

9. Inflows of direct and portfolio equity investment per capita (1970–2000), in U.S. dollars at 1996 prices

Source: Laura Alfaro, Sebnem Kalemli-Ozcan, and Vadym Volosovych, "Why Doesn't Capital Flow from Rich to Poor Countries? An Empirical Investigation," Working paper, November 2005, 62, figure 1, www.people.hbs.edu/lalfaro/lucas.pdf.

Note: Inflows of total equity (FDI and portfolio equity investment) divided by population are based on data from the International Monetary Fund and International Fund Services and are depicted in 1996 U.S. dollars. Data are for 98 countries and averaged over five-year periods. The FDI inflows correspond to direct investment in reporting economy (line 78bed), which includes equity capital, reinvested earnings, other capital, and financial derivatives associated with various intercompany transactions between affiliated enterprises. Portfolio equity inflows correspond to equity liabilities (line 78bmd), which includes shares, stock participation, and similar documents that usually denote ownership of equity. Rich countries include 23 high GDP per capita countries that are classified as "rich" by the World Bank; poor countries denote the 75 remaining countries.

versing themselves, even though the United Nations estimated in its *Human Development Report* of 1997 that it would take only 1 percent of global income and around 2 to 3 percent of national income in all but the most impoverished countries to fund a program to eliminate world poverty.[13] Where the field of comparative international political economy is concerned, these stark facts call for an account of the systemic international inequalities that are their basis. Since the aim of the uneven development or dependency paradigm has always been to furnish precisely such a theory, it has not lacked a prima facie rationale even when some of its formulations have been questioned and found in whatever way to be lacking. The time is certainly right for a revisiting of this paradigm: global capitalism as currently configured confronts less wealthy nations with severe, systemic, and pressing problems, problems that only the uneven development paradigm has sought to depict

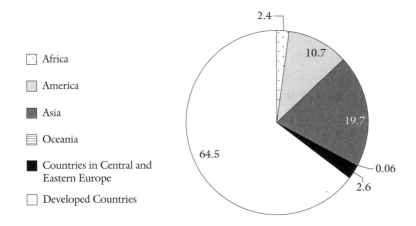

10. Inward foreign development investment stocks by region in 2002

Source: United Nations Conference on Trade and Development, *2004, Development and Globalization: Facts and Figures* (New York: United Nations, 2004), 35.

and analyze in a serious and theoretically comprehensive way. Is there something better for the poorest of the poor than the "triage" prescriptions of the currently dominant capitalist liberal-democratic global configuration? If so, what are the outlines, both practical and theoretical, of this alternative set of possibilities?

The Transnationalization of Financial Capital

THE SITUATION OF THE LESS WEALTHY NATIONS
(EAST ASIA IN PARTICULAR)

It is difficult to do full justice here to the many facets of the epochal transformations that have taken place in extraterritorial financial markets and institutions since the early 1980s.[14] But in noting the more distinctive features of these shifts, it can be seen that in addition to a very considerable increase in the overall volume of transnational capital flows since the 1980s, there has been an equally marked change in the composition of the flows themselves, especially to developing countries since the 1990s, with the Asian crisis of 1997–98 as a decisive factor in marking the economic and social impact of such flows. Capital flows to LDCs were drastically reduced by the Asian crisis. According to Stephany Griffith-Jones, citing IMF figures, net private capital flows to LDCs rose to nearly $240 billion in 1996 (having grown constantly throughout the first half of the 1990s), then decreased to less than $120 billion in 1997, decreased by approximately 40 percent to less than $70 billion in both 1998 and 1999, decreased to less than $10 billion in 2000 (the impact of the Asian crisis being palpably evident in the figures since 1997), and then rose to a not very impressive $31 billion in 2001.[15] This rising or recovering trend has continued; the Institute of International Finance (IIF) reported in 2005 that net private capital flows to emerging markets rose in 2004 to an estimated $279 billion (the highest since 1997), a substantial increase over the 2003 figure of $211 billion and more than double the 2002 total of $125 billion.[16] This rising trend of private capital flows to emerging markets has continued up to 2008; the IIF reports that these flows reached $568.2 billion in 2006, with an estimated $782.4 billion for 2007, and a forecast drop to $730.8 for 2008 as a result of the collapse in the U.S. subprime market.[17] China and Russia (especially its oil and natural gas industries) have been the main beneficiaries of these private capital flows.

It is important therefore to understand the kinds of portfolio investment flow that moved in and out of East Asia in these alternating phases of financial expansion and contraction, even if only to form a notion of the character and magnitude of the crisis of 1997–98 and its aftermath, and what this is likely to entail for a new and modified version of the uneven development or dependency paradigm. (There is of course another reason for focusing on East Asia: it is the economic darling of many advocates of neoliberalism, who love to believe that all the developing world's economic problems would be solved if only more developing countries could become like Taiwan and Malaysia. But we shall see that East Asia's story in regard to financialization, the cornerstone of the currently dominant regime of accumulation, in the end provides few real grounds for such optimism.)

Part of this exponential growth in financialization was a new interest shown by investors, drawn by relatively high interest rates, in Asian stock markets that led quickly to a boom in the East Asian bourses, which petered out very soon after the economic debacle of 1997–98. The scale of this extremely rapid East Asian stock market growth has been noted by Ajit Singh, among others (see chapter 3), where Singh's analysis of the relative times it took the United States and the emerging countries to reach roughly the same capitalization ratios shows that the East Asian economies rose at a much faster pace than the United States did, albeit in an earlier developmental epoch. At the same time, the growing reliance of the East Asian countries on portfolio investment was instrumental in creating the structural conditions responsible for the collapse of East Asian financial markets in 1997–98.[18]

To begin with, there is the sheer disparity of scale between the combined resources of the funds run by financial institutions in the most advanced industrial countries and the market capital of middle-income countries very new to this form of capitalism. As I have noted at several points in this chapter and chapter 3, and as I will note again, the combined market capitalization of high-income countries (HICs) vastly exceeds that of the LDCs. The effects of an imbalance of this kind during a rapid capital movement episode are potentially catastrophic for an LDC, whose stock exchange is likely to be dominated by foreign-owned portfolios. Furthermore, portfolio investors can pull out of markets very quickly, and are prone to do so if short-term performance targets are not met or if other economic indicators are thought to portend weakness (such as the high levels of nonperforming loans in East Asian banking systems that were said to have been instrumental in bringing about the crisis of 1997–98). This is especially true of American mutual funds, which are capable of redirecting their investment flows with possibly devastating consequences for prices in the equity markets of the LDC thus affected.[19]

The behavior of this form of short-term portfolio capital is quite different from that of financial and industrial capital as characterized by Marx, since the virtual autonomy it enjoys in relation to actual economic activity (this being the primary source of its volatility) makes it correspond more to what he calls "fictitious capital" in volume 3 of *Capital*, where it is used to designate a form of capital that creates money in ways completely detached from the productive process and the exploitation of labor.[20] Interestingly, the only advice the World Bank and its representative, Mohsin Khan in this case, were able to give LDCs faced with a potentially damaging reversal of portfolio investment flow is the now familiar refrain "Strive for consistency in the implementation of strong macroeconomic and structural policies, and ensure that borrowed resources are appropriately invested."[21]

A country facing significant withdrawals of foreign portfolio capital will encounter the "usual" problems resulting from pressure on its exchange rates and its balance of payments (with a resulting drain on foreign-exchange reserves) and from the almost inevitable price falls in domestic financial markets. This in turn can result in a weakening of the LDC's financial system, which is more likely if banks and financial houses are closely integrated with the securities sector and have borrowers with a high level of investment in the domestic market; these borrowers will default on their repayments and leave the banks and financial houses facing shortfalls in meeting their obligations, which they may then try to discharge by borrowing abroad.[22] In the longer term, however, the lower-income country relying on relatively large inflows of short-term capital provided by foreign portfolio investment (as opposed to foreign direct investment, which is harder to withdraw quickly), and thus facing the possibility of overnight capital flight when financial markets become volatile, confronts a serious problem of macroeconomic management encompassing, but also extending beyond, the phenomena—runs on its currency, interest rate hikes, a balance of payments and foreign reserves squeeze, and so forth—more immediately visible when capital market volatility starts to become more generally disruptive. For this instability makes it difficult for lower-income countries to pursue independent fiscal and monetary policies and to have a coherent strategy for managing exchange rates.

This is especially so when the lower-income countries involved have only very short periods of time in which to find workable realignments in vast and unstable markets. (In 1995 the portfolio investment market's worldwide transactions amounted to $1.3 trillion daily, or $312 trillion in a year of 240 business days; in 2005 this daily figure reached $2 trillion.)[23] Moreover, as was evident during the exchange rate instabilities after the European Exchange Rate Mechanism debacle in 1992, transnational capital markets are now large enough, and institutional speculators possess sufficient resources that are swiftly interconvertible (banking, securities, and insurance businesses now blend into each other, as indicated by the comprehensive transformation in the United Kingdom of what a couple of decades ago used to be "building societies"), to neutralize the coordinated efforts of even the American and Western European central banks during a financial crisis. Central banks in the LDCs, with resources that are a fraction of their OECD counterparts, have virtually no chance of succeeding where much bigger central banks have failed (and will continue to fail in the absence of more permanent institutional arrangements to control such instabilities).

The LDCs face a constant and seemingly irremovable dilemma in this vast and fluid financial environment. To raise standards in education and increase health service provision and social welfare they may have to pursue an independent fiscal and monetary policy, but this will almost certainly result in exchange rate instability; setting independent exchange rate levels will likewise cause the country in question to have less control over its domestic macroeconomic and monetary arrangements. The three situations—capital mobility, fiscal and monetary policy autonomy, and stable exchange rates— seem therefore to be mutually incompatible, leaving countries, especially lower-income countries, with little or no room to maneuver.

In addition, and the Asian economic crisis of 1997–98 bore this out, portfolio funds, both foreign and local, tend not to go into those sectors, manufacturing and agriculture primarily, that take longer to produce significant yields, but instead find their way into domains where options favoring quick money are more readily available, namely, the stock market and real estate. This is just as likely to be true of an East Asian LDC in 1997 as it is of the United States in 2008.[24] The ideal situation for such threatened LDCs would be a multilateral strategy that is coordinated accordingly, but which still allows a country to use a range of capital controls that give it a degree of macroeconomic and monetary policy autonomy in the face of financial market integration.[25] But the coordination of multilateral efforts to stem capital market instability is difficult to sustain over the longer haul, when the crisis that prompted the initial search for multilateral coordination has dissipated and national self-interest reasserts itself in the absence of institutional forces and principles strong enough (politically and not just economically) to counter such fissiparous tendencies. And so the structural dilemma remains: market integration places a high premium on the coordination of policies between nations, but this coordination is harder to maintain in the longer term because there seems to be no way of obviating tendencies to fall back on national self-interest when it becomes more difficult to support coordinated macroeconomic and fiscal measures for more than a relatively short time. This is clear from the inability of the United States and the European Union to agree on a concerted strategy in dealing with the current financial crisis. The EU countries have shown little or no reluctance when it comes to the direct takeover of banks ("nationalization"), whereas in the United States the specter of socialism has led to a policy of subsidizing banks as opposed to taking ownership of them.

Here of course the HICs have a huge advantage because they have a much better chance of using their economic and political resources to manage such crises in ways not available to their poorer LDC counterparts: they can use these resources to allow their fiscal and monetary policies to operate independently in the short term, and the policies they implement in this connection are not necessarily to the benefit of the less wealthy nations (who in any case enjoy no such freedom to decouple fiscal from monetary policy).[26] For example, the "structural adjustment" package that South Korea had to accept as a condition of getting its IMF bailout during the Asian crisis caused a rise in unemployment because the government had to lower or eliminate its subsidies to state-owned enterprises and set high real interest rates to reduce Korea's current account deficit and keep the won stable. But this did not seem to figure among the IMF's primary concerns, which, as in everything else that comes under its purview, are to safeguard "confidence" in the international banking and trading systems and to preserve and promote access to markets worldwide as an end in itself. In a similar case, the Mexican economic collapse in December 1994 was precipitated in part by high U.S. interest rates imposed by the Federal Reserve to prevent the U.S. economy from "overheating" and to help reduce the size of the country's chronic current account imbalances; however, when U.S. interest rates rose, Mexico's debt situation became unmanageable and the peso went into a free fall.[27]

SOME THEORETICAL CONSIDERATIONS

The absence of a viable system for ensuring adequate macroeconomic management in the face of financial market volatility is a problem that is particularly pressing for LDCs. That absence, however, is the outcome of a more profound failure that results from the convergence or intersection of two other crises: the crisis that accompanied the ending of the postwar Golden Age, when the social and economic costs (inflation in particular) attributed to Keynesian and New Deal and Great Society policies intended to ensure that consumption was somehow always in line with production were found to be "unacceptable" by the Reagan and Thatcher administrations; and the succeeding crisis, when the neoliberal switch of emphasis from fiscal to monetary policy (augmented by an array of supply-side instruments) turned out to be too deflationary, so that monetarism was abandoned in the early 1980s by its leading exponent, the British Conservative government. Since then there has been no adequate system of national macroeconomic management capable of producing sustained noninflationary growth involving no recourse to speculative bubbles (which are short-lived in any case, as evidenced by the U.S. dot-com and the U.S. and British housing market bubbles in the past decade), whether in the United States or elsewhere. The powerlessness of the LDCs in the face of world financial market instabilities must necessarily be seen in this broader and more encompassing context.[28] The prevailing neoliberal ideology, promulgated in the United States but also espoused by multilateral institutions such as the World Bank and IMF, accords priority to keeping inflation low, to avoiding price "distortions," to monetary discipline (though not quite full-blown monetarism after the disastrous 1980s), and to deregulation and liberalization. Neoliberalism has no solutions for exogenous capital market volatility beyond the pious injunction that the affected countries should try always to have "sound macroeconomic fundamentals" and embrace open markets.[29] The components of this ideology were seen by the World Bank and others as the enabling basis of East Asia's "miraculous" economic success. The collapse in 1997–98 of the economies of Thailand, Indonesia, Malaysia, and South Korea (as well as Japan's lingering recession), along with America's need in the 1980s to rely on the short-lived dot-com and housing market bubbles to float the economy, have exposed in the most abrupt and dramatic fashion this ideology's economic and political limitations.[30] It is in this context that a new and modified version of dependency theory has its place, along with the notion that we may be on the threshold of the emergence of a new and somewhat different regime of accumulation (though it is too early to make any predictions).

Whatever happens, the claim made by Giovanni Arrighi and others that Japan and the other East Asian economies constitute a formation that has begun to supersede an American economic hegemony that has lasted for most of the past century can no longer be upheld in this bald and unqualified fashion, if indeed at all. For the immense proliferation of pension, insurance, and mutual funds in the past decade and a half has changed radically the circuits of value realization and accumulation that are at the disposal of the capitalist system, and the crises visited on the LDC economies by exogenous capital volatility are almost certainly a primary outcome of this new state of affairs.[31] The impact of these new circuits of value realization and accumulation on the economies of the LDCs has to be taken into consideration, especially since these nations are confronted unrelentingly by an ideology (the "Washington consensus" identified by John Williamson) which insists that all economic advancement, including progress beyond the most abject poverty and immiseration, must necessarily be market-driven. Moreover, the question at the heart of theories of dependency and uneven development, namely, the possibility of implementing a postcapitalist system of production and accumulation, can be answered only by an analysis of these new and very recent capitalist circuits of realization and accumulation.

Portfolio Capital in Practice

As I stated earlier, the sheer disproportion in the relative sizes of the stock market capitalizations of the HICs and the so-called emerging countries affords the former group of nations more flexibility in dealing with international capital market mobility. As Table 7 shows, in 2002 total stock market capitalization in North America, Europe, and Japan amounted to $19.466 trillion, while the figure for the emerging market countries was $2.525 trillion (out of a world total of $22.810 trillion).[32]

In addition to being the recipients of capital flows dwarfed by the HICs, the scope for economic policymaking in the LDCs is constrained in another way, namely, by the particular forms of the concentrations of accumulated

TABLE 7. Selected indicators of the size of the capital markets, 2002

| | GDP | Total reserves minus gold* | Stock market capital-ization | Debt Securities | | | Bank assets† | Bonds, equities, and bank assets‡ | Bonds, equities, and bank assets‡ (in percent of GDP) |
				Public	Private	Total			
World	32197.4	2513.9	22809.6	16564.8	27005.4	43570.2	40063.2	106443.0	330.8
European Union	8656.7	289.1	5734.3	4930.9	7891.4	12822.3	17654.9	36202.5	418.4
Euro Area	6678.1	207.9	3677.7	4226.1	6000.4	10226.5	12839.0	27040.7	405.3
North America	11216.8	104.9	11625.0	5033.0	14823.3	19506.3	6909.6	38471.7	344.0
Canada	736.0	37.0	570.2	499.6	307.4	807.0	1100.2	2477.4	336.6
United States	10480.8	68.0	11055.6	4533.4	14515.9	19049.3	5899.4	35994.3	344.6
Japan	3973.3	461.2	2095.5	4841.9	2072.7	6914.6	6212.1	15222.2	381.9
Memorandum items									
EU countries									
Austria	206.1	9.7	33.6	156.3	152.6	308.9	278.8	621.3	303.5
Belgium	245.4	11.9	138.7	304.0	256.4	560.4	1000.9	1700.0	690.6
Denmark	172.4	27.0	76.7	100.0	238.2	338.2	425.9	840.8	486.2
Finland	131.9	9.3	138.8	82.1	52.7	134.8	297.4	571.0	435.4
France	1438.4	28.4	1025.6	780.7	1151.3	1932.0	3161.7	6119.3	425.7

Germany	1992.3	51.2	686.0	860.2	2348.0	3208.2	2969.6	6863.8	344.5
Greece	133.4	8.1	66.0	161.2	11.8	173.0	175.9	414.9	311.4
Ireland	122.1	5.4	59.9	30.7	72.9	103.6	195.9	659.4	540.0
Italy	1188.0	28.6	477.1	1208.3	822.8	2031.1	1789.4	4297.5	361.8
Luxembourg	21.1	0.2	24.6	0.0	27.0	27.0	529.4	580.9	2820.4
Netherlands	419.8	9.6	518.6	198.4	669.3	867.7	1345.1	2731.4	650.7
Portugal	122.3	11.2	47.2	79.7	82.0	161.7	174.5	383.4	314.1
Spain	657.3	34.5	461.6	364.5	353.6	718.1	918.0	2097.7	320.2
Sweden	240.6	14.9	179.1	130.7	337.9	359.4	359.4	876.5	364.7
United Kingdom	1565.7	39.4	1800.7	474.1	1445.6	1919.7	3724.2	7444.5	475.2
Emerging markets	7415.9	1513.3	2525.0	1511.8	1062.0	2573.8	6980.4	12079.3	162.8
Asia	3429.4	975.9	1965.7	706.4	820.9	1527.3	4911.4	8404.5	242.2
Latin America	1658.5	161.0	308.5	464.6	178.4	643.0	773.9	1725.4	105.2
Middle East	737.2	132.5	52.5	5.4	13.5	18.9	598.5	669.9	73.4
Africa	450.3	72.9	116.5	47.7	20.8	68.5	315.3	500.4	112.1
Europe	1140.5	189.1	81.7	287.7	28.4	316.1	381.3	779.1	81.8

Source: IMF, *Global Financial Stability Report*, April 2004, 179.

*Data are from Institute for Fiscal Studies. For United Kingdom, excludes the assets of the Bank of England.

† Assets of commercial banks.

‡ Sum of the stock market capitalization, debt securities, and bank assets.

assets in pension and mutual funds in the HICs, especially by the business practices of the managers of these funds, who are concerned solely with their short-term dividends and not in the least with the (longer term) economic and social well-being of the economies in which their funds are invested. These assets are immense. The disproportion between the holdings of these mutual and pension funds and of the less wealthy nations is palpable, if not staggering. To give yet another example, private pension funds in 2001 in the OECD countries, without including insurance funds and mutual funds, amounted to $8.986 trillion, dwarfing the total stock market capitalization of the LDCs ($2.525 trillion in 2002).[33]

Moreover, the forms of capital associated with pension, mutual, and insurance funds have done away with many of the traditional disciplines exercised by ownership at the point of production. The reason for this is that the financial instruments created as part of the burgeoning of such funds are less amenable to established disciplines and forms of regulation (as was clearly evident in the subprime loan market collapse), because the instruments in question are not positioned within relatively stable and organized markets in the ways typical of more conventional forms of financial capital. These instruments are managed by relatively few and largely anonymous fund managers, based overwhelmingly in the United States, the United Kingdom, and a few other countries, and their complexity is often such that they tend to be understood, if at all, by only a few specialists. There are three inevitable outcomes of this situation: (1) the creators of these novel, often hybrid, instruments stand most to benefit from their deployment simply because they are in a position to be maximally cognizant of their intricate workings; (2) since many of these instruments are consciously designed to pass financial risks and transaction costs from the lender to the borrower, LDC financial institutions that borrow through them inevitably take higher risks than their lender banks in the First World (this being part of the prevailing business ideology of "risk transfer"); and (3) as with any financial market innovation, the first users of the mechanism or channel in question tend invariably to profit disproportionally from it: as these mechanisms come to be more widely used the rates of their attendant gains are inclined generally to fall. The power of those who control such funds and the instruments and channels through which they are deployed is therefore massive, and these highly mobile and relatively unconventional forms of capital are very much the locomotive force of the newest regime of capitalist accumulation.

But this expansion in its recent form of transnational portfolio capital does not augur well for the development of the LDCs. There is ample empirical evidence of direct correlations between portfolio capital equity inflow and exchange rate instabilities, as there is of the destabilizing "income effects" generated by stock exchange volatility, of the failure of portfolio inflows in LDCs to be matched by increases in aggregate saving and investment in those countries, and of the propensity of stock markets to favor the survival of large, though relatively unprofitable firms at the expense of their smaller but more efficient counterparts. Other difficulties exist, such as the proneness of financial markets to failure (due to the now well-known information deficits, unenforceable contracts, etc.); the inability of the LDC relying on foreign portfolio capital to use this short-term and speculative capital as part of a long-term macroeconomic strategy; and the susceptibility of such capital to exogenous pressures (shifting U.S. interest rates, the paramountcy of the needs of HIC investors, etc.).[34]

But the most important consideration here is that the transnational financial markets have done nothing so far (nor do they give any indication of doing so in future) to deal with what is perhaps the single most important causal factor in the economic declines experienced by many Latin American and sub-Saharan African countries since the 1980s, declines that in many cases are continuing into the twenty-first century. This is the outcome of the inability of the governments of the countries in question to maintain levels of real investment.

According to the *World Development Report* of 1991, gross domestic investment decreased in the Latin American and sub-Saharan countries as a group in the 1980s, at the same time that both groups experienced their largest declines in growth rate.[35] Trends in these countries twenty years later have improved somewhat, especially where the Latin American growth rate is concerned, though the region as a whole still has a problem with attracting investment.[36] The situation in sub-Saharan Africa in the first decade of the twenty-first century has been less ruinous overall than in previous decades, but this was almost entirely due to better prices for primary commodities such as oil and metals, needed by China and India to fuel their economic growth. Moreover, these improvements took place in only a handful of countries, with South Africa being the main beneficiary.[37]

Why did real investment fall so significantly in these LDCs in the 1980s and 1990s, and why is this situation persisting for so many LDCs in the twenty-first century? Will the exponential growth in transnational financial markets occurring since the 1980s do anything to alleviate the chronically low levels of investment (and output) in these nations? The answer to the second question, given the evidence available so far, is no. In fact, the need of emerging countries to keep real interest rates high in the hope of attracting foreign investor funds by ensuring higher returns for foreign capital and to fall in line with the deflationary intent that is standard to all IMF and World Bank "structural adjustment programs," will, all else being equal, lead to lower real wages. Given continuing high levels of unemployment, this policy will inevitably have negative effects on that country's income distribution. Given also the high existing levels of poverty, a growing population, depressed wages (for the reason just indicated), uneven economic performance, and other possible factors, such as a decline in the quality of land stock (and the almost certain depletion of environmental assets), there is certainly no way that the poorer nations will be able to generate enough savings and investment endogenously to drive any kind of real growth, even if they try to heed the World Bank's injunction to seek their "comparative advantage" (though many nonindustrialized nations have no evident comparative advantage to benefit from) and to maintain open trade and investment arrangements as the optimal way to ensure such growth. Moreover, significant amounts of foreign portfolio capital are not likely to flow in the direction of such countries, even if they seek to implement open trade and market arrangements.

The plight of such LDCs is grim, and given the almost complete absence of institutions and mechanisms designed at both national and international levels to promote long-term investment and financial stability, continued stagnation is virtually inevitable for most of these countries. Many of them have already been consigned, in Samir Amin's words, to a Fourth World that has no significant prospect of advancing even to the threshold of industrialization and of benefiting in any way from current and future expansions of international trade.[38] Richard Kozul-Wright, a senior economist at the United Nations Conference on Trade and Development (UNCTAD), sums up the situation faced by the overwhelming majority of LDCs in a paragraph that is worth quoting at length:

> International trade and foreign capital movements remain largely dominated by transactions among the already-rich countries, and though developing countries have been trading more, all too often they have been earning less from these activities. [Foreign direct investment] has rarely flowed to the poorest countries where economic growth and accumulation have failed to take off or have remained weak and uncertain. . . . Although FDI can incorporate a developing country into internationally integrated production chains, it often confines it to those functions requiring unskilled labour, often the assembly of imported components. . . . The finding that despite a rising share

of world exports of manufactures, the developing countries' share of global value-added (i.e. gross factor incomes) in manufacturing points to FDI as widening, rather than narrowing, the gap between rich and poor.[39]

Regarding the much-touted advances made by China and India in recent years, Kozul-Wright says:

> The economies of a more dispersed and specialized international division of labour have tended to accrue disproportionately to advanced countries and to the foreign owners of capital. This has not ruled out some catch-up performances, most recently and notably in China and India, albeit in both cases, coming from a very long way behind the leading pack. However, in neither case can a strict diet of opening up [to the global market] explain successful growth performance. Rather, local "policy heresies" appear to have helped successfully manage the interface between internal and external integration in a way that has helped perpetuate virtuous growth circles.[40]

In short, the success of China and India is due, if anything, to their willingness to buck the prevailing neoliberal consensus. The fundamental insight of dependency theory—that all claims to the contrary notwithstanding, capitalism is not inherently progressive—appears to be more probative than the cozening neoliberalism of those who insist that open markets and the pursuit of comparative advantage are somehow going to be the salvation of the world's low-income countries.

Dependency Theory Revisited via a Detour through Giovanni Arrighi's Analysis of the Current World-System

Dependency theory has aimed to provide an explanation for the systematic underdevelopment of the nonindustrialized or semi-industrialized nations (thereby filling a lacuna in marxist theories of imperialism, which have tended to focus more on the contradictory nature of capitalist production and its property relations and less on the politically instituted relations of exchange between nations).[41] Dependency theory has done more than this, however, because as one of its corollaries it has the proposition that as long as actually existing capitalism prevails, the LDCs as a group are not in principle going to be the beneficiaries of any structural changes in the international system. But if this is true, then it behooves the proponent of dependency theory to provide an account, however stylized, of the current makeup of this system.

To my mind, the most historically detailed and analytically rigorous analysis of the current regime of accumulation, its relationship to its predecessor regimes, and the conditions being set down now for its possible successor is the one furnished by Giovanni Arrighi in *The Long Twentieth Century*. Advocates of any version of dependency theory must at some point engage with the argument of this exemplary text.

One of Arrighi's aims is to account for the decline in profitability and economic growth associated with the ending of the Golden Age of the Western economies from the 1970s onward. His primary analytical notion is that of a "systemic cycle of accumulation." Adapting Marx's formula for the basic circuit of capital

money → commodities → more money (M → C → M¹)

Arrighi argues that each systemic cycle consists of two phases. One is a period of "material expansion," in which profits are derived largely from the production and traffic in commodities, and which Arrighi takes to be the equivalent of the $M \rightarrow C$ component of Marx's formula. The other cycle is a period of "financial expansion," in which profits come primarily from financial enterprises and not from the extension or intensification of the production and traffic in commodities, and which Arrighi takes to be the equivalent of the $C \rightarrow M^1$ segment of Marx's formula.

Arrighi describes these expansions thus. Material expansions occur because of the emergence of a particular bloc of governmental and business agencies capable of leading the system toward wider or deeper divisions of labor.[42] These divisions of labor in turn increase returns in capital invested in trade and production. Under these conditions, profits tend to be plowed back into further expansion of trade and production more or less routinely, and knowingly or unknowingly the system's main centers cooperate in sustaining one another's expansion. Over time, however, the investment of an ever-growing mass of profits in the further expansion of trade and production inevitably leads to an accumulation of capital over and above what can be reinvested in the purchase and sale of commodities without drastically reducing profit margins. Decreasing returns set in; competitive pressures on the system's governmental and business agencies intensify; and the stage is set for the change of phase from material to financial expansion.[43]

Arrighi identifies four major systemic cycles of accumulation, or "long centuries," in Western capitalism: the Genoese, the Dutch, the British, and the American. He also thinks it possible that Japan or East Asia is on the verge of constituting itself as a successor (fifth) major systemic cycle. In addition, he identifies (in his response to Pollin) three different sources of financial profit that have a particular role in the processes of financial expansion:

1. A source in which "cut-throat intercapitalist competition" creates excessive liquidity that finds an outlet in financial transactions
2. A source in which the significant redistribution of income to capitalists creates conditions for the profitability of such financial transactions
3. A source in which the liquidity generated by this profitability moves from centers that are no longer capable of sustaining material expansion to those that are developing this capability, thereby creating the conditions for the supersession of the previous phase of financial expansion[44]

Arrighi says explicitly, "All financial expansions were eventually superseded by a new phase of material expansion."[45] This may be true of all systemic cycles of accumulation up to the present one; on this there is no need to argue with Arrighi (or with Pollin, for that matter). But unless this characterization of succeeding phases and cycles is to be elevated into a teleology that runs a staunchly dialectical course (a "logic of world economic history" in the manner of Hegel),[46] the possibility must be left open that there may be no recognizable successor systemic cycle of accumulation to the present one, and that the primacy of the current systemic cycle may thus extend indefinitely into the (so far anticipatable) future. Or it may be possible for there to be a series of transformations, however prolonged, of the current phase of financial expansion, so that by the time this series of transitions has progressed far enough there will no longer be a form of capitalism that resembles the presently regnant and American-sponsored systemic cycle, or indeed for there to be anything like a systemic cycle of accumulation in the way characterized by Arrighi.[47]

If these scenarios were to obtain, then Marx's insight that the capitalist has no intrinsic interest in the value of commodities he or she buys or finances so long as the commodities in question can be sold for a profit will be borne out, and the blissfully "utopic" situation for the capitalist, whereby the capitalist moves directly from the initial sum of money to yet more money, to still yet more money, and so on (the circuit $M \rightarrow M^1 \rightarrow M^2 \rightarrow M^3 \rightarrow M^n$), bypassing altogether the production and exchange of commodities (the circuit $M \rightarrow C \rightarrow M^1$), will have materialized. If this new regime of accumulation should be implemented, then, *pace* Arrighi and Pollin, this will have occurred without the accompanying impetus to generate conditions for a new and succeeding phase of material expansion. But how is this possible, given that profits necessarily must at some point come from the production and circulation of commodities? (This is not to suggest that there will no longer be any material or commodity-production expansions if these scenarios occur. A material expansion may take place in future, but it will not do so according to the ebb-and-flow logic outlined in *The Long Twentieth Century*.)

For Arrighi the two circuits or phases of capital are in a relationship of oscillation. To put it somewhat schematically, when capitalists can't make enough profit from commodity production or have overaccumulated as a result of commodity production, they switch to financial transactions; they return to commodity production (only) when the speculative bubbles generated by excessive financial expansion have burst. In other words, Arrighi conceives of the relationship between phases as one of succession or alternation, that is, as an essentially temporal relationship. But a significant body of work on recent international trade and financial regimes seem to indicate that the relationship between financial and productive capital is now primarily spatial, so that what we have in world capitalism today approximates more a complex amalgam of two simultaneously existing subregimes, one that is purely financial and one represented by commodity production and its attendant forms of productive capital.[48]

The huge disparity between the sizes of these subregimes needs to be emphasized again—not just the scale of the pension, insurance, mutual, and hedge funds, but also the sheer volume and value of trading on foreign exchange markets (the world's largest financial market), which as early as 1994 was nearly forty times the daily value of cross-border trade.[49] In 2005 global financial stock totaled more than $118 trillion and was predicted to increase to $200 trillion by 2010. In 2002 the gross value of cross-border equity trades constituted 80 percent of global equity market capitalization, a huge leap when compared to 1989, a year in which cross-border trades constituted 18 percent of a substantially smaller world equity market.[50]

As a result of the important changes that have taken place in the international system of financial markets since the 1970s, including changes in the sources of international credit and a new capital-recycling mechanism, today no single state or public authority has effective control of the international financial system, which was not the case in Arrighi's two most recent systemic cycles of accumulation, the American and the British, which gave markets in New York and London a clear and decisive primacy in those systems of accumulation. The result is a growing regionalization of interest rates and the declining importance of reserve requirements as financial institutions become more hybridized and their resources more interchangeable as a result.[51]

There is therefore no unitary, comprehensive model of how this global financial system (which can appropriately be viewed as an $M \to M^1$ subregime) relates to the production and exchange of commodities (which constitutes a $C \to M^1$ subregime). The dynamics of the relation between these two subregimes as it involves the economic system of a particular country (or group of countries) or region is inflected by path dependency, so that the economic activities that form this particular dynamic necessarily occur within, and have outcomes that are determined by, an always specific structure of political and social relations, a structure which *that* country or group of countries may or may not share with other countries or groups of countries.[52]

Some countries or cities—Hong Kong and Singapore come readily to mind because their economies hinge crucially and overwhelmingly on the provision of financial services and the undertaking of a variety of entrepôt functions—display a very substantial embeddedness in the financial subregime or circuit of capital $M \to M^1$. Countries that are much more dependent on manufacturing—Taiwan and Brazil are good examples—are more profoundly embedded in the commodity-production subregime or circuit of capital $C \to M^1$. Still others, such as the United States (especially) and Japan, evince a powerful embeddedness in both of these subregimes. The forms of embeddedness in these subregimes are inevitably somewhat stylized in this account, since there is no such thing as a pure or perfect regime of financial enterprises nor one of commodity production. And since there is in principle a potential multiplicity of forms of path dependency and embeddedness, different countries can relate in very different ways to one or both of these subregimes. But what of the claim made by Arrighi and Pollin that, in Pollin's words, "the $M \to M^1$ circuit of pure financial deals operates successfully only because this operation always presupposes a newly successful $M \to C \to M^1$ circuit"?[53]

In the account being canvassed here, the financial capital subregime (*FCSR*) can stand in a variety of relationships to the productive or manufacturing capital subregime (*PCSR*), and each such relationship will have its own particular dynamism, though it will certainly be possible for us to categorize the different kinds of relationship and their accompanying dynamism and to formulate principles that govern the relationships and dynamisms under consideration. In dealing with Pollin's question (filtered through my own nomenclature), a great deal will depend on whether the *FCSR* happens to be in a relation of subordination or superordination to the *PCSR*. In a capitalist order, the survival or continued viability of this or that *FCSR* or *PCSR* is wholly contingent on the capacity of that particular subregime to generate continued surpluses. Failure to do this would result in a crisis for that subregime and for the capitalist system which it embodies. This is the only absolute necessity incumbent upon any system or form of accumulation as long as capitalism prevails. To continue to extract surpluses a regime has to enable its agents or instruments to find outlets or markets into which these surpluses can be channeled. Determining the subordination or superordination of an FCSR in relation to a PCSR will therefore require a determination to be made of their respective (and always path-dependent) capacities to generate surpluses. Judged on the basis of the respective scale of the surpluses they have generated, presented in this chapter and chapter 3, there is compelling evidence that since the end of the Golden Age FCSR and not PCSR has been the primary capitalist subregime (though with the current financial crisis this state of affairs may no longer obtain, even in the slightly longer run).

The primacy of FCSR over PCSR in the past two decades is plain to see. So is the fact, given growth of this magnitude, that in that time surpluses in the HICs have been recycled into financial expansion (such as housing and property markets) and not so much into commodity production. With generally weak levels of productive output, the threat of an immense overabundance of commodities being left unsold is thereby reduced. And it is this threat which lies at the heart of the insistence (which appears in Pollin's question) that financial capital can continue to have life only if the system of accumulation it subserves manages to maintain or increases productive output (i.e., incorporates a "successful $M \to C \to M^1$ circuit"). Of course, commodities "have" to be produced, but in the current system of accumulation this is being left to the economies with low labor costs which function therefore as suppliers for the markets of the HICs. Arrighi himself notes this when he says, "[The] main structural feature of the emergent [East Asian] regime remains the provisioning of wealthy markets with products that embody the cheap labor of poor countries." But he then goes on to say, "Nevertheless, the 'informality' and 'flexibility' of the Japanese multilayered subcontracting system, combined with the abundance of parsimonious and industrious labor in the East Asian region, endow Japanese and East Asian capital with a distinctive advantage in the escalating global race to cut labor costs. It is precisely in this sense that the emerging East Asian regime of accumulation is a negation of the old U.S. regime."[54] However, it is clear that there is no such "global race" (let alone one that is "escalating") to cut labor costs, since the FDI that targets such low-cost labor in developing countries is being aimed very specifically at a tiny minority of countries. As I indicated earlier, most of the world's FDI goes to a mere handful of LDCs, most of them East

Asian, while the overwhelming majority of LDCs outside East Asia receive little or no FDI (though Russia and Brazil have started to receive more FDI). There *is* a quest for low-cost labor, granted, and though some features of its general trajectory may conform to the one delineated by Arrighi, it is not by any means a global quest.

On the contrary, the search or "race" for cheap labor has a marked regional structure (Africa and most of Latin America are effectively disqualified from participation from the outset), and its direction within that structure is even more highly selective. Few would deny that the quest for cheap labor subserves the imperative of stocking the markets of the wealthy nations, but the overaccumulations of the wealthy nations are not allowed to saturate commodity-producing domains located in low-income countries (i.e., domains which belong to the *PCSR*); instead, in the currently prevailing capital allocation mechanism these surpluses are plowed back into dealings on worldwide financial markets (the *FCSR*) primarily to fund the U.S. current account deficit. When surpluses do find their way to the less wealthy countries, they do so through the intermediation of these financial markets, which means that they can always be pulled out of the LDCs at extremely short notice.

Attention also needs to be paid to the entirely new configurations of speculative and industrial or commercial capital that now exist. Many corporations nowadays derive profits from speculation as well as the enterprises they are more commonly associated with, and so the need to look for outlets for surpluses in new commodity-producing circuits is less pressing. For instance, since 1993 American Airlines has been hawking its own mutual fund in conjunction with its frequent-flier program, and in the United States the quasi-federal agencies, the now notorious Federal National Mortgage Association (Fannie Mae) and the Federal Home Loan Mortgage Corporation (Freddie Mac), buy up mortgage loans from banks and thrift societies and package these into bonds that are then sold on the securities market, a process therefore known as securitization. As we know only too well, securitization led to the downfall of Fannie Mae and Freddie Mac in 2008.[55] Money continues to be invested in a few developing countries, of course, but it is in the very nature of FDI that it be generated from a foreign source, so the surpluses that accrue from this investment in the LDCs will return to the foreign source in question (usually an HIC).

The East Asian crisis of 1997–98 can be attributed in part to this almost complete reliance on foreign capital, especially on the part of the so-called second-tier East Asian newly industrialized countries (Indonesia, Malaysia, and Thailand). Arrighi's prediction in this regard is quite plausible: the centers of the emerging regime of accumulation will receive a surge of foreign capital drawn to them by the prospect of higher rates of profit than those available at the centers of the declining system. But the heavy reliance of the East Asian countries on foreign investment has several troubling features that immediately qualify any judgment of them as the (collective) potential successors of the dominant but ostensibly fading U.S. regime. In 1991–93 Malaysia had an annual average ratio of FDI to gross domestic capital formation of 24.6 percent. This also accounted for its high services account deficit ($6.7 billion) in 1995, caused by foreign companies repatriating their profits. Malaysia also had a problem with low total factor productivity, which grew at an annual rate of only 2.2 percent between 1991 and 1996. At the same time, Malaysia had a massive credit expansion, averaging over 30 percent a year between 1994 and 1997 and constituting around 160 percent of its GDP, with bank loans alone approaching 57 percent of GDP. In Thailand in 1997, every dollar exported contained 43 cents of imported materials, so dependent were its export-oriented manufacturing sectors on imported parts. Thailand also had a large foreign debt total of $90 billion. Indonesia had a foreign debt total that stood at $60 billion at the time of its IMF bailout in 1997. Nonperforming loans in the Southeast Asian banking system amounted to approximately $73 billion, over 13 percent of Southeast Asian GDP.[56] Even a decade after the crisis of 1997–98 these hardly seem like nations belonging (with Japan and China) to the regime of accumulation seen by Arrighi and many others as the potential successor to the possibly declining U.S. regime.[57]

Together, the features that most strongly define actually existing world capitalism point inexorably to the relative autonomy of financial (and "fictitious") capital from productive capital, that is, the autonomy of the FCSR from the PCSR. The embeddedness of a national economy in either or both of these subregimes is strongly path-dependent; for the economy of a particular nation, this may either enhance or reduce the autonomy of the FCSR in relation to the PCSR, or vice versa. But in reality there is no such thing as an absolute autonomy or an absolute integration of these subregimes: financial capital markets and regimes and productive capital markets and regimes are necessarily related to each other, because funds are free to move between them and policies made in regard to one necessarily affect the other.

At the same time, the world capitalist system that has emerged since the end of the Golden Age is in crisis because the surpluses yielded by the FCSR enable those national economies most deeply embedded in it to escape many of the disciplines that are imposed on those economies which function by being embedded primarily in the PCSR (let alone the stark inequities that confront those in the Fourth World, which belongs to neither subregime). The most telling illustration of this is the accomplishment of the United States in getting its massive current account and federal budget deficits subsidized by the domestic surpluses of other countries. These countries must convert their surpluses into low-yielding U.S. Treasury bills so that they can hold official reserves of U.S. dollars as a safeguard against sudden reversals in capital flows. But then they have to borrow money at higher rates to finance their own development.[58] Only a country as widely and powerfully embedded in the *FCSR* subregime as the United States can grant itself this option, which must make the United States, now able to comport itself as the "investor aristocracy" of this world capitalist system, an object of envy for many a poor country struggling with its fiscal deficits but with no financial market resources at hand to bring it this kind of miraculous but nonetheless ultimately chimerical economic relief.[59]

Worldwide economic polarization in its current manifestation is driven more by the divorce (always politically instituted and maintained) between financial and productive capital, and less by the mechanisms of unequal exchange as typically understood in dependency theory. In the typical account, unequal exchange exists because of an international division of labor which allows the HICs to commandeer industrial productive capacity while consigning LDCs to the production of primary commodities (this being the phenomenon of compulsory maldevelopment described by Samir Amin and others in the dependency and uneven development school), because international trade on these terms can never be mutually advantageous. However, in the account being canvassed here, while there still is unequal exchange—it being undeniable that even in the era of financial capital (and its fundamental divorce from productive capital) the less wealthy countries function essentially as producers of primary commodities and as providers of cheap labor—the main source of international economic polarization today is precisely the autonomy of finance capital from productive capital. This autonomy establishes asymmetries between the high- and low-income countries that appear to be deeply entrenched. So the question remains whether, and if so to what degree, these asymmetries are surmountable.

Surmounting International Economic Polarization

The development policy prescriptions—trade and price liberalization, deregulation, privatization, and closer links with the world economy—of international financial institutions such as the World Bank and the IMF, as well as those nations, primarily the United States, responsible for underwriting the neoliberal Washington consensus, are largely irrelevant to the economic situation of the LDCs, many of whom are still struggling with varying degrees of success to make the long-term structural adjustments necessitated by the major recession and debt crisis of the 1980s, the boom-and-bust crises of the 1990s and today, and the market volatility associated with these upheavals. According to these international institutions and wealthy countries, swimming with the tide of global economic integration is the only way forward for the poorer nations of the South. The dependency and uneven development paradigm has long been associated with the proposed delinking of the economies of the South from those of the North.[60] This delinking strategy is commended because of the conviction of those upholding the uneven development paradigm that the situation of the lower-income countries cannot be improved structurally within the terms of the prevailing regime of accumulation. As we have seen, a judicious scrutiny of the available evidence is hardly likely to controvert this conviction. With the kinds of financial and monetary control afforded by delinking and with more democratic political institutions, LDCs can at least pursue more consistently, if not more seriously, the project of an economic liberation that hopefully will start to bring to an end the newest form of economic dependency.

CHAPTER 5

The Possibility of a New State I
Delinking

The analysis of the current regime of accumulation provided in chapter 4 supports the proposition that economic relations between the world's rich and poor countries are structurally defined by fundamental asymmetries that make the extraction of surpluses from the LDCs, whether directly or by more complex circuits of accumulation, a pervasive condition for the economic advancement of the wealthy countries. The outcome of this entrenched situation is a systemic inequality, affecting both economic and social conditions, which greatly impedes the advancement of a large number of LDCs. Any attempt to conceive of a viable liberation for the impoverished masses of women, children, and men from this condition of economic and social privation (it may perhaps be better characterized as a mode of pauperization) must therefore focus on the causes of this inequality in order to furnish practical proposals for its immediate amelioration and ultimate elimination.

Why Delink?

The economic advancement of the world's HICs, located mainly in the North, has gone hand in hand with the progressive impoverishment of the citizens of its less well-off countries, located mainly in the South (where 85 percent of the world's population live). It follows from this that the removal of this North-South polarization, which at its root is class-based, must be the goal of any project of liberation.[1] In this chapter I argue that the best way to remove this fundamental polarization, from the point of view of the countries of the South, is through a strategy of delinking. The economic development of the nations of the North under capitalism has so far required the South to "adjust" to the economic aspirations of the North. The array of strategies associated with delinking proposes that this economic subordination on the part of the South should no longer be the case, that is, that the economic development of the South must on the contrary follow strategies no longer requiring it to make systemic "adjustments" whose basic rationale, whether explicit or merely tacit, is the economic advancement of the North. To think otherwise is to acquiesce in a reality where the gap between North and South, already pronounced, will only grow, with calamitous consequences for even larger numbers of human beings in the South.[2]

It is easy for (uninformed and sometimes ill-intentioned) critics of the delinking strategy to portray it as an autarkic severing of links with the rest of the world, akin to the dreadful vision Pol Pot tried to impose on Cambodia, or the one which prevailed in Albania ("the world's most secretive state") in Soviet times, or in North Korea today. However, the Albanian, North Korean, and Cambodian scenarios are very far from the proposals advanced by proponents of the delinking strategy.

Proponents of delinking claim that economic advancement for the nations of the South will take place only when these nations are able to pursue their own policies for developing productive systems appropriate to the needs of their people, while at the same time establishing internal political conditions for overcoming economic and social inequality, and then using the logic of this (new) system of productive and social relations to structure their dealings with the advanced capitalist countries. The initial aim is to find alternatives to the prevailing "structural adjustment" policy advocated by neoliberalism, which compels the nations of the South to trim their policies to the demands of international capital, and thus to the detriment of the social and economic interests of the majority of their people.[3]

The current system of accumulation is at root a structure of exploitation, no more and no less, and so delinking is premised on the need to find immediate alternatives to this structure of exploitation. This exploitation is not only economic, but also extends into the spheres of social and cultural recognition for those who are exploited.[4]

Recently, Lance Taylor, who has made a number of careful criticisms of the World Bank over the years but who is hardly to be regarded as a marxist, has recommended a partial delinking on "narrowly technical grounds."[5] Taylor has analyzed extensively the data regarding the open trade and capital market strategies of a cross-section of fifty lower income countries (going as far back as the economically more propitious 1960s) and found few gains and some losses accruing from these exogenously oriented policies. The same conclusion is drawn by Mark Weisbrot, Dean Baker, and David Rosnik in their assessment of the "development" policy favored by multilateral institutions such as the World Bank and IMF over the past twenty-five years:

> The past quarter century has seen a sharp decline in the rate of growth for the vast majority of low- and middle-income countries. Accompanying this decline has been reduced progress for almost all the social indicators that are available to measure health and educational outcomes. . . .
>
> Indeed, some economists have recently concluded that more "policy autonomy"—the ability of countries to make their own decisions about economic policy—is needed for developing countries.[6]

The "policy autonomy" Weisbrot et al. commend is not sufficient, though it is certainly a good start for some LDCs. Policy autonomy does not necessarily take into account those actual market linkages which serve to disadvantage the LDCs, and unless something is done *systemically* to deal with these linkages that work to the detriment of the South, very little will be achieved.

Taylor has helpfully proposed that LDC countries should dispense on a piecemeal basis with linkages to the markets of the North that bring "the least benefits" or exact "the greatest costs," concluding that a limited and selective autarky of this kind offers them a better bet for economic survival. As Taylor puts it, "The inwardly oriented resource allocation strategy seems the least risky, especially for large countries."[7]

Given that openness to global capital flows makes an LDC more vulnerable to external shocks and to the potential onset of financial crises such as the one that occurred in East Asia, it would seem to be in the best interests of the LDCs to buck the wisdom of the neoclassical consensus and attempt a strategic and selective delinking along the lines recommended by Samir Amin, Lance Taylor, and others. This would at least place the LDCs in a better position to exert greater control over their macroeconomies as they implement development policies that are endogenously oriented, as opposed to placing their faith in roller-coaster financial markets that have the LDCs at their mercy ("by the throat" may be the more apt metaphor).

So the first step in a delinking strategy would be a cost-benefit analysis of all the linkages that a particular LDC has with the countries and institutions of the North. The example of Argentina a few years ago, which decided to pay off all its debt to the IMF in order not to have to submit to the IMF's structural adjustment requirements, shows that it is possible to escape the tutelage of the institutions integral to the "Washington consensus."[8] Like-wise Venezuela, which has never had to accept IMF assistance, in 2006 paid off all its loans to the World Bank, again in order not to be beholden to that institution. The exemplar for these countries, at least when it comes to in-dependence with regard to such organizations as the IMF, World Bank, and WTO, is of course Cuba, which despite the long-standing U.S. embargo and the peremptory withdrawal of aid from the USSR at the time of its dissolu-tion, nonetheless has child mortality, literacy, and general educational and health levels that match those of most OECD countries, and certainly the United States. The question of maintaining or severing such linkages with the countries of the North will have to be utterly pragmatic ("Is this really to our people's benefit or not?") and based strictly on the national or regional interests of the LDC in question.

The guiding principle in such decisions to continue or to abandon link-ages with the capitalist metropolitan centers is the need to revise, and if nec-essary discard, the international regulatory framework, superintended by such organizations as the IMF, the WTO, and the World Bank, which governs trade relations between the LDCs and the wealthy countries of the North. This regulatory system works overwhelmingly to promote the interests of the North, and the LDCs will have to find the means to ensure more, and fairer, access to the markets currently monopolized by the economically ad-vanced countries.

Another requirement will be the complete reorganization of the inter-national financial system, whose current disposition is very much to favor speculation on the part of private investors in the wealthy countries at the expense of the poor citizens of the LDCs. If the LDCs are to benefit from fi-nancial arrangements which promote longer term investment in productive activities, then it will be evident to all but the most biased observer that the current regime of accumulation, which privileges short-term speculation to the detriment of just about everything else, will have to be drastically refash-ioned. Priority will have to be accorded to those forms of financial activity which allow productive investment to be steered in the direction of countries such as Mali and East Timor, which hardly figure in the thinking of stock market strategists and fund managers in London, New York, or Zurich.

In addition, the world's poorest LDCs will have to be afforded resources that enable them to keep their exchange rates fairly stable, as opposed to fluc-tuating at the whim of central banks in the wealthy countries of the North (which is the United States, basically). No Third World country should face radically diminished economic prospects and the impoverishment of its people simply because the U.S. Federal Reserve wants to lower or raise interest rates in order to "soft-land" the domestic economy or to make a dent in the massive U.S. current account deficit. The most satisfactory outcome for the countries of the South would be a regionalized system of exchange rates, potentially able to serve as an LDC bulwark against opportunistic shifts in the monetary policies of OECD countries (especially U.S. monetary policies).[9]

To reiterate a point already made, development is highly path-dependent. That is, it is more likely to occur if it is imposed in appropriately sequenced phases. Thus, to cite a banal example, financial openness is not likely to be of immediate benefit to a peasant-based society with little or no access to stock market capitalization; of far more use to such a society will be debt reduction, suitable enhancements in agricultural technology (though not of the agribusiness variety!), and a more equitable system of land distribution as opposed to wholesale privatization of utilities. As Samir Amin has repeatedly pointed out, the overwhelming majority of the people of the South are peasants; in fact 3 billion (i.e., 50 percent) of the world's population are peasant farmers. To state the obvious: to a rural population entirely lacking in utilities such as water and electricity, an IMF-imposed privatization of utilities is worthless.[10]

Crucial here is the issue of agricultural productivity. Farmers in the developed North, with access to the latest technologies associated with widespread agricultural industrialization, have very high levels of productivity in relation to those of peasant farmers, only a small segment of whom have access to rudimentary mechanization and who are thus able to benefit in small ways from the so-called green revolution. (Not that the green revolution has been an unqualified boon for poor farming populations in the countries of the South. Many of this revolution's "gains" have been sequestered wholesale by multinational agribusiness corporations to the immediate and total detriment of poor farmers.) The overwhelming number of peasant farmers in the South have no access even to basic technologies; as a result, says Amin, the ratio of productivity of the most technologically advanced tier of agricultural production (in the countries of the North and West) to that of the poorest forms of peasant agriculture (in the South), which stood at 10:1 before 1940, is now approaching 2,000:1.[11]

Compounding this state of affairs is the decline of prices in the agricultural sector in relation to prices in the industrial and service sectors to one-fifth of their level fifty years ago. The question of uneven development is thus first and foremost an agricultural question. Open and deregulated markets, along the lines proposed by the WTO, would not be of much use to the overwhelming majority of these three billion peasant farmers. Their predicament is tersely summed up by Amin in the following terms:

> One can imagine that the food brought to market by today's three billion peasants, after they ensure their own subsistences, would instead be produced by twenty million new modern farmers. The conditions for the success of such an alternative would include the transfer of important pieces of good land to the new agriculturalists (and these lands would have to be taken out of the hands of present peasant societies), capital (to buy supplies and equipment), and access to the consumer markets. Such agriculturalists would indeed compete successfully with the billions of present peasants. But what would happen to those billions of people? . . . What will become of these billions of humans beings, the majority of whom are already poor among the poor, who feed themselves with great difficulty? In fifty years' time, industrial development, even in the fanciful hypothesis of a continued growth rate of 7 percent annually, could not absorb even one-third of this reserve.[12]

The only viable alternative for this 50 percent of the world's population is for peasant agriculture to be maintained for several decades, while modern technologies and methods are introduced and agricultural productivity in the South is raised. With this rise in productivity more peasants in the South can move from subsistence farming to the higher value-added industrial and service sectors, in this way avoiding immediate immiseration and the precipitous collapse of their supporting social networks. However, the policies now being pursued by the international financial organizations and the governments of the North are quite the opposite of the sane and rational proposals made by Amin and others. These policies, premised on the "need" for a wholesale market deregulation in world agriculture, will have even more calamitous consequences for those whose lives are already precarious. Even now, as was seen in previous chapters, the lot of those living on less than two dollars a day is being made worse by such policies.

The preponderance of the peasant agricultural sector in the South is matched by an equally strong tilt toward urban-based industrial production in the metropolitan countries (mainly in the North). As Amin points out, four-fifths of the urban dwellers in the advanced countries are workers engaged in some form of industrial production. But even here there is precariousness, since a large segment of these workers are engaged in low-wage and "informal" modes of labor with little or no social protection. Table 8 depicts the distribution of the world's urban population. The popular (or working) classes constitute 75 percent of the world's urban population, with

TABLE 8. Percentages of total world urban population

	Centers	Peripheries	World
Wealthy and middle classes	11	13	25
Popular classes*	22	54	75
Stabilized	(13)	(11)	(25)
Precarious	(9)	(43)	(50)
Total	33	67	100
Population involved (billions)	1	2	3

Source: S. Amin, "The Conditions for an Alternative Global System."

*Amin makes a distinction between the middle and popular classes (*classes populaires*). The latter consists of a segment in reasonably well–waged and guaranteed employment (i.e., they are "stabilized"), while the rest belong to the "precarious" segment.

the "precarious" component accounting for 40 percent of the popular classes in the metropolitan "center" and 80 percent in the countries of the "periphery," that is, about 60 percent of the global popular class. In other words, the precarious popular classes form around 50 percent of the world's urban population and a great deal more than this in the countries of the periphery. There are now 1.5 billion individuals who belong to this precarious group, which presents a massive problem for the world's poor countries as they struggle with huge expansions of already crowded cities, growing social and economic inequality, insufficient access to globalized markets for their commodities, and a shortage of investment to promote economic and social development in these countries.

Structural Considerations

The systemic inequities faced by the LDCs, captured by statistical data of the kind just presented, can easily be taken to represent phenomena that are merely transitory, "blips" that will be ironed out when the LDCs get with the program that the neoliberal consensus has decreed for them. According to this neoliberal consensus, the problems confronting the LDCs are remediable in principle primarily because LDC economies are beset by "market disequilibria" which need to be "corrected," and the principal impediment to this correction is the failure of the LDCs to adopt "good policies" that allow markets to function without interference or impediment. This contention, however, takes no account of the pervasive structural hurdles that confront poorer countries in actually existing capitalism (as opposed to the fantasies about open markets that possess the minds of those who advocate neoliberalism).[13] The LDCs, and indeed all countries whose economic fates are tied to actually existing capitalism, face a seemingly insurmountable obstacle posed by an ingrained logic of capitalism which operates in two ways, one tending to promote underconsumption and the other overaccumulation.

First there is the problem posed by a systemic propensity to underconsumption in the capitalist economies. This propensity can be explained by a simple arithmetical example, derived from the pioneering work of Baran and Sweezy.[14] Suppose the total output of a particular economy is 100, with wages constituting 50 percent and profits 50 percent, and that in this economy workers' consumption is 50 percent, while the consumption of the economy's capitalists is 25 percent, and investment is a further 25 percent. We then suppose that this distribution changes to a ratio of 40:60 between wages and profits, and that the capitalist consumption and the investment figures remain unchanged. Since workers cannot consume beyond their wages, total demand in the economy would be only 90 percent, as opposed to the initial 100. But if the state then has an expenditure of 10 percent, raised by taxing profits or by borrowing, then the output figure will be 100, with after-tax profits constituting 50 percent, while the wage bill remains at 40 percent. Neither the total output nor the share of post-tax profits in this economy would have changed in regard to the initial situation, even though consumption is now at 40 percent as opposed to the initial 50 percent. This built-in propensity toward underconsumption is never visible since it is effectively concealed by state intervention. Baran and Sweezy argued that this was a defining feature of post–World War II capitalism, when the immense military expenditures of the West (and especially of the United States) compensated for this inherent tendency toward underconsumption.

The root cause of this susceptibility to underconsumption in the capitalist system is a "law of the motion of capital" identified by Marx, namely, that as surpluses are acquired by capitalists who then use these surpluses to expand production, output will rise in due course and accumulation will be enhanced. At the same time, the bargaining power of labor increases, and with this improved bargaining power wages tend to rise. Capitalists respond to this rise in wages by introducing labor-saving technologies, which, because they release workers into the pool of the unemployed, will cause wages to fall again. But while capitalists now have reduced wage costs thanks to the introduction of labor-saving machinery, this machinery has to be paid for, and consequently investment in capital goods on the part of capitalists has to go up. The enhanced profitability made possible by a declining wage bill is countered by the growing costs of investing in labor-saving technology. The response on the part of the capitalist is to reduce labor costs, which generates surpluses that can then be invested in expanded production, and the whole cycle is set off again. This time, however, there are fewer workers to lay off (the labor-saving technology having ensured this). So each subsequent round of labor-saving technology enhancement releases workers from an ever-diminishing workforce. In time, the labor force will be so drastically reduced that no more surpluses can be extracted from the few (or no) workers left.[15] At the same time, the cost of investing in capital goods to make up for a progressively reduced labor force has also gone up. Profits will then fall, inevitably, and so necessarily will the wage pool, and with it effective demand. Falling wages and declining consumption are thus a built-in tendency in the capitalist system: in Marx's words, there is "a natural tendency for the rate of profit to fall."[16] A similar logic, premised on a frantic drive to reduce wage costs in order to boost profitability, underpins the current corporate disposition to downsize by resorting to offshore outsourcing.

Second, this account of the falling rate of profit is complemented by another explanation, also Marxian, relying on the notion of a competition between firms which results in overproduction and overcapacity (the overaccumulation thesis). According to this explanation, whose foremost proponent in recent years has been Robert Brenner,[17] the decline in the rate of profit which confronts capitalist enterprises has its basic cause in the fairly constant disposition of producers to enhance profitability by deepening capital, that is, resorting to cheaper and more effective forms of production while maintaining output. But even as they do this, producers have to disregard, more or less, the capital that has already been sunk into their enterprise. This already encumbered capital ("fixed capital") constitutes an inflexible cost that cannot be driven downward. Producers will seek to maintain their competitiveness by reducing prices, but given that they cannot avoid the unbending costs of their fixed capital the inevitable outcome is a decline in aggregate profitability. The insight here is that investment in labor-saving technology, designed to save profitability, only increases the ratio of fixed capital to wage costs. Brenner says that the very measures taken by capitalists to maintain profitability, measures which are rational for them to take individually, fail to overcome the problems that squeezed profits in the first place and have the added effect of impelling further measures, again sensible and necessary when undertaken individually but which when taken in the aggregate put yet another brake on (aggregate) profitability. Confronted with reduced profitability some firms will persist in their enterprises rather than look for more lucrative alternatives, while other, lower cost producers will find it profitable for them, individually, to move into these areas despite their overall reduced profitability. The result is a downward spiral of overcapacity and overproduction, entailing a (further) reduced profitability and leading inexorably to declines in investment and output growth, as well as in the rate of wage increase. These declines in investment and real wages lead to declines in productivity and effective demand in both Departments I and II; this in turn puts even more curbs on profitability. The only remedy for this situation—a restoration of profitability—is for large enough numbers of high-cost, low-profit firms to be dislodged from lines facing overcapacity and overproduction with their attendant reduced profitability, and placed in higher profit lines (23–24). The corollary of this interfirm state of affairs, when extended to competition between national economic blocs, is that a particular capitalist bloc will prevail only to the extent that it "achieved a certain rationalization and revitalization, largely through shedding redundant, ineffective capital and intensifying labour" (38, 254). Thus works "the malign invisible hand" that for Brenner more accurately characterizes the nature of capitalist competition than "the benign invisible hand" of Adam Smith (23).

The tendency of the rate of profit to decline is countered in a number of ways by firms and the governments that support them. Immense amounts of government money underpin an assortment of tax exemptions, scaled-down tax assessments, liberal depreciation write-offs and tax credits, price maintenance policies, loan guarantees, payments in kind, research and development grants, insurance subventions, marketing services, export subsidies, irrigation and land reclamation projects, the tolerance of premeditated (and sometimes blatantly illegal) corporate overcharging on government contracts, and other, virtually unlimited forms of government beneficence to private industry (such as the no-bid contract system that has been such a boon to Halliburton and its subsidiaries in Iraq), immediate bailouts when firms fail through their own greed and incompetence (such as the huge Savings and Loan bailout of the 1980s in the United States and the bailout of several collapsed investment banks on Wall Street in 2008), various privatizations and deregulations that swell corporate balance sheets (such as the swathe of privatizations that took place in the United Kingdom in the 1980s and 1990s, when deliberately underpriced state assets were virtually given away to private investors, while at the same time the investment banks handling this multi-industry sell-off made a killing from bloated commissions paid by the Conservative governments of Margaret Thatcher and John Major), and of course the military expenditures ("military Keynesianism") cited in the arithmetical example provided by Baran and Sweezy. These strictly exogenous interventions (and only a mere handful have been listed so far!), whose effect is to combat falling profit rates, represent externalities, in the sense that they are basically *political* measures existing outside the purview of markets and their associated forces, but which are clearly intended by their protagonists to sway the functioning and performance of markets themselves.[18]

The dire economic situation of the countries of the South is not therefore simply a result of the LDCs encountering hurdles to free trade as they struggle to deal with the economic and social impact of globalization, or their current lack of "efficient" and "effective" institutions, or their inability or unwillingness to open themselves to the "competitive discipline" of markets, or a combination of all these. Unless significant steps are taken to remedy the structural causes of underconsumption and overaccumulation (or systemically created uneven accumulation, since the sub-Saharan countries are confronted by chronic disaccumulation) there is little that can be done in the longer term for the world's poor countries as long as the prevailing system of capitalist accumulation is not overturned. The fact of the matter is that despite increased private equity financing and foreign direct investment, the LDCs transfer more resources in the aggregate to their developed counterparts than they receive from those countries. According to the UN's *World Economic Situation and Prospects 2006*, "This pattern of negative transfers has lasted for about ten years and reflects the growing export surpluses of developing countries. The magnitude of these transfers has risen steadily from about $8 billion in 1997 to $483 billion in 2005. Net transfers to the poorest countries in sub-Saharan Africa are still positive, but also on the decline, reaching $2 billion in 2005, down from $7.5 billion in 1997."[19] Moreover, as the *World Economic Situation and Prospects 2008* indicates, overall world economic growth is not likely to increase in 2008; in 2004 the world economy grew at the rate of 4 percent, declining in 2005 to 3.2 percent but growing to 3.8 percent in 2007, while it is expected to decline to 1.8 percent in 2008, with 2.1 percent forecast for 2009.[20] Even here there are danger signs, since, as the UN report points out, the LDCs in recent years have benefited from higher export commodity prices, and this favorable situation cannot be expected to last in the long run. At the same time, LDCs that have to import oil and agricultural products to fuel development are going to have to deal with the adverse effects of the higher cost of oil and food imports. Underconsumption and overaccumulation (and persistently uneven patterns of accumulation) are absolutely integral to capitalism, and the question of overturning them is therefore willy-nilly the question of working for a postcapitalist system for the organization of production and the circulation of the goods. Anything else might as well be called "business as usual," and "business as usual" has invariably spelled disaster for the world's poor countries.

Options for the Countries of the South

The countries of the South are not in a position to secede at one stroke from the global economic system. Their immediate objective, as I said earlier in the light of the findings of Lance Taylor and others, is an abandonment of specific links that are of little or no benefit to them, while retaining those links that are obviously beneficial. The current alignment of the capitalist system will not allow for anything approximating to an effective degree of redistribution between rich and poor countries, and the only way to deal with this situation is for the poor countries to begin to make practical decisions about linkages with the wealthy countries that will for once be in their own interests.[21]

The next step in this process of overcoming the worldwide polarization that works against the poor nations has to be a regional consolidation of (poor) countries interested in forming a bloc capable of resisting the inevitable repercussions that will ensue from taking measures associated with delinking: the cancellation of aid, pulling out of short-term capital, diplomatic sanctions, and so forth. It is interesting that such a bloc, admittedly ad hoc, is in the process of being formed in Latin America, where a visible alliance is now being formed between Cuba, Venezuela, and Bolivia, with Argentina's policies toward the IMF showing that while it has not explicitly aligned itself with this group, its policy orientation nonetheless is fully accordant with the objectives espoused by this left-oriented group of Latin American nations. A more formal alignment of South American nations would obviously be the next step for these countries, as indeed would be a similar alignment among the sub-Saharan African, the Central Asian, and the Pacific Island nations. We should not be sanguinely utopian about the possibilities of setting up such alignments; the pressures on such countries to cut deals with the rich nations to promote their own economically specific interests are going to be very difficult for them to resist.

A corollary of the position being taken here is that the impetus for change in the capitalist world-system is not likely to come from the predominantly prosperous North, which has little or no incentive to bring about a significant, let alone radical, transformation of this system, but rather from the South. No individual or group in power in the United States, European Union countries, or Japan and China has anything significantly at stake in enabling the poorer countries of the South to move beyond the systemic pauperization that now confronts them. What we have at present is the pretense (and it is this and nothing else) that what is in the interest of the world's rich countries is also somehow in the interest of the countries of the South. The available evidence suggests that this is not true. The countries of the South have to seek to bring about this deep-seated transformation before it will register significantly with the nations of the North. At the same time, this should not preclude the formation of alliances with progressive forces in the North, but the terms of this alliance formation should always be those promoting the interests of the poor nations of the world.

Of course a great deal more than alliance or bloc formation can and should be undertaken. For one thing, there could be the implementation of a global system of taxation, for example, by taxing any income derived from resources that belong to the global commons, such as midocean fisheries or mineral resources. This income can then be divided among nations according to their income level. The militarization of the planet, overwhelmingly spearheaded by the United States, is a colossal waste of economic resources. The money devoted to militarization will make an immediate and significant difference if it is directed instead to the project of improving the lot of the world's poorest peoples.[22] These proposals are explicitly political, and they once again bear out the point that transforming the situation of the world's poorest people will in the end require a complete shift of political orientation, one that supplants liberal capitalism, resting as it does on a laissez-faire dogmatism, with economic and social arrangements that will be less dangerous to those whose basic needs show no chance of being met by the system now in place.[23]

PART II

CHAPTER 6

Models of Liberation I

The Politics of Identity

I have already argued (see chapter 2) that the life-world of the individual subject is constituted by an amalgam of semiotic assemblages whose mutual permeation produces an overall effect that gives the individual in question his or her social and cultural subjectivity. This proposition was reinforced by the argument that particular phases of capitalist development always serve as the enabling conditions for the emergence and solidification of these social and cultural life-worlds. These enabling conditions are provided by capitalism's mode of societal regulation, which comprises the apparatuses (education, the legal system, religious institutions, media and communications networks, etc.) that produce the forms of subjectivity and the structures of desire and sentiment essential for continued capitalist production and accumulation. These apparatuses produce the subjectivities and forms of desire and sentiment of vast numbers of men and women through the creation of a doxa which "normalizes" the functioning of the capitalist system. I have also argued (see chapter 3) that the late 1960s and early 1970s saw the demise of the dominant form of capitalist production and accumulation, associated with the "virtuous spiral" of high levels of employment, abundant wages and welfare expenditures, the rise of a culture of mass consumption, and nearly three decades of relatively benign business cycles. In those decades, these conditions conduced to the possibility of a relatively effective working-class politics. At any rate, this system of production and accumulation depended on a concordat between capital and labor which allowed the working classes a share in the economic gains that ensued from this virtuous spiral. This paradigm of production and accumulation, depicted in some circles as the Fordist regime of capitalist accumulation, was superseded by a series of developments whose cumulative effects have come to be associated with the rise of a post-Fordist, neoliberal globalization. With this shift the postwar compromise between labor and capital was jettisoned, and the conditions for an effective working-class politics seemed to disappear with the Reaganite and Thatcherite derailment of this concordat. As one would expect from the foregoing, a shift of this magnitude, from one paradigm of capitalist development to another, was bound to be accompanied by a fairly radical transformation of the political core of the life-world of the individual subject.

There are two slightly divergent positions on the rise of a "new" politics at the end of the 1960s or in the early 1970s. According to the first, the spreading prosperity associated with the postwar Fordist dispensation made a class-based politics and its associated identities less indispensable for the broad mass of working people; as the economically propitious times associated with this dispensation took root in the late 1950s and continued into the 1960s (the Conservative British prime minister of that time, Harold Macmillan, campaigned on the slogan "You never had it so good!"), an increasingly prosperous working class had less and less need to rely on worker-based forms of action to secure and consolidate financial and social gains, important though these worker-based initiatives had been for establishing the initial phases of post–World War II prosperity. This relatively well-paid, and overwhelmingly white and male, working-class stratum was able on the whole to protect its financial position as the downturn of the 1970s and 1980s manifested itself, and gravitated in fairly significant numbers toward the neoliberal policy regimes of Reagan and Thatcher. For these blue-collar Reaganites and Thatcherites, the so-called affluent workers, the Thatcher and Reagan regimes were more attuned to the aspirations of those seeking to retain the gains accruing from the postwar economic expansion than the option represented by what seemed like a confiscatory social democracy or played-out Keynesian "welfare statism" apparently unable or unwilling to change with the times. Lower taxes, reduced public expenditures, and the trumpeted ideology of a "more competitive economic environment" (mixed in with ample doses of populist authoritarianism!) were more to the liking of this emerging "postproletarian" echelon than the previous policy regime's Keynesian adherence to what appeared to be (to these working-class supporters of Reagan and Thatcher) a progressively more ossified and dysfunctional (and costly) welfare state. The Reagan-Thatcher *Gleichschaltuung* owed its energies to the political conjuncture that arose in response to the economic decline experienced in the advanced industrial countries in the 1970s and 1980s, and this neoconservative ascendancy exacerbated the drift away from traditional forms of working-class identification which had started to emerge during the peak period of postwar prosperity.[1]

In those earlier decades, in the 1960s in particular, the civil rights, feminist, peace, ecology, and gay liberation movements started to find increased scope for collective action, often deriving their impetus from the example set by Third World liberation movements at a time when the prosperous West (the North-South axis would become more truly germane after the worldwide debt crisis of the 1970s) seemed to be ever more deeply immersed in the joyless satisfactions afforded by the burgeoning consumer society.[2] At the beginning the civil rights, feminist, peace, ecology, and gay liberation movements coexisted with an older New Left that had also drawn inspiration from the various Third World militancies; when the influence of the New Left and the trade union movement started to wane in the 1970s and 1980s, the new social movements associated with the struggle for peace and the resistance against environmental despoliation, as well as racial, gender, and sexual discrimination, soon showed themselves to be the only forces capable of opposing in any concerted way the depredations of the Reagan and Thatcher regimes.[3] The new social movements rarely became much more than ad hoc coalitions when they acted together, but the 1970s and 1980s would certainly have been an even bleaker time for the cause of a progressive politics if these groups had not been able, however fitfully and haphazardly, to impede the full-blown consolidation of the neoliberal and populist-authoritarian hegemony. With the emergence of the new social movements and the falling away of the old, class-based political arrangements, however, very different possibilities for organizing a politics directly motivated by the quest for liberation came to the fore. This development was further intensified in the late 1980s and 1990s by the rapid proliferation of ethnic and national identities in Eastern Europe and the countries of the former Soviet Union and the rise of groups campaigning for immigrant rights in Western Europe. More will be said about this in the remaining parts of this chapter.[4]

While this account of the rise of a new politics in the 1960s and 1970s relates its emergence to the collapse of the Fordist-Keynesian mode of regulation that had prevailed since the end of World War II, a second kind of account prefers to characterize the rise of this new politics in terms of a more specifically national situation. Thus, it is held that it was the quest for a specifically American national identity in World War II which propelled the broader search for kinds of political identification not based on class or class fractions. According to David Palumbo-Liu, whose account is retailed here, the war effort necessitated the creation of the notion of an American identity wide and powerful enough in its appeal to draw the general population into the sweeping war mobilization. Palumbo-Liu regards Margaret Mead and Ruth Benedict as the primary protagonists in this endeavor.[5] Working for the U.S. Office of War Information and the Office of Strategic Services during World War II, Mead and Benedict used the resources afforded by their disciplinary field (cultural anthropology) to arrive at an understanding of the "American national character" that appealed to the category of "distinctiveness" to show what it was about the American ethos that enabled those who belonged to it to possess the qualities that made these individuals typically and characteristically "American." At the same time this culturally sanctioned understanding had to be sufficiently elastic to accommodate large numbers of immigrants who wanted to belong to this ethos, in this way acquiring the badges and emblems that would enable them to be regarded as properly American.[6] After the war this liberal definition of the American national character, while retaining some of the enfranchising propensities inherent in its original formulation, was nonetheless significantly transformed under the combined pressures of urbanization, the growth of the federal bureaucracy, and capitalist expansion (later on the ideological battles of the cold war would become an important causal factor in bringing about this transformation), and in so doing caused the earlier and still relatively roomy notion of an "American distinctiveness" to be superseded by a tighter "American exceptionalism" that had to operate in a context defined by the new postwar multipolar internationalism.

America's postwar role as a superpower required it to be set apart from its actual and potential competitors, that is, to retain the differences that made it ostensibly distinctive, while the post-1945 multipolar international regime enjoined that these competitor nations in turn be allowed to preserve the differences that accounted for their own national specificities. Ideally, differences would be retained without being construed and acted upon in ways that would allow these differences to become sources of conflict and instability. As Benedict said, "The tough-minded are content that differences should exist. They respect differences. Their goal is a world made safe for differences, where the United States may be American to the hilt without threatening the peace of the world, and France may be France, and Japan may be Japan on the same conditions."[7] The preservation of difference becomes a virtue, to be upheld and promoted along with the proposition that the world is a better place for allowing differences to coexist. In this way a newly engineered American feeling for nationality, a largely romantic sentiment serving as the primary impetus for the formation of an American identity serviceable for wartime needs, is translated into the realization that others (the French, the Japanese, etc.) are likewise entitled to have aspirations toward nationality.

However, this new cosmopolitical regime, whose cosmopolitanism was attenuated by the fact that it largely envisaged a world dominated by America and (Western) Europe, soon had to accommodate a phalanx of newly independent African and Asian nations that were not going to acquiesce in a geopolitical order constrained (for them) by the terms and conditions of a taken-for-granted Euro-American political and cultural supremacy. Rationales now had to be found for inserting the countries of an evolving Third World into this "post-Bandung" international order, an undertaking which required the mitigation of the "problems" caused by the more or less intractable cultural differences which ostensibly set apart these newly independent countries from their counterparts in the West (and East). The Third World's inclusion in this order further spurred the zigzagging growth and modification of the previously instituted geopolitical logic based on the principle of a coexistence of differences. There ensued from the implementation of this geopolitical logic a multiculturalism which gathered speed from the 1970s onward, as the cold war ended and the world economy was rapidly internationalized. The strategic prescriptions embodied in this many-faceted and vigorous multiculturalism quickly took over from those motivating the more decorous and less supple cosmopolitanism that had been enjoined by Mead and Benedict during the war as notions of a "world culture," "cultural diversity," "cultural sensitivity," and so on gained prominence in the political and cultural vocabularies of this new multicultural template. This template lay at the heart of a whole range of new activisms conducted on behalf of a democratic extension of the principle of difference. Palumbo-Liu shows compellingly how it was an acute anxiety over these activisms which prompted the creation of such bodies as the Trilateral Commission, whose 1975 report, *The Crisis of Democracy: Report on the Governability of Democracies to the Trilateral Commission*, contained an essay by Samuel Huntington that prefigured his later *The Clash of Civilizations and the Remaking of World Order*.[8] This multiculturalism, arising in the 1960s and 1970s and becoming fully institutionalized in the 1980s, but with its roots in the restrained inclusiveness of a World War II cosmopolitanism (which enjoined that difference was fine as long as implementation of its principles accorded with the requirements of the relatively self-contained American ethos of the 1940s and 1950s), is one of the primary bases of the new politics that succeeded the dethroned political culture of the Fordist-Keynesian dispensation.

The politically motivated quest for an identity, however, has in numerous instances a provenance that long antedates the 1970s and 1980s, that is, the period generally associated with the onset of the new politics that on the face of it has transcended the need for political identifications based on class affiliations. It is important, therefore, to say precisely what the difference is, qualitatively, between these long-antecedent quests for a politically salient conception of identity and the much more recent quests which stem from the dethronement of a class-based politics. Tracing the particular specification of an identity (and its cognate expressions and forms) back to the Second World War, or to 1707 (the time when a recognizably British identity first emerged in something like a full-blown sense), is important and salutary, but an undertaking of this kind simply begs the question of how an identity-forming conjuncture was able to materialize in the 1960s and 1970s, and in this way set itself apart, however tentatively, from the previous attempts to constitute the earlier versions of the identity under consideration. For instance, if there was an attempt to constitute the beginnings of a recognizably British national identity in 1707, it becomes more than a matter of curiosity to ask what in principle makes a British identity espoused nearly three centuries ago qualitatively different from the British identity envisioned in the 1970s and 1980s, when Mrs. Thatcher, by bringing into play a collective fantasy of an insular sovereignty with its accompanying notion of a narrow British identity, was able, through the mobilization of these fantasies, to convince many voters of her resolve to put the "Great" back into "Great Britain."

A remotely plausible answer to this question has to acknowledge that something manifestly different took place in the 1960s and 1970s at an architectonic level (which, among other things, allowed Mrs. Thatcher to "be" the Mrs. Thatcher of this rebarbative fantasy) and that a very different kind of political logic was animated by this change, a logic whose basic elements were supplied by a putative world culture (one existing more as an ideal than as an actuality, since it is impossible to imagine what a truly global culture would be like). At any rate, this would be the ideal of a culture capable of accommodating a distinctively new species of universalism, one that exists in a novel relationship with the newly recognized particularisms that happen to mark all the necessarily *partial* cultures to which we now belong (the American, the Brazilian, the British, the Samoan, the Sudanese, the Thai, and so forth).[9] The pressure exerted by this inescapable need to negotiate between the numerous partial cultures, whose clamorous amplitude has become one of the established features of the post-1960s conjuncture (and is the source par excellence of the anxieties of someone like Samuel Huntington), is precisely what establishes the difference between the current situation and its predecessors.[10]

The Politics of Identity

The politics of identity seems to be one of four main options for organizing a politics directly motivated by the quest for liberation, the others being the politics of subjectivity, the politics of the event, and nomad politics. Each of these is to be identified with a particular conceptualization of the transformations responsible for altering the social and cultural life-worlds of individual subjects, and each conceptualization sponsors a specific vision of the forms of collective liberation needed by these subjects. There are several conceptions of liberation even within marxism itself, this in turn reflecting the near certitude that a collective liberation, should it occur, is not likely to be confined to a single, well-defined political trajectory.[11]

A politics of identity that is no more than an extension of the liberal parliamentary democracy (in some quarters it is called "capitalist democracy") which dovetails so smoothly into actually existing capitalism has to be discounted from the outset as the putative source of a genuinely revolutionary social and political project. No collective social transformation that is all-inclusive in scope can be both mutual and comprehensive while having no way of extricating itself from actually existing capitalism. Only a version of identity politics that does not cohere with the lineaments of actually existing capitalism would be genuinely compatible with this putatively revolutionary project. Since a "pro-capitalist" or "non-anticapitalist" identity politics does not suffice, a theoretical model of an identity politics compatible with this revolutionary project is relatively easy to come by. The conceptual core of this anticapitalist identity politics would be as distant as possible from its non-anticapitalist counterpart. Two considerations obtrude at this point.

First, it is necessary to confront the argument that no politics of identity can be anticapitalist in principle, for two reasons: (1) identity politics emerged root and branch from a conjuncture which militates against the possibility of a broad-based anticapitalist politics and is therefore a symptom of this failure rather than an antidote to it; and (2) conceptually, identity politics is necessarily a version of an ultimately ineffectual politics of difference, and as such will never be able to infuse a movement with the antagonistic power needed to fend off the depredations of capitalism. An identity politics, according to this view, can never be anything more than a compromise formation; it is on this account constrained to be a politics of consolation that cannot aim for the overthrow of the very system that has enabled and limited it at the same time. As such, it has to be discounted from the outset as one of the paradigms for an anticapitalist revolutionary politics. Or so this argument goes.

Second, the previous objection notwithstanding, even if it can be shown that it is possible for an identity politics to be a viable part of an anticapitalist political formation, concerns necessarily arise over the character of the specific contributions an identity politics can make to a formation of this kind. For, clearly, very many things can conceivably contribute to an anticapitalist politics, ranging from a large-scale insurrection to mounting a campus campaign against corporations who employ sweatshop labor, or a campaign to resist the peremptory eviction of tenants of rental properties that have been foreclosed without the tenants' knowledge in the 2008 subprime housing loan crisis, or a campaign to hold Wall Street financial delinquents and Washington lobbyists responsible for their malfeasances in this same crisis.

The argument that the politics of identity is unavoidably an adaptation of the politics of difference, and that it will not be able to inspire a movement capable of resisting capitalism, is made by those who contend that a politics based on difference will never be sufficiently adversarial or antagonistic: a particular manifestation of the politics of difference can differ only from its competitor manifestations, and this does not even imply anything about the desirability of the difference under consideration. It cannot account for the weight of the difference made by that particular difference, something borne out by the always irresolvable arguments that arise when someone or some group insists that he or she or it has such and such a character because of the particular identity he or she or it happens to have. A group which insists that it is X by virtue of possessing identity Y affirms only that it is not something else (say, Z) because anything that is Z typically does not happen to possess Y, the condition of being X. In other words, to be different from X is only to be identical with that which is not the same as X.[12] While this purely logical argument against the politics of identity carries some conviction (at any rate for those who are apt to be convinced by purely logical arguments of this kind), it is nonetheless problematic to the extent that it implies that logic is all that one needs where identity is concerned, and that we need not be too troubled by the fact that struggles over difference are more likely than not to be political struggles, so that in many cases these struggles can have the supplanting of capitalism as their focus. However, there are historical instances in which anticapitalist struggles have clearly incorporated a racial or ethnic component; one thinks here of the politically significant alignment between the South African Communist Party and the African National Congress in the struggle against apartheid, or the Zapatista struggle in the Chiapas region of Mexico. In both cases, the struggle against racism in South Africa and the struggle undertaken on behalf of the indigenous people of the Chiapas region, to combat racism or the victimization of indigenous peoples is perforce to be in opposition to the structures of capitalist exploitation which serve as the underlying practical logic for this racism or ethnic victimization.

Hence it is the convergence of an antiracist or cultural and ethnic struggle with anticapitalist resistance which can lend force and popular legitimacy to *both* forms of resistance. In which case, the challenge for marxism is to find theoretical models and political configurations which conduce to an alignment between these two sets of political forces, one of which does not possess any kind of anticapitalist orientation. The objection that identity politics owes its existence to a conjuncture which has precluded the possibility of an effective anticapitalist politics is therefore much more significant than the merely conceptual objection just raised (and disposed of): if an anticapitalist politics is not feasibly in prospect, then any hoped for convergence between the politics of identity and an anticapitalist struggle is just a straw in the wind.[13]

It is important to note that the virtually unquestioned normative position assigned to capital is apt to cause a misunderstanding of its dynamic. For instance, it is invariably held that the "laws" of capital set objective and unalterable limits to economic behavior, so that any breach of these limits (e.g., ignoring market forces, flouting the so-called rules of competition, not promoting private enterprises in order to featherbed the public sector) is deemed to cause quite unacceptable economic and social consequences (such as capital flight, failing stock markets, currency collapses, disastrous effects on job allocation, rising rates of poverty). But these outcomes in no way show that these limits are inviolable, nor do they demonstrate that the "laws" of capital are immutable. On the contrary, this indicates only that capital has already been given a position of primacy in an existing political and economic struggle. It in no way follows from the fact of this primacy that capital's position never was, and never is going to be, assailable. The limits of capital are not the limits of the universe (which is to say that they are not metaphysical).[14]

Acknowledgment that the supremacy of capital is always a primacy that derives from a political and social struggle is important for the analysis of the causes of the decline, or demise, of an effective anticapitalist politics, as well as the saliency this politics bestows on class-based movements and agents. The claim, made primarily by those eager to say that politics today is no longer about right and left, that politics today necessarily transcends class and class affiliation, only reflects the fact that the social antagonisms inherent in capitalism have mutated in a way which requires them to be presented to us as something that does not involve class and class position.

In the United States, for instance, the impact of the recent collapse of the dot-com and housing market bubbles on the working classes is never referred to by politicians in these terms; the euphemism "the challenges facing working families today" is always used instead. Interestingly, the superwealthy who live off investment incomes are never referred to as "nonworking families," since to refer to them in this way would be to let the proverbial cat out of the bag and to concede that there are a significant number of Americans who make money, lots of it, without having to work, which is precisely what the capitalist system in its current form is intended to accomplish for its beneficiaries but cannot admit at the ideological level. The idea that the politics of identity has replaced an old class-based politics can thus be accepted only if it is granted at the same time that this development is still part and parcel of an ongoing antagonism with the forces of capital, and that this ideological disappearance of class is itself the result of a continuing conflict necessarily taking place at the level of an enduring class antagonism. What America needs more than anything else is the real possibility of a public acknowledgment that there *is* an American working class, and that there also are nonworking families, not because they can't get work (the fate of many who are poor), but precisely because nonworking families of this ilk are so rich they do not need to work. A profound ideological shift will occur when ordinary Americans realize that nonworking Americans also include segments of the financial oligarchy whose investment portfolios are voluminous enough to free them from the need to undertake wage labor.

The suggestion that the politics of identity is anchored in a conjuncture of a "post–New Left politics which has (thus far) not been able to supply the lineaments of a comprehensive politics of liberation—in which case an identity politics cannot hope to be part of a movement decisively opposed to the prevailing hegemony unless it is part of an overall emancipatory politics that is devised and implemented in order to serve as a condition for an adequate identity politics—is more or less implicit in the writings of Paul Gilroy and Wendy Brown.[15] A much more damning criticism of identity politics is made by Slavoj Žižek, who argues that "multiculturalism" (which for Žižek is pretty much a surrogate expression for the politics of identity) is nothing less than "the ideal form of ideology" for global capitalism, a form of colonization that does not, however, require the colonizing agency of the nation-state metropole.[16] Žižek goes on to say:

> Multiculturalism involves patronizing Eurocentrist distance and/or respect for local cultures without roots in one's own particular culture. In other words, multiculturalism is a disavowed, inverted, self-referential form of racism, a "racism with a distance"—it "respects" the Other's identity, conceiving the Other as a self-enclosed "authentic" community towards which he, the multiculturalist, maintains a distance rendered possible by his privileged universal position. Multiculturalism is a racism which empties its own position of all positive content (the multiculturalist is not a direct racist, he doesn't oppose to the Other the *particular* values of his own culture), but nonetheless retains this position as a privileged *empty point of universality* from which one is able to appreciate (and depreciate) properly other particular cultures—the multiculturalist respect for the Other's specificity is the very form of asserting one's own superiority.[17]

Multiculturalism, in Žižek's view, is an ideological screen for an unparalleled homogenization of culture brought about by global capitalism and its necessary accompaniment, our economically privileged liberal-democratic society, coupled with the apprehension, however empty-headed, that the now ubiquitous capitalist order is not going to be supplanted. Multiculturalism, says Žižek, allows our critical energies to have a stand-in target: instead of having us direct these energies at global capitalism itself, multiculturalism takes the battle for cultural difference to be the "real" conflict, thereby leaving untouched the fundamental homogeneity brought about by worldwide integrated capitalism (which is left unquestioned by the denizens of multiculturalism). Instead of finding ways to confront, in an informed way, the systemic depredations of the Wall Street tycoons over the course of a century or more in American capitalism, it is easier for many Americans to succumb to the economic banalities and non sequiturs of a co-opted ignoramus like "Joe the plumber" (the quintessential emblem of a fictitious anti-elitism promoted above all by representatives of the current American plutocracy) in the 2008 U.S. presidential campaign.

A position similar to Žižek's is to be found in a work written primarily from a national and global security perspective, Philip Bobbitt's grandly titled *The Shield of Achilles: War, Peace, and the Course of History*, where the proposition that the "market-state" has now emerged as the dominant form of state organization is harnessed to the thesis that the market-state is becoming "more meritocratic, more multicultural, and more secular" as a result of a propensity to decentralization that cannot be contained.[18] According to Bobbitt, the market-state, unlike its precursor formation, the nation-state, no longer aims to provide universal welfare for its inhabitants; having imposed market-driven limits on what it can undertake on behalf of its citizens, this state prefers instead to optimize, through deregulation and privatization, their opportunities as they deal with "freed-up" markets and their forces. The market, especially the global market, becomes the effective arbiter for the activities of the state and its citizens, diluting in this way the sovereignty that had hitherto resided in the state and its apparatuses. With this diminution of state sovereignty, it becomes possible for a range of entities beyond the nation-state, among them multinational corporations and even organizations like Al Qaeda, to function as "virtual" states. One of the scenarios for the shape taken by the American market state, by then fully decentralized thanks to constitutional amendments, at some time in the future (2025? 2050?) is envisaged by Bobbitt in the following quasi-retrospective terms:

> In the United States, cultural groups were allowed, by constitutional amendments that altered the application of the 14th Amendment, to transform states to their own liking. *This led to considerable migration within the United States as its citizens sought congenial states that catered to religious, ethnic, and political preferences.* All these new "states" retained an open trade relation with the rest of the United States much like the one that prevailed in Europe within the E.U., and all adhered to a common defense policy with the rest of the United States under a much-shrunken defense establishment. Only their state constitutions were radically different: some permitted a union of church and state; some allowed the prosecution of "hate speech" and forbade books and movies that reinforced racial or gender stereotypes; some reintroduced corporal punishment; while others forbade capital punishment. There were feminist states where women were given certain affirmative benefits, including requirements that a certain number of officeholders and corporate board members be women; there were religious fundamentalist states that forbade commercial transactions on the Sabbath, required prayer in schools, and outlawed the sale of alcohol; there were ethnic states where English was a second language; *and so on. In short, the new states permitted a closer match between the values of a certain polity and its legal rules—a reaction, it may be said, to the market-state's indifference to cultural values.*[19]

The scenario Bobbitt conjures of a putative multiculturalism taking root in the fully federalized American market-state accords with Žižek's analysis of the key premise motivating the politics of multiculturalism. Žižek takes this fundamental category, multiculturalism, to be that of the empty universal, a "homologous utopia," in which the United States becomes the demographic enactment of the "chain of equivalence" (between liberals, feminists, religious fundamentalists, political and cultural conservatives, ethnic separatists, protagonists of lifestyle niches, and so on) that underlies this identity-based politics. The empty universal, because of its vacuity, can be infused with any content as long as all the contents involved are taken to be "equivalent."[20] The problem with this particular invocation of the chain of equivalence is that even in a leftist politics like that of Laclau and Mouffe, the crucial dimension represented by the stark realities of capitalist economic exploitation and the power structures inherent in its attendant liberal-democratic governmental apparatuses are occluded or drastically de-emphasized.[21] A politics of some kind may be involved in establishing the condensations and shifts that activate the chain of equivalence, but in the end no anticapitalist struggle is genuinely enjoined in this form of identity politics. This impoverishment or evisceration of the political is especially evident in the extreme libertarian vision of utopia delineated by Robert Nozick in *Anarchy, State, and Utopia*.[22] As David Runciman has pointed out, Nozick's "metautopia" amounts to an apotheosis of the decentralized multiculturalism visualized by Bobbitt, and it is instructive to examine it for this reason alone.

Anarchy, State, and Utopia frames a conception of the "minimal state" that is compatible with a whole range of communal options, which for Nozick are subject only to the proviso that individuals should be free to join and free to leave these communities. The Nozickian minimal state is confined to "the narrow functions of protection against force, theft, fraud, enforcement of contracts, and so on" (ix), since "a state or government that claims . . . allegiance . . . must be *neutral* between its citizens" (22; Nozick's emphasis). Arguing against anarchism, which prescribes no state, and a state form that exceeds the bounds permitted by the minimal state (especially in the provision of social welfare), Nozick delineates a vision of the minimal state that can serve as a "framework for utopia." In setting out the conditions for this utopia, he begins with the anodyne observation, delivered with more than a touch of rhetorical artifice, that there is no form of an ideal society that would be shared by the following amorphous collection of individuals, all of whom happen to be renowned: "Wittgenstein, Elizabeth Taylor, Bertrand Russell, Thomas Merton, Yogi Berra, Allen Ginsberg, Harry Wolfson,

Thoreau, Casey Stengel, The Lubavitcher Rebbe, Picasso, Moses, Einstein, Hugh Hefner, Socrates, Henry Ford, Lenny Bruce, Baba Ram Das, Gandhi, Sir Edmund Hillary, Raymond Lubitz, Buddha, Frank Sinatra, Columbus, Freud, Norman Mailer, Ayn Rand, Baron Rothschild, Ted Williams, Thomas Edison, H. L. Mencken, Thomas Jefferson, Ralph Ellison, Bobby Fischer, Emma Goldman, Peter Kropotkin, you, and your parents" (310).

In this "utopia of utopias" (the phrase is Nozick's) there will be communities that consist of "visionaries and crackpots, maniacs and saints, monks and libertines, capitalists and communists and participatory democrats, proponents of phalanxes (Fourier), palaces of labor (Flora Tristan), villages of unity and cooperation (Owen), mutualist communities (Proudhon), time stores (Josiah Warren), Bruderhof, kibbutzim, kundalini yoga ashrams, and so forth" (316). As long as they adhere to the absolutely unobtrusive framework of rights that overarches these communities, "anyone may start *any* sort of new community (compatible with the operation of the framework) they wish. (No community may be excluded, on paternalistic grounds, nor may lesser paternalistic restrictions geared to nullify supposed defects in people's decision processes be imposed—for example compulsory information programs, waiting periods.)" The supervening minimalist regime of rights and rules remains impartial and detached from these communities, and their members simply get on with their lives, as environmentalists, communists, computer gamers, vegans, religious fundamentalists, practitioners of tai chi, devotees of blue grass music, antivivisectionists, and so forth. So in this utopia there is a fundamental evasion of the political, and moreover there can be no real need for politics: one simply goes to a place where it is possible to live with people who share to a significant enough extent one's political and cultural preferences.[23]

This Nozickian vision of an eerily depoliticized state coheres with the picture sketched by Bobbitt of a multicultural United States brought into being by a modified Fourteenth Amendment, in which the most significant action undertaken by an individual appears to be his or her migration to a "congenial state," thereby allowing the individual in question to live, "by choice," in this or that community of ethnic separatists, antivaccinationists, train spotters, s & m devotees, owners of fighting dogs, or one run by IBM or General Electric or Al Qaeda or whatever. It would therefore not be unfair to view Nozick's proposals for a metautopia as the culminating point or utopia for any identity politics, and at the same time as the integral reductio ad absurdum of a politics of identity organized according to the tenets of a liberal multiculturalism. "You do your thing, and I do my thing". . . .

Bobbitt is justifiably anxious that market-states, whose raison d'être is the promotion of the market and its institutional trappings, are not likely to produce on an adequate enough scale "public goods" of the kind needed to ensure the ultimate survival of these states, let alone promote the well-being of the overwhelming majority of their inhabitants. In a similar way, the conceptual difficulties which vitiate Nozick's "utopia of utopias" also illustrate graphically the ultimate bankruptcy of any rights-based regime not accompanied by a substantive conception of human well-being. The following conclusion is therefore inescapable: a true utopia (though heterotopia is the favored notion in this argument) would be one that underwrote in principle a fairly substantive conception of human well-being, even as it addressed the very considerable problems that attend any search for a substantive conception of this kind. This substantive conception will conceivably, or even necessarily, allow a place for the politics of identity, but it would not be one that conformed to the rights-based principles (in the case of Nozick) and the rational calculus of state power (in the case of Bobbitt) that underlie, whether explicitly or implicitly, their respective multicultural utopias.[24]

Another Politics of Identity?

The preceding section indicated that the politics of identity needs to remove itself from the auspices of a liberal multiculturalism if it is to be theoretically plausible and practically efficacious from the standpoint of a substantive politics of liberation. Any situation involving the constitution of political identity whose logic is derived from a framework that approximates Nozick's metautopia or Bobbitt's radically decentralized federalism is not going to deliver specifications of this identity adequate to the needs of the project of liberation (unless of course "liberation" for religious fundamentalists, environmentalists, animal rights activists, gays and lesbians, pacifists, ethnic separatists, and so forth consists precisely in being able to belong to a community composed of individuals professing pretty much the same political-cultural affiliation as oneself; there are circumstances, for instance, in which one's sense of being a victim is likely to be diminished by belonging to a separatist movement of this kind, and that being able to live with many others like oneself therefore amounts to a "liberation" for such putative victims).[25] It will be important to consider whether the new social movements, vaunted in certain quarters as vehicles for a hoped for substantive liberation, are nonetheless trapped in a nexus of historical and political forces that will culminate inexorably in an uncongenial (from the standpoint of those who propound a substantive liberation) utopia of utopias with a philosophical character and geopolitical trajectory of the kind charted by Nozick and Bobbitt, respectively. Providing an answer to this question requires us first to take into consideration at least five features of *identity* as a category with an important function in political-philosophical and social-historical discourse.

The first feature is that identity as a category is attended by an undeniable plurivocity, which in turn poses the question of what it is that notions as disparate as the following have in common: "German European identity" (as counterpoised to, say, "Welsh European identity"), where the context involved is that of national identities;[26] "European Muslim identity" (as counterpoised to, say, "European Christian identity"), where the context involved is that of religious identities;[27] "African Ibo identity" (as counterpoised to, say, "African Kikuyu identity"), where the context involved is that of putative ethnic identities; "Indian male identity" (as counterpoised to "Indian female identity"), where gender considerations operate in conjunction with the category of the nation and the national; "northern Californian identity" (as counterpoised to, say, "southern Californian identity"), where the region and regional differences are the operative background categories, albeit in ways that may be lost to many non-Californians; "white South African identity" (as counterpoised to, say, "black South African identity"), where the context is supplied by notions of racial difference (the situation would be very different if "white South African identity" were counterpoised to, say, "white Botswanan identity"); "Afrikaaner South African identity" (as counterpoised to, say, "British South African identity"), where the distinction between South Africans of Dutch and British descent supplies the operative context; the identities of retirees or senior citizens (as counterpoised to those identities reflecting other demographic or subcultural niches, such as "skateboard kids," "young professionals," "Generation Xers," "soccer moms," "rednecks," "weekend warriors," "disco queens," "dot-commers," and so forth); "British identity circa 1707" (as counterpoised to "British identity circa 1945"), where the difference involved is specified in terms of different historical epochs; "New York Jewish identity" (as counterpoised to "Russian Jewish identity"), where it is differences within a religious tradition that provide the operative framework for glossing the identities in question; and so forth. The demarcations at work in this cursorily drawn list of identities are only a cross-section of a more extensive range that is virtually inexhaustible in scope (what about identities associated with professions or the pursuit of leisure activities, or within specific institutions and industries?). Of course the identities of all but a very few individuals áre formed as a result of an extensive crisscrossing concatenation of a substantial set of the different elements belonging to the range referred to above.[28]

It should be evident from all this that the concept of identity carries the freight of a considerable history, going back at least three or four centuries where its provenance is concerned. This history influences any use of the concept, sometimes in ways that escape the attention of even the most sophisticated of these users. As Michael Herzfeld has pointed out in his useful précis of the concept of identity, such groundbreaking works as C. B. Macpherson's *The Political Theory of Possessive Individualism* and Louis Dumont's *Homo Hierarchicus* show compellingly that the notion of an identity, in this case a specifically European identity, is replete with assumptions derived from the ideologies of individualism that emerged in Europe with the onset of modernity.

This individualism went hand in hand with the accepted wisdom that the defining marks of the (Western) individual are property ownership and an imputed rationality, and as the age of empire began these were augmented with the supposition of a racially inflected European colonial superiority that was rapidly disseminated from the metropolitan centers to Europe's colonial possessions.[29] Any careful invocation or application of the concept of identity has no alternative but to take this previous history into consideration. These days, when there is widespread awareness, among the denizens of the academy at any rate, of the problematic ideas and dubious impulses which lie behind the logic of this "colonial difference," it is relatively easy to use the academy's array of critical tools—made available to us by Edward Said, Gayatri Chakravorty Spivak, Homi Bhabha, Stuart Hall, Enrique Dussel, the Subaltern Historians Group, among others—to eliminate such assumptions of a European (and white) superiority from this or that application of the concept of identity. But even when helpfully cleaned out in this way, the concept of identity still tends to retain some of the other unhappy features of its initial European background, in particular the one involving presumptions about self-autonomy, presumptions tied in this case to the conviction that identity is inexpugnably about some kind of "self" who is a self precisely by virtue of *possessing* that particular identity.[30] Herzfeld suggests that the best way to avoid this parochialism, which fails to recognize itself for what it is because it generalizes these distinctively European particularities and, whether wittingly or unwittingly, takes them to be constitutive of the category of *identity* as such, is for us to be appropriately circumspect when the category of an identity is employed.

This critical circumspection can take several forms, but these will center

primarily on the question of the particular interests that are served by espousing a certain identity and the conditions under which that identity is
sustained. These would include the interests that are served and not served
by contesting the identity in question, with particular attention being paid
to the differences between the local, regional, and national levels in ascertaining the nature of these interests.[31] An inquiry of this kind places a particular
emphasis on the contexts in which notions of identity are used and focuses
less on the difficulties associated with an intrinsic conceptual content (i.e.,
the matter of an identity concept's *logic*) than on the outcomes of its particular conditions of employment (i.e., the matter of this concept's *pragmatics*).
The concept of an identity encompasses a number of distinct but sometimes
overlapping strands or elements, but whatever these are, they are the product
of a dynamic that is irreducibly political.

The identity of something is always the product of the desire, necessarily
social and political, in which that thing happens to be invested and which
effectuates the identity in question through the dynamic of this production.
The overall configuration of markers usually associated with the possession
of a particular identity (gender, racial, ethnic, national affiliation, and so
forth) are the outcome of this desiring production. But how does the bearer
of an identity come to be produced? How does one become an exemplary
bearer of "African Americanness," "Anglo-Saxonness," "Turkishness," "Turk-
ish womanness," and so on? In all the representative cases, identities are produced through processes of differentiation, so that "Turkishness" (say) is
produced through its differentiation from "Lebaneseness," "Japaneseness,"
"Mexicanness," and so forth. In the end, therefore, it is the putative border
between one's own ethnos, race, nationality, gender, and so on and the *ethnos*,
race, nationality, and gender of some "other" that produces the identity associated with one's ethnicity, race, gender, and national affiliation. These barriers between *ethnoi*, races, nationalities, and genders are not impermeable,
however; they are more like a see-through screen or piece of too-wide net-
ting, evocative of Hegel's famous distinction in the *Logik* between the two
kinds of exteriority to an identity concept, that is, the insuperable "barrier"
(*Schranke*) and the more porous "limit" (*Grenze*).[32] If cultural barriers are not
insurmountable and are really perishable limits (in the Hegelian sense just
specified), then it becomes harder to insist on the absolute distinction between "being English" and "seeming to be English" (this being another way
of stating the insight behind the problematic of a postcolonial "hybridity"
posed by Homi Bhabha's famous locution "not quite/not white"). For here
we run into the difficulty identified by Hegel, namely, that of providing a

specification of an identity concept (*Grenzenbegriff*) in terms of its internal determinations, that is, within its "limits."

The presence of a conceptual barrier between being English and being Fijian and being Nigerian, say, makes the difference between them relatively easy to specify: we simply use the operation of negation, and in so doing are able to determine that to be English is not to be Fijian and not to be Nigerian, and so on. However, when it comes to grasping the concept "being English" within its limits (in Hegel's technically recondite sense of "limit"), its internal determinations become harder, if not impossible, to enumerate satisfactorily. What marks someone as "being English" when there are undeniably many different kinds of individuals who appear to qualify for this designation? Playing cricket? But there are many English who don't play cricket. And besides, Pakistanis and West Indians also play cricket. What about being a subject of the Queen of England? But New Zealanders are also subjects of the Queen of England. Eating roast beef and Yorkshire pudding? But what about those who happen to be (English) vegetarians? Liking televised darts, snooker, sheepdog trials, and lawn bowls? One will find quite a few English men and women who evince a profound distaste for these activities, whether televised or not.[33]

Specifications of identity depend on the dialectic of identity and difference, which in turn pivots on the operation of negation. Its effectiveness as an instrument for demarcating between any "them" and any "us" is necessarily circumscribed and provisional, especially when the operation of negation is difficult to perform. Hence being *yokozuna* (grand champion) in sumo wrestling was long regarded as a quintessential marker of "Japaneseness" until Akebono became grand champion, when the knotty circumstance of his being an American from Hawaii (originally named Chad Rowan) posed a conundrum for many traditionally minded Japanese followers of sumo. Hegel was aware of this problem nearly two centuries before the *gaijin* (foreigner) Chad Rowan became *yokozuna*, when he suggested that negation does not in itself enable one to specify a concept's determinations: a rose is not a lily and not a daisy and not a daffodil, but saying that something is not a lily in no way indicates what it is that makes a rose a rose, since being George W. Bush or being the Gobi Desert or being invisible is just as compatible with being a nonlily as being a rose is. So when Chad Rowan acquired what had hitherto been as "authentic" a marker of "Japanese" identity as anyone could reasonably hope for, the use of negation to demarcate "being (authentically) Japanese" from "being (authentically) American" became unavoidably problematic. Those who insist on the strict separation between the "authentic" and the "inauthentic" in such cases are unavoidably engaged in the interminable labor of distinction production. This work may be relatively easy to undertake when the demarcation between "being American" and "being Japanese" is instantiated through Ronald Reagan and Emperor Hirohito (where this demarcation retains the character of a Hegelian conceptual barrier, and the use of negation to arrive at a specification, however attenuated, of "being American" and "being Japanese" is still possible). However, in pursuing this Hegelian tack, once "being American" and "being Japanese" are approached in terms of their conceptual limits, what exactly are the conceptual determinations of "being American" (especially in the case of Akebono/Chad Rowan) or of "being Japanese" (again in the case of Akebono/Chad Rowan), especially now that Akebono/Rowan has taken Japanese citizenship? And what, moreover, if these determinations are such that they can never be viewed convincingly in terms of the logic of mutual exclusion? It is conceivable, for instance, that (the accident of birthplace aside) Akebono, who now speaks fluent Japanese, has Japanese citizenship, and is married to a Japanese woman, could possess more of the internal determinations of Japaneseness than, say, the child of a Japanese business executive who came to the United States as an infant, grew up in this country and decided to remain here, and who now prefers North Carolina barbecued pork to any other food, has started to lose his or her fluency in Japanese (this being yet another spin of the needle that oscillates between the "authentic" and the "inauthentic"), and has married a white American from Rocky Mount, North Carolina. This needle spins interminably because no Japanese person possesses fully all the appropriate internal determinations that constitute the concept of "being (properly) Japanese," and this not because the Japanese are a particularly "hybrid" people (for the purposes of discussion they could just as well be Tunisian or Zambian), but because, as Hegel pointed out, the full set of internal determinations of any concept, when apprehended at its limit, can be approached only asymptotically. To be authentically Japanese or French or Samoan is always possible, certainly, but this never amounts to anything more than someone's being in effect sufficiently Japanese or French or Samoan. Desire and fantasy, and above all politics, must unavoidably do the rest, as writers on nationality and ethnicity from different fields and theoretical orientations, such as Benedict Anderson, Anthony D. Smith, Etienne Balibar, and Slavoj Žižek, have been telling us.

The concept of identity (it would be more accurate to refer here to "identities") itself has a variegated history, which has to be taken into account as part of the attempt to do justice to the politics behind the formation and dissemination of identities. The question "Who is this (person)?" is a function of the question "What kind of person is this?," and the need to consider the issue of "the kind of thing X is or the kind of thing Y is" when addressing the question "Who is X or Y?" makes it clear that all individual identities are necessarily a function of their collective counterparts.[34] The politics of identity pivots on the premise that identities are based on differences that are entitled to be regarded as legitimate (or even celebrated). This premise can be granted, and in itself is entirely uncontroversial. But what is problematic, given the essential derivability of individual from collective identities ("no specification of an individual identity without consideration of its basis in a collective identity"), is the further assertion that the politics of collective identities can be bypassed or overlooked when dealing with individual identities. Of course the identities of groups based on ethnic, racial, gender, religious, national, and age differences (as well as the identities of environmental rights groups, animal rights activists, gay and lesbian rights groups, taxpayer protest groups, "fat acceptance" groups, etc.) are collective identities in the necessary but nonetheless trivial sense mentioned earlier (since belonging to a group necessarily confers on one a collective identity). But what is controversial about the politics of identity is the (further) claim that groups and individuals who define themselves by adverting to differences based on considerations of ethnicity, race, gender, religion, nationality, age, and so on have interests that cannot be secured or promoted by more generalized forms of agency, such as class or some kind of affiliation with state formations. So the crucial question here is whether any politics of collective identities is a politics that involves at some necessary level these more comprehensive and inclusive forms of agency (most notably, class or class fractions or a connection with state formations).

The existence per se of groups who derive their identity from differences based on considerations of ethnicity, race, gender, religion, nationality, age, sexual orientation, body size, and so on cannot be said to depend directly on these more inclusive kinds of agency. As I indicated earlier, the identities of these groups can be established purely and simply on the basis of the (Hegelian or quasi-Hegelian) logic of identity and difference; hence one is entitled to be represented by the National Association for Fat Acceptance because one is not thin, the American Association for Retired Persons because one is not a thirty year old, and so on. But the existence of states of affairs or situations in which these concerns regarding ethnicity, race, gender, religion, nationality, age, sexual orientation, body size, and so on become salient depend for their existence on structures that are more encompassing than those which underlie the immediate constitution of identity-based groups. It is clear, for instance, that these identity-based groups have as preconditions for their existence the emergence of a modern sense of individuality and subjectivity, since it is this modern sense of self which enables individuals to see themselves as the "owner" of an identity.

It is also evident that conceptions of national identity depend for their existence on the formulation of citizenship rules that connect individuals to a particular *ethnos*, in this way enabling these individuals to understand themselves as the "citizens" of a nation affiliated with that particular *ethnos*, and that there is a crucial link between forms of identity and apparatuses of identification which would not exist but for a long and prior history of categories and collectivities.[35] More generally, the possession of an identity depends on a formation of a very wide range, something akin to Foucault's *dispositif* or grid of intelligibility, which consists of rules, invariably not available to members of the dispositif in question, that make available to these individuals modes of visibility and expression that would not exist if the dispositif in question had not been in place. Hence, and these are two examples that come randomly to mind, someone living in medieval Paris would not be able to regard himself as "French" because his dispositif would not have given such a person the opportunity to conceive of himself as a member of the "French nation" (there being no French nation at that time), just as a contemporary of St. Paul would not have had a notion that his beliefs about Jesus from Nazareth constituted a "religion" in the way that Christianity, Buddhism, and Hinduism are today customarily viewed as "religions" (the notion of religion belonging essentially to a modern dispositif which used the category of "a religion" to denote a well-defined repertoire of practices and convictions that belong to a particular "people").

For all these reasons, therefore, more wide-ranging forms of agency and subject formation, and the resources of identity associated with these forms of agency and subjectivity, are absolutely necessary for the functioning of any politics of identity, including one of the kind that has existed since the 1960s. But from the standpoint of a marxist conception of liberation a further kind of affirmation is needed, namely, that the structures typically underlying these more expansive forms of agency and subjectivity must in some way involve class or class fractions, and through this, to be connected with the prevailing regime of capitalist accumulation. The important question here involves the nature of this connection that identity-based groupings have to the system of capitalist accumulation. It has to be emphasized that the connection between an identity group and the capitalist regime of accumulation is not a direct one: any attempt to depict struggles involving race, gender, ethnicity, sexual orientation, or religious affiliation as being "really" about class and capitalist exploitation is simply not plausible. The position developed in this book stresses the crucial mediation that is represented by the life-worlds to which subjects belong and whose function is integral to the operation of the mode of societalization required by capitalism. The state and its apparatuses are the primary vehicle for this mode of societalization, and the mode of societalization in turn orchestrates the life-worlds which provide the basis for the formation of subjects and agents (and thus of their identities).[36] Identities are formed through the operation of a range of mechanisms that function at multiple levels, and any suggestion that all struggles involving identity are somehow class struggles "in disguise" is to be resisted. To see why this suggestion needs to be guarded against it is important to consider the role played by struggles involving identity.

Identity Struggles

Any struggle is conducted, potentially, at many levels, and each of these levels may involve a range of transformations of the consciousness of those involved in these struggles. Michael Mann has proposed a typology of working-class consciousness that can be suitably modified to provide a classification of the main kinds of subjectivity and agency involved in struggles:[37]

1. Simple *identity*—the definition of someone as a member of a particular group, carrying with it a simple awareness of taking part in the activities of that group in concert with others belonging to it.

2. *Opposition*—the perception that by virtue of belonging to one's group, one is likely to be opposed by those whose interests are not served by the activities of one's group. The sense of identity and opposition tend to reinforce each other.

3. *Totality*—the acceptance that *identity* and *opposition* contribute to the constitution of one's overall social circumstances and the entire society of which one is a member.

4. An *alternative society*—the objective that a struggle will culminate in if it moves through all its stages. However, as Mann says, "True revolutionary consciousness is the combination of all four, and an obviously rare occurrence."[38]

The movement from (1) to (4) involves the capacity to connect one's immediate experience to a conception of underlying structures and finally to strategic conceptions of an incisive alternative to one's society. For marxism, though not necessarily the politics of identity as such, the movement from (1) to (4) takes place when antagonisms in the domain of production are coupled with the emergence of a collective oppositional consciousness, and it is only when these conditions are in place that protagonists will have the capacity to gravitate toward a socialist understanding of the transformation of society.[39]

A politics of identity which does not allow for a progression through all four of these stages will not suffice as a theory of (complete) liberation. Of course, any kind of social and political advance (involving, say, identity and opposition) is to be welcomed in a world ruled by an amalgam consisting of plutocratic elites, organizations such as the IMF, World Bank, and WTO, which serve the interests of these elites, and a substantial clutch of international business organizations. Too often marxists have dismissed and overlooked struggles simply because they appeared to involve and sanction experiences based only on identity and opposition, but not totality and a conception of an alternative society. In any case, Mann's typology will provide a set of norms for any assessment of a particular movement's (or program's) potential when it comes to serving the many causes whose convergence is the crucial ingredient in any advance toward a decisive liberation.

CHAPTER 7

Models of Liberation II

The Politics of the Place of the Subject

The politics of subjectivity can be associated, primarily though not necessarily exclusively, with any politics premised on the notion of a fundamental reciprocity between a subject, or the "place" of that subject, and the putative "other" of this subject or subject-place.[1] Jacques Derrida is the most notable exponent of the thought of such a politics, though where Derrida is concerned Emmanuel Lévinas is very much the background force inspiriting this line of ethicopolitical reflection. Any discussion of this politics of subjectivity has to acknowledge from the outset what Derrida himself has insisted, albeit with the meandering twists and spirals typically associated with his rhetoric of deconstruction; for example, "I will propose an abrupt deceleration, but in order to speak to you about urgency";[2] "Indeed (to further tangle the threads of this prehistory) I almost began this introduction precisely with the problem of translation. But did I avoid doing so? Have I not already done it?";[3] "I will push hyperbole beyond hyperbole."[4] The discourse of the subject, says Derrida, while necessary and unavoidable, nonetheless has to be comprehensively renovated (though for Derrida no such conceptual renovation can control the conditions under which it is undertaken, nor have power over the consequences that ensue from this undertaking), so that it behooves us to speak of the "effect" or "trace" of the subject rather than the subject per se.[5]

For all that he has said about the need for a radical reconstitution of the discourse of the subject, and of the complementary need to conceptualize the subject as the outcome of a doxa or strategy that "produces" it, Derrida resists any suggestion that the subject has been "liquidated" in his writings, or in those of Lacan, Althusser, Foucault, and Heidegger, who are widely regarded as exemplary thinkers of "the end of Man." Far from it: the subject is for Derrida the name of the irremovable power that poses the primordial question to which the *who* that is the subject is in effect the inescapable answer. Where Derrida is concerned, the only answer that can be given to the question "Who?" has to be something that emerges from a place approximating to that of the subject.[6]

We must resist the urge to contrast Derrida's work just before his death, with its fairly clear emphasis on retaining the place of the subject, with his earlier work, which in places seems to favor an antihumanism that commends a "decentering" of the subject. Already in 1966, in his lecture "La structure, le signe et le jeu dans le discourse des sciences humaines," Derrida contrasted two "interpretations of interpretation," one which does not try to pass "beyond man and humanism," and the other which does. He refuses to gloss the difference between these two positions as one requiring a choice to be made between them. To have to choose between these "interpretations of interpretations" in this way is to fail to see that there is an irreducible commonality which exists between them that allows their difference to be established in the first place (the ground of this commonality being supplied by the famous Derridean quasi-concept of the "supplement").[7] In a lecture published in English in 1968 as "The Ends of Man," Derrida again distances himself from an antihumanism of the kind more typically associated with Althusser and Foucault, arguing as he did in "La structure, le signe et le jeu" that a choice between this antihumanism and the kind of "anthropologism" associated with the writings of Heidegger and Sartre is as false as it is problematic.

Making use of Nietzsche's distinction between the "superior man" (*höhere Mensch*) and the "overman" (*Übermensch*), the former still distressed over the loss of the truth of Being while the latter accepts this loss joyfully in an "active forgetting," Derrida argues that there are perhaps two "ends of man": one still vestigially anthropocentric, embodied in the figure of the höhere Mensch, and the other resolutely postanthropocentric, embodied in the figure of the Übermensch. Derrida suggests that we may be suspended between these two ends of man, and that there is no ultimate basis for choosing between them. In the first case, we confront the being who, embodied in the Nietzschean figure of the superior man, stands guard over the sarcophagus of the metaphysics of existence, feeling a palpable grief at the demise of the man of metaphysical humanism, but only too aware that this is a vigil over a corpse that cannot be revived; in the other, the overman leaves the dead to themselves and escapes to another threshold that is beyond Being and Man. But, says Derrida, each of these ends of man is just as much ours as the other. To escape in the manner of the overman is impossible, since the very attempt to leave behind the corpse of Being has to retain its place of burial as exactly that locality *from* which one has to break away. To flee from the presence of the dead is still to be pervaded by the spectral presence of the dead. (The tenor of this argument about the "never truly left behind" is something of a formula or "postulation," the kind of term Derrida would probably prefer. One thinks here especially of his *Specters of Marx*.)[8] The place of the subject and its attendant metaphysics of being are thus never really left behind in Derrida's writings, though they are subjected to a consistent and painstaking deconstruction, a deconstruction that began as early as "La structure, le signe et le jeu" in 1966 and which has manifested itself in everything he subsequently wrote on the subject.

The subject who is submitted to this deconstruction arises from a "space" of responsibility that is antecedent to the subject's emergence and its identification with the self, with the consequence that "the relation to self, in this situation, can only be difference, that is to say alterity or trace. Not only is the obligation not lessened in this situation, but, on the contrary, it finds in it its only possibility, which is neither subjective nor human. Which doesn't mean that it is inhuman or without subject, but that it is out of this dislocated *affirmation* [thus without 'firmness' or 'closedness'] that something like the subject, man, or whatever it might be can take shape."[9] For Derrida, and in "Eating Well" he is simultaneously at his most Heideggerian and Lévinasian, the *who* that becomes the subject is the one who answers to the other in this situation of primordiality (this representing the legacy of Lévinas), the other in this case being the one who poses to the one who becomes the subject the primal question of its being (this being Derrida's rendition of the Heideggerian *Dasein*).[10] The call from the other is thus the basis of the subject's constitution, and the responsibility of heeding or overlooking this call is for Derrida the core of this event of subject constitution.

The gravamen of the argument in "Eating Well" is that deconstruction, as is necessarily the case with anything that belongs to metaphysics or epistemology, is situated within the remit of a philosophy of the subject. This assertion may be difficult to reconcile with the antihumanist impulse that clearly motivated some areas of Derrida's earlier work, *De la grammatologie* being perhaps the exemplary instance of this seeming hostility to any kind of philosophical or political anthropocentrism. In "Eating Well," however, Derrida has moved beyond an unqualified repudiation of the anthropocentric principle, primarily (and here I agree with Herman Rapaport) by espousing a logic of recognition of the kind that belongs to the distinguished tradition extending from Hegel to Sartre, but which would not typically be associated with the author of *De la grammatologie*.

This logic of recognition was expanded in "Eating Well" to include the possibility of one's recognition by animals and not just human beings. For Derrida, if one can be recognized by an animal, it clearly follows that the operation of the logic of recognition is not limited to the domain of the human, with the crucial implication that the animal is situated in principle in the very place where the subject is. The place of the subject is willy-nilly the space of the parahuman, but, equally, the space of the parahuman (the appropriate way to characterize the "beingness" of the nonhuman animal) is for Derrida coextensive with the place of the subject. The upshot is that the demarcation between the human and its beyond is destabilized, and both the human and its "animal" exteriority can be placed within the ambit of the subject.[11]

If the disposition of the philosophical humanist is first and foremost to buttress the philosophy of the subject, and in so doing to retain what the concept of the subject is intended to secure philosophically—namely, the fundamental insight that the source of meaning does *not* reside in some structure or unconscious and impersonal principle, but rather in some locus of reciprocity or primordial response (however deconstructed the latter are)—then what deconstruction necessarily accomplishes is the simultaneous modification and retention of the place of the subject or subjectile. For Derrida this place is retained even as it is deconstructed.

Deconstruction destabilizes the boundary between belief and skepticism, reason and madness, calculation and spontaneity, text and context, human and nonhuman, the metaphysical and the premetaphysical, and so forth. But Derrida's retention of the place of the subject or subjectile even as deconstruction is pursued comes from the inescapable realization that the very posing of the question of this destabilization has to involve a *who*, in this case a *who* that bespeaks inescapably the place of the subject or subjectile. For to pose the question of what is at stake when a boundary is questioned or its notion entertained is perforce to posit a conviction, no matter how provisional or tentative, that the boundary in question operates in this or that way, that it has this or that significance, and this in turn automatically implies that there is a putative *who* that will be addressed by this boundary's notion, a *who* that can potentially be "convinced" to whatever degree and in whatever way by that which happens to be posited by the notion in question.

The acknowledgment of the philosophical pertinence of the *who* is, in a roundabout way, Derrida's way of rendering Heidegger's Dasein: some mode of being-in-the-world (the core of any definition of Dasein) is necessarily involved when there is the mere possibility of a question being posed about the one who poses the question. Where Derrida and the Derridean "Heidegger" are concerned, the very possibility of formulating a question presupposes the prior affirmation of the conditions, always involving a mode of being-in-the-world, which make it germane for that question to begin to be posed by the one who poses it. These conditions include the mode of being-in-the-world of the one who ventures the question as well as that of its putative addressee (these can of course be one and the same individual).[12]

But this *who*, while occupying the logical or "grammatological" space of the subject, does not for Derrida possess in any significant way or degree the features typically taken to define the subject of classical metaphysics and epistemology. This *who* cannot be this classical human subject because the grammatological space is the space of Derrida's deconstructed, and thus parahuman, subject, and this subject is for both Derrida (and the Derridean "Heidegger") the equivalent of a singularity that is beyond all the categorizations that are involved in the constitution of the classical human subject. The following passage from "Eating Well" is unambiguous on this point:

> Under the heading of *Jemeinigkeit*, beyond or behind the subjective "self" or person, there is for Heidegger a singularity, an irreplaceability of that which remains nonsubstitutable in the structure of *Dasein*. This amounts to an irreducible singularity or solitude in *Mitsein* (which is also a condition of *Mitsein*), but is not that of the individual. This last concept always risks pointing both toward the ego and an organic or atomic indivisibility. The *Da* of *Dasein* singularizes itself without being reducible to any of the categories of human subjectivity (self, reasonable being, consciousness, person), precisely because it is presupposed by all of those.[13]

Two claims can be embodied in the proposition that the "*Da* of *Dasein* singularizes itself without being reducible to any of the categories of human subjectivity (self, reasonable being, consciousness, person)." One is that there are in fact several philosophies of the subject, to wit, the humanist subject, the subject of writing, the subjectivity instituted by Dasein, the subject as the one designated by the *who*, and so on, each governed by a separate logic but with no overarching principle to bring them together into a single, coherent whole. The other claim is that the singularity designated by the *who* is constituted in such a way that it can *never* be taken to be a subject (in the full-blown senses underwritten by these philosophies of the subject), because the *who*, here more appropriately designated as a subjectile, comprises myriad objects and part-objects, without any intrinsic rationale or metaphysical accord to unite these parts into a "philosophy" of the subject as such. While these two claims can be used to complement each other, they in no way necessarily imply each other. It is possible after all to insist that there is an irreducible plurality of philosophies where the subject is concerned, with no overarching rationale to unify them into a comprehensive account of the subject (in this case one would in effect be maintaining that there is no ground for a theory of the subject), without accepting the proposition that the "subject" is a mere *façon de parler*. (The person who accepts this proposition would not even be able to affirm that there is a subject capable of functioning as a theoretical object.) In other words, to determine that the subject is a mere *façon de parler*, one would have to demonstrate why the assertion that there is such a thing as a subject lacks plausibility in a fairly decisive way, perhaps by showing in a nontrivial manner that singularities or subjectiles are all that really exist, and that a subjectile is necessarily an amalgam of objects and part-objects lacking an a priori unifying principle which can elevate these object and part-object components into a subject.

The difference between these two positions can be stated thus: in the first case, the place occupied by the subject is not ontologically void, but the matter of choosing between different conceptions of the subject is nonetheless permeated by an evident undecidability; in the second case, the place occupied by the subject *is* ontologically void because the subjectile (whose mode of being cannot be rendered into anything like that of a subject) resides in its place, and the question of undecidability cannot therefore even begin to arise. But even if the claims embodied in these two positions do not imply each other (and for analytical purposes they are perhaps best kept apart), it is still possible to assert them both. Indeed the imprints of both are to be discerned in Derrida's "Eating Well."[14] It has to be noted, however, that the Derrida of "Eating Well" and "To Unsense the Subjectile" has swung toward the second of these two perspectives on the subject and subjectile, without repudiating the notion, especially canvassed in his earlier writings, that the theory of the subject, qua theory, is permeated by a fundamental undecidability.

In "Eating Well," "To Unsense the Subjectile," and the long essay "Finis," Derrida takes as his launching point Heidegger's elaboration of the concept of "nothingness" (*Nichtigkeit*) in *Being and Time*.[15] The analysis of "thrownness" provided in *Being and Time* identifies being with the Nothing and the Not because Dasein (i.e., that which accounts for the "beingness" of one's being) has no control over the ground of its being. In Heidegger's "analytic of *Dasein*," thrownness is presented as an existential structure which defines Dasein; by virtue of being "thrown" Dasein is confronted by unconditional possibilities that would exist even if you or I did not, from which Heidegger concludes that these possibilities can have no ultimate meaning for us. Absolute possibility thus has a basis in something that Dasein itself cannot entirely dispose of, since to be a being is to find oneself thrown into *some* possibilities, and thus never into *all* possibilities, and so possibility in its fullest amplitude has a ground which cannot be encompassed by Dasein. In being thrown, Dasein can only project itself in the face of possibilities it cannot contain or be fully in command of, and as such it lacks the fixity or completeness of being it would need to have if it were to be an "essential" being. Lacking essential and comprehensive being, Dasein's only indispensable possibility is the impossibility of essential and comprehensive being, and has thus to be characterized as "nothingness": to be thrown is necessarily not to have command over all possibilities, over the ground of one's being, and this ground, in its absolute opacity to Dasein, must therefore constitute itself for Dasein as an insurmountable nothingness. Dasein is a nothingness not able to make possibility into its own defining possibility. A final nonrelation to possibility is Dasein's only possibility. An irremovable structural nullity therefore defines Dasein, and the voice of conscience (*Stimme des Gewissens*) for Heidegger is a voice addressed to us in the realization that the world is fundamentally meaningless because of this nullity.[16] For Heidegger, I am someone, that is, some being, but the "beingness" of the being that I am is not given to me as an essence even as I heed the call of conscience. My life is the project constituted in response to this call, but this project has to construct its ground in the awareness that no such ground is given in advance, and that this lack of "givenness" where being is concerned is the very thing that gives life its character as "project."[17] There is no ground from which one responds, soberly and responsibly (these being the hallmark of Heideggerian "authenticity") to the call of conscience.

This Heideggerian existential thrownness, having its ontological corre-late in the doctrine of nothingness and issuing as it does in the claim that our essence can never be given to us, is taken by Derrida to provide the lin-eaments of the concept of the subjectile. The subjectile is the being who is not in possession of its being, the one who, like the Artaud depicted in "To Unsense the Subjectile," has passed beyond the need to have an essence.[18] By passing beyond the need to have an essence, the subjectile, like Heidegger's thrown individual, is the exemplary deconstruction of the rational animal that the metaphysical tradition has typically taken as a defining feature of the human.[19]

What then determines who or what can be located in those spaces and places of the question to which humans and animals alike ostensibly belong, all with the warrant, supplied by Derridean deconstruction, to be considered subjects or subjectiles? The Derridean answer is *ethics*, understood here in a sense that makes it integral to the political. But, and this is the gist of the passage from "Eating Well" cited earlier, this ethics or politics will be driven by a theory of singularity, and the features that define this theory will lie at the heart of this ethics or politics. The notion of a singularity is virtually indispensable for any political philosophy seeking to obviate the endlessly problematic polarity between the "individual" and the "collective" that is essential to the Hobbes-Rousseau-Hegel tradition of reflection on the state and sovereignty, and so Derrida certainly possesses one of the key theoretical elements for providing an alternative to this tradition.

The Ethical and Political Singularity

For Heidegger, as we have seen, the call (*Ruf*) of conscience is a call that each individual heeds (or fails to heed) without having an essence to serve as a ground for his or her response to this call. The call of conscience forestalls any attempt at human self-mastery or self-possession, and as such the call (though for Heidegger this call is issued in silence) is fundamentally ethical and political.[20] The call of conscience is a call to responsibility, as the follow-ing passage from *Being and Time* makes clear:

> The statement that *Dasein* is at the same time the caller and the called has now lost its empty formal character and its obviousness. *Conscience reveals itself as the call of care*: the caller is *Dasein*, anxious in thrownness (in its already-being-in . . .) about its potentiality-of-being. The one called is also *Dasein*, called forth to its ownmost potentiality of being (its being-ahead-of-itself . . .). And

what is called forth by the summons is *Dasein*, out of falling prey to the they (already-being-together-with-the-world-taken-care-of . . .). The call of conscience, that is, conscience itself, has its ontological possibility in the fact that *Dasein* is care in the ground of its being.[21]

In other words, the call of conscience is an event which discloses to us Dasein's fundamental character as care. In this event of disclosure, I find that I am thrown into a past that is not entirely at my disposal, but which, as the groundless ground of my future, nonetheless constitutes the basis for my potentiality of being, a potentiality from which I construct my life as a project. Only in this way can I avoid leading the kind of life in which I fail to realize that Dasein confronts me with choices between which I have to choose, even though there is no ground for making these choices. The individual is thus confronted with two ways of being, one authentic (exemplified by the willingness to make the choices that inevitably face us) and the other inauthentic (exemplified by the flight from the need to choose). Responsibility, as one would expect, consists in not turning away from this need to make choices.

Lévinas, having accepted that Heidegger had undermined irretrievably any pretension that metaphysics (and ontology specifically) could serve as the "first philosophy," would take this call of conscience and locate it in an explicitly ethical structure, in this way turning ethics into the "first philosophy" that ontology could never be. For Lévinas all subjects are such by virtue of the call made by the other, with justice then being defined as one's irreducible responsibility for the other. Despite Derrida's firmness in maintaining that the postdeconstructed subject begins with a constituting nonidentity with itself, he still accepts the Lévinasian principle that its underpinning as subject (albeit a deconstructed subject or subjectile) comes precisely from a call made by the other, and the corollary of this principle that justice is one's irreducible responsibility for the other (though Derrida would emphasize that this responsibility is exercised in the face of the undecidability that pervades one's relationship with the other).

The problem with Derrida's position here extends all the way back to Heidegger. If ethics and the ethical (for simplicity's sake we can use some bald nomenclature that Lévinas would have been far more comfortable with than Heidegger, who was unrelenting in his repudiation of tidy designations), and also politics and the political, derive from this constitutive feature of Dasein's structure, its typical mode of being-in-the-world, then there is an unavoidable sense in which the politics that is legitimated or entailed by this conception of the subject is a politics of decision vitiated by Heidegger's (and *perhaps* Derrida's) inability to tell us how the (seemingly always solitary) subject or subjectile moves from ever-present undecidability to concrete political decision.[22] This is especially the case if one is talking of the subjectile who, as Herman Rapaport points out, is marked by a certain "autism." It is not apparent how the individual who happens to be defined by this autism is going to be able to function satisfactorily as protagonist in any kind of nontrivial collective political project.[23] This difficulty will be addressed later, after further discussion of Derrida's positions.

There is a troubling voluntarism at the heart of Heidegger's conception of Dasein, and a number of commentators have noted a profound philosophical hankering after individual authenticity that reflects Kierkegaard's influence on Heidegger.[24] The Derridean equivalent of Heidegger's thrownness is the "interminable experience" which Derrida associates with "a sort of nonpassive endurance of the aporia," this endurance being for Derrida "the condition of responsibility and of decision."[25] The "endurance of the aporia" is subtended by a "structure of nullity" that has remarkable affinities with the structure displayed in *Being and Time*. This Heideggerian reprise is evident in the following passage from *Aporias*:

> The antinomy here better deserves the name of aporia insofar as it is neither an "apparent or illusory" antinomy, nor a dialectizable contradiction in the Hegelian or Marxist sense, nor even a "transcendental illusion in a dialectic of the Kantian type," but instead an interminable experience. Such an experience must remain such if one wants to think, to make come or to let come any event of decision or of responsibility. The most general and therefore indeterminate form of this double and single duty is that a responsible decision must obey a *duty that owes nothing, that must owe nothing in order to be a duty*, a duty that has no debt to pay back, a duty without debt and therefore without duty.[26]

Derrida goes on to draw out the implications of the assertion that the ethical decision is not bound up with a "determinable or determining knowledge, the consequence of some preestablished order" (17). Rather than maintaining a relation to a determination derived from an order of this kind, he proposes that the ethical decision (and presumably this holds for the political decision as well) be seen as an interruption of the preestablished order and the determinations issuing from it, while still retaining a relation to this interruption and that which it interrupts. The threshold of this interruption resembles a "borderly edge" and corresponds in Derrida's scheme of things to the Heideggerian "limit situation" (*Grenzsituation*), which for Heidegger is the place in which being displays itself to Dasein when Dasein is resolute in the face of the nullity of existence.[27]

At the threshold of this borderly edge the maker of ethical and political decisions is faced with a twofold duty. On the one hand, his or her decision and its accompanying responsibility, constituted as they are by the "unconditionality of the incalculable," cannot be shielded by the assurances and certitudes provided by knowledge, the institution of a program, or some kind of appeal to reason.[28] At the same time, and this is the aporia in the exercising of a genuine responsibility, these conditions for the making of the decision in question cannot simply be discarded: they guide the decision while remaining "radically heterogeneous" to the calling that solicits the decision and its accompanying responsibility in the first place. Decision and responsibility have, simultaneously, the character of a passage and a nonpassage, as the one summoned to decision has to bar himself or herself from the guarantees afforded by "typical forms," such as knowledge, reason, and programs, while at the same time realizing that no wish or decree can cause these to be jettisoned.

The person who decides has thus to live in the undecidable while acknowledging the presence of principles and conditions that bespeak the very presence of the decidable. To decide is to do so in the active presence of these "typical forms" *and* the power of the undecidable that makes every truly ethical and political decision into a singular event, but without having at our disposal any principle that enables us to determine how we are to make the passage from the undecidable to the determinate and vice versa. Derrida takes this "aporetic structure" to be integral to politics and the political, contending that there will be no ethics or politics without the "inexhaustible singularization" that stems from the operation of this "aporetic structure" (*Aporias* 20). To quote Derrida from *The Other Heading*:

> These conditions can only take a negative form (without X there would not be Y). One can be certain only of this negative form. As soon as it is converted into positive certainty ("on this condition, there will surely have been event, decision, responsibility, ethics, or politics"), one can be sure that one is beginning to be deceived, indeed beginning to deceive the other.
>
> We are speaking here with names (event, decision, responsibility, ethics, politics) of "things" that can only exceed (and *must* exceed) the order of theoretical determination, of knowledge, certainty, judgment, and of statements in the form of "this is that," in other words, more generally and essentially, the order of the *present* or of *presentation*. Each time they are reduced to what

they must exceed, error, recklessness, the unthought, and irresponsibility are given the so very presentable face of good conscience.[29]

In other words, politics and ethics can only be engaged in a realm that combines, in a way that is unavoidably aporetic, the typical and the singular, and the practices associated with the political and the ethical can be undertaken only in a conditional mode, with conditions being specifiable in a strictly negative form (meaning that the conditionals in question can indicate only necessary but never sufficient conditions). Two features of this account stand out.

First, all ethical and political decisions are marked by an epistemological insufficiency whose source is ontological. Epistemological insufficiency has its origin in a lack of ontological sufficiency that structurally conditions *all* situations in which decisions are made. Second, and this is a corollary of the previous trait identified with Derridean ethical and political decision making, the individual making such decisions, confronted by this omnipresent epistemological insufficiency and its underlying lack of ontological sufficiency, has to deal with a "limit of truth" that stems in the end (and this is where Derrida shows himself to be Heidegger's greatest disciple) from the sheer unavailability of ontological knowledge concerning the ego, consciousness, person, the soul, the subject—that is, all the premises of metaphysics.[30] A thinking of *being* without the prop of metaphysics would have to be a thinking that goes beyond being, resulting in an attempt to acknowledge the "place" occupied by that which "bestows" being. But any thinking which broached this subject would have to face a set of aporias that cannot be dissolved or circumvented. This axiom of Heidegger's thought is the starting point of all the positions taken by Derrida on the ethical and the political.

A thinking of the ethical and the political is for Derrida inexorably bound up with the "experience of the aporia" and the thinking conducted on behalf of this experience. For both Derrida and Heidegger this is an experience of being faced with a limit, of arriving at that limit. The experience of this event poses the question of the one who experiences this arriving at the threshold of limit, of the singularity of this being who arrives at the limit. The nature of the limit is such that the new *arrivant* "comes to be where s/he was not expected, where one was awaiting him or her without waiting for him or her, without expecting *it* [*s'y attendre*], without knowing what or whom to expect, what or whom I am waiting for—and such is hospitality itself, hospitality toward the event" (*Aporias* 33). Not only is the new arrivant affected by the threshold which he or she approaches, but the very experience of the threshold itself is affected by the approach of the new arrivant. This occurs because the new arrivant brings out, in his or her approaching of the threshold, the possibilities residing in the threshold that had only been latent until the emergence of the arrivant. Derrida alights on the performative character of this disclosure of possibility: the possibility brought into the open by the arrivant comes in the form of "an invitation, a call, a nomination, or a promise (*Verheissung*, *Heissen*, etc.)" (33). The crux of this disclosure of possibility resides for Derrida in the figure of the subjectile, or what he calls (in *Aporias*) "the absolute *arrivant*":

> The absolute *arrivant* does not yet have a name or an identity. It is not an invader or an occupier, nor is it a colonizer, even if it can also become one. This is why I call it simply the *arrivant*, and not someone or something that arrives, a subject, a person, an individual, or a living thing, even less [a] migrant. . . . Since the *arrivant* does not have any identity yet, its place of arrival is also de-identified: one does not yet know or one no longer knows which is the country, the place, the nation, the family, the language, and the home in general that welcomes the absolute *arrivant*. (34)

The absolute arrivant is "not an intruder, an invader, or a colonizer, because invasion presupposes some self-identity for the aggressor and for the victim." Denying that the absolute arrivant can serve as a "legislator" or "the discoverer of a promised land," Derrida depicts the arrivant, a being "as disarmed as a newly born child," as one who cannot be identified with any telos or eschatology, since this being "exceeds the order of any *determinable* promise" (*Aporias* 34; emphasis in original). Although the arrivant cannot be reduced to any of these terms, he or she nonetheless makes all these possible, "starting with the humanity of man, which some would be inclined to recognize in all that erases, in the *arrivant*, the characteristic of (cultural or national) belonging and even metaphysical determination (ego, person, subject, consciousness, etc.). It is on this border that I am tempted to read Heidegger. Yet this border will always keep one from discriminating among the figures of the *arrivant*, the dead, and the *revenant* (the ghost, he, she, or that which returns)" (35). The reference in this passage to Heidegger is significant, because Derrida states unambiguously in the paragraph following this passage that he is using the figure of the arrivant to rethink the notion of Dasein. Just as Heidegger used this notion to deconstruct the anthropologism that is the taproot of Western metaphysics, Derrida seeks to complement and reconstitute the Heideggerian Dasein through his account of the arrivant. Heidegger used the existential analysis of Dasein's being-toward-death to undo ontotheology, the essence of the superordinate system of possibility that made the so-called ontic sciences (biology, anthropology, historiography, psychology, etc.) possible, by analyzing death as the "possible impossibility" which, because it cannot be absorbed by this system of possibility (death being the cessation of all possibility for Dasein), represents its untranscendable and aporetic limit. In a similar way, Derrida's absolute arrivant is an "impossible possibility" that marks the limit of a seemingly invulnerable system of representation. The notion of a radical finitude lies at the heart of the analytics of Dasein, and Derrida's conceptualization of the absolute arrivant derives from the extension and deepening of this notion to a number of existential situations not considered by Heidegger in *Being and Time*. These are the situations of "mourning and ghosting (*revenance*), spectrality or living-on, surviving," the situations par excellence when it comes to defining the subjectile or absolute arrivant.[31]

Derrida follows Heidegger in asking the question, From where does possibility emerge for Dasein (in the case of Heidegger) or the subjectile or arrivant (in the case of Derrida) when they face up to the aporetic limit represented by the ground of Dasein's or the arrivant's possibility? The answer, for both Derrida and Heidegger, can be found only by making recourse to the self-constitution of Dasein and the arrivant. This question of self-constitution—and here Derrida includes the self-constitution of the ego, person, conscious being in a way that Heidegger would perhaps not countenance—is posed in terms of the question of the "mineness" (*Jemeinigkeit*) of the being of Dasein and the arrivant. This is how Derrida answers this question: "If *Jemeinigkeit* . . . is constituted in its ipseity in terms of an originary mourning, then the self-relation welcomes or supposes the other within its being-itself as different from itself. And reciprocally, the relation to the other (in itself outside myself, outside myself in myself) will never be distinguishable from a bereaved apprehension" (*Aporias* 61). Derrida calls this necessary proximity to the other in one's self-constitution "the reciprocal axiom," and suggests that the apprehension of death, whether of my own death or the death of an other, is always instituted by a "mineness" that is circumscribed by the ego or even the conscious "I." The reciprocal axiom cannot be suspended; to mourn, and the certitude of death makes mourning inevitable, is necessarily to not have oneself be there for the other or the other be there for oneself. Mourning, from which there is no escape, is thus irreducibly political: "There is no politics without an organization of the time and space of mourning, without a topolitology of the sepulcher, without an anamnesic and thematic relation to the spirit as ghost [*revenant*], without an open hospitality to the guest as *ghost* [in English in the original], whom one holds, just as he holds us, hostage" (61–62).[32] In this conceiving of the possible that is the core of the "existential analysis of death," "being-possible" is shown to be the "being proper to *Dasein*." To await oneself at the limits (and this is necessarily bound up with an awaiting of the other) is to engage in something that is unavoidably destabilizing. Derrida identifies three structures or modes in this waiting at the limits constituted by the waiting for death (a waiting we are consigned to whether we like it or not): (1) "awaiting oneself in oneself"; (2) "waiting for the *arrivant*," so that one waits for someone else; and (3) waiting for each other (*s'attendre l'un l'autre, l'une l'autre*; *Aporias* 68).

Having a relation to death is impossible, says Derrida in a necessarily laborious formulation, because death is the showing as such of that which cannot appear as such, and so we are able only to name the one thing which appears in death: (the event of) a being's physical or corporeal perishing.[33] Death, the "possible impossibility," is for Derrida the limit at which one waits, since the state of affairs that would make this waiting cease can never materialize. The only thing that would preempt this waiting is the provision, at the point when life is ebbing, of more life, and yet more life, all adding up to endlessly extended life, and this of course can never happen for a mortal being. Sooner or later we find ourselves at the place of this aporetic limit. But it is also the place where one is awaited. At this aporetic limit, a place that cannot be chosen (even the one who chooses voluntary euthanasia, say, only alters the time at which he or she comes to this place), the place of the one who waits and the one who is awaited can be exchanged, interminably, since this is a destination to which no one belongs. No one can be "at home" at the threshold where all possibility ceases. In this place, then, all are arrivants. For Derrida we are kept by this secret, a secret that bespeaks a true democracy, since all belong to this place, even if none of us is "at home" in it.

Singularity and Politics

A fundamental presupposition of Western metaphysics is that of an irrevocable stability of conceptual deployment. Metaphysics is possible only if judgment, adequate judgment, is possible, and stable boundaries between concepts and nonconcepts or failed concepts are thus its sine qua non. However, this requirement that there be a certain fixity to the boundaries that exist between the concept and the nonconcept cannot be met by any final guarantee, and Derrida (like Heidegger) shows in text after text why judgment, and thus also metaphysics, never have ultimate possession of what they need conceptually and so can never insist that the distinction between concept and nonconcept is as stable as it is typically taken to be. There will always be an "outside" or "surplus" to metaphysics that unhinges the very principle of such a stability.

If the needed distinction between concept and nonconcept is unstable tout court, then any fixity that attaches to it can emerge only as the resultant of our practices and, by virtue of this, the always contingent arrangements that underlie these practices. These practices generate concepts and bestow on them their conditions of intelligibility, and it is from this ground that the notion of a singularity derives its force. This insight has been operative in Derrida's thinking from the beginning, and his much (and in some cases willfully) misunderstood claim in *De la grammatologie* that "there is nothing outside of the text [*il n'y a pas de hors-texte*]" encapsulates the principle of an intertextuality (as Derrida's defenders are wont to maintain in their efforts to protect him from the accusation that he is a pernicious "idealist" of the text). But also, and perhaps more significantly for our purposes, this formula can be understood to encompass the principle, integral to Derrida's understanding of conceptual practice, that "everything" is *inside* the text.[34] This "everything" would include historical, social, political, and economic considerations that bear on a text's conditions of intelligibility and truth, and the claim that "there is nothing outside of the text" can then be taken to imply that this (Derridean) theory of textuality and conceptual practice is in effect a theory of ideology. That is, the text proffers a world, which may be the real world or an alternative to that world, in which certain interests are deemed desirable or worthwhile and legitimated in the process, while others are overlooked or sidelined and therefore delegitimated.[35]

With a constitutive instability pervading the operation of concepts, every conceptual operation is susceptible to deconstruction, that is, the constant permeation of our practices, and not just our textual practices, by what Derrida calls *différance*. This in turn connects with the subject's character as an absolute singularity. Subject constitution takes place in a field of practices suffused by the *quasi-transcendental* that is différance, and the unreserved Heraclitean passage of différance submits everything to effects that decompose and reconfigure whatever it is that comes within its orbit.[36] The strategies that enable the movement of différance (these strategies are not, however, identical with the "event" of the movement of différance) to be what it is are themselves susceptible to the passage of différance (this being the nub of deconstructive practice), so that the enterprise of critique or analysis is itself subject to deconstruction. The upshot is that while metaphysical principles are placed in abeyance by différance, différance cannot function as a "better" metaphysics than metaphysics itself; if it did, différance would have to become an alternative metaphysics, and in doing this, it would have to become the presence that it cannot be (since différance is itself the condition of presence, and as that which has to "be" in order to enable presence, it cannot itself be present). If the event of the subject's constitution is subject to the movement of différance, then this event has to originate in an undecidability that is absolutely primal. The subject qua singularity or subjectile exists because the elemental undecidability that ensues from différance always calls for a stabilization, however brief and rudimentary, in the face of the undecidable. Whether the realm is meaning or politics, values or metaphysics, any stability of concept or judgment, no matter how provisional or ephemeral, has to follow from a resolve in the face of this measureless undecidability to let concept X designate this but not that or permit judgment Y to involve the affirmation of this and this but not that or that. At any rate, concepts are deployable and judgments issuable only because of a prior occlusion or stilling of this originary undecidability, thereby enabling us to disregard the imprints of the ceaseless flux that arises from this absence in principle of the decidable.[37]

This occlusion or stilling of the chaos of the undecidable is not in itself irresponsible. There would be no lived world without it; quite the reverse, responsibility counsels that this flux be immobilized in order to make the determinations that are needed to make life livable. It is this flux that makes ethics possible, since ethics and politics are not possible without the real possibility of making determinations, the "art" of discrimination being integral to ethics. Geoffrey Bennington, perhaps Derrida's most faithful and still rigorous interpreter, and also his coauthor and translator, has said the following about this opening for the ethical:

> This possibility of ethics in undecidability and inventivity is not itself (yet) ethical or political, but is, beyond good and evil (as Derrida said of writing in 1967), also the impossibility of any ethic's *being* ethical. But if this opening is not yet itself ethical, it gives both a principle for judging (any ethical or political judgement that closes off this condition of undecidability is *ipso facto* suspect) and a principle for the infinitisation of ethics and politics. This infinitisation, which takes place each time finitely, is also called justice. For all metaphysical doctrines of ethics and politics close off the undecidable at some point: political and social philosophies of all colours project teleologies whereby politics and morals are oriented towards their end (in social justice,

virtue, transparency, etc.), whereas the deconstructive construal cannot but suspend this teleological thrust (this has made it suspect to many commentators) with its radical appeal to a future (the coming of the undecidable singular event) which will never be a present (this future that is not a future present determining the claim from the earliest work that the future is necessarily *monstrous*, i.e. formless) although it always happens *now*. This appeal to an irreducibly futural future (the interminably *à-venir* or to come) suspends deconstruction always this side of any ethical or political *doctrine* or *programme*. But Derrida is prepared to link this thinking to that of a democracy which is the ethico-political figure of the never-absolute, never-present dispersion of *différance*. Far from preventing ethico-political decisions of the most concrete and pressing kind, this democracy to-come would be the condition of possibility of all decisions, and simultaneously the condition of impossibility of any self-righteousness about them.[38]

This passage draws out in yet another way some of the implications of the Derridean premise that with the impossibility of a direct route to the absolute (this being precluded by différance, since any contiguity with the absolute would arrest the passage of différance), all who approach the threshold of the ethical and the political do so as arrivants. The engagement with the undecidable undertaken by each subject or arrivant is thus absolutely singular: if différance is unending movement, shuttling between the transcendental ("the political," in this case) and the empirical (i.e., "politics") in order to interrogate both in terms of a quasi-transcendental that neither can hope to encompass, and which therefore has the capacity to suspend both realms while also propelling them in entirely unanticipated directions, then all political and ethical engagement has the potential to take directions that are novel and distinctive. The absence of finality, except when this is instituted, whether overtly or tacitly, in order to impede the passage of différance (thereby only making this a finality that can always be "undone" by this quasi-transcendental), means that all politics and ethics partakes of the singular. Everything that defines the political (i.e., the transcendental plane superordinate to concrete political activity) as we encounter it in the political forms and processes explicitly manifested in everyday life, and this quotidian practical politics as it is interrogated by the metaphysics of the political (in this way connecting again with the inexhaustible passage of différance), always brings with it the possibility of an encounter with the other. Our respective encounters here are always with this other, a "not me" in "me," that is the sine qua non of any engagement with the political and the ethical.

One must qualify, if not dismiss outright, the impression that this un-ending shuttle between the two planes, productive as it is of the irreducibly singular, generates in all kinds of new and interesting ways a politics and ethics in which subjects are constantly confronted with novelties and fresh challenges that derive ultimately from the movement of différance, situations which then have to be dealt with through an exercise of the subject's will. The passage of différance does not turn politics into voluntarism and politi-cal logic into a logic for an orchestration of the will in the face of the flux associated with the "dance" or "play" that is différance, where responsibility takes the form of a "resolute" exercise of the will as the subject deals more or less nimbly with an endless succession of contingencies and "accidents."

Derrida's positions on the political and the ethical clearly militate against the view that politics and ethics involve, at their core, what is in essence an exercise of the will (though for Derrida they certainly do not preclude this willfulness). For Derrida, the political subject motivated by a sense of respon-sibility is more likely than not to be claimed by a tradition that he or she ap-proaches as an inheritance to be adhered to even if aspects of this inheritance are challenged or repudiated.[39] Here Derrida wants to use the deconstruc-tion of the metaphysics of concepts, and this eo ipso includes the concept of the political, to show that a deconstruction of metaphysical concepts is itself necessarily political, and that this vigilance in the domain of metaphysical concepts in turn enjoins, through a kind of osmosis or contagion of practice enabled by différance, an active vigilance in the complementary sphere of an everyday politics, that is, what counts as politics in the more commonplace senses of the term. This connection between deconstruction and the political is explicitly made by Derrida in his celebrated claim that "justice is the un-deconstructible condition of deconstruction," which palpably implies that at least one of deconstruction's conditions is insusceptible of deconstruction, and that this irremovable condition is justice (and hence politics) itself.[40]

The assertion that a specific politics (a politics incompatible with the re-quirements of justice would be ruled out, peremptorily, as a condition of deconstruction) is the unfettered condition of deconstruction shows decon-struction to be situated at the core of the political, and vice versa. Decon-struction operates at the behest of a specific conception of justice or respon-sibility as a condition of discharging its other responsibilities. But how do we get from this somewhat generalized conception of justice, with its attendant politics, to more practical concerns having to do with peace and war, the causes of famine, racism, the merciless exploitation of women and children, the making of decisions and the determining of courses of actions, and so forth? After all, valuable though it is to find a politics crisply and rigorously at work in the throes of deconstructive practice (i.e., the realm of the onto-logical), it remains the case that this generalized politics can operate only in terms of a transcendental horizon and thus have no visible connection with practice and commitment (i.e., the realm of the ontic).

Derrida has declined to use deconstruction as a guide for developing precepts and principles that can inspire conduct. As he sees it, any attempt to use deconstruction to generate political and ethical precepts that will be "useful" for individuals in the daily round of their lives is inherently problematic: if used in this way, deconstruction vitiates an important condition for the making of real decisions, since decisions are truly made only when they are arrived at in the face of the undecidable, and not because a moral or political calculus is available that can be applied by rote.[41] Decisions in the non-aporetic sense of the term, for Derrida, can be made only in a context subtended essentially by the undecidable; if it were otherwise, one would simply be adhering to a course that had been predetermined, and this would be no real decision. In stressing the indispensability of this place of the undecidable for a genuine ethics and politics, Derrida adverts to a set of modalities sanctioned by the undecidable—the possible, the conditional, the "perhaps"—that are indispensable accompaniments to the making of real decisions.[42] Bennington characterizes this position of Derrida's in the following way:

> Derrida will say that an event that occurs on the condition of the perhaps *lifts* that condition (but remembers it *as* its condition): "If no decision (ethical, juridical, political) is possible without interrupting determination by getting into the *perhaps*, on the other hand the same decision must interrupt the very thing that is its condition of possibility, the *perhaps* itself." Radicalising this thought about events in general in the context of *decisions* leads to a reinscription of the concept of decision away from the concept of the subject to which it is traditionally bound.[43]

Derrida's stress on the "perhaps" goes hand in hand with a significant demarcation made between the *subject* and the *event*, harnessed here to the aim of having the subject displaced by the event. The subject needs to be displaced, according to Derrida, because the intactness of the traditional subject, premised on notions of self-sufficiency and autonomy, makes every decision undertaken by this quintessential embodiment of rationality and sovereignty into something that is fundamentally extraneous to the beinghood of the subject. As he puts it, a decision made by this subject is "an accident that leaves the subject indifferent." By contrast, the event "will surprise both the freedom and the will of any subject, in a word surprise the very subjectivity of the subject."[44] A genuine decision is one that dislocates the intact subject by inserting into the being of the subject the order of the event, which then serves as an exteriority to the subject, inciting in the subject a passivity or receptivity which conduces to an out-of-jointness that makes the one who decides into a subjectile. The subject, in the account Derrida proposes, is no longer to be viewed as a "most real" which effectively turns the world into a secondary reality that has to derive its substance from the being of this immovable bulwark. The following crucial passage from *Politiques de l'amitié* indicates that in the process of being interrupted by this exteriority, the being of the-one-who-decides becomes an arrivant even in regard to itself: "In principle absolutely singular, in its most traditional concept, the decision is not merely always exceptional, *it makes an exemption of me*. In me. I decide, I make up my mind, sovereignly, would mean: the other-me as other and other than me, *makes* or *make* an exception of the self-same. This presupposed norm of any decision, this normal exception does not exonerate from any responsibility. Responsible for myself before the other, I am first of all and also *responsible for the other before the other*."[45] Derrida here turns the Heideggerian diremption of the Dasein of the subject by the nullity of Being into an axiom according to which the subject's correspondence with itself is interrupted by the passage of différance (différance being, among the many things that it is, Derrida's casting of this Heideggerian diremption into the form of a quasi-transcendental), so that the decision made by the subject becomes ethical at its core. In coming to a decision, I am drawn into an "event" in which the other is positioned as a *not me* in an ineliminable adjacency to *me*, so that my deciding is the outcome of an oscillation between the two poles of the *me* and the *not me*, and the *me*, by virtue of this diremption which consigns the self into an exile from itself, is thus an arrivant responsible for the arrivant that is the other (in me). "Home," according to this conception, is the singularity which emerges from this event in which a subject constructs a place in order to deal with its constitutive exile from self and from other, as much as this subject or subjectile is constructed from this place, and as a result is able to issue a welcome in spite of this exile. Home, the place created by the law of unlimited hospitality, is where this responsibility for the other can be discharged, where one or more arrivants can be welcomed unreservedly. This absence of reservation results from the accompanying absence of a determination that bestows on the arrivant an "essence" or an "anticipation" which serves to neutralize the "otherness" of the one who is the stranger.[46] Hospitality and responsibility have to be without ground, and this nonexistence of ground is due to the movement of différance.

As I said earlier, différance is the quasi-transcendental that is ultimately responsible for this crucial and originating lack of a ground for politics and ethics. With this primordial absence of a ground, undecidability becomes an all-enveloping condition for the emergence of democracy: democracy arises when the myriad singularities that elude incorporation into an Absolute or All are then free to be organized in ways that make them insusceptible to being dragooned by an organization or individual acting solely at the behest of a doctrine or program. Democracy is possible for the Derridean only when forces preemptive of the possible are warded off and a ubiquitous and yet enabling uncertainty is installed in the realm of the ethical and the political. Politics is possible only when a threshold of hesitation or reserve allows the political subject opportunities to experience the displacements and reorientations integral to any process of transformation and renovation.

Politics beyond Politics?

A fundamental gap between the undecidable as the concomitant of the quasi-transcendental différance and the event of making concrete ethical and political decisions is integral to Derrida's deconstruction of the metaphysics of the political, a metaphysics that has prevailed from the time of the Greeks to Carl Schmitt. This gap may make Derrida vulnerable to what looks like a telling objection advanced by Simon Critchley, who believes that Derrida cannot show how the subject or subjectile, in this account, is going to be able to move from the all-encompassing undecidability so pivotal for deconstruction to the making and implementation of concrete political decisions. How is one to surmount the aporias arising from the chasm between the transcendental or quasi-transcendental basis of undecidability, with its supervening logic of generalization and generalizability, and the "facticity" of everyday decision making, with its logic of the sheerly singular?

One way of responding to an objection of this kind is to argue that those who find it compelling fail to see that Derrida's insistence on the separation between the quasi-transcendental and the empirical, which seemingly mirrors the Heideggerian distinction between the ontological and the ontic, is intended not so much to create an impasse between the transcendental and the empirical (as these critics of Derrida contend), but is instead a way of *not* absolutizing the distinction between the transcendental and the empirical particular.[47] Identifying the features of the aporetic logic which governs the passage between the quasi-transcendental and the empirical does not of itself prohibit commerce between the two, but instead displays the terms and conditions that subtend this movement, in this way indicating the compromises, oversights, evasions, and commitments which attend the making of this or that connection, no matter how distended or intervallic, between the quasi-transcendental and the empirical. Derrida in effect provides the lineaments of a conception of the contingent and the singular in his elaboration of the "nonconcept" of différance, the whole point of which is not to close off the empirical and the transcendental from each other, but rather to allow the outlines of the always contingent underpinnings of any traffic between the two to be acknowledged and acted upon. This passage or oscillation between the empirical and the quasi-transcendental is then the context, a context itself necessarily outside the purview of the "factically" political and the ethical, from which the factically political and ethical singular emerges.

This context underlies the encounter between me and an other, in which we confront each other as arrivants. Or more precisely, it is the other's other that, as a third party involved in the interchange between the other and me, who confronts the other in me.[48] The complexity ensuing from the "being there" of this third party in the encounter between the other and me makes justice possible, maintains Derrida, because the presence of an other in me and in my other makes it impossible for our relationship to be governed by the principles of a normativity whose overall character has been determined absolutely in advance. The singularity of the event of such an encounter owes its existence to this radical undermining of the notion that the encounter has an essential structure in which everything is given in advance (herein lies the gist of Derrida's critique of Lévinas). For Derrida, justice is possible only because the other is singular and because the event of my engagement with the other has a character that is not set in advance. The trajectory of this encounter has to partake of the undecidable and the interminable to ensure that no finality can set limits to justice. If the other is welcomed because he or she happens merely to embody some principle, or because hospitality to the other is decreed programmatically, then my encounter with the other cannot be animated by a true justice or spirit of hospitality. Limits can be set to the factical extension or applicability of programs and principles, but if this were to be the case, justice and hospitality would be vitiated in the process.

This response to his critics notwithstanding, Derrida still has a problem with the everyday or factical dimensions of the political. Even if it is granted that those of his critics who accuse him of driving an absolute wedge between the transcendental and the empirical are mistaken because he is, on the contrary, interested in conceptualizing in as rigorous a way as possible the metaphysical (and para-metaphysical) assumptions underlying the interchanges between these two domains, there remains the question of the nature of the conceptual practice involved in establishing a Derridean delimitation on traffic between the two domains. A conceptual practice, as well as having a specific structure, culminates in a specific outcome or outcomes, and the outcome of Derrida's conceptual practice in taking the demarcation between the transcendental and the empirical to function as the fulcrum for conceptualizing an adequate enough notion of an ethical and political possibility raises questions that cannot be ignored. What happens when the Derridean notion of the subjectile or arrivant is inserted into the realm of the factically or actually political?

Especially toward the end of his life, Derrida did address political questions of undeniable consequence; the imprisonment of Nelson Mandela, immigration (the status of the so-called *sans papiers* or undocumented foreigners) in France, genocide, human rights, racism, European unification, and Algeria are among the themes dealt with in the texts of the past two decades or so. But for all this, except perhaps in the eyes of his more fervent admirers, there is something curiously unsatisfactory about this body of writings. There is of course the fondness for the elusive and the aporetic, the unbridled zest for etymological twists and turns (the affinity with Heidegger in this respect has been much noted, though Derrida lacks the ponderousness of his German predecessor), conjuring up the proverbial image of a dog chasing its own tail. But this is a minor foible when pitted against the seriousness and palpable rigor of the work being done in such texts as *Politiques de l'amitié*, *Spectres de Marx*, *Apories*, and *Rogues*.[49] At the same time, it is important that we continue to pose the question, which as we have seen is vital to any consideration of the sustainability of the project of liberation, of an openness, a "*certain* openness" (this would be Derrida's preferred idiom when characterizing this openness) to the possibility of the emergence of a specific kind of collective subject (since liberation will require the activity of this subject on a significant scale). And not just any collective subject, but a collective subject capable of initiating a range of transformations that can have an impact in areas as diverse as Burkina Faso and Washington. In reflecting on this possibility, it has to be borne in mind that a philosopher can reflect on the political in at least two ways, given the perspective on liberation canvassed earlier.

One option, and it need not be explicitly chosen, conceives of the political solely or primarily as a conceptual entity or philosopheme. The other, and again it is a preference that, philosophically, need not be voiced for what it is, requires that this thinking of politics involve not only the analysis of concepts, but also the pursuit of a specific historical and political task, namely, the project of a collective human liberation premised on a decisive supersession of the capitalist system of accumulation.[50] A reflection or discourse of the latter kind on the singularity of political practice will have three foci: (1) a subject or addressee; (2) the discourse itself, which will take the form of the formulation of a particular political problem, and which has its own conditions of intelligibility; and (3) an object, which is the concrete situation addressed by the discourse and is the place that circumscribes its conditions of possibility. The pursuit of a collective human liberation involving a supersession of capitalism will clearly require this discourse to be one that addresses the question of the possibility of revolutionary transformation, of creating a state or society not finally constrained by the imperatives of capitalist accumulation. Those addressed by this discourse, its putative subjects, would be those who would be affected by this possibility of transformation. Its object would be the historical and political conjuncture which enables or blocks this possibility, in this case a particular arrangement of classes and their always uneven relations to the mechanisms of capitalist development.

Framed in this way it is difficult not to conclude that Derrida's is a thinking that remains entirely at the level of the philosophical. Of course, there are the vaunted declarations of Derrida himself and several of his commentators that the whole point of deconstruction is to show how this boundary between philosophy and its "outside" is fundamentally unstable and aporetic. For Derrida, as we have seen repeatedly, the boundary between a concept (philosophy or metaphysics in this case) and its outside is unavoidably caught up in the movement of différance, and so no mastery over the placement of this boundary is achievable in principle. The origins of this boundary, or any boundary for that matter, have inserted into them the elemental disruption represented by différance, and this absolutely precludes any attempt to impose a philosophical rectitude or discipline on the course taken by différance. But this claim with regard to the all-encompassing undecidability affecting the operation of any philosopheme can itself never escape, fully, philosophy or metaphysics. While the efficaciousness of the philosopheme can have no ground in a "presence," as Derrida maintains, the realization of this inevitability has to be generated within a frame that encompasses the philosopheme in question *and* its outside, or even the totality of philosophemes and their outside. And this frame will have to contain within itself the mark of philosophy or metaphysics; it cannot escape this fate. Derrida has never shirked the implications of this leitmotif or axiom of deconstruction. On the contrary, he has said repeatedly that the abyss which lies on the other side of a boundary or limit is the only place from which an infinite and unqualified responsibility, and thus ethics and politics, can emerge. With the impossibility of mastery or appropriation, every subject and subjectile has to accept responsibility for what transpires at this necessarily disconcerting limit: "You reach the edge from which what once seemed assured is revealed in its precariousness, its historical breadth—without necessarily disappearing or collapsing." He goes on to say, "In 'this' place . . . you must find yourself, hear yourself out, yourself and your reader, beyond all reckoning, thus at once saved and lost."[51] To not acknowledge the challenge posed by this inescapable moment of decision is to fail to heed the call of responsibility, and thus to be a stranger to the ethical and political.[52] (Failing to heed the call of responsibility is an impeccably Heideggerian way of expressing the matter, but then Derrida's conceptualization of the theme of a summons to responsibility is close to Heidegger's.) Derrida also says that in this "iteration" of responsibility at the abyssal limit, responsibility itself, though it remains an ideal in its form as a summons, is inevitably compromised and its tenets adhered to only incompletely.

This summons is where singularities materialize and intersect, where "manners of living, voices, writing, of what you carry with you, what you can never leave behind" converge to create an "'*old new language*,' the most archaic and the newest, unheard of, and thereby at present unreadable."[53] Derrida insists that the production of singularities is governed by a logic which makes it impossible for the ego, or any center of consciousness, to function. At the same time it is hardly deniable that an irremediable abstraction has seeped deep into this account of the constitution of the singular. For Derrida, the singular comes into being at exactly the moment when the aporetic limit is reached. Or perhaps more precisely, this moment is the occasion and also the stimulus for the emergence of the singular. Approaching the threshold of the limit thus becomes the indispensable condition for the emergence of any singularity. But what happens when this moment draws near? Then, says Derrida, one confronts the undecidable, always, and this unavoidable encounter is then the impetus which moves the subject or subjectile away from any kind of fixity (admittedly this is a fixity displaying itself primarily or perhaps even exclusively at the level of concepts), so that what was previously thought to be immune to the impress of the contingent is now brought within contingency's reach. The inevitability of this encounter with contingency is thus the vital and indispensable horizon for generating singularities.[54]

Ontological difference is the womb from which the singular emerges. The subject's or subjectile's situation as a singularity is conditioned, as a matter of conceptual logic and hence axiomatically, by the movement of difference. But who or what is the one addressed or constituted by this movement of the undecidable? The one so addressed or constituted is for Derrida the one whose being is permeated by what Bennington has called "the event of alterity" (i.e., the event which constitutes the singularity):

> Derrida's many more or less visible interventions in concrete political situations . . . are to this extent not merely the circumstantial acts of a philosopher elsewhere, and more importantly, developing theories of knowledge, but continuous with each act of deconstruction from the start, always more or less obviously marked by a strategic event of decision in a given context. *This does not provide a theoretical model for politics so much as it strives to keep open the event of alterity which alone makes politics possible and inevitable, but which political philosophy of all colours has always tried to close.*[55]

The conceptual practice intrinsic to the kinds of political intervention undertaken by Derrida, and subjected to rigorous reflection in his texts, conceives of politics as taking place primarily, though by no means exclusively, as a context-given "event of decision." Events of decision involve, potentially, many different kinds of subject (individual, collective, national, transnational, local, gendered, sexual, legal, and so on), depending on the nature of the discourse that makes possible the instantiation of the subject in question. But the absolute priority accorded "the event of alterity" does seem to indicate that the subject brought to this point of decision is typically the solitary individual. Moreover, the crux of this encounter with alterity is not necessarily to further a project of liberation (however one defines that project), but, rather, whether or not the one immersed in this encounter is able, through this encounter, to "keep open the event of alterity." If political circumstances, those of an impending revolutionary situation, say, necessitate in whatever way a foreclosing of this prized event of alterity, then the clear implication of this passage (and indeed all of Derrida's oeuvre) is that this revolution must be deemed to have failed in some sense, even if—and this is an entirely plausible scenario—the revolution in question improves in very visible ways the lives of large numbers of women, men, and children!

Elevating the event of alterity into an untranscendable horizon for the constitution of the political clearly has counterintuitive consequences with regard to the realm of the materially political. The event of alterity is the condition that makes possible the emergence of a singularity, but the singularity comes into being by "making politics possible," and presumably not by accomplishing anything else in the realm of "actually existing" politics. It would seem that in Derrida's account one becomes a singularity by taking a decisive step in what is irretrievably a *metaphysical* politics, or the metaphysical dimension of politics, in which "being political," purely and simply, is co-extensive with "keeping politics open." And making the opening of politics a prized and nonnegotiable principle even when human beings may be dying as a result of actions taken in the world of an actual politics is undeniably counterintuitive. But to pose the question again: What kind of singularity is it that emerges from this confrontation with the event of alterity associated by Derrida and his followers with the passage of différance?

Given all the above, this can only be a singularity constituted at a fairly high level of abstraction: politics is kept open, yes, but open in ways that could prompt anyone becoming a singularity, or having already become a singularity, to overlook what happens in a situation involving the welfare of actually existing subjects. After all, the singular individual owes his or her singularity to a movement, that of différance, whose primary orientation or guiding impulse is not really the transformation of the world but the keeping open of politics. It could be argued of course that this openness of the political is precisely an enabling condition of this sought-after material transformation. But were this argument to be made, the question of the gap between the event of alterity and this project of material transformation would still arise; furthermore, the principle that only the event of alterity is needed to constitute singularities is left untouched by this counterargument. To see that this account of the constitution of the singular is beset by a troubling detachment from the situations of a concrete politics, we can contrast this view of the singular with the one to be found in the writings of Gilles Deleuze.

For Deleuze, any entity is what it is, or is able to become what it was in the process of becoming, because it is the outcome of an always specific convergence of forces. It transmits forces and receives other forces, and the plexus of these forces makes up the constitutive power of the individual (the notion of a "constitutive power" being borrowed from Spinoza).[56] The individual, as the event that results from this convergence of forces, is also a singularity. No individual receives or transmits forces in *exactly* the same way as other individuals; if they did, individuals would be qualitatively indistinguishable from each other; that is, there would be no individuals. However, the individual's "nature" as this singularity, as opposed to that singularity or that other one, is always due to a precise concatenation of forces. What makes Abraham Lincoln the singularity that he is, is the amalgam of forces having to do with his being born in a log cabin in Illinois, his decision to abolish slavery, his speech at Gettysburg, his assassination, and so on, to encompass a veritable myriad of such powers, some received and others transmitted, and coming together to constitute the event "being born in a log cabin," "deciding to abolish slavery," "speaking at Gettysburg," "being assassinated," and so on, so that "Abraham Lincoln" names the resultant of all these events. A powerful empiricism is at work in this conception of a singularity, an empiricism which derives from the insistence that singularities result from an always particular constellation of material forces, a materialism which is missing from Derrida's definition of a singularity in terms of its relation to an insistent structural event of alterity generated by the passage of différance.[57]

If we return to the delineation of a conceptual practice congruent with a project of radical social and political transformation, then Derrida's unraveling of the horizon from which *all* philosophies of the political must begin will have as its subject or addressee the one who is the subjectile or arrivant. But of course *all* are arrivants when facing the event of alterity that is the mark of an irreducible contingency: George W. Bush and Nicolas Sarkozy, as well as the Zambian copper miner and the Chicana hotel chambermaid in Los Angeles. Of course each of these individuals will, or will not, be confronted by their respective events of alterity in quite different ways. But this thinking of the event of alterity has to reckon with an inescapable feature of this encounter with alterity and its capacity to bring one to the realization that we are all arrivants, namely, that the Zambian copper miner, say, is in all likelihood going to have a vastly different understanding of his beinghood as an arrivant from the understanding possessed by George W. Bush (and this not merely because the Zambian miner did not go to Yale, did not come from a wealthy family firmly positioned at the heart of his country's ruling elite for generations, etc.). This commonplace draws attention to the need for a view like Derrida's to be complemented by something like a theory of ideology, or at any rate to have at its disposal the wherewithal to accomplish what it is that a theory of ideology is intended to achieve. For the Zambian copper miner and the talentless plutocrat in the White House are situated in completely different life-worlds. (Who can fail to acknowledge this?) And this realization has at least one major consequence with regard to the status quo: George W. Bush will in all probability acquiesce to this status quo, whereas the Zambian miner will in all likelihood not find it so congenial. Quite different subject formations and quite different modes of decision making are at stake here, and conceptual practice has to begin by acknowledging this if it is to succeed as conceptual practice.

The Derridean could argue, however, that this criticism misses the point: what the Derridean deconstructionist seeks to provide is a specification, at the logico-metaphysical level of the condition of possibility, of an always-not-yet-decided, so that decisions regarding practices and their outcomes are never yet made by the one who faces the event of alterity. Decisions can be made only when "the ordeal of the undecidable" has been submitted to, and from this ordeal emerges a "hesitation," referred to by Derrida as "a messianic hesitation," which "does not paralyze any decision, any affirmation, any responsibility. On the contrary, it grants them their elementary condition. It is their very experience."[58] But there is a logical chasm between a depiction, no matter how detailed or persuasive, of the conditions of possibility for making ethical and political decisions (i.e., what Derrida seeks to delineate) and the ideological implications and practical outcomes of making particular ethical and political decisions (what our account of a conceptual practice accordant with a project of radical transformation enjoins). The quest for just social and political arrangements is a defining feature of any such project, but setting down logical conditions for the pursuit of justice will show only what is necessary at the formal level for the implementation of an emancipatory project. It will not be substantial enough to imbue this project with the concrete propositional content needed to demarcate adequately between the respective life-worlds of the Zambian copper miner and George W. Bush. This incapacity is crippling for any project of radical social and political transformation, since no such project can hope to get off the ground without having the means to identify the features that distinguish, systemically, the life-worlds of those who are exploited from the worlds of those comfortably positioned at the depths of the structure of domination which subjugates those whose basic condition is that of being exploited.[59]

The *discourse* of a conceptual practice capable of sustaining a project of liberation will be one which formulates a particular political problem, or set of problems. In the case just referred to it will concern itself with the political ramifications of a situation marked by fundamental asymmetries of power that create the life-worlds of the Chicana hotel chambermaid and Zambian copper miner and George W. Bush, and which constitute the chambermaid and the miner and the president as social and political subjects. There is no hint in any of Derrida's works, even in *Specters of Marx*, of the necessity for such a discourse.

The *object* of this conceptual practice will be the concrete situation addressed by the discourse, which functions as the place circumscribing its conditions of possibility. For our purposes, this place will be the respective life-worlds of the Zambian copper miner, the Chicana chambermaid in Los Angeles, and George W. Bush, and the crucial question for the one who engages in this conceptual practice will be one that focuses on the asymmetries of power that, among other things, are responsible for perpetuating a fundamentally inequitable situation which allows these life-worlds to be maintained in their existing form. Conceptual practice, at any rate the conceptual practice of anyone invested in a project of radical emancipation, will pivot on this need to replace these life-worlds with significantly different alternatives.

Toni Negri did not mince words in his response to *Specters of Marx* when he said that Derrida's insistence on "solitary transcendental horizons" when expounding his conception of justice means that he had nothing really to say about exploitation and the forms of capitalist regulation that subtend this exploitation. Negri is absolutely right, not necessarily about the "solitary transcendental horizons," but certainly about the absence of a Derridean reckoning with the structures responsible for an actually existing exploitation. The tragedy of the politics of subjectivity (at least the Derridean version thereof) is that it has no way of inserting the subject into the domain of the actually political.[60] We are left instead with a paralyzing Kierkegaardian pathos that provides no way of imagining resistance at the level of a politics of collective action. The alternative to this pathos is a militancy based on a materialism of the singularity that is the subject. At issue here is the crucially important distinction between, on the one hand, forming or constituting a subjectivity, or putting in place the conditions responsible for its emergence (these having in Deleuze's case to do essentially with a specific accumulation or aggregation of forces), so that this subjectivity, or the conditions underlying its presence, is already the outcome of a palpable politics (the transmission and reception of these physical forces being always already ordered by a politics), and, on the other, providing a quasi-metaphysical elaboration of this subjectivity or set of conditions (this having in Derrida's case fundamentally to do with a response to the event of alterity), and only then broaching the question of a politics that conforms in principle to this constituting logic or set of enabling conditions. Derrida's writings on the political approximate more closely to the latter position, those of Deleuze and Guattari to the former.[61] One is a politics that can be addressed or alluded to only *after* a fixity or blockage has been undone by keeping things open to the passage of différance; the other is a politics that, materially and therefore politically, comes *before* the passage of différance and provides conditions for any manifestation of alterity. For proponents of the latter position, it is necessarily the case that before the movement of différance there is politics. For those who take this position, Derrida and his followers have put the proverbial cart before the horse and preempted the possibility of a militant politics.

CHAPTER 8

Models of Liberation III

The Politics of the Event

The politics of the event, associated here with Alain Badiou and, to a somewhat lesser extent, Slavoj Žižek, finds the possibilities of a reinvigorated militancy in the political reorientation opened up by a particular kind of singularization, one stemming from an encounter with the Real or a truth-event (the primary exemplars of this kind of singularization for Badiou being such figures as St. Paul and Lenin). From these distinctive singularizations there emerge possibilities of a rupture with the baneful reality of the present; in turn such ruptures provide the potential for anticapitalist political interventions. Several of his commentators have noted that Badiou's truth-events tend to be remarkable and rather splendid (St. Paul's conversion, the French Revolution of 1789, the Bolshevik Revolution of 1917, and the events of May 1968), as well as being associated with obviously charismatic personages (Lenin, Mao, St. Paul), and Simon Critchley and others have criticized Badiou for what seems to be a kind of political romanticism.[1] The other seeming problem with a politics of the exceptional event is that it is the American right, and to a lesser degree the New Labour government in Britain, that are now using the category of the exceptional event to mobilize the very considerable resources of power and coercion that are at their disposal after September 11, 2001. September 11 is clearly the American right-wing and British New Labour obverse of Badiou's 1968 truth-event, as evidenced by such claims as "Things can never be the same again after the attacks in New York and Washington," "From now on everything is different," and "After September 11 we have to fight the terrorists on their own soil," used by George Bush and his handlers not just to mobilize American public opinion as a response to Al Qaeda, but also to promote the Republican Party's overall right-wing domestic agenda. In Andrew Bacevich's eloquent words, "President Bush will bequeath to his successor the ultimate self-licking ice cream cone. To defense contractors, lobbyists, think-tankers, ambitious military officers, the hosts of Sunday morning talk shows, and the Douglas Feith–like creatures who maneuver to become players in the ultimate power game, the Global War on Terror is a boon, an enterprise redolent with opportunity and promising to extend decades into the future."[2]

There is of course something cynical and opportunistic about this right-wing exploitation of the event of September 11. As is clear from the way the Bush administration has used this emblematic event to let itself off the hook for using torture at Abu Ghraib and Guantánamo, to justify the invasion of Iraq, to curtail civil rights in America, and even to make a case for oil drilling in the Alaskan wilderness and for maintaining military ties with "authoritarian" Central Asian regimes, the event of September 11 is in the eyes of many a fraudulent rationale for pursuing a foreign and domestic policy accordant with the objectives of the neoconservative faction that dominated policy formation in the Bush administration. September 11 is, palpably, no truth-event in the sense used by Badiou. But the fact that those who rule us have fabricated, and probably will continue to fabricate, "truth-events" of the kind associated with the right's vision of September 11 is hard to gainsay. (The 2008 presidential campaign of John McCain and Sarah Palin provides more than enough evidence for this kind of duplicitous "evental" production.) There must therefore be at the very least a critique of this appeal to truth-events by the right which can serve as a complement to the left's own descriptions of the truth-event. The basis of such a critique is to be found in some of Badiou's more recent writings, where he states explicitly that "not every transformation or becoming is a truth and consequently dependent upon a founding event and a fidelity to this event."[3]

The left's attempts to mobilize a countervailing power to this right-wing assimilation of the appearance of the truth-event have to involve the insistence that some things really have remained the same in spite of something like September 11, that, for instance, the exigent claims of justice and the cause of equality, which are marks of the genuine truth-event, have not been abolished or shelved by the events of September 11. As the American country singer and anti–death penalty campaigner Steve Earle reminded an audience in London a few days after September 11, "George W. Bush did not stop being stupid on September 11th."[4] If September 11 is the appearance of the truth-event par excellence for us today (and I entertain this proposition as a somewhat dubious position, no matter how much one may abhor personally the killing of innocent people in New York and Washington that day), then this is its profoundly fundamental truth, its "axiomatics": that the world will not be a better place for the majority of human beings as long as our leaders continue to provide forms of bogus psychic relief for the bewildered and confused, as well as the plainly nasty substratum that exists in every electorate, since these forms (inducing a war fever over Iraq in the case of Bush, conducting a xenophobic campaign against asylum seekers in the case of the former Australian prime minister John Howard, making specious appeals to human rights and riding the late Princess Diana and the late Queen Mother "effect" in the case of Tony Blair) are utterly disabling, even in the shortest of short runs. The truth-event has an inviolable impetus toward the liberation of all human beings that takes it in a quite different direction from the Right's dragooning of these events. This insight of Badiou's, focused on addressing the question "What is it to have a radical commitment to justice and equality?," needs to be taken seriously in any characterization of the truth-event that avoids the attempted appropriation of it by the right.

The Politics of the Truth-Event

The core of Badiou's conception of the truth-event resides in his desire to make the radical militant integral to the left's understanding of political agency. The account he gives of this radical militant is subtended by the following axioms. The most significant of these axioms is embodied in the assertion that radical commitment is structured by truth, or more specifically, a truth procedure. This truth procedure, part of Badiou's "science of the multiple in general," has two characteristic features: it combines a dimension of subjectivity with an adherence to strict universality. The truth procedure begins as part of a "situation" (the term is Badiou's), constituted in a particular time and place, which is structured by rigorously egalitarian principles; it is these egalitarian principles which set this truth procedure totally apart from the Right's attempts to construct truth-events.[5] The structure of the ensuing commitment is not enabled or constrained by any psychological or social canons or principles, since for Badiou only a properly universal truth can be the adequate source of a genuinely radical commitment, and is thus not to be understood as a function of this or that subject's personal psychology or social beliefs or values.

A situation provides constraints marked by an inevitable specificity, but the truths that prompt assent from a subject are capable of gaining the adherence of anyone who happens to be in that particular situation. Even if it happens to be induced from a particular situation, the character of a truth does not depend on any existing forms of power, knowledge, or awareness. Not having any need to depend on prevailing configurations of power and judgment, a truth is necessarily novel in relation to the situation from which it emerges, and the subject's being is constituted precisely by his or her relation to this novelty, which therefore represents a departure from the status quo. This departure from the status quo is for Badiou exactly what constitutes an "event." The axiomatic logic of the situation, according to Badiou, is that of "infinity-minus-one," that is, the unique "void" which, in Badiou's axiomatics, is the nonenumerable and unnamable that is the ground for the antagonisms, revolutionary discipline and fidelity, and radical nonconformity that characterize a militant politics. If something lends itself to being named and enumerated, it can be fully identified and described by our prevailing encyclopaedias of knowledge, which purvey little more than opinion, and so cannot provide the impetus for the creation of a genuinely transformative social and political movement.

At this "evental site" (*site événementiel*) the certitudes afforded by existing paradigms of knowledge (i.e., opinion) are suspended, and the truth that emerges from the event's "possibility of the impossible" will possess the capacity to generate radical dispositions on the part of individuals who are attuned to the event's potentiality.[6] Such individuals are constituted as the subjects of this event's truth. The militant subject is thus someone who maintains a fidelity to an event's consequences. The truth is then the assemblage that emerges from the event's genuinely novel ramifications and outcomes. The subject's fidelity to the event's consequences is identified with the capacity to reconfigure the situation's self-organization qua the situation that it is, all the while maintaining a disciplined adherence to the intellectual contours and practical implications of the event itself. This disciplined adherence has to be universal: anyone acting on behalf of the interests of a particular group in a situation only manages to reflect a certain kind of partiality and not anything like a genuinely universal interest. It would be a mistake, however, to see Badiou as the proponent of a Habermasian universal communication. As Badiou sees it, in an "actually existing politics" in which electorates are invariably encouraged to converge on a mythical "center" which in reality reflects only the more or less concealed partiality of ruling-class interests masquerading as universal principles, those interested in a genuinely universal politics have to separate themselves from this mythical center, and in so doing will give the impression of lacking impartiality. The defenders of a real universality then seem (to the upholders of this sham political consensus) to be one-sided and partial, if not downright biased. To quote Badiou:

> Democracy thus inscribing itself in polls and consensus necessarily arouses the philosopher's critical suspicions. For philosophy, since Plato, means breaking with opinion polls. Philosophy is supposed to scrutinize everything that is spontaneously considered as "normal." If democracy designates a normal state of collective organization, or political will, then the philosopher will ask for the norm of this normality to be examined. He will not allow for the word to function within the frame of an authoritarian opinion. For the philosopher everything consensual becomes suspicious.[7]

A subject constituted by a genuinely universal politics will recognize that the truth of a cause will hold indifferently (which is not to say that the proponents of this truth will themselves be indifferent in its pursuit) for all who belong to the situation in question; the truth is "generic" and thus will not discriminate between individuals.[8] For a militant politics, every individual counts as one, and the only real interest is a universal interest. Its pure generic character notwithstanding, the truth of an emancipatory politics, as the possibility of the impossible, pits "that which is not yet in being, but which . . . thought declares itself able to conceive," against the bland formations of consensus, the ersatz universality promoted by the regnant liberal order.[9]

Repudiating a kind of universalism founded on the premises of liberalism, Badiou finds the possibilities of an alternative militant universality in the singularizations opened up by the encounter with the truth-event in question. Central to this point of view is the proposition that the generic quality that necessarily inheres in the being of all that exists is not discernible except through the exceptional commitment of those who emerge as subjects by virtue of being opened to the event. This exposure to the truth-event will reveal Being to be pervaded by a fundamental multiplicity that is nonetheless universal. The truth-event will therefore be at odds with any politics based on identity, since identity divides subjects from each other and is therefore incompatible with the axiom of equality. Or, as Badiou succinctly puts it, "Politics can only think as the thought of all."[10]

His assertion that "politics can only think as the thought of all" notwithstanding, Badiou maintains that true politics is inextricably conjoined to the exceptional, since only the exceptional can motivate a politics not circumscribed by the apparatuses of the state. It is this stress on confronting the exceptional that prompts some friendly critics to chide him for what seems like political romanticism. While this Schmittian politics of the exception or the exceptional event does not nullify Badiou's insistence that a genuine politics adheres to the principle "Everyone can occupy the space of the political, if they decide to do so," it does cause some difficulties for anyone who agrees with Badiou's metapolitics.[11]

Badiou maintains that the fundamental premise behind the politics of representation, that is, the politics associated with the great thinkers of liberalism (preeminently Rousseau, Kant, and Hegel), is fatally flawed. For Badiou it is axiomatic that *all* can participate in a democratic political process, and so a politics premised on a contest to be the representative of those who must then agree to be "the represented," this being the procedure constitutive of political liberalism, is to be rejected. Against the bifurcation of the representative and the represented required by liberal-democratic parliamentarianism, Badiou suggests that there is really only one political actor: the *we* that is constellated by a political procedure driven by the imperatives of liberty, equality, and fraternity (especially fraternity). Indeed, the dichotomizing of the political actor required by the so-called parliamentary democracies has as one of its main consequences a rendering transcendent of the state's political power, for it is the state that provides the mechanisms of sovereignty which allow a select few to become representatives and a great many others to be the merely represented. Parliamentary liberalism, which regards the state as the indispensable core of sovereignty, can never challenge the state, and so it only obscures the realities of the fundamental power which lies behind this sovereignty and allows it to perpetuate itself. Parliamentary liberalism therefore pits abstractions such as "the people" and "the masses" against the state, with the state possessing all the instruments of coercion and persuasion for organizing its citizens into "the people" or "the masses."

To a considerable extent, however, the critique of capitalist parliamentarianism in terms of the unacceptably abstract model of sovereignty and representation it presupposes, which is the crux of Badiou's metapolitics, is somewhat dated. Contemporary capitalism has bypassed this model of sovereignty and representation, even if it still clings to the husk of the parliamentary system. The revolutionary transformations in financial accumulation discussed earlier in this book have had several important political results, the most significant of which has been the bypassing of capitalist parliamentarianism's system of representation. With the emergence of financial capital as the primary instrument for the furthering of accumulation, at the expense of those drawing wages and salaries, the notion of a "stakeholding society" has arisen to enfranchise not just private citizens, but also corporations and financial organizations; these bodies are alleged to have just as much of a stake in civil society as the represented individual citizen. When financial corporations are considered to have just as much of a stake in society as citizens, it becomes relatively easy for those in power to suggest that it is the primary responsibility of citizens to vote for policies and parties which at the very least do not disfavor corporations; the flawed presumption here is that the interests of corporations and the interests of citizens coincide perfectly if only the right "fix" can be found. Hence the repeated and sometimes hysterical warnings of financial market collapses and currency market tumbles that supposedly serious publications such as *The Economist* and the *Wall Street Journal* issue when a party or candidate with even mildly redistributionist policies looks like getting elected.[12] As Prabhat Patnaik points out, "freedom" in such a context is tacitly or even overtly equated with the freedom of corporations to engage in accumulation with as few constraints as possible. When this happens, political representation is radically modified, and those elected as representatives in fact represent corporations as much as, if not more than, they represent individual citizens.

This development is exacerbated by the fact that electoral campaigns, which in the advanced industrial countries are overwhelmingly television-based nowadays, depend more and more on corporate subventions for their publicity campaigns. One does not have to be a Ralph Nader to acknowledge that politicians in the United States, for instance, represent business interests as much as they purport to represent their constituents. Badiou, however, with his refusal to consider the realm of economic interests, may have given up the chance to register the impact of this powerful transformation wrought by financial capital in recent decades. When the state can no longer distinguish between the interests of civil society and those of the business corporations, the entire political prospectus of those who purport to represent "the people" in liberal democracies must be regarded with at least a modicum of initial suspicion.

But how is politics to be "de-statified" in the way required by Badiou? Can a revolutionary politics in the current conjuncture hope for a complete displacement of the state? Badiou's antistatism has something in common with Hardt and Negri's *Empire*, but it is not difficult to see that the notion of a preemptive de-statification is somewhat implausible.[13] To his credit, Badiou came to change his mind on this putative de-statification. Where he once accepted the orthodox marxist position, a position incidentally also adhered to by classical liberalism, that affirmed the necessary exteriority of the state with regard to the domain of the political, he now believes that a complete de-statification of this kind is impossible. To quote Badiou:

> We tended to leave the state outside the field of politics in the strict sense. Politics unfolded according to the interests of the masses, and the state was the external adversary. This was our way of being faithful to the old communist idea of the withering away of the state, and of the state's necessarily bourgeois and reactionary character. Today our point of view is quite different. It is clear that there are two opposed forms of antistatism. There is the communist heritage of the withering of the state on the one hand; and on the other there is ultraliberalism, which also calls for the suppression of the state, or at least its reduction to its military and police functions. What we would say now is that there are a certain number of questions regarding which we cannot posit the absolute exteriority of the state. It is rather a matter of requiring something from the state, of formulating with respect to the state a certain number of prescriptions or statements. I'll take up the example I gave a moment ago, because it is an example of militant urgency. Considering the fate of the *sanspapiers* in this country, a first orientation might have been: they should revolt against the state. Today we would say that the singular form of their struggle is, rather, to create the conditions in which the state is led to change this or that thing concerning them, to repeal the laws that should be appealed, to take the measures of naturalization [*regularization*] that should be taken, and so on. This is what we mean by *prescriptions against the state*. This is not to say that we participate in the state. We remain outside the electoral system, outside any party representation. But we include the state within our political field, to the extent that, on a number of essential points, we have to work more through prescriptions against the state than in any radical exteriority to the state.[14]

In a word, Badiou's requirement is that we work against the state rather than regard the state as being wholly exterior to the political domain. The proposition, now accepted by Badiou, that the state is not a pure exteriority in respect to the political is salutary and plausible. But some critics have noted that there is a strongly reformist tinge to Badiou's proposal concerning "prescriptions against the state," namely, that "the singular form of their struggle is . . . to create the conditions in which the state is led to change this or that thing concerning them, to repeal the laws that should be appealed, to take the measures of naturalization [*regularization*] that should be taken, and so on." Is this all that can be done against the state?

The other notable feature of Badiou's conception of the militant, and indeed of his entire treatment of the political, is a rigorous separation between politics and economics, coupled with his insistence that the economics only records or analyzes the status quo, and thus has no part to play in any conceptualization of a radical political alternative to the status quo:

> Any viable campaign against capitalism can only be political. There can be no economic battle against the economy. We have economist friends who analyse and criticize very well the existing system of domination. But everything suggests that on this point, such knowledge is useful, but provides no answer by itself. The position of politics relative to the economy must be rethought, in a dimension that isn't really transitive. We don't simply fall by successive representations, from the economy into politics. What kind of politics is *really* heterogeneous to what capital demands? — that is today's question. Our politics is situated at the heart of things, in the factories, in a direct relation with employers and with capital. But it remains a matter of politics — that is to say, of thought, of statements, of practices.[15]

There is a troubling convergence between Badiou's refusal of the state (though he later modified his position to acknowledge that the state is not a pure exteriority), for example, his injunctions not to vote, to stay outside "party politics," and this absolute repudiation of any "transitivity" between the political and the economic.[16] Granted that the key principle here is the need to maintain a "heterogeneity to what capital demands," but the restriction of politics to "a direct relation with employers and with capital," coupled with the abstention from any state-supervised politics, effectively severs political subjectivity from the situations that make up "political *and* economic objectivity." Not that there is a readily identifiable "subjectivity" and "objectivity" here, but to keep them apart in the way that Badiou does overlooks the fact of capital's immense complexity as an assemblage of assemblages. Or if one prefers a more Hegelian-Marxist way of putting things, he elides the central part played by the vast network of mediations in the functioning of the capitalist system.

Militancy is absolutely essential for an emancipatory politics, but it is hard to see how it can be sufficient if it is severed so radically from any "transitivity" with the economic domain and the apparatuses of the state. Emancipation will require, at least in the beginning, a complete restructuring of the state, among other things, and it is hard to conceive how this can be accomplished if the political is severed from the economic, and the political (which for Badiou is always another name for the aleatory realities of *a* politics) is then confined strictly to "direct relations with employers and with capital." The state provides the crucial enabling conditions for the realization of economic surpluses, and as such is foundational for contemporary capitalist appropriation.[17] But let us consider again the matter of the event and its connection to truth. There may be something here that, for Badiou, is able in principle to acknowledge the decisive relation of politics to the economic dimensions of capitalist accumulation.

Truth, Truth-Effects, and Politics

Badiou has recently hinted that his earlier demarcation between a "situation" that is in principle capable only of generating opinion and of conserving the status quo and an "event" capable of furnishing new axioms of thought and practice as well as a genuine universality is perhaps too rigid.[18] In his *Logiques des mondes*, he identifies four kinds of transformation: "a modification (which is the mode of being of the objects of the world), a fact (which is a transcendental novelty, but one endowed with a low degree of intensity), a singularity (a transcendental novelty whose intensity is strong, but which has few consequences), and an event (a singularity with consequences of maximal intensity)."[19]

This is an ontological schema, and as such it provides us with a framework for reflecting on the nature of transformation in principle, although clearly something else will be needed for a more comprehensive and yet concrete notion of the political event. Badiou is of course aware of the need for this further requirement, and he goes on to say that "in order to arrive at a new type of existence with regard to a given problem (the status of sexual difference, the future of Palestine, the resurrection of music after serialism, etc.), it is necessary to possess, at one and the same time: a certain transcendental regime of intra-worldly modifications, the shock of an event, the constitution of a new subject, the rule-bound consequences of this constitution, and so on" ("Afterword" 236). The problem here, however, lies not so much with the ontology of modification or transformation per se (as much as some have quarreled with him over his choice of set theory as the means of displaying the logic of this ontological framework), but rather with the criteria used to identify the event whose defining feature is that of the "shock," that is, the quality of being able to thwart any kind of predictability with regard to the prevailing order of reality, and then the well-known Badiouian principles of liberty, equality, and fraternity. This inevitably takes politics away from the realm of ontology (indispensable though ontology is when it comes to specifying the conditions subtending the presentation of objects as such) into the domain of what can only be regarded as a history of the present, or a version of standpoint theory having the concrete practices of political agents as its focus.

Badiou is certainly aware of this need for something like a history of the present or of standpoint theory, even if he does not quite use the nomenclature of either. But the insights embodied in these positions are certainly compatible with his own formulations. For instance, he has made it clear that there has to be a "concrete analysis of change," while maintaining that it is precisely "a certain transcendental regime of intra-worldly modifications, the shock of an event, the constitution of a new subject, the rule-bound consequences of this constitution, and so on" that provide the basis for this "concrete analysis of change" (236).

Badiou also suggests that this "concrete analysis of change" has to be undertaken via "the construction of a truth." As he sees it, only the recourse to this construction avoids the "logic of interests of the human animal." Human interest is all-pervasive, which entails that we find ways to overcome this "logic of interests," which is "the logic of the (very many worlds) inhabited by this crafty, cruel, and obstinate animal. In other words, because only this construction [of a truth] is trans-human." Badiou adds, "All I am doing here, in fact, is corroborating some very old speculative statements. Plato: philosophy is an awakening, ordinary life is nothing but a dream. Aristotle: we must live as immortals. Hegel: the absolute works through us. Nietzsche: we must free the overman within man" (237).

Badiou argues that only the construction of a truth, which for him only philosophy can accomplish, will enable us to avoid "an anthropology of finitude" that does no more than ratify the accomplishments of "this crafty, cruel, and obstinate animal." So any proposal, such as mine, which calls for Badiou to take the path of a history of the present or some kind of standpoint theory in order to provide a "concrete analysis of change," must involve philosophy if it is to do justice to "the desire, forced by an evental outside, to move beyond the resignation of established beliefs" (237). The choice for Badiou, therefore, is simple but momentous: either resignation to the status quo or the enabling of a truth, generated philosophically, which, because it is philosophical, allows the power of an event to force the otherwise resigned human animal to awaken itself and desire another, better world. This truth can come only from a concrete event, albeit one which avoids the taint of an anthropology of finitude.

It is axiomatic for Badiou that truth is evental. That is to say, a truth is such that it is generated by a happening with implications that defeat the human urge to repeat and to calculate:

> For the process of a truth to begin, something must happen. What there already is, the situation of knowledge as such, only gives us repetition. For a truth to affirm its newness there must be a *supplement*. This supplement is committed to chance. It is unpredictable, uncalculable. It is beyond what is. I call it an event.
>
> A truth appears in its newness, because an evental supplement interrupts repetition.[20]

If a truth can emerge only as a pure novelty, this being a fundamental principle for Badiou, it is nonetheless the case that the truth in question has to be appropriated by a subject in order to be what it is, and it is this process of appropriation which makes truth properly ethical. Truth is ethical because it constitutes a situation in such a way that the subject of that truth is drawn powerfully into a response that is irreducibly faithful: "The fact that the event is undecidable imposes the constraint that a *subject* of the event must appear. Such a subject is constituted by an utterance in the form of a wager. The utterance is as follows: 'This has taken place, which I can neither calculate, nor demonstrate, but to which I shall be faithful'" ("The Ethics of Truths" 250, Badiou's emphasis).

It is here that Badiou must face the question of the structure of this wager. How does the movement from the undecidability of the event to the occurrence of the wager take place, not just "empirically," but also as a matter of processual logic? Does every manifestation of the undecidable result in a wager? The undecidable certainly creates the structural possibility of such a wager, but what else has to take place for this (mere) possibility further to be consolidated into a formation in which a subject can respond to a wager of the kind posited by Badiou? Clearly, though not necessarily in a way that is self-explanatory, the subject has to be affected in significant ways by the implications of the event under consideration. There has to be a reckoning with the effectivity of the event on the part of the subject, which in turn involves an estimation of the effects of the truth that brought the subject to the point of confronting the wager that he or she must now make. But what enables truth to possess this effectivity? What is it about truth that, ontologically, elicits the response of fidelity, that prompts the decisive break with routine and the hollow repetition of the status quo that market democracy finds so congenial? Badiou does not shirk these or similar questions. His possible response to them hinges on the basic insight that when the event of truth occurs, the subject opens himself or herself to the diremption or rupture represented by this event, and as a result the rupture functions as the basis for an acknowledgment on the part of this subject that a fundamental transformation has taken place.

With the onset of this fundamental transformation, the subject can then proceed to verify or disconfirm the occurrence of this transformation by embarking on an investigation of the forces that enable this transformation to be what it is; in the process this investigation becomes a moment of conversion for that subject. The truth becomes the truth when the subject is launched on this process of investigation and conversion, when the truth procedure "induces" the subject into fidelity to the event and its implications. For the subject to do this, he or she must construct a truth by making a choice (the core of the wager) "within the indiscernible." There is something in every truth procedure that requires the deed of creation to be incalculable as to the enabling basis of the truth thus being generated. Badiou is worth quoting at length at this point:

> But what is a pure choice, a choice without a concept? It's obviously a choice confronted by two *indiscernible* terms. Two terms are indiscernible if no effect of language permits their distinction. But if no formula of language distinguishes two terms of the situation, it is certain that the choice of having the verification pass by one rather than the other can find no support in the objectivity of their difference. It is then an absolutely pure choice, free from any presupposition other than that of having to choose, with no indication marking the proposed terms; the choice by which the verification of the consequences of the axiom will first pass.
>
> This means that the subject of a truth demands the indiscernible. The indiscernible organizes the pure point of the subject in the process of verification. A subject is what disappears between two indiscernibles. A subject is the throw of the dice which does not abolish chance, but accomplishes it as a verification of the axiom which founds it. What was decided concerning the undecidable event must pass by *this* term, indiscernible from its other. Such is the local act of a truth. It consists in a pure choice between two indiscernibles. It is then absolutely finite. ("The Ethics of Truths" 250–51, Badiou's emphases)

This passage calls for some elaboration in terms of an example or two.[21] Resorting to Badiou's favored set-theoretic armature, one can define an event in terms of its self-intactness or self-correspondence with regard to its being,

$E \ \varepsilon \ E$, such that from the event E a grounding and enabling statement p can be derived, $E \rightarrow p$, which is another way of saying that E is the cause of p. Further implications can then be drawn from the basal statement p. When E is the cause of p, the upholder of p cannot be indifferent to E: if she is indifferent to E, then she has no ground for affirming p.[22] Once E is belief-causing, then the believer who assents to p on the basis of E has in some sense to maintain a fidelity to E as a condition of adhering to the conviction that p (is the case) as well as being faithful to all that is entailed by p.

At the same time, assenting to p on the basis of E is an act distinctive in at least a couple of ways. First, there is the disjunction between p as such and p as asserted in this or that particular situation; "It is snowing" may be true for me in Manhattan today but not for my sister in Burlington, Vermont, and vice versa. But the relation of p to its localized situation of enunciation is never given in p as such.[23] This relation of p to its localized situation stands outside of p, and so cannot be named or designated by p; even if the statement "It is snowing in Manhattan right now" contains an explicit reference to Manhattan and to the falling of snow at this time, there is nothing in "It is snowing in Manhattan right now" which establishes a relation between this statement and the situation in which snow is now falling in Manhattan. Indeed, this relation can only be the outcome of a specific assembling of factors and conditions from the congeries of speech and cultural forms, personal dispositions, collective structures, and so on that make up the situation under consideration. The relation between a statement, a speaker, a time, and a place has to be assembled in a specific way, and can never be deduced from the statement alone. Second, from the relation of a statement p to its "founding" event E (i.e., $E \rightarrow p$), it cannot be inferred from p itself that it has this founding relation to E. Since E is the ground of p, the relation between E and p necessarily has to stand as an exteriority to p that cannot be named by p. Thus, such notions as "insurrection," "guerrilla formation," and "transcontinental class struggle" had to await the event that goes by the name "Che Guevara" to receive their distinctive cast when used in the context of Cuba's contribution to insurrectionary struggles in Bolivia and Angola in the 1960s and 1970s.[24]

A situation, then, has to undergo an extractive operation before it can yield a truth or set of truths. In this extractive operation, components of the situation are "forced" in ways that create, out of the incompleteness of the situation (an incompleteness that pervades truth itself), the possibility that "permits anticipations of knowledge concerning not what is but *what would have been if truth is brought to completion*."[25] A structure of anticipation is created as a result of this extractive operation. A truth cannot be described or identified as it is now, but once a condition exists in which a truth will have been, then, as a result of this extractive or forcing operation, it can yield many possible kinds of knowledge because the truth in question would have been brought to its point of completion (which for Badiou is exactly what forcing involves). That a truth permits interventions of a certain kind as it takes its course is the very thing that allows knowledge to emerge and to be constructed, in which case the truth is not something that one knows, but is rather the condition which enables the various encyclopedias of knowledge to be created and circulated. Where truth is concerned, therefore, it is true to say that one knows only *after* the event. One knows one has fallen out of love only after one has fallen out of love; Richard Perle, the leading American neoconservative, knew he was a neoconservative only after his conversion from being a disciple of the cold war Democratic senator Scoop Jackson to being the Republican neoconservative he now is.

Given that a forcing has to take place in order for statements to be extracted from a situation, and that a fundamental undecidability pervades the underlying basis of this extraction, there is always the possibility of variation in the generation of statements and the kinds of interventions (scientific, political, amorous, artistic) which issue forth from this or that forcing. (Badiou, incidentally, pits this philosophy of irreducible and infinite variation, which accepts stark incommensurabilities between forms of being, against the tradition of vitalist philosophy associated with Spinoza and Deleuze, which in Badiou's eyes always allows the unity of relations between these forms of being to trump incommensurability.)[26] What in Badiou's scheme of things enables a truth to have this efficacy?

Forcing enables the components or elements of a situation to be propelled by an event from the void into the domain of an expressible knowledge. The event discloses the void of a situation and in so doing keeps at bay the possibility that the subject's powers of expression can bridge the gap between the unnamed situation and the modes of speech about it. This revelation of the void is an incitement to truth, since the subject must now respond to what has been revealed with regard to the void. In fidelity to the event, the subject has to strive to find resources of expression or symbolization that enable a connection to be built up between the unnamed void and the domain of names and designations. Those placed in that situation then have to take sides with regard to the named event which they now confront: Are they going to be in favor of it, or are they going to be against it? Interventions are constituted by this taking of sides, and the subject is constructed by the "investigations" he or she undertakes as a consequence of taking sides with regard to the event.[27] For Badiou, the truth that is at issue in this taking of sides adheres strictly to the law of the excluded middle; that is, a statement is either true or false, with no possibility of a middle between truth and falsity. Badiou has no truck with those who espouse a perspectivalist conception of the truth, or those who, in the manner of Foucault, maintain that truth is an "effect" of a "regime of practices." There is a huge technical literature on the law of the excluded middle, too large to delve into in a work like this, but Badiou's devotion to the law of the excluded middle has momentous consequences for his conception of politics.[28]

Badiou's conception of truth, wedded as it is to the law of the excluded middle, is in turn derived from his adoption of a particular version of set theory, which must now be looked at more closely. In a short but perspicacious review article on *L'Être et l'événement*, the late Jean-Toussaint Desanti dealt with the choices made by Badiou when it came to using set theory as the basis for his ontology. Desanti's discussion, as befits a philosopher of mathematics, is technically recondite, but the nub of his argument centers on Badiou's use of the Zermelo-Fraenkel (ZF) system of set theory to provide the basis for his ontology. The crux of Desanti's position is the defining feature of a set, namely, that a set has no intrinsic "meaning," but is defined by the elements or members that belong to it; that is to say, it is defined extensionally and not conceptually or intensionally. In other words, in logical symbolism $\{x| x$ is the forty-third president of the United States$\}$ is the same set as $\{x| x$ is George W. Bush$\}$ because their respective members are the same individual, in this case the person named "George W. Bush" who happens to be the forty-third president of the United States. Moreover, set membership is determinate, so that it is always the case that any possible member of a set is either in that set or not in it, with no place for any kind of imprecision or ambiguity. These are not the only principles required to make ZF work, but together they render it inevitable that Badiou's "intrinsic ontology" (the term is Desanti's) will exclude by definition the question of its "margin."[29]

The margin in this case refers to a form of writing that is beyond or in excess of ontological writing (i.e., set theory), but which is nonetheless essential to ontological writing. The realm of ontological writing, as we have seen, consists simply of rules and procedures for the constitution of sets and their membership, and as such it can do no more than indicate the items that populate the field designated by the intrinsic ontology (items such as George W. Bush, leaves, dogs, texts, hijackers, musical scores, Madame Curie, hydrogen molecules, prime numbers, and prime ministers). An intrinsic ontology cannot, by virtue of its confinement to ZF, deal with the vital questions lodged on its margins, to wit, such questions as "what was said; what was thought; what we would need to re-think; what we should try to do in order to live" ("Some Remarks" 62).

Desanti is convinced that Badiou needed to resort to Paul Cohen's notion of "forcing" to deal with this problem of the margin that cannot be dealt with solely by employing the resources of set theory.[30] Desanti then tells the following parable to illustrate the nature of the problem created by this commitment to set theory:

> Imagine that there are people obliged to move about in a territory whose border they cannot cross because this border is so contrived as to push them back however close they come, each and every time they approach it. They would soon begin to suspect that this effect has its source on the other side of the border. They would in fact have no choice but to believe this, for since there are no clues within their own territory allowing them to point to the source of this effect, the latter is all the evidence they have for the existence of the border. It would be as though their border was "infinitely" distant for them: they would be incapable either of reaching or crossing it. Nevertheless, this border would still constitute a "beyond" because its effect would not be produced from within the bounds of their territory. In order to designate their situation as one of *subjection*, of assignation to this strange territory, we simply call these people (they could be "human," but that is of no importance here) "subjects." But since "being subjected to the territory" means "being subjected to what lies beyond it," these particular people would end up trying to fashion some way of designating, or marking, what might be going on in this beyond, all the more so because they would come to attribute an infinity of effects, which they would undergo as "subjects," to the effect of the border itself. As subject to these effects, however, they would be unable to mark or specify their points of origin within their own territory. . . . Such a subject must express the connection between an "internal infinite" and an "externalized infinite"—an "indiscernible real" but one which, again as subject, it has to "mark." ("Some Remarks" 64, emphases Desanti's; translation modified)

Desanti presses his critique by saying that set theory or intrinsic ontology can provide only the means for expressing an "internal infinite," and as such has no way of accounting for what lies beyond the border of the territory mentioned in his parable. In order to have access to the "externalized infinite" that lies on the other side of the border, the subjects of the territory need, at the very least, theoretical instruments that set theory, limited as it is to the internal infinite, cannot deliver on its own. But what other resources are needed by the inhabitants of Desanti's fabled territory if they are to avoid the fate of an irremediable confinement within its bounds? Desanti's proposal is that Badiou needs another "basic ontology" if he is going to be able to ensure adequate ontological access to the externalized infinite. He ends his review of *L'Etre et l'événement* at this point, but it is a point that remains well taken, and it behooves anyone interested enough to pursue the question of the ability of Badiou's theoretical armature to do justice to this externalized infinite.

Some supporters of Badiou have shown that his writings subsequent to *L'Etre et l'événement* have reflected important shifts in his position as he has tried to overcome the limitations of that book's ZF set-theoretic ontological apparatus. Peter Hallward, who has access to Badiou's unpublished papers, suggests that Badiou's interest in category theory is integrally bound up with his attempts to deal with the recalcitrant externalized infinite.[31] Badiou's recourse to category theory is thus indispensably a part of this search for a way to complement ZF set theory in order to include, but also to move beyond, the internal infinite of ZF set theory, and by so doing to find the means to accommodate this problematic and thus far excluded externalized infinite. Category theory differs from set theory in a number of important respects. The most notable of these is the fact that category theory is attentive to considerations of meaning and semantics (i.e., intensionality, as opposed to the exclusively extensional orientation of set theory), as indicated in figure 11.

The arrows in figure 11 express relationships between such categories as "progressive citizen," "the Bush administration," "critics of the Bush administration," and "the prison at Guantánamo" in terms of the symmetrical relations of "endorsement" and "disapproval." As Hallward says about any diagram of this kind, which can connect progressive and nonprogressive individuals or groups or can be inverted to express the position of the nonprogressive citizen, any disapproval (and here I refer to my own example and not the one given by Hallward in *Badiou: A Subject to Truth*) of the Bush administration's policy on the internment camp at Guantánamo Bay, whether expressed in concrete actions taken or merely declamatorily, has as its corollary an endorsement of those groups critical of the Bush administration, and vice versa.[32]

This somewhat cursory account shows that one of the fundamental differences between set theory and category theory is that while the former is derived from and regulated by its axioms, the character of this or that category can be specified only by a process of empirical inspection. Thus,

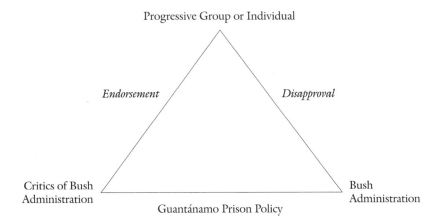

Progressive Group or Individual

Endorsement   *Disapproval*

Critics of Bush
Administration

Bush
Administration

Guantánamo Prison Policy

11. *Source*: Adapted from Hallward, *Badiou: A Subject to Truth,* 317.

where our Guantánamo prison example is concerned, it is entirely an em-pirically contingent matter that the Bush administration's policy of housing "enemy combatants" in an offshore location so that they will not fall under the juridical purview of the American legal system has (even in the United States) attracted much criticism up to now; however, it is entirely conceiv-able that such opposition on the part of progressive citizens will disappear if the Guantánamo prison regime is drastically reordered so as to bring it into line with international law, hard though it is to imagine how this can be done at a location like Guantánamo Bay. While category theory permits the kind of empirical pinpointing that set theory does not, it has to be acknowl-edged that Badiou himself understands the relation between the two types of theory in a way that seems to preclude the possibility of any straightforward alignment between, on the one hand, intrinsic ontology (focused here on Desanti's internal infinite) and set theory and, on the other, category theory and the externalized infinite. For Badiou, as Hallward points out, has always insisted that category theory is not some kind of supplement to set theory; in Badiou's words, "For me, set theory is still today the only consistent on-tology that I know of."[33] Category theory's function is thus to elucidate the logical implications of an already made ontological decision, and this because the sole domain of category theory is a possible universe, while set theory can be entrusted the function of deciding a particular real (as opposed to a merely possible) universe.[34] Hence, where our Guantánamo prison example is concerned, knowing that there is an opposition between the Bush admin-istration and its critics on the legality of the prison, and maintaining that progressive movements are structurally disposed to oppose the Bush administration's policy regarding the prison, in itself shows only that a choice is there to be made between the options available—in this case, a choice between siding with the administration and opposing it.

All that category theory can do here is to lay bare the structure of the possible options confronting the potential chooser. It cannot operate at the level of ontological decision, which for Badiou is necessarily a level that involves reference to truth, that is, the real universe as opposed to the merely possible universes of category theory. Thus, if there is a world that includes the set or class of canines, then since cats, horses, and birds are not extensionally identical with regard to canines, and since the identity of a set is determined exclusively by its membership, the set $\{x|\ x$ is a canine$\}$ cannot be the same set as $\{x|\ x$ is a feline$\}$. In other words, given that there are dogs in the (real) world, and dogs are nonfelines, dogs and cats cannot, ontologically, belong to the same class in this (real) world. Category theory therefore only elaborates the premises that underlie set theory. It cannot in principle augment these premises, nor can it breach in any way the principles undergirding classical logic, and in particular the principle of bivalence integral to that logic which insists that the true is irreducibly opposed to the false, and vice versa, with no possibility of any kind of "in between." So for Badiou the canons of set theory are superordinate over those of category theory; the latter can amplify, but in no fundamental way extend, the ontologic sanctioned by set theory and classical logic in general. Accepting that this is the only warranted relation obtaining between set theory and category theory, however, will plunge Badiou back into the problem that Desanti identified with his ontology, namely, that since the objects encased by this ontology are limited to those compatible with what ZF set theory itself permits, and thus can be defined only extensionally, Badiou's ontology cannot deal with the externalized infinite. Badiou's axiomatic ontology therefore seems doomed to remain within the confines of the territory with unapproachable boundaries adverted to in Desanti's parable. What this entails for a viable conception of truth is something we have to consider in due course.

While it is possible to go back and forth on the question of the externalized infinite in particular, and a suitable axiomatic for truth in general, the choice on these matters comes down ultimately to two views of the logic of multiplicity, one Platonic and the other Aristotelian (according to the terms of art provided by Badiou), or in Hallward's lapidary formulation, "the subtractive austerity of Number over the seductive plenitude of Nature," referring to Platonism and Aristotelianism, respectively.[35] The two logical or ontological traditions thus identified are:

— *Platonism* or Unicity (ontological, of *the* void) — Canons of classical logic; difference results from being and is localized; standard set theory expressed in first-order logical notation; relations are determined internally by their terms.
— *Aristotelianism/Leibnizianism* or Plurality (of voids) — Canons of intuitionist logic; difference results from action and movement and is globalized; category theory; relations are external to their terms.[36]

There is no procedure that can vindicate a putative choice between these two ontological traditions, since someone's being a Platonist or an Aristotelian/Leibnizian is precisely what predetermines the ontological commitments made by those who happen to count themselves as Platonists or as Aristotelians. There is therefore no such science or philosophy as "meta-ontology," and in the absence of the means of adjudication afforded by a metatheory, the choice between the two traditions is groundless from a strictly ontological point of view. For Badiou, it follows from this that the choice of an ontology can result only from a decision that is without a basis that is transcendental or that is indebted in some kind of primordial way to the ultimately arbitrary conventions of language. The decision setting axiomatic ontology in motion is an event or Act (this Act, a "pure" decision, is arbitrary, albeit in a way that differs from the arbitrariness of Saussurean linguistic conventions). With the occurrence of the Act, the process of a fidelity to an event can begin, and with this fidelity, whose primary structure is provided by truth and its procedures, thought also can begin, and thought for Badiou has an inherently logical or axiomatic structure.[37]

Badiou's aim here is to outline a version of Platonism that lends itself to a plausible rapprochement with the undecidable and the arbitrary, one which enables the axiomatics linked to the former to superintend the latter notions, though Badiou does acknowledge that conceptions of the arbitrary and the undecidable belong more appropriately to the alternative ontological tradition associated with Aristotle and Leibniz.[38] This contention is then fleshed out via the claim that for Badiou only Platonism bestows on the notion of possibility the maximal degree of logical breadth. This claim underlies Badiou's stern refusal to admit that non-Platonism, with its commitment to a constructionist ontology, is superior to Platonism because the Aristotelian/Leibnizian tradition keeps its notion of the possible wide open simply because it is always susceptible to construction. As Badiou sees it, the Platonist commitment to the law of the excluded middle entails that anything which is not false is then true and nothing else, and that anything which is not logically impossible is logically possible. And so for Badiou Platonism's understanding of the possible is wider than anything permitted by the constructionist approach favored by non-Platonism.

Having eschewed the law of the excluded middle, which always requires that truth or falsity be the only admissible logical constraint on possibility, the non-Platonist schools of thought have to gloss possibility in terms of its sheer constructability, and so possibility comes to be equated with what is deemed conceivable by the one who happens to be doing the constructing. But if possibility is collapsed into conceivability, and given that conceivability is moreover a patently psychological notion, it follows, according to Badiou, that the non-Platonist must permit the always variable facts of this or that psychology to determine how much scope is then to be accorded the concept of possibility. The structure of this argument against the non-Platonist point of view is essentially that of a reductio ad absurdum. To elaborate: while it is logically possible for a human being to swim, unaided, across the Atlantic Ocean (in the sense that no logical contradiction is involved in making this supposition), it is nonetheless plausible to believe that for most of us it is inconceivable that a human being be physically capable of such a feat. In which case, the notions of (logical) possibility and (psychological) conceivability simply do not overlap. Furthermore, it is also evident that possibility, when compared to this psychologically based conceivability, is really the more logically capacious notion. To this extent, therefore, Badiou is right: Platonism, as he characterized it, appears intrinsically to be less capable of being ensnared by the vagaries of human psychological capacity or incapacity. (This psychology is also for Badiou an element of the despised anthropology of finitude.) And so, if one agrees with Badiou in seeing little option but to accept Platonism, the only tenable position requires us to accept that anything is possible as long as it is not logically impossible.

The problem with Platonism, its initial persuasiveness notwithstanding, is that it still does not provide the wherewithal for dealing with the externalized infinite invoked by Desanti in his critique of Badiou.[39] It is a minimum condition of dealing with the externalized infinite that there be some way of registering more than just the extensionally marked objects of the internalized infinite, these being the only generic objects recognized as legitimate by an axiomatic set theory governed by Platonist principles. But what will it mean to proceed beyond extensionally defined objects? The only alternative for those wanting to make such a move beyond extensionality is to accept the principle of intensionally defined objects, that is, granting that there has to be an active incorporation of the Aristotelian/Leibnizian tradition of ontology, since it is this tradition, rather than its Platonist counterpart, which permits intensional objects. This tolerance of intensionality, though, is exactly what Badiou will not countenance. This is a seemingly intractable impasse, unless it is possible for axiomatic set theory to be elongated in some way that enables acquiescence in the principle of intensionality. Desanti's hunch on this issue comes immediately to mind, namely, that Badiou borrows Paul Cohen's notion of "forcing" to extend axiomatic set theory beyond the realm of extensional objects. However, this suggestion faces an immediate problem: forcing is Badiou's way of allowing objects to be orchestrated in configurations that exceed the structures of conventional knowledge, but he still insists that these objects, no matter how reconfigured, remain extensionally defined and subject to the laws of classical logic.[40] It is by no means clear, however, that the externalized infinite can be approached adequately if the instruments of this approach are constrained by the requirement that only extensional objects meet the test of absolute logical propriety. There is a built-in parsimony to Badiou's ontology that seems to resist any openness to intensional objects. The axiom of extensionality basically confines an ontology to objects that lend themselves to immediate or easy recognition as existent objects. For instance, if extensional objects are the only objects permitted, then $\{x|\ x$ is my paternal grandfather$\}$ and $\{x|\ x$ is Gilbert Surin$\}$ are easily extensionally equivalent, since both my paternal grandfather and the individual named Gilbert Surin are existent objects. However, if intensional objects are also permitted, then, to choose a familiar example from mythology, $\{x|\ x$ is a winged horse$\}$ and $\{x|\ x$ is Pegasus$\}$ are (intensionally) equivalent. (They would of course also be extensionally equivalent for Badiou.) But what would happen if we had to adjudicate a situation in which, say, I came along in a fit of complete ontological derangement and insisted that $\{x|\ x$ is a winged horse$\}$ and $\{x|\ x$ is my grandfather Gilbert Surin$\}$, and moreover that I also happened to believe with utter conviction that in this instance $\{x|\ x$ is a winged horse$\}$ and $\{x|\ x$ is my grandfather Gilbert Surin and not Pegasus$\}$? To preclude such incongruities Badiou would have to restrict his ontology to palpably existent objects, and in so doing banish such entities as winged horses, but in the process he would necessarily preempt the possibility of gaining ontological access to the externalized infinite (which presumably is populated by a plethora of intensional objects). However, as Hallward has pointed out, Badiou is committed to an understanding of extensionality which stipulates that a set is defined entirely by its elements, with no restriction being placed on how those elements are related or combined. This definition of extensionality is therefore sufficiently capacious to permit sets to have intensional objects as their members as long as they meet the appropriate combinatorial constraints on the formation of sets.[41]

But this flexibility leads to some counterintuitive results. It is possible for $\{x|\ x$ is believed by Kenneth Surin to be the greatest chess player ever$\}$ and $\{x|\ x$ is Gary Kasparov$\}$ to be identical sets because x in both cases is Gary Kasparov. But $\{x|\ x$ is the greatest Azerbaijani chess player ever$\}$ should also be identical to these two sets, since the Baku-born Kasparov is also Azerbaijani. It is possible, however, for me to assent to $\{x|\ x$ is believed by Kenneth Surin to be the greatest chess player ever$\}$ and $\{x|\ x$ is Gary Kasparov$\}$ but not $\{x|\ x$ is the greatest Azerbaijani chess player ever$\}$ because I happen to have the mistaken belief that Kasparov is Russian or Georgian or Ukrainian or whatever, with no thought that he might really be Azerbaijani. So, while according to the axiom of extensionality in its purest form, all of $\{x|\ x$ is believed by Kenneth Surin to be the greatest chess player ever$\}$, $\{x|\ x$ is Gary Kasparov$\}$, and $\{x|\ x$ is the greatest Azerbaijani chess player ever$\}$ are in fact the same set, in actual fact the belief-set that can properly be imputed to me should not include $\{x|\ x$ is the greatest Azerbaijani chess player ever$\}$ and $\{x|\ x$ is Gary Kasparov$\}$. Of course, the upholder of the expansive version of the axiom of extensionality could argue, and would be right to so argue, that had I been better informed about Kasparov's place of origin I would see my mistake and immediately acknowledge that $\{x|\ x$ is the greatest Azerbaijani chess player ever$\}$ is also the same set as $\{x|\ x$ is believed by Kenneth Surin to be the greatest chess player ever$\}$ and $\{x|\ x$ is Gary Kasparov$\}$. This possible escape route for the upholder of the roomy version of the axiom of extensionality, tempting though it may be, nonetheless begs the question whether it is more important to retain the axiom of extensionality come what may, or to give an accurate account of someone's specific and localized belief-set. There is no clear-cut rule here: in some cases, given the highly localized nature of belief-sets, we may want to use category theory to do the work of displaying the logic of the belief-set in question, while upholding the axiom of extensionality as an overarching logical principle, but in others we may deem it more important or useful to give an accurate account of someone's belief-set, maybe even dispensing with the axiom of extensionality (anathema though this would be to Badiou and his followers).

The decision to grant primacy to the characterization of someone's belief-set, with the need to make intensionality absolutely central, may require the suspension of the axiom of extensionality, and with it the law of the excluded middle, so that the principle of truth-effects, as opposed to truth or falsity *simpliciter*, becomes a perfectly acceptable ontological option (as much as Badiou and his followers may oppose any such move, involving as it does a clear repudiation of the axiom of extensionality). Whatever decision is made here, it will be hard to insist that once intensional objects are permitted by an ontology, the law of the excluded middle and a strict version of the axiom of extensionality will be easy to uphold and to apply. For it is evident that they won't: once intensional objects are permitted, it then becomes more difficult to maintain that statements are either true or false, with no options in between such as "partially true," "somewhat false," or "not entirely true." Once such "vague predicates" are permitted in the domains of truth and falsity, we have to grant that truth-effects exist, and not just the two truth-values "true" and "false." This would involve a concession on Badiou's part, since he categorically precludes the inclusion of truth-effects in his ontology.

The notion of a truth-effect is considerably more elastic than that of truth or falsity per se. A truth-effect is what it is as soon as someone is disposed to act on the conviction that the statement in question is accepted as true, or false, or probably true, or not entirely true, and so on. The crucial question for those who accept the existence of truth-effects is the connection between the conviction that something is true or false and the plausibility of the conviction in question. Thus, for instance, my conviction that my employer is treating me badly is likely to have the effect of increased resentment on my part and an unwillingness to take on extra responsibilities at work. But a truth-effect does not convey any information about the nature of the grounds or the rationale(s) someone may have for holding a particular conviction; in the example just given, my conviction that my employer is treating me poorly, while it may have undeniable effects, does not in any way signal that I have genuinely good or genuinely bad reasons for possessing this conviction. It cannot be denied that someone can believe that he or she is being badly treated even when that is not the case, and that someone can think that he or she is being well treated even when that is not the case. Certainly one can believe that one's employer is being good to one and for that truly to be the case; equally, the judgment that one is being badly treated could be supported by the fact that one is indeed being badly treated by one's employer. These scenarios lend themselves fairly easily to the kind of representation enabled by category theory, which is able to acknowledge from the outset that there is no necessary match between someone's beliefs and the grounds that justify the holding of those beliefs, though, all else being equal, for most of the time someone's beliefs are not hugely incoherent. The polar alternative to the presumption that individuals are generally right in their beliefs would be to suppose that persons are likely to be mistaken a great deal of the time with regard to most of their beliefs and, more generally, that rational beings as a generality could hold massively incoherent beliefs.[42] The upshot of this principle is that if I am likely to be right most of the time in my judgments about the way things are, then I have to grant the same assumption to other putatively rational beings.

A truth-effect, therefore, arises when a rational being holds a statement to be true, and as a consequence accepts that certain entailments are generated by adhering to the truth of the statement in question, though of course no statement is true (or false) simply because someone happens to believe that it is true (or false). The basic insight here is that it makes a difference when a belief is held to be true, as opposed to false, and vice versa, though as just stated, someone's holding a belief true in no way ensures that it cannot be false, and vice versa. The only alternative to upholding these truisms would be to suppose that as a matter of generality it makes little or no difference to us whether our beliefs are true or false, though a better way of stating this may be to say that most of us care whether or not we are warranted in holding the convictions we possess, the possibility of self-deception notwithstanding.

Truth-Effects and Political Outcomes

Given these truisms concerning truth-effects, a political system can be viewed as an immense and overdetermined amalgam of truth-effects, and any truth-effect (or set of truth-effects), depending on historical and social circumstances (these of course always being political), can be prevented from displaying itself (or themselves). A truth-effect does not produce automatically, and hence cannot guarantee, its own mode of actualization; it cannot of itself banish the historical conditions, whatever they may be, that could in principle preempt its realization as a truth-effect.[43] A truth-effect, in this account, is the product of desire, often having the force and character of a "project," in this case a project motivated by a particular arrangement of this constitutive desire or striving. For instance, the event of Nelson Mandela desiring his freedom (and thus the abolition of apartheid) results in a truth-effect, or in a set of truth-effects, because this desire functions as an enabling (though not a sufficient) condition for the removal of all that stands in the way of the realization of that desire. We could call this a "truism" of the logic of desire, inasmuch as to desire that X be the case is to aim to make true or realize all that conduces to the attainment of X. Or, if we go back to Desanti's fable, the inhabitants of the territory who believe that some power outside the borders of that territory is preventing them from approaching its boundaries will very likely also believe that some form of agency situated on the other side of its borders is the source of the mysterious force that is being exerted on them. Their belief that this statement is true will probably set in motion a plethora of other convictions and actions, such as the desire to get rid of this outside agency or to neutralize its power, or to turn this power on their enemies, and perhaps to communicate with it, and even to create systems of knowledge about it. Such desires and beliefs have a clear analogue in the behaviors of those denizens of this planet who do not doubt that there is intelligent life elsewhere in the universe, or who believe that their actions are being guided by a supernatural power. Equally, the belief that the world needs to be transformed radically will potentially carry with it a range of accompanying practices and convictions. A truth-effect, then, is likely to initiate beliefs and actions on the part of its subjects which structure desire in ways that promote the realization of a state of affairs identified as the "truth" of that situation. This characterization of the close connection between a truth-effect and the desire to bring about the state of affairs that realizes the truth at issue is very similar to Badiou's description of the fidelity procedure.

The subject of a fidelity procedure is prompted by the event, which inserts a break in the normal course of things, to make an intervention in a situation. By virtue of making this intervention, the subject is confronted with the task of making new choices, and in the course of making these choices, the event is named. A case in point is the French Revolution, where a situation of generalized dissatisfaction with the monarchy was turned by the decisions and actions of Danton, Marat, Robespierre, and others into the event that came to be named the French Revolution. Their fidelity to the event led to the broadening circulation of specific forms of militancy, thereby enabling Danton, Marat, Robespierre, and their confreres to form new alignments and disengagements with regard to the original event, in this way releasing even more forces that took the event in ever newer directions and created yet more forms of fidelity for the subjects facing the event.[44] This account of the event and fidelity to the event is obviously compatible with the characterization of a truth-effect being given here. Thus, where the French Revolution is concerned, the forms of desire activated by the widespread dissatisfaction with the monarchy led Danton, Marat, Robespierre, and others to envisage the lineaments of a constitutional republic, though this revolutionary vision was soon to be undermined by Napoleon Bonaparte.

It is clear from this that any treatment of liberation or militancy as a concept has to place an undeniable centrality on the conditions underlying the production of the truth-effects of this or that system of liberation. A nearly universal detestation of the French monarchy on the part of the populace put in place the conditions that generated the truth-effects to which Danton et alia were able to respond. In turn the forms of desire associated with these revolutionary responses and the patterns of fidelity created in the process led to other new situations, and these in turn generated novel truth-effects and new forms of desire. But why is it important for this question to be raised?

It behooves the writer on liberation or militancy as a concept to pose this question because no practice of liberation, nor any theoretical formulations stemming from that practice, can view the seeker of liberation as someone who settles for life just as it is (i.e., has "adjusted" to the normalcy that in Badiou's thinking requires the rupture introduced by the *novum* of the event before this baneful reality can be pushed to one side). This is precisely the point at which the question of the conditions that subtend the production (or the dissolution) of truth-effects arises in all its force. For the difference made to life by any practice conducing to liberation depends crucially on the emergence or the suppression of the conditions that effectuate "truth."

This provides only a horizon, albeit one that is salutary and absolutely indispensable, for a resuscitation or sustaining of the "desire for the new" (the *novum*). A great deal more needs to be said about this ontological horizon, but I will conclude by indicating briefly how I think this account of truth-effects and its underlying ontology has some advantages when compared to Badiou's account of the truth-event.

What this ontology of truth-effects possesses is something that Badiou cannot provide, constrained as he is by his intellectual indebtedness to Plato and Sartre. To be more specific: there are many ways of relating truth to the real or the concrete. Far from there being a dialectical relation between truth and practice, truth and practice form an endless relay: at one moment truth is plugged into practice, at another practice is plugged into truth. And there is a potential multitude of such relays, not Badiou's unitary relation of the truth-event to the fidelity of the follower. To be fair, Badiou does allow that there are many ways of exercising this fidelity, hence his resort to category theory in his more recent work. But at the same time it is clear that for Badiou the event of truth stands as some kind of surd exteriority to be embodied in the life of the militant. Truth, however, is much more malleable and protean than this. It is known by its effects, and these are immensely plentiful and variable. A Platonism like Badiou's cannot accommodate this insight. A more suitable alternative may be the Aristotelian/Leibnizian logical tradition that Badiou views as the alternative to this Platonism.

Conclusion

A countervailing politics should not seek to predicate itself on the event of exception, and for this reason would seek a radically different ontology that enabled us to organize signs in new ways, as well as finding new theoretical operations and formulations. It would also discover novel and sometimes disturbing styles for organizing gestures and actions and expressing dissatis-factions, in many places and in many times. After all, even as tacit structures for the disclosure of revolutionary possibility taken in the most abstract sense, the events that go by the names "St. Paul" and "May 1968" mean nothing for most of the inhabitants of the earth. The import of these notions may be implicitly universal, but they are not pragmatically available to those who lack a basic familiarity with the foundations of Christianity or the thwarted revolution of 1968. Finding ways, in their specific locations and contexts, of getting rid of the shah of Iran, or Margaret Thatcher, or George W. Bush, or the tyrannical junta in Myanmar/Burma on the contrary possesses a saliency that is politically less elusive. To accomplish such things, urgently needed patterns of revolutionary opportunity will have to be sought, and hopefully found, in theoretical formulation as much as on the streets. But it is not clear that we need the singularization of an exceptional event for such a politics, as much as a great deal of what Badiou says is sane and salutary for any kind of militant project (e.g., his conviction that nothing good can come from a situation which has the fingerprints of state control all over it). Also, by making politics sensitive to the plight of people like the *sans-papiers* and other detainees (as opposed to viewing it in terms of the machinations of power-mongers in parliamentary and congressional chambers), Badiou has brought to the forefront the increased likelihood that capitalist parliamentarianism is itself now falling into desuetude.

CHAPTER 9

Models of Liberation IV

The Religious Transcendent

The conceptions of liberation discussed so far are premised on notions that are rigorously immanentist; they make no appeal to any principle or force that cannot be accounted for entirely in terms that are located in historical and social processes that are "this-worldly" in the strict sense of the term. But it should not be presumed without further reflection that a conception of liberation is not able in principle to accommodate positions involving an appeal to the transcendent.[1] If there can be a viable account of liberation based on some kind of recourse to the transcendent, then it would be perfectly legitimate to pose the question of the proper form of such a theory of liberation based on this recourse. The line of argument I consider here begins by assuming that there can be such an appeal to the transcendent (on the grounds that no logical canons are breached by the mere making of such an appeal) and proceeds to examine the claim that the transcendent, construed theologically, can serve as the basis for an adequate account of liberation.

A suitable, perhaps the most suitable candidate for an approach to liberation based on an invocation of the transcendent is the "universal pacified myth" of the vision of Christianity underwritten by the Radical Orthodoxy movement. In this chapter I broach the question of the transcendent in terms of the formulations integral to the Christian mythos, inasmuch as I do not discount from the outset the plausibility of the position of those who profess to stand within the circle of faith. The most important upshot of this acknowledgment is the centrality that has to be accorded to the notion of incarnation in setting the absolute norm for any Christian account of representation and linguistic mediation. For the incarnation to make sense, there has to be the presupposition that representation and mediation, ultimately, are divinely sanctioned and, by virtue of this, are wholly adequate (at any rate for those who dwell within the circle of faith).[2] The basis for this presupposition is not difficult to grasp, inasmuch as if the reality of godness cannot be expressed in language, then agnosticism is the only logical outcome. This in turn poses the question of the ground for affirming this ontological affinity between the divine reality and language; for those who stand within the circle of faith, the answer lies in upholding the incarnation, or the doctrine of creation (more specifically, the view that the created order is made in the divine image, or *imago dei*), or both. The doctrine of analogy then becomes the most appropriate way to elaborate and to secure, theologically and philosophically, this fundamental insight into the basic expressibility of godness.

The doctrine of analogy operates by maintaining that we can impute to godness whatever qualities would need to be possessed by the supreme and absolute reality capable of being the author of the entire created order. Wisdom would of course be one such quality, and so wisdom can be attributed to godness, though since the divine being possesses its attributes in the mode of infinity, godness possesses wisdom in the mode appropriate to the divine infinity, whereas creaturely beings possess this attribute in a finite mode. Hence there is an infinite qualitative distinction between the modes in which the two qualities are respectively possessed.

It is clear, therefore, that any conception of language congruent with the Christian mythos will rely fundamentally on the *via analogia*, as opposed to a Scotist, Spinozist, or Deleuzean univocity of language. For if the incarnation or the doctrine of creation is to serve as the normative underpinning for a Christian conception of expression and representation, then godness has to be capable in some way of being rendered in terms of semiosis. But at the same time, since godness is infinite, and thus axiomatically transcendent with regard to any finite order, this infinitude (*the* transcendent) necessarily ensues in a transcendence that exceeds the bounds of semiosis. Linguistic univocity, by contrast, would require that statements about godness be made in exactly the same sense in which they are made with respect to creaturely beings (or so the philosophico-theological argument in support of the via analogia goes). Transcendence, in the sense that calls for the reality of *the* transcendent to be acknowledged, thus becomes the absolute requirement of the Christian mythos. It is important to recognize this, because no mere exteriority can suffice to serve as this transcendent; no mere invocation of, say, *difference* or supplementarity or undecidability or sublimity will suffice, these being some of the favored candidates for the role of an exteriority to semiosis in contemporary philosophy and philosophical theology. Only a metaphysics of participation (in the divine Being), and the via analogia that is its linguistic correlate, can serve as the principle of connection between immanence and the transcendent.[3]

This being so, the constituting relation of the Christian mythos (in particular) or the discourse of a full-blown ontological transcendence (in general) to the convictions of Christian militants such as St. Paul and St. Ignatius of Loyola must be retained if we are to make sense of the activity of such militants. So while Alain Badiou's book on Paul brims with powerful insights, his suggestion that Paul's theological beliefs be consigned to the realm of "fable" cannot be taken as it stands, especially by those who profess to be Christians.[4] Which is not to suggest that these Pauline beliefs should then be taken to be literally true. But coming from someone who for Christians embodies in an exemplary way the central tenets of the Christian mythos, Paul's statements about godness are to be construed analogically, which is not to imply that they are true, since the doctrine of analogy is a theory of meaning and not a theory of truth. Though, like every theory of meaning, it presupposes that certain things are true (especially about meaning!).

To place this analogical construal on Paul's statements about godness requires at the very least that the ontology of participation be accepted as the bedrock of Paul's theology (even if Paul himself did not explicitly use the language of participation). The theological espousal of the language of participation will in turn militate against the characterization of Paul's theological language as "fable" (at any rate for those who are convinced of the tenability of the language of participation as a way of connecting the immanent with the transcendent). Of course acceptance of the metaphysics of participation is confined to those disposed from the beginning to a certain religious or theological orientation, and there cannot be any presumption that those outside the circle of faith, someone like Badiou, need adhere to such a metaphysics. But when it comes to making sense of Paul's discourse, the language of participation can properly be assumed. To not do so would be to accept that a large part of Paul's discourse is simply incoherent (this may be what the appellation "fable" basically asserts), save those parts of it that testify to his exemplary militancy. A lesser injustice would be done to Paul's discourse about the divine if it were understood in terms of the via analogia and then deemed, for whatever reason, to be largely devoid of truth, than for most of it to be taken as a fable except for those "acceptable" components of it that pertain to his consummate militancy.[5]

For the reasons just indicated, the conception of the transcendent required by the Christian mythos cannot be disregarded even if we are seeking to provide an account that is confined strictly to the political import of the writings of such Christian militants as Paul or Ignatius of Loyola. Accepting the via analogia as the basis of this discourse, however, requires that scrutiny be directed at the via analogia as such. The claim advanced by members of the Radical Orthodoxy theological movement is that only the via analogia can provide a safeguard against nihilism, nihilism being the inevitable fate confronting a Scotist, Spinozist, or Deleuzean univocity of language. The upshot of this claim is that none of the immanentist models of liberation being considered in this book (the politics of the subject, the politics of identity, the politics of the event, nomadology) is ultimately satisfactory because they all result inexorably in nihilism. In the words of Conor Cunningham:

> If metaphysics (the science of Being) is to be metaphysical it must dissociate itself from philosophy and continually demand theological discourse on the question of Being. Metaphysics must escape philosophy because the latter's forms of explanation will violate each question supposedly asked. It must also demand theological discourse on the question of Being because only theology, which appeals to transcendence, can offer a form of explanation that will escape the aporias of philosophical explanation. Metaphysics exists only between this refusal and this demand.
>
> Such an upshot would enable metaphysics to be metaphysical, and philosophy to be philosophica, *viz.*: purely descriptive. To be so philosophy would have to reposition itself with regard to theology, deferring to the latter's mode of discourse, yet in so doing opening up a space for its own articulation. Only in this way will there be ever be metaphysics and philosophy proper.[6]

The tacit assumption on the part of such theological critics of immanentism is that only a model of liberation based on *the* transcendent is able to avoid the snare of nihilism, and therefore that these transcendence-based models are free of the pitfalls that attend their immanentist counterparts. As can be gleaned from Cunningham's remarks, an immanentist metaphysics, by virtue of its abjuration of theology, can only result in aporias. The only way out for metaphysics, then, is to be subordinate to theology, that is, to a discourse involving a necessary resort to the transcendent. But are these transcendence-based conceptions themselves free from significant objections?

The Via Analogia

The following set of claims will be hugely tendentious in the eyes of some, but the espousal of the via analogia ostensibly militates against Christianity's "universal pacified myth" in at least one respect, namely, that the via analogia necessarily acknowledges a hierarchy among beings, specified in terms of a being's proximity in principle to the Godhead (angels being nearer the Godhead than humans, humans than other creaturely beings, and so forth), so that there is, and here one resorts to the language of Spinoza and Nietzsche, the inevitable possibility of the sad or reactive passions arising when a being is lower down the ontological hierarchy. For with analogy there is always a primary and a secondary analogate, so that some kind of *via eminentiae* becomes absolutely unavoidable, with one subject (the primary analogate) "producing" the other (the secondary or derivative analogate), at any rate "conceptually," through the unavoidable mechanism of the analogy of concepts. In such a divinely instituted hierarchical order, some created beings will necessarily be more eminent, ontologically, than others simply by virtue of the divine fiat.

Christianity could forestall this pathos of *ressentiment* by adhering strictly to its Platonist philosophical antecedents, this Platonism in effect allowing a relationship of "peaceability" to be maintained between the primary and the derivative analogates, so that the eminence of the primary analogate does not cause a violence of intractable "difference" between it and its derivative analogates. But the price of this has to be the incorporation into Christianity of a version of the doctrine of preestablished harmony.[7] By sanctioning the equivalent of a preestablished harmony between levels of being, the unavoidably Platonized Christian mythos obviates the pathos of ressentiment that is bound to exist between the different levels of being (which an analogical doctrine is required to posit). But do we want to adopt some version of the doctrine of preestablished harmony?

Christianity's peaceableness is thus guaranteed only when there is logically prior commitment to the ontological requisites of a preestablished harmony (in fact, acceptance of this divinely ordained harmony becomes an ontological condition for being a Christian), since this is the only way to preempt absolutely the occurrence of the sad passions. This preestablished harmony is thus vital for Christianity; its ineluctable weddedness to the great chain of being, without which it cannot operate the via analogia, is at once its power and its weakness. As I said, this problem for Christianity's universal pacified myth arises because hierarchies necessarily impose difference. But it could be argued that difference in itself is not necessarily to be identified with an inevitable ontological violence, since there can always be a peaceable difference. (According to Radical Orthodoxy this is precisely the ontological core of Christianity's universal pacified myth.) This is so because, on this account, only Christianity is capable of providing a metaphysical legitimation of a difference that does not result in ontological violence; only Christianity can furnish an ontological backing for hierarchy that does not involve recourse to terror. But if I am right, it can make this claim only because of its prior adherence to some version of the doctrine of preestablished harmony.

There is an interesting implication here: it has to follow from this that difference as difference will be peaceable only when all become Christians, for only then will there be the possibility of a universal and peaceable acceptance of difference. The Christian mythos will work only when all are guided or constrained by it, which means that the via analogia can plausibly serve as the basis for Christianity's universal pacified myth only when the whole world is converted or somehow drawn to the Christian mythos.[8] Christianity bestows harmony, the peaceability that surpasses all peace, through its "essence," which raises the question of whether harmony can be given in this way, or whether, as urged by the Scotists, harmony can come only from the striving of collectivities whose efforts are organized by the operation of a will guided by eros (a question I shall return to shortly). Univocity, the Scotist doctrine par excellence, is disavowed by Radical Orthodoxy, but it could be argued that it alone is capable of securing the principle of an accord among beings without overriding difference in the process, because for univocity (at least in its Scotist-Deleuzean rendition) difference resides purely and simply in the repetition of singularity, with no hierarchy among the singularities.[9]

Second, there is the matter of what comes first: the universal myth that founds peaceable difference or the solidarity with other human beings, out of which comes the development and consolidation of a rationality that enjoins peaceability. The Christian mythos requires the first of these alternatives, whereas the Stoics and David Hume, as well as Deleuze and Guattari, are to be aligned with the second of these choices. The problem with the immanentism of the position identified here with Stoicism and Hume and Deleuze and Guattari (and it happens also to be my own position) is that solidarity is never attainable by desiring solidarity as an end in itself. (The desire for solidarity for its own sake seems to be an inherently tragic desire, as when one seeks absurdly to make friends merely for the sake of the principle of having friends.) Thus a politics that never gets beyond the principles integral to the political is doomed to futility.

The whole point of politics is not to abolish the political (this being an equally tragic gesture), but rather to use the domain of the political as the means to get to those things—solidarity, compassion, and the negation of cruelty—that imbue the political with its constituent power, and which therefore cannot be engendered by the political itself, even if the political is absolutely necessary for the realization of solidarity, compassion, and the negation of cruelty in their active and practical forms. The political derives its strength and character precisely from this constituting exteriority. The desire named "the political" has always to be the desire for that which the political itself enables (this being the place where the political has its necessity), but which the political cannot bring into being by itself. The world is not yet ruled by the requirements of solidarity, compassion, and the negation of cruelty. They are thus real without being actual; that is, they are virtual. It is the political as it is presently constituted (viz., the dovetailing of economic neoliberalism with political neoconservatism described earlier in this book) which stands in the way of their actualization. If the political is able to move to a new and different constitution, then solidarity, compassion, and the abandonment of cruelty will move from being real to being actual. They are real now, however, because they act on the present constitution of the political, which has to work ceaselessly to keep at bay those forces which, if they could be given free rein, would bring into being a collective state of affairs in which solidarity, compassion, and the abandonment of cruelty can actually flourish. "Actually existing politics" wards off this radically new politics which will allow this new Earth to manifest itself: a new politics, a new form of being, though one that is already real without being actual.

Christianity is founded on a logic that affirms the rationality of a desire grounded in something beyond that which we know and desire, and to this extent it is ontologically disposed to acknowledge the exteriority premised on self-surpassing desire, the desire that gets beyond what desire itself can know or anticipate. This is a truly remarkable ontological asset (if one can speak of it in this way), since it enables Christianity ceaselessly to move beyond the limits necessarily constituted by the given (this movement being another name for the exteriority adverted to in this book). This is something that liberalism never really can do. Slavoj Žižek is therefore quite right to insist that Christianity and marxism are the only two real metaphysical alternatives to liberalism.[10]

Faced with the ultimately spurious choice of harnessing marxism to the ontological lineaments of Christianity (it should also be noted that for John Milbank this is the only viable ontological option open to marxist socialism),[11] or trying somehow to make marxism compatible with liberalism ("the management of difference that has always to be placed within limits in order to facilitate this bureaucratic administration of difference": this aptly expresses liberalism's metaphysical nucleus), Žižek has clearly opted for the former. But are we confined to two, and only two, alternatives: on the one hand, a marxism functioning concordantly with Christianity in the manner advocated by Milbank and Žižek, or, on the other, a marxism which, because it has no real way of engaging with its exteriority, can only become a disposable appendage of liberalism (albeit one with a bit more struggle tacked on to it than liberalism typically permits)? How is the project of liberation to come to a proper acknowledgment of the exteriority constituted by this self-surpassing desire? Here we should end where we began, that is, with the figure of Kant.

Kant broke with his scholastic precursors when he declined to view Being as the transcendental of the transcendentals, and instead made truth and judgment function in place of Being in his first *Critique*. Kant failed to see, however, that the notions of truth and judgment cannot really perform this surrogate function, for two reasons. First, making judgments always presupposes other judgments, and these in turn presuppose yet other judgments, and so forth.[12] Second, the use of truth and judgment to serve as quasi-transcendentals depends in any case on a harmony of the faculties that simply cannot be justified by reason.[13] So imagination (i.e., aesthetics) displaced judgment in Kant's third *Critique*, as he made the *Critique of Judgment* complete the transcendental argument that could not be completed by his first *Critique*. Feeling then inevitably becomes the organizing principle for completing the transcendental argument, since only feeling can harmonize the faculties. Just as important is another consequence of this Kantian shift from judgment to the imagination and feeling, which is that the sublime, necessarily lodged in the noumenal for Kant, becomes for him the only place for the properly ontological. German idealism then took over this axiom regarding the imagination as the proxy for the transcendental of transcendentals. It is perhaps noteworthy that the contemporary interest in the "unpresentable" (the writings of Lyotard, Lacoue-Labarthe, Derrida, and Nancy come readily to mind in this connection) is really an extension of the exemplary philosophical pattern established by Kant.[14] But this pattern has now run its course: today what is presentable in the popular culture is precisely the "unpresentable" as it is displayed in the phenomena which go under such labels as "panic culture," "trauma culture," "hyperreality," and "the matrix."

But how does one philosophize this momentous transformation, important as it is for any thinking about the absolute exteriority that is the meta-physical (though not the practical!) place from which any kind of movement toward a revolutionary transformation will have to issue as thought? What lies beyond this historic change, which in effect requires the very present-ability of the sublime, where its being the sublime (i.e., the unpresentable) has become paradoxically the precise condition of its presentability? With the now normative reinsertion of the sublime into the realm of feeling and sensibility in this paradoxical movement (Kant in any case having prepared us for this shift with his linking of the sublime to time), the imagination has to yield to sensibility (or so it would seem); or, more precisely, it would appear that feeling and the passions have supplanted the imagination at the level of the faculties. Kant's faculties, if we retain them, now necessarily re-late to each other through affectivity and the structures of affect (though, as we shall see, Gilles Deleuze is almost certainly right in calling this "pathos" rather than affect per se).

Indeed, nowadays it is affect, or rather pathos, and overwhelmingly these, which preselect judgment for its availability as (largely spurious) judgment. One only has to watch the evening news on American local television to get a glimpse of how pathos conditions what is presented to the viewer as judg-ment or a putatively "true" record of events; it is a commonplace observation to note that these evening news bulletins typically recount an endless succes-sion of trivial episodes, rendered (ephemerally) significant only by the largely inconsequential realization on the part of the viewer that, say, "this happened in the next town down the interstate," "this happened two blocks away from where I live," "I shop at the supermarket where this break-in took place," "I went to school with the sister of this burglary suspect," and so on, as each news bulletin catalogues one or more traffic accidents with only minor in-juries, a grandfather being bitten by a neighbor's dog, a local teacher's arrest for driving while under the influence, the death of the mayor's mother, the new patrol car purchased for the town police, a cute puppy being taken to the animal shelter, and so on, ad nauseam. Admittedly, very little judgment seems to go into the presentation of these stories, but what scarce judgment there is, is entirely at the disposal of the need to get viewers to identify af-fectively with the images being purveyed on the television screen. Judgment is thus deliberately subordinated to a lamentable and utterly impoverished orchestration of pathos.

If all this is symptomatic of the wider culture, then certain philosophi-cal conclusions likewise become inescapable. One such conclusion would be that the sheer unpresentability of pathos, even in a popular cultural form like the American local television news, has the inevitable effect of enabling pathos to float around like an untethered balloon, so that affective intensity is left to be as uncoded and unconstrained as possible. Judgment in the proper, though not entirely unproblematic, sense of the term is bound to the claims of truth, and truth itself is based on the strict exclusion of those possibilities that run counter to the truth in question (the truth of "I flew to Chicago yesterday for a three-day stay" implies that I did not fly to New York or San Francisco yesterday, that I did not go to Chicago by car or train, that I did not travel to Chicago today or the day before yesterday, and so forth), whereas an uncoded pathos is not constrained in this way by even the most minimal of the exigencies of truth. The free-floating quality that inheres in pathos means that pathos can easily attach itself to incompatible statements: an American whose son or daughter is serving in Iraq can thrill to the announcement that "Rumsfeld is doing a great job" at a military parade in which the erstwhile U.S. secretary of defense is surrounded by flags, patriotic music, floating balloons, and confetti, and still feel annoyed and upset the same day when he or she reads the headline "U.S. Soldiers in Iraq Lack Proper Equipment" in the local newspaper. The pathic effects of statements can be experienced without any intrinsic connection being made to the constative properties of the statements in question, in which case the constative character of the statement effectively becomes functionally unpresentable, as the uncoded and unbounded sensibility trumps even the imagination in the appropriation of such statements. The overall effect is one of a pervasive depoliticization, as citizens can have all kinds of warm feelings about any politician under the sun regardless of the policy decisions he or she makes ("Ariel Sharon is a true man of peace," "Ronald Reagan was the greatest American president of the twentieth century," "Silvio Berlusconi has restored pride in Italy," "Tom De-Lay is a man of absolute integrity," and so on). To get back to Kant.

Kant's circumscription of reason had thus effectively broken down by the time he got to the third *Critique*, when he was forced to concede that the faculties cannot be regulated in their employment. Henceforth there could be no preestablished harmony of the faculties. Deleuze has a passage on the groundbreaking implications of Kant's "emancipation of dissonance" that is worth quoting:

> This is no longer the aesthetic of the *Critique of Pure Reason*, which considered the sensible as the quality that could be related to an object in space and time; nor is it the logic of the sensible, nor even a new logic that would be time. It

is an aesthetic of the Beautiful and the Sublime, in which the sensible takes on the autonomous value for itself and is deployed in a pathos beyond all logic, and which will grasp time as it bursts forth (*dans son jaillissement*), at the very origin of its thread and its vertigo. This is no longer the Affect of the *Critique of Pure Reason*, which linked the Self to the I in a relationship that was still regulated by the order of time; it is a Pathos that lets them evolve freely in order to form strange combinations as sources of time, "arbitrary forms of possible intuitions." It is no longer the determination of an I, which must be joined to the determinability of the Self in order to constitute knowledge; it is now the undetermined unity of all the faculties (the Soul), which makes us enter the unknown.[15]

This unconstrained deployment of all the faculties inevitably politicizes any undertaking involving knowing, feeling, and doing, although this is a conclusion that Kant himself failed to draw. (In this sense Kant is symptomatic of the culture that prevails today, where affect is pervasively depoliticized.) A very significant philosophical opportunity opened up by the "dissonant accords" (the phrase is Deleuze's) introduced by Kant in the *Critique of Judgment* comes with the accompanying acknowledgment that it is not reason which leads us to the real, but rather the will guided by eros, so that reason is produced as an effect that emerges from the will's striving. Kant thus opened a way that led back to Scotus and Spinoza, and from these figures a trajectory could be launched that takes us forward to Deleuze.

The Scotist axioms that reality is to be approached by the will guided by love and that reality is constituted by worlds of singularities, events, and virtualities, and not of subjects and objects, allow all these items to be "expressively" distributed: all kinds of possible worlds, extending to a potential infinity, can express the same singularity, event, or virtuality, so there is from the beginning a complete preemption of any bureaucratic administration of these "expressive" distributions and the worlds in which they are located. The very constitution of reality is politicized, but not in the sense that involves, necessarily and from the beginning, a coercive reining in, a stultifying management of this multiplicity by the negative power of the state or sovereign. The distribution of expressivities is governed by a logic of ceaseless proliferation, one which is freed from any ontological dependence on the categories and principles of classical representation and the anthropological presuppositions which guided the previous architectonic of reason and the politics sustained by it. With this uncontainable production of expressivity, there is an absolute "beyond" for all that is given. As the horizon for the critique of anything that is given, this beyond is precisely the exteriority needed for any viable project of liberation.

The sublimity that manifests itself in the popular culture as the ever greater expansion of an uncoded pathos at the expense of truth and reason therefore represents a profoundly missed opportunity for the general culture. The "de-transcendentalization" of truth could have instituted an alternative cultural political regime in which truth and affect would have been jointly guided by the will linked to eros, and thus powerfully politicized. Instead, will and eros were themselves displaced by a vapid sentimentality that gave an uncoded pathos a virtually unlimited field for expansion. A critique of the popular culture can thus no longer be premised on the hope that truth can somehow be brought back into service as a transcendental capable of disciplining pathos. For what it is worth, the horse that is pathos has now fled the stable, and there is no point in bolting the stable door. It is not transcendentally maintained truth that will recode this uncoded pathos from now on, but the will guided by eros, though we cannot be certain that even the latter represents a realistic cultural political option in advanced capitalist societies. To repoliticize what has so far been massively depoliticized will be something akin to a revolutionary undertaking.

A New Ontological Script?

For the remainder of this chapter, it is important to examine whether a wholly immanent ontology, with the will guided by eros as its Scotist pivot point, can serve as the exteriority to the political which a hugely depoliticized contemporary politics desperately needs to possess if it is to be capable of motivating a viable project of liberation.

As I pointed out in the previous section, this Scotist-Spinozist-Deleuzean ontology posits an infinity of expressivities and their associated possible worlds in a way that is at once rigorously immanent and materialist, and also rigorously politicized. Without being transcendent (there being no universal subject and universal object for it to transcend), this ontology serves as a transcendental field for the becoming of new multiplicities, each new multiplicity being potentially another name for a new kind of political agent living for a liberation that the old sovereignties are now unable to forestall.[16]

It has been objected to this Scotist-Spinozist-Deleuzean ontology that it is really a species of nihilism. Once it is assumed or asserted, so this objection goes, that all finite being folds back into the virtual, then an inevitable devaluation of finite particularity has to ensue, since the virtual can only be the void into which is collapsed the entire array of differentiations that is the ground of each particularity. In the absence of an ultimately sustainable ground for differentiation, particularity is irretrievably undermined, and without a real particularity this ontology has no alternative but to end up by positing the One into which all finite difference is poured and totally abolished. Scotus, Spinoza, and Deleuze, their philosophical pleas on behalf of particularity notwithstanding, thus end up being disciples of Plotinus, the first great philosopher of the One.[17]

The argument that this Scotist-Spinozist-Deleuzean ontology can only culminate in a nihilism of the void does not take a crucial feature of Deleuze's ontology into account. Deleuze is quite explicit that the void of deterritorialization does not exist on its own, but rather exists necessarily in a triptych of dimensions, in which there coexists a dynamic and mutually determining relationship between the three levels that consist of (1) the monism of a pure perceptual moment, (2) the dualism of composition in which pure perceptual moments are unified or "made into one" to form such objects as a raindrop or a forest, and (3) the void, which is a pure *act* of separation or division that divides things endlessly, so that the raindrop can become a molecule of oxygen that can then become something else, as it enters ever new circuits of causality, and so on. *This* book did not emerge from the void, but from an assemblage with a particular process of causality that allowed paper, the act of writing, print technology, the present state of the publishing industry, the author's inculcation into a particular matrix of thought production and intellectual practice—what we in the academy call "scholarship"—to operate conjointly to produce *Freedom Not Yet*. And with its insertion into a new circuit of causality, this book can in turn become a text for an examination, a doorstop, kindling for a bonfire, or a paperweight. (A friend of mine who once lived in a cockroach-infested apartment told me that for a long time Deleuze and Guattari's *A Thousand Plateaus*, a weighty tome, was his favored implement for bringing a scurrying cockroach to a dead halt.) The existent object arises only as the outcome of such dynamic interactions, and any notion that Deleuzean objects emerge from the pure void and disappear into it when they cease to exist (as this or that object) is therefore incorrect. The Deleuzean void always exists simultaneously and in conjunction with the other two dimensions, namely, the moments of evanescent experience and the unity of composition.[18] There is no all-encompassing void constituting an absolute exteriority to the object for this particular ontological tradition. As a result, the problem that is usually taken to be insurmountable for proponents of the absolute void, namely, how the logico-metaphysical transition from the nothingness of the void to the presence of existent objects is to be understood, does not apply in Deleuze's case. Quite simply, for Deleuze there is no absolute void, and the question of the movement from sheer nothingness to the plenitude of existing objects does not arise for him.[19]

Alongside this objection to an immanentist ontology voiced by the supporters of the *analogia entis* is another, related objection, to the effect that both Scotus and Deleuze have no way of conceptualizing the transition from pure possibility to actuality, since they do not acknowledge a mediating principle, invoking the notion of participation (as the analogy doctrine does), to enable the transition from possibility to actuality. According to this objection, if the existent object does not participate in that from which it emerges, its emergence can only be surd and arbitrary. This argument for the centrality of analogical participation can be used against those who uphold notions of univocity and immanentism only because it begins with the assumption that these notions have to begin from possibility, which then has to be converted somehow into actuality. But Deleuze follows Scotus in making an important distinction between *possibility* and *potentiality*. *Possibility* encompasses the range of what a thing can become without ceasing to be itself, and if something is merely possible, it is not actual (though of course it has to be possible if it is to become actual). *Potentiality*, by contrast, is act, active, and actuality.[20] Potentiality, unlike possibility, is a state of power, in this case the power of producing the state of affairs that actuates the possibility in question. Potentiality already presupposes an active causal nexus from which the actuated entity can emerge. And so Deleuze and his philosophical predecessors are able to avoid the objection that, with no ontological basis for appeal to the principle of an infinite Being who can convert possibility into actuality, this school of thought is left with an actuality that is simply a ghostly ontological facsimile of mere possibility.

But is this ontology derived from Scotus, Spinoza, and Deleuze really compatible with marxism, understood here as a theoretico-practical armature requiring both revolution and socialism? The ontological script that can be written out of this delineation of the immanent field of the multiple is certainly compatible with a marxist conception of liberation. Some would argue that while Deleuze can accommodate theoretically the notion of revolution, socialism, which requires that transformation to a new order of social being, cannot be encompassed by a philosophy which, in the eyes of such critics, conceives of order strictly in terms of "metastability," and so has to accept the principle that all order is ultimately arbitrary. For if order is no more than metastability, it can never amount to more than a momentary arresting of chaos, and socialism needs more for its realization than just the suspension of the basal flux.[21]

For Deleuze, however, the attainment of socialism is inherently bound up with struggle, in this case, the struggle to construct an assemblage that is finally able to escape the constraining power of the capitalist state. The socialist assemblage would be one premised on a counterpower that can be directed against the powers of the state assemblages. And here the insight that these state assemblages are not fixities, but at best only metastable structures, has the tremendous advantage of allowing the conceptualization of their fundamental impermanence. As Brian Massumi points out, if metastability imposes order, this order is never more than a contingent arresting of disorder. The next (socialist) order will come, unless the apparatuses of the capitalist state are able to continue to forestall its arrival.[22] And only a politics (for me a marxist politics though it could well be a politics of a radical but nonmarxist variety) can put in place the conditions that will allow the supplanting of the apparatuses of the capitalist state.

We cannot be sure, however, that this strictly immanentist ontology is compatible with Christianity, which seems to be wedded irreducibly to an ontology of the transcendent. But the possibility of Christianity's being able to incorporate an ontology of unqualified immanence is one that cannot be ruled out tout court. Or it may be that we cannot after all obviate the transcendent, despite what I have argued in this chapter, in which case Christianity's ontological preeminence is guaranteed, as John Milbank and others have argued. Either way, we know that it is possible for us to delineate convincingly the terms of a conceptual basis for a notion of liberation that is unrelentingly immanent. What this actually portends for conceptions of liberation so far premised on the transcendent is really another story. For the moment, the immanent ontology of liberation certainly bypasses liberalism, but, as I noted earlier, we cannot be so certain that it does the same with regard to Christianity. The only important consideration here, though, is whether this immanent ontology can undergird a marxist conception of liberation, and regardless of what this portends for Christianity as an ontology, this is all that a philosophical marxism needs.

CHAPTER 10

Models of Liberation V

Nomad Politics

Nomad politics, which can readily be identified with Deleuze and Guattari's nomadology, has two primary virtues.[1] First, unlike its counterpart politics of the exceptional event (associated in chapter 8 with the writings of Alain Badiou), it does not rely on the extraordinary event to provide a basis for the convergence of collective agents around a project of liberation.[2] The crowds who seemingly emerged out of nowhere to restore Hugo Chávez to the presidency of Venezuela after he had been deposed in a coup, or the similar crowds of protesters at several G8 summits (these now tend to be held in out-of-the-way mountain or island resorts in the hope of thwarting protesters), both constitute nomadic formations whose actions are regarded by some as harbingers of significant future political transformations.[3] Second, and in a more philosophical vein, nomadology has the great merit of bypassing the problematic of representation identified earlier with the model of sovereignty underwritten by the "previous" politics, that is, the model which requires an orchestration, primarily through the mediation of the state, of the throng of individual wills into a single collective will or body politic. As I pointed out earlier, this assembling of the hodgepodge of individual wills into "the people," who are then represented by the sovereign or parliamentary body, is regarded by proponents of this liberal-democratic political tradition as the essential, indeed transcendental condition for effective political action.[4] In nomadology, this axiom of liberal-democratic political action is totally dispensed with (since in reality all it delivers is a merely symbolic "unity in diversity") because the logic of the nomad's political being cannot but be structurally autopoetic; as I already mentioned, nomadic formations direct themselves according to their own powers and their own histories. It should also be noted that overlaps are possible between nomadology and the politics of the event, this convergence being very evident in the work of Deleuze and Guattari, for instance, who take nomadology to provide the logic for a project of struggle but who also accord certain events (e.g., the foundation of the Paleolithic state, May 1968) a decisive political significance.

As we have seen from the discussions in the preceding chapters that have focused on the politics of identity, of subjectivity and the place of the subject, and of the event, the kinds of reflection embraced by the thinkers placed under these rubrics have as their common *problematique* the question of the character of political subject in the conjuncture of a "postpolitical" politics. Postpolitical politics is still a politics; even in an epoch in which the traditional mechanisms of political representation (identified in this book with the tradition that extends from Hobbes, via Rousseau and Kant, to Rawls) have been supplanted, there is still the need to ensure the continued production of social cooperation, this being an absolute requirement for continued capitalist accumulation. In the advanced capitalist economies, as was seen in part I, these days the production of social cooperation is undertaken primarily by the service and information industries, whose primary aim is the promotion of the imperatives of capital.

The Production of Social Control

The need to maintain constant control over the forms of social cooperation in turn requires that education, training, and business never end: the business time scale is now 24/7; the Tokyo stock exchange opens almost as soon as the one in New York closes in an unending cycle, training is "on the job" as opposed to being based on the traditional apprenticeship model (itself a holdover from feudalism), and education becomes "continuing education," that is, something that continues throughout life and is not confined to those aged six to twenty-two. As I noted earlier, this essentially dispersive propensity is reflected in the present regime of capitalist accumulation, where production is now metaproduction; that is, in the advanced economies it is no longer focused on the use of raw materials to produce finished goods, but rather on the sale of services (especially in the domain of finance and credit) and products that involve cultural and symbolic production. Social control is no longer left to schools and police forces, but is now also a branch of marketing, as even politics has become "retail politics," in which politicians seek desperately for an image of themselves, or for some "hot-button" issue, to market to largely passive and apathetic electorates ("Doesn't George W. Bush look absolutely great in blue jeans?"; "Tony Blair sweats too much when he is on TV"; "Aren't Sarah Palin's glasses fantastic?"; "Let's have the Ten Commandments put up in Alabama courthouses"), and when public opinion specialists and spin doctors (Dick Morris in the case of Bill Clinton, Karl Rove for George W. Bush, Alistair Campbell for Tony Blair) are more important to prime ministers and presidents than are capable and wise civil servants. Recording, whether in administration or business, is no longer based on the written document kept in the appropriate box of files, but on computerized spreadsheets, bar codes, and other forms of electronic tagging.[5]

The implications of these developments for state theory are momentous. The state itself has become fragmented and compartmentalized and has accrued more power to itself in some spheres while relinquishing power totally in others. But however much the state has mutated in the era of control societies, it still retains the function of regulating, in conjunction with capital, the "accords" that channel social and political power. In his Leibniz book, Deleuze maintains that state and nonstate formations are constituted on the basis of such "concerts" or "accords."[6] These accords are organizing principles which make possible the grouping into particular configurations of entire arrays of events, personages, processes, institutions, movements, and so forth, such that the resulting configurations become integrated formations. As a set of accords or axioms governing the accords that regulate the operations of the various components of an immensely powerful and comprehensive system of accumulation, capital is situated at the crossing point of all kinds of formations, and thus has the capacity to integrate and recompose capitalist and noncapitalist sectors or modes of production. Capital, the "accord of accords" par excellence, can thus bring together heterogeneous phenomena and make them express the same world, that of capitalist accumulation.

Accords are constituted by selection criteria which specify what is to be included or excluded by the terms of the accord in question. These criteria also determine with which other possible or actual accords a particular accord will be consonant (or dissonant). The criteria that constitute accords are usually defined and described by narratives governed by a certain normative vision of truth, goodness, and beauty (reminiscent of the so-called medieval transcendentals, albeit translated where necessary into the appropriate contemporary vernacular). A less portentous way of making this point would be to say that accords are inherently axiological, value-laden. What seems to be happening today, and this is a generalization that is perhaps somewhat tendentious, is that these superposed narratives and the selection criteria these accords sanction, criteria which may or may not be explicitly formulated or entertained, are being weakened or qualified in ways that deprive them of their force. Such selection criteria, which tend to be policed by the state, usually function by assigning privileges of rank and order to the objects they subsume ("Le Pen is more French than Zidane"; "Turks are not Europeans"; "English is the official language of West Virginia"—the polite equivalent of "Get out of here if you want to speak Spanish at a West Virginia government office"), as the loss or attenuation of the customary force of such accords makes dissonances and contradictions difficult or even impossible to resolve, and, correlatively, makes divergences easier to affirm. Events, objects, and personages can now be assigned to several divergent and even incompossible series. The functioning of capital in the control societies thus requires that the state become internally pluralized.

The transcendental principles which subtend the constitution of the social order are embodied in what Deleuze and Guattari call the *socius*. In *Anti-Oedipus*, the socius is said to be necessary because desiring-production is coterminous with social production and reproduction, and for the latter two to take place desire has to be coded and recoded, so that subjects can be "prepared" for their social roles and functions. The socius is the terrain of this coding and recoding. Another rationale for the socius stems from the part it plays in consolidating the capitalist order. Desire is simultaneously enabled and limited by capital, which frees it from its previous embodiments or codings so that it can be placed at the disposal of capitalist expansion; after this decoding by capital, desire is then reined in or recoded so that it can subserve the novel requirements of capitalist production.

Coding or "inscription" is thus central to the constitution of the socius, and Deleuze and Guattari respond to the crucial question of the "surface" on which this inscribing takes place by invoking the notion of the Earth. The Earth precedes the constitution of the socius and is the primordial unity or ground of desire and production. As such the Earth is the precondition of production, while also being the object of desire. The first form of the socius has therefore to involve a territorialization, undertaken by a "territorial machine," which parcels out the Earth into segments of social meaning.

Once territorialization has occurred, it becomes possible for social machines (the core of the socius) to operate. Social machines have humans as their parts and are essential to the generation of cultural forms, which are needed to link humans to their (technical) machines. Social machines organize flows of power and desire by coding them. There are all kinds of flows: different kinds of humans, vegetation, nonhuman animals, agricultural implements, flows that involve bodily functions and organs, and so on. Nothing escapes coding, and so nothing can escape the purview of the socius.

If the socius is a megamachine (a machine that regulates other machines), the fuel that drives this machine is desire, though desire is shaped and orchestrated by its insertion into this megamachine. In modern societies the nature of this insertion of desire into the social megamachine has been significantly transformed. To facilitate the functioning of capitalism, flows have had to become more abstract, since in order to work capital requires intersubstitutability, homogeneity, relentless quantification, and an array of exchange mechanisms. Hand in hand with this abstraction goes a privatization of the social, since a systemic overvaluation of the individual ("Each and every one of you matters to me" is the slogan of the typical huckstering politician on the campaign trail) is required to compensate for the massive collective disinvestment that takes place in the social as a result of the inexorable growth of the processes of abstraction. The vehicles of this privatization are ruled by the Oedipus principle, which functions as a kind of transcendental regime for the investment of social desire. Other principles, primarily concerned with morality and punishment but also with death and cruelty, are also effective in this domain.

In dispensing with psychoanalysis as the ontology for this constitution of the socius, Deleuze and Guattari find it necessary to replace Freudianism with another ontology of social constitution. This alternative, called by them "schizoanalysis" or "nomadology," begins by refusing any kind of transcendental principle purporting to serve as the ground of the socius. In place of the logic of necessity and continuity that characterized previous ontologies of the social, Deleuze and Guattari opt for one that is marked by "ruptures," "limits," "singularities," "ironies," and "contingencies." The traditional logic displaced desire as the motor that drives the social megamachine, and its replacement would have to reinstall what was pushed aside. Schizoanalysis or nomadology would provide a new conception of experience and desiring-production, emphasizing forms of experimentation not constrained by the ego or Oedipal structures, as well as the need to create new forms of collective (as opposed to merely individual) liberation. This liberation would not, indeed could not be sponsored by either the state or capital.

Nomadology

Using the writings of Georges Dumézil as their initial template, Deleuze and Guattari provide a fascinating narrative when addressing the question of political sovereignty in the plateau titled "Treatise on Nomadology."[7] Invoking Dumézil's dualism of the shaman-king and the priest-jurist, they go on to say:

> Undoubtedly, these two poles stand in opposition term by term, as the obscure and the clear, the violent and the calm, the quick and the weighty, the terrifying and the regulated, the "bond" and the "pact," etc. But their opposition is only relative; they function as a pair, in alternation, as though they expressed a division of the One or constituted in themselves a sovereign unity. "At once antithetical and complementary, necessary to one another and consequently without hostility, lacking a mythology of conflict: each specification at any one level automatically calls forth a homologous specification on another. The two together exhaust the field of the function." They are the principal elements of a State apparatus that proceeds by a One-Two, distributes binary distinctions, and forms a milieu of interiority. It is a double articulation that makes the State apparatus into a *stratum*.[8]

Deleuze and Guattari take Dumézil's personifications, at once complementary and mutually reinforcing, of the magician-king and the jurist-priest to constitute the two-pronged function of the state. They also follow Dumézil in opposing this state apparatus, and thus the figures of the magician-king and the jurist-priest, the counterforce represented by the war machine (the apparatus typically employed by nomads). The respective properties possessed by the state apparatus and the nomadic war machine can be tabulated in the following manner (for these properties, see *A Thousand Plateaus*, 352–60):

STATE APPARATUS	WAR MACHINE
sovereignty (*pouvoir*)	power (*puissance*)
law	event
fixity of Being	ontological innovation
gravity	celerity
the public	secrecy
binary distributions	multiple becoming
permanence	evanescence
conservation	power of metamorphosis

milieu of interiority	milieu of exteriority
internal, biunivocal relations	external relations
polis	*nomos*
semiology	strategy, pragmatics
"striated" space	"smooth" space
coding and decoding	territorialization and deterritorialization
king, jurist	warrior, prophet
concentration	dispersion
strategies of exclusion	resistance, openness
"arborescent"	"rhizomatic"
hierarchical	nonhierarchical
identity	transformation
individuality	singularity
false plenitude, empty repetition	facing the void
delimitation	immeasurability
Goethe, Hegel	Kleist, Artaud
apparatuses of power	packs, bands
theorems	problematics
formal concentration of power	solidarity
religion	offenses against gods and priests
harmony	rhythm
architecture, cooking	music, drugs
history	geography
measured time (*chronos*)	indefinite time of event (*aeon*)
Egyptian state	Moses
man	"becoming-woman"

Deleuze and Guattari caution against viewing the opposition between the state apparatus and the nomadic war machine in strict binary terms:

> The problem is that the exteriority of the war machine in relation to the State apparatus is everywhere apparent but remains difficult to conceptualize. It is not enough to affirm that the war machine is external to the apparatus. . . . What complicates everything is that this extrinsic power of the war machine tends, under certain circumstances, to become confused with one of the two heads of the State apparatus. Sometimes it is confused with the magic violence of the State, at other times with the State's military institution. . . . So there is a great danger of identifying the structural relation between the two poles of political sovereignty, and the dynamic interrelation of these two poles, with the power of war. . . . Whenever the irruption of war power is confused with

the line of state domination, everything gets muddled; the war machine can then be understood only through the categories of the negative, since nothing is left that remains outside the State. But, returned to its milieu of exteriority, the war machine is seen to be of another species, of another nature, of another origin. (355)

For Deleuze and Guattari, the law of the state is despotic and priestly in its most fundamental impulses, and anything like an interpellation (admittedly an Althusserian notion that Deleuze and Guattari would certainly not want to use) of the subject is perforce conducted in congruence with those "theorems" sanctioned by the state's despotic and sacerdotal orders, these sacred or quasi-sacred orders persisting even when the polity in question is a liberal democracy with an accompanying normativity ostensibly resting on entirely secular premises.[9] Ethico-political subjects interpellated in this way will therefore be caught up in a transcendental validation of their subjectivities; for Deleuze and Guattari, legitimation at the hands of the state always places the subject at the mercy of an *arché*, or founding principle, that requires the citizen to be created in the image of the state's figures of sovereignty, in this case the overarching despot and priest. The outcome will in any case be a thousand little despots, a thousand little priests, all defined as model citizen subjects.

The state, in this account, is the product of thought, in this case a thinking which is inextricably linked to a desire that for Deleuze and Guattari is ubiquitous and endlessly productive: "Everything is production: *production of productions*, of actions and of passions; *production of recording processes*, of distributions and of co-ordinates that serve as points of reference; *production of consumptions*, of sensual pleasures, of anxieties, and of pains. Everything is production, since the recording processes are immediately consumed, immediately consummated, and these consumptions directly reproduced."[10]

The implications of this position are profound and radical, and they point to, among other things, a significant difference between a standard and almost normative reading of Foucault and the authors of *Capitalisme et schizophrénie*. Deleuze and Guattari clearly accord great importance to desiring-production (as indicated by the passage above). But this undeniable saliency of desiring-production does not translate into the primacy of the modes of production as such, which is what one would expect of a more conventional marxist or marxisant thinking. Instead Deleuze and Guattari bestow this primacy on the so-called machinic processes, that is, the modes of organization that link myriad kinds of "attractions and repulsions, sympathies and antipathies, alterations, amalgamations, penetrations, and expressions that affect bodies of all kinds in their relations to one another" (*A Thousand Plateaus* 90). The modes of production depend on these machinic processes for their constitution (435).

The upshot is that the modes of production are always themselves the product or derivation of a ceaselessly generative desire: what enables each mode to be constituted is an always specific, indeed aleatory aggregation of desires, forces, and powers. The organization of productive desire gives the mode of production its enabling conditions, and not vice versa, as is the case in some of the more typical marxisms. In arriving at this formulation, though, Deleuze and Guattari are very much in line with what Marx himself said about the necessity for society to exist before capitalism can emerge in anything like a fully fledged form: a society-state with preexisting surpluses has already to exist if the (capitalist) extraction of surplus-value is to take place. To quote Deleuze and Guattari: "Marx, the historian, and Childe, the archaeologist, are in agreement on the following point: the archaic imperial State, which steps in to overcode agricultural communities, presupposes at least a certain level of development of these communities' productive forces since there must be a potential surplus capable of constituting a State stock, of supporting a specialized handicrafts class (metallurgy), and of progressively giving rise to public functions. This is why Marx links the archaic State to a certain [precapitalist] 'mode of production'" (*A Thousand Plateaus* 428). The state, in other words, gives capital its "models of realization" (434). But the state that provides capital with the models it needs in order to be effectuated is already functioning even before it manifests itself as a concretely visible apparatus. The state, in this case the Paleolithic state, destroys or neutralizes the hunter-gatherer societies that it came to supersede, but before this happens there has to be a necessary point of convergence between the state and the hunter-gatherer troupes. This point of convergence, which the troupes ward off and anticipate at the same time, designates a situation or space in which, simultaneously, the existing hunter-gatherer formations are dismantled and their successor state formations put in place. In the words of Deleuze and Guattari, the two sets of formations unfold "simultaneously in an 'archaeological,' micropolitical, micrological, molecular field" (431).[11]

The state achieves its "actuality" through a complex and uneven process involving the arresting or caging of nonstate formations, so that both state and nonstate formations exist in a field of perpetual interaction. This interactive field, in the parlance of Deleuze and Guattari, is irreducibly "micropolitical" or "molecular," and so state formations, which for them are quintessentially "macropolitical" or "molar," are not positioned in a field that has already been transformed by the state apparatuses or their prototypes into something that is (now) exclusively macropolitical or molar. It is virtually an axiom for Deleuze and Guattari that before, and alongside, the macropolitical there is always the micropolitical. The state has perforce to interact with the micropolitical.

This is at odds with a certain interpretation of Foucault (regarded as the exemplary philosopher of the micropolitical) which views micropolitics to be a relatively new development arising more or less strictly in response to forms of power, preeminently biopower, that did not exist before the onset of the most recent phases of modernity. While it is not quite clear whether Foucault himself should be saddled with this view, it remains the case that for Deleuze and Guattari the state apparatuses always emerge in a "molecularized" field that the state never entirely contains or neutralizes. The appearance of the state cannot therefore be the outcome of its own efficacy, of any inherent propensity on its part to generate its own enabling conditions. Whatever its powers, autogeny is beyond the power of the state to accomplish. Micropolitics have therefore always been antique in its provenance, and the state came about as an invention designed to arrest these micropolitical forces. Moreover, as an invention, the state necessarily had to be "thought" before it could begin to be efficacious in any social and political field.[12]

But the state has to deny this irremovable factitiousness of its "origins" and present itself precisely as its "opposite," that is, as an unthought (at any rate where origins are concerned): "Only thought is capable of inventing the fiction of a State that is universal by right, of elevating the State to the level of de jure universality" (*A Thousand Plateaus* 375). Thought confers on the state its character of a singular and universal form, the fullest expression of the rational-reasonable (*le rationnel-raisonnable*). The foremost exponent of this "thought" behind the genesis of the state is of course Hegel, who explicitly views the state as the embodiment of the universal, as the realization of reason, and thus as the spiritual community that incorporates all individuals within itself. Against this view, which derives the state from the rational-reasonable, Deleuze and Guattari hold that it is the rational-reasonable itself that is derived from the state. The state provides the formal conditions for the enactment of the rational-reasonable (375–76), and thought (as the primary instantiation of the rational-reasonable) in turn necessarily confers on the state its "reason" (*lui donner, necessairement "raison"*; 556 n. 42). Reason or thought becomes the province of the state in this Hegelian (or quasi-

Hegelian) view, and Deleuze and Guattari therefore propose a wresting of thought from the state and a complementary returning of the state to thought, in the form of an acknowledgment of the state's irreducible fictiveness.

The archaic state that arose from a recoding of the primitive territorial codes of the hunter-gatherer troupes instituted an organized production associated with the creation of "a particular kind of property, money, public works" (*A Thousand Plateaus* 448). But this archaic state was not able to prevent a substantial quantity of "decoded flows" from escaping:

> The State does not create large-scale works without a flow of independent labor escaping its bureaucracy (notably in the mines and in metallurgy). It does not create the monetary form of the tax without flows of money escaping, and nourishing or bringing into being other powers (notably in commerce and banking). And above all it does not create a system of public property without a flow of private appropriation growing up beside it, then beginning to pass beyond its grasp; this private property does not itself issue from the archaic system but is constituted on the margins, all the more necessarily and inevitably, slipping through the net of overcoding. (449)

This epochal transformation confronted the succeeding state apparatuses with a new task. Where the previous state form had to overcode the already coded flows of the hunter-gatherer groups, the new state apparatuses had to organize conjunctions of the decoded flows that had been escaping their archaic predecessor. These became the apparatuses of a polynucleated and more complex kind of state. But even here the state could not prevent decoded flows from escaping (yet again), and the most recent versions of these flows attained an "abstract," "generalized" conjunction which overturned their adjacent state apparatuses and created capitalism "at a single stroke" (452–53). Capital thus represents a new and decisive threshold for the proliferation of flows, and this capitalist "force of deterritorialization infinitely [surpasses] the deterritorialization proper to the State" (453). But capital's superiority in this regard did not spell the end of the state. Instead, the state underwent a further mutation, and the modern nation-state was born.

The State and Capital

The relation between the state and capital is thus one of reciprocity. Capitalism is an "independent, worldwide axiomatic that is like a single City, megalopolis, or 'megamachine' of which the States are parts or neighborhoods" (*A Thousand Plateaus* 453). The state form is not totally displaced by the "worldwide, ecumenical organization" of capital, but in its modern manifestation it has become a "model of realization" for capital. As such, it is the function of each state today to "[group] together and [combine] several sectors, according to its resources, population, wealth, industrial capacity, etc." (454). Under capitalism, the state serves "to moderate the superior de-territorialization of capital and to provide the latter with compensatory re-territorializations" (455). The state becomes a field for the effectuation of capital, and it does this by reharnessing and reorganizing flows which capital brings together and decomposes (221). Capitalism will even organize and sustain states that are not viable for its own purposes, primarily by crushing minorities through integration and extermination (472). The primacy of capital manifests itself at the highest level of abstraction: capital is an international organization that can organize with a prodigious resourcefulness the various state formations in ways that ensure their fundamental "isomorphy" (which is not to be confused with "homogeneity" in Deleuze and Guattari's scheme).

International capitalism is capable of bringing about the isomorphy of very diverse forms and their attendant forces. As I noted earlier, Deleuze maintains that cultural and social formations are constituted on the basis of "concerts" or "accords."[13] These accords or organizing principles make possible the grouping into particular configurations of whole ranges of phenomena, such that the resulting configurations become integrated formations. As a set of accords or axioms governing the accords that regulate the operations of the various components of an immensely powerful and comprehensive system of accumulation, capital is situated at the nodal point of a plethora of formations, and thus has the capacity to integrate and recompose capitalist and noncapitalist sectors or modes of production.[14] Capital, the "accord of accords" par excellence, can bring together heterogeneous phenomena and make them express the same world, that of capitalist accumulation. Thus in Malaysia, for example, the accord or set of accords that controls the high-tech world of downtown Kuala Lumpur (the location of what was until recently the world's tallest skyscraper) and the accord (or set of accords) that constitutes the world of Stone Age production to be found among the tribespeople in the interiors of eastern Malaysia (Sabah and Sarawak) are not intertranslatable (or not directly or immediately so). But what the accord of accords created by capitalism does, among myriad other things, is to make it possible for the artifacts produced by the indigenous peoples of these interior regions to appear on the tourist markets in downtown Kuala Lumpur, where they are sold alongside Microsoft software, Sony camcorders, and Macintosh PowerBooks. The disparate and seemingly incompatible spheres of production and accumulation represented by downtown Kuala Lumpur and the interior regions of Sabah and Sarawak (which are only about five hundred miles from Kuala Lumpur) are rendered "harmonious" by a higher level accord or concert established by capital, even though the lower level accords remain (qua lower level accords) disconnected from each other. Each lower level accord retains its own distinctive productive mode and its associated social relations of production, even as it is brought into relationship with other, quite different modes and social relations of production (each with its own governing ground-level accords) by the meta- or mega-accord that is capitalism in its current world-integrated phase. The concerto grosso brought about by this prodigiously expansive capitalist accord of accords enables the lower level accords to remain dissociated from each other while still expressing the same world, the world of the current paradigm of accumulation. In a country like Malaysia, and indeed anywhere else in the world, every and any kind of production can thus be incorporated by the capitalist algorithm and made to yield a surplus-value. This development has effectively dismantled the intellectual terms of the age-old debate about precapitalist modes of production and their relation to a successor capitalism. This debate was concerned, in the main, with the putative laws that underlay the supersession of the precapitalist modes by their capitalist successors, but the question of this supersession has become moot in the current phase of accumulation: as the case of Malaysia illustrates, the precapitalist modes can continue to exist in precisely that form but at the same time are inserted into a complex and dynamic network that includes, in the spirit of a vast and saturating ecumenism, all the various modes of production, precapitalist and capitalist alike, so that they function in concert with each other, in this way promoting the realization of even greater surplus-values.[15]

Accords

Accords are constituted by selection criteria, which specify what is to be included or excluded by the terms of the accord in question. These selection criteria are being weakened or qualified in ways that deprive them of their force. The selection criteria that ground an accord assign privileges of rank and order to the objects they subsume ("John McCain is more American than Barack Obama"; "Toledo is a quintessentially American town in a way that Miami is not"). The disappearance or weakening of the traditional criteria that buttressed such accords makes dissonances and contradictions difficult or even impossible to resolve; concomitantly, divergences become easier to uphold. Events, objects, and personages can now be assigned to several divergent and even incompossible series, a phenomenon spectacularly demonstrated by Lautréamont's uncannily surrealistic definition of reality (or beauty) as "the chance encounter between a sewing-machine and an umbrella on a dissecting-table."

Such a Lautréamontean, culturally sanctioned disposition in the present day, conducing as it does to a traffic in all kinds of incompossibilities and divergences, is becoming increasingly commonplace. As each of us takes the opportunity to negotiate for the fifteenth or hundredth or whatever time the several historical avant-gardes, the writings of Borges, cyberpunk, the matrix, and so forth, we become familiarized with the propensities of a Lautréamontean consciousness in ways not available to a learned and cosmopolitan person living as recently as fifty years ago. Thus, for instance, we have a whole genre, magical realism, predicated on the logic of incompossibility (something can be a bird and Simón Bolívar at the same time and, even more "implausibly," at the same point in space); there is a new technological form based on the same logic (such as the morphing that Michael Jackson underwent in his video *Thriller*),[16] as well as entire schools of music which use tones in series that escape or block any kind of resolution by the diatonic scale (as in the work of John Cage, Toru Takemitsu, and free improvisational jazz).[17] Such examples can be multiplied according to one's taste.

This pervasive weakening of the force of these "transcendental" accords, and of the narratives and images which sustain them, may be associated with the collapse of a number of once widely entrenched distinctions; the boundaries between public and private, inside and outside, before and after, political left and political right, and so on have all become difficult, if not impossible, to uphold. In the process, however, accords thus detached from the narratives and other conditions capable of guaranteeing their stability likewise become "impossible." We may be living in worlds that are no longer predicated on any real need to secure and maintain accords, worlds characterized by sheer variation and multiplicity (but still functioning according to an axiomatic, i.e., capital, that ensures their fundamental isomorphism in the face of this uncontainable diversity), worlds that partake of a neo-Baroque perhaps more "truly" Baroque than its predecessor, as Deleuze maintains in his book on Leibniz. Or rather, these are worlds in which the work of accords is now done emblematically and allegorically, so that there is no real accord for what it is that, say, constitutes "Englishness" (or perhaps more accurately, there is now the realization that our accords determining what it is that constitutes "Englishness" rest on an ineliminable fictiveness, so that these accords lack any kind of transcendental legitimation). In the absence of anything approximating to a transcendental backstopping, "being English" can be designated only ascriptively or emblematically, that is, nonabsolutely, as when Queen Elizabeth II (who has as much claim to be regarded as German) is so easily allowed to "count" as "English," while supporters of the Conservative politician Enoch Powell, a British and intellectually upscale version of the *poudjaiste* Jean-Marie Le Pen, were able to cavil nastily over whether a London-born son or daughter of a Jamaican immigrant could justifiably be regarded as "English."

The ascriptive or emblematic imputation of Englishness would allow it to be placed into at least a couple of divergent series. There would be Enoch Powell's grimly robust and settled series, which would effectively confine Englishness to him and his benighted ilk, but other, more expansive series would count as English the London-born children of Jamaican immigrants, the half-American Winston Churchill, the Canadian-born English tennis player Greg Rusedski, and the Japanese-born novelist Kazuo Ishiguro. Crucial to this more ascriptive way of assigning or determining identities is the abandonment of the concept in favor of description (a move delineated by Deleuze in his Leibniz book). Typically, the specification of an identity requires that the identity under consideration be determinate in regard to a concept ("being a communist," "being Irish," "being an economist," or whatever), a concept whose range of applicability is regulated by certain criteria of belonging. These criteria are motivated and underpinned by accords of the kind described earlier, and the breakdown of these accords means that the concepts they support and organize can be replaced by descriptions. Hence, for example, in place of the concept "being an English person" one could have the descriptions "Queen Elizabeth II conducts herself as an English woman," "Greg Rusedski is the Canadian-born tennis star who plays for England," "the Japanese-born anglophone Kazuo Ishiguro is a novelist," and so forth. Such descriptions, as opposed to the concept "being English," would allow Englishness to be used ascriptively or emblematically, so that it could be placed, depending on the particular instances involved, in two or more divergent series. This substitution in principle of the description for the concept would be a not inappropriate way of acknowledging the emergence of a new intellectual and cultural condition (we could call it the time after the end of the Empire, which is our time undeniably) in which it has become more difficult than ever to claim that there really are transcendental accords which subtend this or that way of designating Englishness.

The worlds opened up by *Capitalisme et schizophrénie* are worlds whose accords are characterized in very decisive ways by the kinds of allegorizing and emblematizing propensities just described. These are worlds marked by the "systemic" loss of transcendental accords; they are worlds that are perhaps seeing the exponential growth of the capacity to accommodate what Deleuze and Guattari call "the anomalous" (*l'anomal*). The anomalous, in their view, "has nothing to do with the preferred, domestic, psychoanalytic individual. Nor is the anomalous the bearer of a species presenting specific or generic characteristics in their purest state; nor is it a model or unique specimen; nor is it the perfection of a type incarnate; nor is it the eminent term of a series; nor is it the basis of an absolutely harmonious correspondence. The anomalous is neither an individual nor a species; it only has affects, it has neither familiar nor subjectified feelings, nor specific or significant characteristics" (*A Thousand Plateaus* 244). The realm of the anomalous lies between the domain of "substantial forms" and that of "determined subjects"; it constitutes "a natural play full of haecceities, degrees, intensities, events, and accidents that compose individuations totally different from those of the well-formed subjects that receive them" (253).[18] The upshot is that each individual is a potentially infinite multiplicity, the product of a phantasmagoric movement between an inside and an outside.[19]

All this amounts to the lineaments of a new and interesting theory of the place of the subject in the cultures of contemporary capitalism. *Capitalisme et schizophrénie* approaches this theory of the subject via a theory of singularity, the category that more than any other goes beyond the "collective versus individual" dichotomy that is essential to the Hobbes-Rousseau-Hegel tradition of reflection on the state or sovereign. This account of singularity, and here I must be very brief and schematic, can in turn be connected with the theory of simulation given in Deleuze's *Logique du sens* and *Différence et répétition*, since for Deleuze simulation (or the simulacrum) is the basis of singularity.[20]

In a universe of absolute singularities, production can only take the form of a singularity; each singularity, in the course of production, can only repeat or proliferate itself. In production each simulacrum can only affirm its own difference, its distanciation from everything else. Production, in this account, is a ceaselessly proliferative distribution of all the various absolute singularities. Production, in Deleuze's nomenclature, is always repetition of difference, the difference of each thing from every other thing. Capitalism, though, also embodies a principle of repetition. The axiomatic system that is capitalism is predicated on identity, equivalence, and intersubstitutivity (this being the logic of the commodity form as analyzed by Marx). In which case, repetition in capitalism is always repetition of the nondifferent, or rather, the different in capitalism is always only an apparent different, because it can be overcome and "returned," through the process of abstract exchange, to that which is essentially the same, the always fungible. Capitalism, as *Capitalisme et schizophrénie* indicates, effects an immense series of transformations ("deterritorializations"), only to make possible more powerful recuperations and retrenchments; it breaches limits only in order to impose its own limits, which it "mistakenly" takes to be coextensive with those of the universe.[21] The power of repetition in capitalism is therefore negative, wasteful, and ultimately nonproductive. Capitalistic repetition can therefore be said to be nonbeing in Spinoza's sense, a conclusion that Deleuze and Guattari do not hesitate to draw.

In the scheme of *Capitalisme et schizophrénie*, capital is constitutively unable to sustain a culture of genuine singularities, even though it creates the conditions for the emergence of a culture that could, with the requisite transformations, mutate into such a culture of genuine singularities, a culture, however, that will necessarily be postcapitalist, which has the capacity to produce such singularities.[22]

Intrinsic to the notion of a singularity is the principle that a common or shared property cannot serve as the basis of the individuation of X from all that is *not-X*: if I share the property of being over six feet tall with anyone else, then that property cannot, in and of itself, serve to individuate either me or that person. A singularity, the *being-X* of that X that makes X different from all that is *not-X*, cannot therefore unite X with anything else. Precisely the opposite: X is a singularity because it is not united to anything else by virtue of an essence or a common or shared nature. A singularity is a thing with all its properties, and although some commonality may pertain to this thing, that commonality is indifferent to it qua singularity. So Félix Guattari will have the property "being French" in common with other people, many millions of them, in fact. But a singularity is determined only through its relation to the totality of its possibilities, and the totality of possibilities that constitutes Guattari is the totality of an absolute singularity. If another being had each and every one of the possibilities whose totality constituted and thus individuated Guattari, then that being would perforce be indistinguishable from Guattari. This being and Guattari would be the same person.

In a time when transcendental accords can no longer really give us our worlds, Deleuze and Guattari believe we have to look for worlds that give us a different basis for the construction of solidarities, worlds in which a new kind of politics can find its raison d'être. This politics will start from the realization that our criteria of belonging are always subject to a kind of chaotic motion, that our cultures have always told us an enabling lie when they denied this, and through this denial have made possible the invention of nation-states, tribes, clans, political parties, churches, perhaps everything done up to now in the name of community. The reader of Deleuze and Guattari may have the feeling, both dreadful and exhilarating at the same time, that *that* time, the time up to "now," has begun inexorably to pass. But we still need our solidarities, now more than ever. They are indispensable for any politics capable of taking us beyond capitalism. These solidarities, however, will be based not on the securing of transcendental accords; capitalism, that most revolutionary of forces, has moved that possibility into desuetude. Our solidarities will be predicated instead on what the reader of Deleuze and Guattari will know as the power of singularity, a power still perhaps in search of its appropriate models of realization.[23]

Since this politics still awaits its models of realization, the power of singularity, which despite the absence of these models is still precisely that, a power, can only manifest itself as the undertaking of a certain risk, the "playing of uncertain games," all the things that conduce to the "revolutionary-becoming" of people who have not yet made the revolution their explicit agenda. What will be the relation of this revolutionary-becoming to the project of the state? Can the solidarities associated with these singularities be regimented, and thus neutralized, by the state in ways that preempt insurmountably the prospects of any kind of revolutionary transformation?

The flows of power in the current social and political dispensation are fluid and relatively open, even as they are powerfully managed and contained by the elites who rule us. This development underlies the increasingly widespread perception that governments in the advanced industrial countries wield more and more control despite the simultaneous prevalence of ideologies of deregulation, privatization, and "getting the government off the backs of the people" (the mantra of Ronald Reagan, among others). And so it looks increasingly as if the notion of representation which made the previous kind of "citizenship politics" possible has now been supplanted, even as the instruments which underpin it are treated as sacred objects. There is perhaps no better example of this than the U.S. Constitution, traduced by an ever expanding capitalist depredation even as its traducers profess their undying veneration for this old document.[24] The blocking of any passage through the philosophy and politics of representation underlying such developments will have significant effects not only on our conceptions of citizenship, but also on our related notions of ethnicity, race, patrimony, clan, nation, and sovereignty. These notions have deeply ingrained personal resonances that will continue to be felt despite the criticisms directed by philosophers and theorists at the concept of representation. But if the philosophy of representation no longer works, and its limitations are impossible to conceal, what should be put in its place? The invention of something different (such as the Deleuzean notion of a political desire or form of willing based on singularities not regulated by transcendental accords) to put in place of the system of representations that has governed thinking and practice about ethnicity, race, patrimony, clan, nation, and sovereignty, these representations being the cornerstone of the *epistéme* or *mentalité* that has prevailed since 1776 or 1789 or 1492 (used here as emblematic markers), will have to be an immense collective undertaking, perhaps spanning many generations. The core of this system of representation is its imperative that all are required to "belong" in some way or other to the various collectivities superintended by this system's logic. An enabling political desire will free us from the need to continue to make this a world where all are required to belong to such collectivities.

State power is of course the most significant impediment to the realization of this emancipatory undertaking. The state identifies, counts, and assigns to its various classificatory systems countless numbers of human beings, all as part of its administrative remit, and the pressing question for the Deleuzean account of political desire is its capacity to mobilize desire in ways that make possible an obviation of state power. The world is changing even as we reflect on it. The collapse of the Soviet Union has been largely instrumental in the emergence of a U.S. hegemony. As a result, the antagonism between capitalism and bureaucratic socialism has been replaced by a range of struggles among competing brands of capitalism (German social market capitalism, the Blairite Third Way, American free market capitalism, Japanese corporatism, and so on). Here the outcome is still uncertain, as indicated by the continuing world economic stagnation and the wars being fought by the Bush administration and its allies. Despite this uncertainty, there are a number of trends in the international system that appear to be fairly consequential. Preeminent among these is a more active role in this system for regional as well as local states, and these are being accompanied by new structures of cultural identification that are tied to regions or subregions rather than nation-states (such as the various "separatisms" associated with the Basques, Catalonians,

Chechnyans, Kurds, Corsicans, Irian Jayanese, Sri Lankan Tamils, Punjabi Sikhs, Kashmiris, Eritreans, and the people of Aceh).[25] One outcome of this development is the increased coexistence of the transnational and the inter-local, with the nation-state having a transformed but still noteworthy function as the apparatus that manages the flows between them. Conceptions of sovereignty and citizenship are being modified in the process, especially since the state system is de-emphasizing govern*ment* in favor of govern*ance* and *metagovernance* as older and more expansive official state institutions are scaled down or sidelined and administration increasingly becomes the process of organizing flows between a range of agencies and networks of power and information (viz., governance) and of devising the "axioms" to link together and harmonize all these structures and movements (viz., metagovernance).[26] Conceptions of citizenship, and their attendant forms of political desire and agency, become increasingly flexible and compartmentalized.

The state will only slowly be replaced or restructured. In failed states such as Somalia, for instance, a state form of some kind will need to be introduced prior to the pursuit of its possible supersession, and this because no viable system for the allocation of resources exists in the Somalias of this world, and the possibility of revolutionary transformation in such countries pre-supposes the existence of such a system to serve as a conduit for decision making. A countercapitalist project of the kind delineated in *Capitalisme et schizophrénie* is not likely to succeed unless the social movements that are its vehicle are able to operate at the level of the nation-state (though they would certainly not be confined to working at this level).[27] Of course this counterproject has to be efficacious at other levels if it is to be successful, including the education, taxation, and bureaucratic systems, and also show itself capable of sustaining "a more general vision of the democratization of societies and their political and economic management."[28] But this counter-project, for the less-developed countries at any rate, is a project that involves the mobilization of a new and different kind of popular national movement. Here an important distinction between the state apparatus and the nation is to be made. Samir Amin has plausibly argued that the appropriation of the state apparatus is usually the object of a country's national bourgeoisie (who will reconcile themselves to recompradorization by external capitals as long as it will leave the state apparatus in their hands), while the construction of the project of national liberation involves not only delinking (needed to avert recompradorization) but also the formation of a "popular hegemonic alliance" among the people.[29]

The construction of a comprehensive national popular alliance, functioning autonomously of the state system, will furnish the stimulus for adopting a different kind of allocation strategy, one premised on a (selective) delinking, and embarked upon with the purpose of transmuting the state apparatus (since the state is the institutional assemblage that has final control of the regime of growth, and indeed there can be no properly constituted regime of growth without the involvement of the state). The first priority therefore is a "destatized" collective national liberation project, the success of which will then lead to a reconstitution of the state itself. Most existing proposals for economic and political reform in the less-developed countries view the reform and reconstitution of the state as the principal objective whose attainment will then lead to a whole range of other benefits ("efficient" economic development, protection of human rights, the upholding of democracy, etc.). This is to put the proverbial cart before the horse, since in many LDCs the state is merely an instrument at the disposal of the ruling elite (who tend invariably to be the recipients of the substantial personal benefits to be derived from subservience to the Washington consensus). It will therefore be necessary to have an alternative and non-state-oriented base within the LDCs in question from which the project of state reform can be initiated and sustained.

Capitalisme et schizophrénie is perhaps best viewed as a compendium of political knowledge, nonmolar and nonarborescent in aspiration and putative scope, which furnishes axioms for the pursuit of the revolutionary project of surmounting capitalism. Deleuze and Guattari insist that there are no pregiven laws to shape or entail this outcome; only struggle, and failures always accompany successes in struggle, can do this. The only other alternative is acceptance of the current finance-led, equity-based growth regime with its concomitant American hegemony and continuing worldwide economic polarization. This line of argument is taken up in chapter 11, where I argue that the poorer countries have no option but to choose a strategy of selective "delinking" from the economies of the metropolitan center.

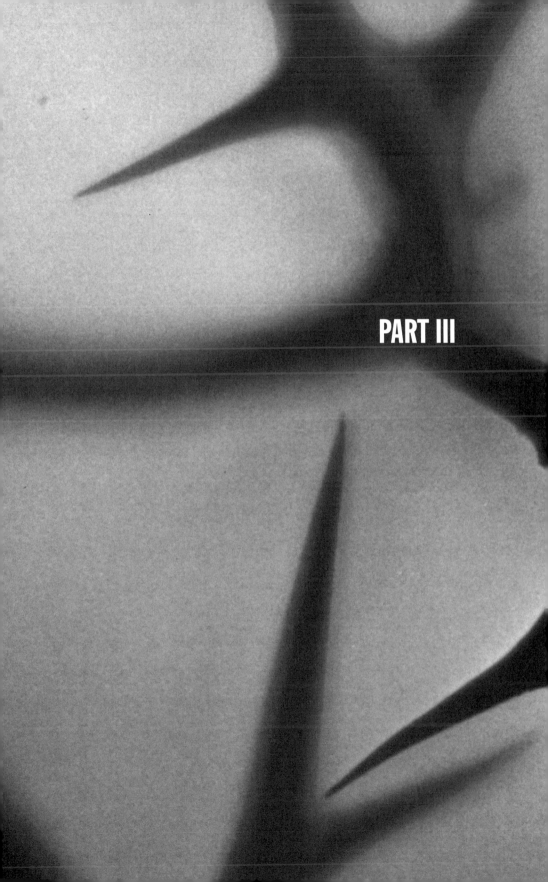

PART III

CHAPTER 11

The Possibility of a New State II

Heterotopia

Where discussions of utopia are concerned, the warning given by M. I. Finley is particularly apt: "Ever since Thomas More gave the world the word Utopia early in the sixteenth century, a semantic cluster has grown round it, or perhaps I should say a spectrum of meanings, of great range and complexity, and of no little confusion."[1] Consideration of the notion of utopia, both as a concept designating a particular kind of reflection ("thinking about a better future," "thought that confounds social pessimism," "thinking that necessarily involves the criticism of ideology"), or as the more or less practical implementation of some scheme or blueprint for a better world ("concrete utopia," "the utopian design of institutions"), tends to be conducted in terms of one tense ("the future") and one modality ("the possible" as against "the impossible" or "absolutely unrealizable").

When cast in these terms, the concept of utopia is marked by a temporal specification signaling a radical break between an existing state of affairs and one that is still to be realized: the time that is properly utopian is always the time *after* some previous time deemed to be nonutopian. If this is not the case, then the utopian is glossed in terms of a *now* that is so completely adequate that it cannot be improved upon or superseded in some fundamentally decisive way. In the latter case, the pattern of temporality is admittedly somewhat altered, but its import remains the same; that is, when the present is regarded as an apotheosis or culminating point, we can hope only to maintain it in its present form, in which case any transformation of an existing state of affairs can amount only to a decline or fall from this current state of supreme excellence, and so in principle the future can only continue to be "the same" as the present or else amount to a decline or worsening in relation to the present. In both cases, however, and this is the crucial point, a gap is necessarily posited between a better or best possible state and a worse or worst possible state. In the one case the putatively good state exists in the future (in which case the better or best possible state is yet to come), and in the other it exists now (in which case the future cannot be the sphere in which any real improvement occurs and is more likely than not to be regarded as dystopian). These propositions are clearly exemplified in the following quotation from Oscar Wilde's essay *The Soul of Man under Socialism*, so famous that it appears as a motto on nearly every website dealing with the subject of utopias: "A map of the world that does not include Utopia is not worth even glancing at, for it leaves out the one country at which humanity is always landing. And when Humanity lands there, it looks out, and seeing a better country, sets sail. Progress is the realisation of Utopias."[2]

Implicit in Wilde's characterization is the proposition that utopia is a destination to be arrived at or moved toward, and that this movement is inextricably linked to a certain conception of progress, so that "landing" necessarily takes the form of a progression from one state or condition to another, with the clear implication that the preceding state is ostensibly a less good "country" than its successor, the place or condition of plenitude or perfection. Regardless of what may be said about this narrative of progress canvassed by Wilde, utopia is construed in it as a "departure" made from a place or occasion that is qualitatively inferior to the subsequent place or occasion of "landing." The assumption at work in this somewhat commonplace logic of the utopian is that of an inverted relation to the situation of a currently existing society, so that the utopian is depicted by the adherents of this logic as a state of affairs necessarily involving improvements upon existing social arrangements, or, even more radically, the pursuit or implementation of utopia is thought to require the complete overturning of these arrangements in their present form.[3]

Utopia versus Heterotopia?

The question of the relation of the utopian to existing social forms has been a vexed one throughout the history of utopian thought. An interesting comparison can be made between the respective positions of Finley and Foucault. Finley, who concludes his essay with Wilde's declaration "A map of the world that does not include Utopia is not worth even glancing at," clearly endorses the logic of the utopian just mentioned, with its emphasis on the inextricable bond between the utopian and conceptions of social progress. Foucault, by contrast, argued in his little essay on "heterotopias" that utopias, unlike heterotopias, are "fundamentally unreal spaces."[4] Finley, in contrasting the notion of utopia with myth (such as the myth of a Golden Age or a Garden of Eden), maintained that utopia has a practical and active relation to "reality," and that this relation is crucial to any transforming influence that the utopian imagination may have upon existing social formations.[5] Foucault has a quite different emphasis, and characterizes heterotopic places as "real places—places that do exist and that are formed in the very founding of society—which are something like countersites, a kind of effectively enacted utopia in which the real sites, all the other real sites that can be found within the culture, are simultaneously represented, contested, and inverted. Places of this kind are outside of all places, even though it may be possible to indicate their location in reality. . . . Between utopias and these quite other sites, these heterotopias, there might be a sort of mixed, joint experience" (24). Foucault's paradigmatic example of the heterotopic site, "a mixed, joint experience," is the mirror. Giving a twist to the Lacanian thesis of the mirror stage, as well as Merleau-Ponty's concept of a "chiasmic" structure which enables beings to "slip into each other," and merging these insights with the kernel of Bataille's notion of a "heterology" to form what he calls a "heterotopology," Foucault writes:

> The mirror is, after all, a utopia, since it is a placeless place. I see myself there where I am not, in an unreal, virtual space that opens up behind the surface; I am over there, there where I am not, a sort of shadow that gives visibility to myself, that enables me to see myself there where I am absent: such is the utopia of the mirror. But it is also a heterotopia in so far as the mirror does exist in reality, where it exerts a sort of counteraction on the position that I occupy. From the standpoint of the mirror I discover my absence from the place where I am since I see myself over there. Starting from this gaze that is, as it were, directed toward me, from the ground of this virtual space that is on the other side of the glass, I come back toward myself; I begin again to direct my eyes toward myself and to reconstitute myself there where I am. The mirror functions as a heterotopia in this respect: it makes this place that I occupy at the moment when I look at myself in the glass at once absolutely real, connected with all the space that surrounds it, and absolutely unreal, since in order to be perceived it has to pass through this virtual point which is over there. (24)[6]

The heterotopia identified by Foucault in this passage is notable for the way it is premised on a particular conceptualization of the relation or passage between an "inside" and an "outside" that transcends, even while working its way through, the dichotomy between the real and the unreal. At work here, therefore, is a certain conception of the *virtual*, which functions as a modal category that bypasses the relationship of contrariety typically said to exist between the possible and the actual (and about which more will be said shortly).

At the heart of this passage between the inside and the outside is a movement between a succession of images, in this case the various images of oneself "over there" in the mirror (the outside) and the complementary images of oneself "over here" (the inside). This movement or oscillation between these sets of images is really a movement between perspectives, at each of which a particular ensemble is constructed out of these images by the perceiver.[7] "Heterotopia" is thus the name of the orchestrating principle which links these perspectives into an amalgam that makes it possible for their associated ensembles to be enfolded into each other, this enfolding being the outcome of an organization of forces in the perceptual field that results in the concretely indivisible composite that is "I." More generally, and taking into account forms of organizing forces that have nothing specifically to do with perception, this organization or process is precisely what generates the structural "site" of this or that heterotopia. A radical constructivism therefore underlies Foucault's characterization of heterotopia, and this constructivism is generalized by him to encompass all heterotopias, and not just those manifestations of heterotopia in the domain of perception.[8]

Heterotopias possess a modality, that of the virtual, which is quite different from the modality characteristic of utopia; utopia belongs in principle to the realm of a possibility that, qua pure possibility, awaits its potential actualization in some future, a future that will come to be utopia's present when this actualization in fact takes place. Unlike the purely possible, however, the virtual is real, but somewhat like the possible, it is not actual (although it does not share any other properties with the possible). Only a state of affairs which had been possible can be actual; the virtual, by contrast, is a pure exteriority that is adjacent to, and inextricably bound up with, all elements in the actual, while not in any way partaking of the actual. The actual acts on the virtual, since the virtual constitutes a basis for the emergence of the singularities which manifest the virtual in the domain of the actual.[9] The event from which a singularity (which, as a singularity, is neither individual nor personal) comes to exist eludes its manifestation in that singularity even as it is brought to expression in it; here Deleuze and Foucault adhere to the Stoic doctrine which affirms that the event is real without being actual. The virtuality that is heterotopia takes shape when a world is constituted by a certain ontological genesis. A measure of philosophical abstraction is unavoidable in providing a description of this ontological genesis, but since the structure of heterotopia is rooted in the structure of this ontological genesis, this description must be a part of the delineation of the heterotopic place.

Ontological Genesis and the Structure of Heterotopia:
Some Ideas of Gilles Deleuze

A world exists when it can be populated by one or more singularities.[10] These singularities, which are potentially infinite in number, are selected as a result of an operation in which a singular point is extended to encompass a range of "normal" points. This extension occurs until another threshold of singularity is encountered, and a world is constituted and actualized when this and other singularities extend over that particular range of normal points. Singularities are actualized in a world, and also in the individuals who belong to that world. These modes of actualization are several, according to Deleuze: "To be actualized or to actualize oneself means to extend over a series of ordinary points; to be selected according to a rule of convergence; to be incarnated in a body; to become the state of a body; and to be renewed locally for the sake of limited new actualizations and extensions" (110).[11] What is actualized is also expressed, and what is expressed is a world that is composed of "differential relations and of contiguous similarities" (111). At this point Deleuze introduces the Leibnizian idea of an *incompossibility*. According to Deleuze, a world is formed when a series depending on a particular singularity converges with a series which depends on another singularity; this convergence then defines compossibility. Conversely, when the series in question diverge, another world emerges, one that is incompossible with the first. The concept of incompossibility cannot be derived from the notion of contradiction: the state of affairs in which George W. Bush does sanction the occupation of Iraq is incompatible with the one in which he does not sanction the occupation of Iraq, not because these two propositions contradict each other, but precisely because of the incompossibility that obtains between the world in which Bush sanctions the invasion of Iraq and the one in which he does not. Hence when one of these worlds is actualized, the other state of affairs cannot arise, and vice versa. But it is entirely a matter of political and historical contingency whether or not Bush sanctions the invasion of Iraq; hence the propositions expressing these two states of affairs are not logically contra-dictory. Though of course once one of these worlds is actualized (in this case the one in which Bush *does* sanction the occupation of Iraq), the other (in this case the world in which Bush does *not* sanction the occupation of Iraq) cannot be brought to the point of actualization.

This structure of incompossibility also governs the emergence or onto-logical genesis of the heterotopian situation. Thus the world in which Bush does not (or better still, is unable to) sanction the invasion of Iraq is hetero-topian with regard to the world, which happens to be the actual world, in which he does have this capacity (and did in fact choose to exercise it). The form of this ontological genesis is quite different from the form that sub-tends the emergence of utopia. As was seen earlier, the proponents of utopia typically view it as a destination to be arrived at or moved toward, so that this movement is inextricably linked to a certain conception of "progress." The premise behind this somewhat commonplace logic of the utopian is that utopia stands in an inverted relation to a currently existing (nonutopian) situation. By contrast, the notion of heterotopia makes no such presump-tion of this inverted relation to the actually existing world or any state of affairs in this world. In fact, Foucault's characterization of the heterotopic place as a "mixed site" in which a virtual element contends with an element that happens to have been actualized is an apt description of this ontologi-cal genesis. In the case of the Bush-sanctioned invasion of Iraq, there was a point at which the world in which Bush sanctioned this invasion and the one in which he did not were both actualizable. It is now widely agreed that any refusal on the part of Tony Blair to be Bush's accomplice in this invasion, combined with less pliable dispositions on the part of the U.S. Congress and the United Nations (What if many more countries in the Security Council were able in the end to share the position of the skeptical French?), as well as outright hostility from the Arab world to the prospect of an American invasion (What if every Arab country followed the example of Turkey in not allowing its territorial space to be used as a springboard for the American invasion?) would have created a political situation in which an American invasion of Iraq would have been difficult to mount for obvious political and strategic reasons. Over time, however, the series constituted by these putative events (which of course did not transpire) diverged from the series associated with Bush's sanctioning of the invasion of Iraq. In a word, the two worlds in question came to be incompossible. Before this, though, there was a period of political contestation which, in slightly different circumstances, such as the subsequently preempted mobilization of the forces potentially opposed to the Bush administration's invasion, could have resulted in the actualization of the world, a properly heterotopian world, in which Bush would not have been in a position to sanction an invasion of Iraq.

Why is this heterotopian ontological genesis seemingly so important for political thought? In thinking about this question, we have to ask if it is not indeed the case that the heterotopian ontological genesis invoked here has a counterfactual structure which, given the essential nature and function of counterfactual structures, can only be seen to be as constitutively "unreal" as the very utopian structure being challenged here.[12]

Any significant argument on behalf of the notion of the heterotopian thus has to reckon in some way with the theoretical contours of this counterfactual structure. In the case of heterotopia, the putative heterotopian state of affairs, though real and existing, nonetheless functions as a kind of countersite to the domain of the actually existing (here I follow Foucault to the letter), and can therefore be appropriately expressed by a counterfactual condition of the following kind: "If this heterotopia (i.e., this countersite) existed, then George W. Bush would not be made president." Again, it is possible for the antecedent of this conditional to be accepted as true ("Heterotopia exists") and the consequent nonetheless to be rejected ("If heterotopia existed, then George W. Bush would [still] be made president"). Of course it would be logically impossible to affirm both these consequents simultaneously, since the consequent of the following statement is clearly contradictory: "If this heterotopia existed, then George W. Bush would not be made president *and* George W. Bush would (still) be made president." But no affirmation of heterotopia in itself enables us to determine which particular wing of this consequent is true or likely to be true. Of course, those inclined to accept that heterotopia is by its very nature oppositional and counterhegemonic would in all probability be inclined to say that, given the kind of policies he espouses, George W. Bush would not really be in a position to be made president if (this) heterotopia existed. But there is a fundamental undecidability in this counterfactual structure that Foucault himself never addressed in his essay on heterotopia: the affirmation made with respect to a particular situation that it constitutes a heterotopian state of affairs does not in itself enable us to claim that it has this or that character in any strict or exclusive way. In this respect the heterotopian structure is unlike its utopian counterpart, inasmuch as utopia, by virtue of its defining logic of the inverted relation in regard to the real world, is able to possess a rather more specific character than the ostensibly heterotopian space does. In a utopian world, or at any rate for most of those who are disposed to believe that such a world falls within the limits of conceivability, George W. Bush would *not* be made president. That is to say, when identifying a utopian space, one would have to profess that utopia requires that George W. Bush not be made president, or else (and one can imagine a fervent Bush supporter saying this) one would say that Bush's being made president is absolutely compatible with, or is indeed required by, the affirmation of utopia. (Granted that the latter state of affairs is less likely to happen than the former, especially since supporters of the Republican Party tend to view utopias as being of interest only to communists, dreamy idealists, charlatans, and so forth.) Heterotopia, by contrast, seems to be much more amorphous: its constitution cannot be specified through the operation of dialectical negation in the way that is constitutively the case with the inverted relation of the utopian condition. So how are we to identify the lineaments of the heterotopian "space," given its inability to determine in anything like a precise way the character of a particular and specific political orientation?

Heterotopian Space?

In the heterotopian space, it is transparently obvious that there is no such thing as a single or straightforward relation of this space to the real world. This is clear from Foucault's description of what he calls "heterotopology," when he says of this "simultaneously mythic and real contestation of the space in which we live" that "there is probably not a single culture in the world that fails to constitute heterotopias. This is a constant of every group" (24). What is said here of heterotopia cannot be affirmed with regard to utopia, no matter how elastic a definition of utopia is espoused, since it is obvious that the utopian imagination is fairly strictly confined to the modern period in Western thought, representing as it does the core of a secularized version of Judeo-Christian eschatology.[13]

Foucault categorizes heterotopias into two basic kinds. On the one hand, there are "crisis heterotopias," located in "privileged or sacred or forbidden places, reserved for individuals who are, in relation to society and to the human environment in which they live, in a state of crisis: adolescents, menstruating women, pregnant women, the elderly, etc." (24). He goes on to say:

> In our society, these crisis heterotopias are persistently disappearing, though a few remnants can still be found. For example, the boarding school, in its nineteenth-century form, or military service for young men, have certainly

played such a rôle, as the first manifestations of sexual virility were in fact supposed to take place "elsewhere" than at home. For girls, there was, until the middle of the twentieth-century, a tradition called the "honeymoon trip" which was an ancestral theme. The young woman's deflowering could take place "nowhere" and, at the moment of its occurrence the train or honeymoon hotel was indeed the place of this nowhere, this heterotopia without markers. (24–25)

This account of the crisis heterotopia depicts it as a kind of liminal space, very much akin to the sense of liminality made well-known by Victor Turner, that is, as a situation in which a decisive threshold comes to be crossed, so that at the point of crossing the individual involved is betwixt and between, neither what he or she had been but still not yet what he or she is in the process of becoming. The liminal space is the place where identities are dissolved and reconstituted.[14]

Contrasted with the crisis heterotopia is the "heterotopia of deviation," in which "individuals whose behavior is deviant in relation to the required mean or norm are placed. Cases of this are rest homes and psychiatric hospitals, and of course prisons; and one should perhaps add retirement homes that are, as it were, on the borderline between the heterotopia of crisis and the heterotopia of deviation since, after all, old age is a crisis, but is also a deviation" (25). Other examples of heterotopic spaces given by Foucault are the utopian colony, theaters, cemeteries, cinemas, gardens, saunas, motels, and holiday resorts. It is fairly obvious that these heterotopic zones are not necessarily political (though in fairness it has to be acknowledged that Foucault himself does not maintain that they are intrinsically political); some such zones may be, but it is hard to conceive of the typical retirement community clustered around a golf course or a Club Med resort as a location where any kind of immediately recognizable or concerted political activity is likely to take place.[15] The space of heterotopia is preeminently a space where what Foucault calls "local strategies" prevail, and while his emphasis on the breaching of norms is evident in his delineation of heterotopia, this emphasis does not on its own signal the crucial or indispensable presence of political activity on the part of the inhabitants of that heterotopia. It is hard to deny that the transgression of norms, in itself, can be merely reactive or amount to no more than a gesture of consolation motivated by feelings of disempowerment and nihilistic rage, rather than any real sense that the society in question can be decisively transformed on a more or less systematic scale.

What needs to be added to this conception of heterotopia if it is to be tilted conceptually in the direction of a systemic transformation of society as a whole, that is, the understanding of emancipation or liberation presupposed by a less orthodox marxism? (We need to leave open here the real possibility that Foucault was himself the adherent of a "deviant" marxism.)

In other words, the notion of a heterotopia is not in itself essentially political or apolitical; rather, a putative heterotopia would be in a position to warrant this appellation of "the political" if and only if certain other conditions, to wit, those warranting this appellation, happen to enable the heterotopia in question. There is an irreducible contingency that attaches to the notion of a heterotopia, and the question of a heterotopia's being political is one that can be resolved only if the underlying conditions for this heterotopia *are* in themselves political. But what would have to be in place for a heterotopia to be political in this more robust sense? Moreover, what would be the nature of the seemingly deviant marxism, whether faithful to Foucault or not, that kept open a place for this politically inflected heterotopia?

Reverse Causation and the Place of Heterotopia

If we return to the notion of the heterotopian as something that is virtual rather than actual, it will be possible to acknowledge that a heterotopian reality would be incompossible with respect to the world, the actual world in this case, in which it is possible for hundreds of millions to go hungry, to face diseases that are eradicable, to suffer in wars that need not be fought, to toil in conditions that amount to a modern serfdom, or, in the example cited earlier, a world in which it is possible for George W. Bush to be made president. This incompossible world, real but alas not yet actual, would be one in which none of these things would be tolerated or countenanced; that is, it would be a reality in which there was a determined and wholehearted attempt on the part of governments, international agencies, and private organizations to provide the mass of human beings with food, jobs, relative peace and a guarantee of personal security, reasonably adequate health provision, passable housing and shelter, a minimum level of education, and living environments that are not inimical to human well-being. To ask where we would find this heterotopian world is somewhat misleading, in that the question presumes that there is, in actuality, a specific place where George W. Bush cannot be made president, where there are enough jobs and food for the mass of impoverished human beings, and so on. But it is evident that no such place is to be found on any significant scale, at least not in the actual world. However, if we make the assumption that this virtual world, incompossible with the actual world, though it is real, is nonetheless prevented from actualizing itself, then we make the kind of claim that is common in certain fields of physics, biology, and economics which entertain the notion of a reverse causation.

To be more specific: in a reverse causality, an event located in the future can act on the present, or the present can act on the past. This runs counter to the traditional image of the "arrow of time," in which the flow of events is always from past to present to future, with present becoming past as the future becomes present. There are numerous rationales for reverse causation. One is mathematical, as exemplified in Henri Poincaré's recurrence theorem, according to which any isolated dynamic system whose total energy is unchanged will return arbitrarily in time to one of its initial sets of molecular positions and velocities; thus no process is irreversible, and so in time (i.e., given a very long time) the coffee spilled on my jacket will return to the cup that contained it, and the liquid coffee now returned to its cup will in turn decompose into its initial components of coffee beans, grains of sugar, and powdered milk.[16] Another case comes from economic theory, where Partha Dasgupta and others have sought to address the well-known conundrum of the relation between environmental despoliation and poverty. While it can be postulated that a significantly degraded environment will conduce in all probability to greater poverty on the part of its inhabitants, the reverse causation also holds, inasmuch as the poor are often more likely to degrade the natural environment in their quest for the mere necessities of life, by raiding forests for firewood, practicing slash-and-burn cultivation, and so on.[17] In the case of the political domain, the action of a reverse cause takes place when some ostensibly "future" state of affairs, the communist revolution, say, is warded off in the present by the forces that keep capitalism in place. If the forces responsible for maintaining capitalism weakened or were displaced in some other way, then, all else being equal, the communist revolution would no longer be impended. Hence the state of affairs known as "communism" is already active, it preexists, even though its actualization can lie only in some as yet unspecified future, because even as this future event it represents a limit for the expansion of capitalism. Capitalism is what it is precisely because it has to be organized in such a way that it can keep at bay those forces which, if they are not weakened or dissolved by already existing capitalism, would bring about the communist revolution. The revolution, which is yet to occur, is already active as a reverse cause that already existing capitalism has to contend with, and dispel with some success, if capitalism is to continue to exist.[18]

Where the principle of heterotopia is concerned, the notion of a reverse cause can be invoked to suggest that heterotopia, though not actual, is nonetheless the situation that capitalism has to ward off in order to continue to be what it is today. So heterotopia is active as the virtual but "inactual" state whose explosiveness capitalism has to contain and neutralize, since failure to restrain the potentially irruptive power of heterotopia would result in the demise of capitalism. But capitalism continues to be what it is, it retains its efficacy, precisely because it has been able to construct the right kinds of mechanisms to keep heterotopia (revolution, in other words) at bay. Heterotopia is thus integral to the operation of capital, to its self-organization, since without heterotopia capitalism cannot exist. The capitalist order is an effect that has heterotopia as its cause, though the latter is virtual and not yet actual.[19] The heterotopia in which George W. Bush cannot be made president, in which jobs and food are available for those whose lives are for now destroyed by poverty, and so forth, enables capitalism to be what it is by stimulating a capitalist counterpower to the heterotopian situation that would be actual were it not for the exercise of this baneful counterpower.

This ontology of heterotopia, if one can call it that, in turn facilitates a counterpart epistemology of the revolutionary event. It does not do this by placing at our disposal "knowledge" of what is going on in the hearts and minds of some future revolutionary subject (this would be a kind of bad utopianism!) or the hidden dimensions of a political process, but rather by furnishing a reason whose primary theoretical operation is fundamentally that of a subtraction. What, bit by bit and here and there, do we need to do in order to take away from capitalism that which makes it possible for it to be so pervasively efficacious? This is perhaps the question par excellence that is posed by this application of the notion of a reverse causality.

Broaching in the way that we have done here the question of marxism's fundamental because constituting relation to the project of liberation (i.e., heterotopia's raison d'être) in turn poses the question of marxism's position in regard to the supersession of capitalism, since it is axiomatic for all schools of marxism that liberation inextricably involves a countervailing action directed at the capitalist system of production and accumulation. But doesn't capitalism exercise its dominance in many modes and at many levels, not all of which give the appearance of being commanded by the forces and agents of capitalism? Can't it plausibly be presumed, moreover, that specifically anticapitalist struggles are not the only ones germane for the construction of heterotopia?

As I argued earlier, it is a mistake to assume that anticapitalist struggles require one to de-emphasize or disregard struggles in other contexts not typically associated with forces and formations integral to capitalism, such as struggles for gender and racial equality and campaigns against discrimination based on sexual orientation. Heterotopia needs these kinds of struggle just as much as it needs anticapitalist struggles, even if one acknowledges that anticapitalist struggles have a catalytic effect on these other kinds of struggle. There are those who will argue that mass movements with an emancipatory, and thus explicitly or implicitly heterotopian intent existed long before the emergence of the capitalist system. The implication is that marxism, whose raison d'être is overwhelmingly the critique of capitalist political economy, is not sufficiently encompassing as a result of this singular and restricted focus to do real justice to these precapitalist radical alternatives and the varied heterotopian movements that were their vehicles. Heterotopia has always existed, even in precapitalist formations.[20]

Arriving at Heterotopia

Here it is perhaps best to begin by discussing a specific example regarding the economic delinking of the so-called peripheral capitalist economies from those at the metropolitan core (a position endorsed in chapters 4 and 5). I argued that one of the distinctive features of the current globalized world-system is a burgeoning of financial markets and financial capital, and that this is where the newest versions of primitive accumulation are taking place. In the past primitive accumulations tended to take the form of a movement into precapitalist formations, subsuming them in the process under the logic of capitalist accumulation and production by taking advantage of docile and often newly proletarianized labor forces, in this way making it possible for these newly capitalistic economies to yield surplus value for those who "invest" in them. By contrast, in the current regime of accumulation dominated by financialization, primitive accumulation takes place when countries that are already capitalist, but that are usually located in the "semiperiphery," free up their already capitalist economies by opening them to overseas financial markets based overwhelmingly in New York, London, Frankfurt, Tokyo, Hong Kong, and Singapore (but especially New York and London). The first movers into a new financial market tend to accrue higher returns than latecomers. This is the absolute basis of financialized primitive accumulation: the brokers and investors who pioneer a new market can reap benefits that will not be available to market actors who come after the first-comers. This development has taken place without the proletarianization required of earlier primitive accumulations.

At the same time we have seen that these new financialized regimes bring very few benefits to the countries who have freed up their economies in this way. Financial markets constrain home government economic policy, since these governments are expected to promote investor confidence by ensuring fiscal solvency, keeping inflation low, and adopting investor-friendly monetary policies (these measures being sanctioned by the prevailing neoliberal consensus upheld by the U.S. government, the IMF, and the World Bank). Government noncompliance with what financial markets want can be severely punished. Hence in 2002 interest rates on Brazil's public debt rose to prohibitive levels as it looked increasingly likely that the left-wing candidate Lula would be elected president. (Some skeptics would say that Lula ceased to be left-wing the moment he was elected.) Speculators withdrew from the Brazilian real and its bond markets, and Brazil's credit rating was downgraded to the levels of Nigeria and Argentina. In the end Brazil had to seek an IMF bailout and implement the austerity measures typically required by the IMF as a condition of granting a loan. As Dani Rodrik, from whom the example of Brazil is taken, points out, "Investors were in effect telling the electorate: you have the vote, but we have the ability to crush the economy. Once elected, Lula was faced with a choice between exacerbating the financial crisis or outdoing the financial conservatism of his predecessor. He chose the latter."[21]

As we have seen, countries yielding to the rules of this neoliberal consensus on open financial markets are usually subjected to chronically unstable inflows and outflows, as well as debt spirals. A heterotopia for countries like Brazil in 2002 (and now) would be one in which they are no longer dragooned by this destructive financial system. Achieving this would require a considered withdrawal from the deleterious aspects of a global market system that impoverishes huge numbers of Brazilians, a course of action not without its own risks and costs. But there are no clear benefits for Brazil from continued participation in internationally integrated financial markets. To quote Rodrik:

> The net benefits of the "business-as-usual" strategy are quite unclear. . . . Under current rules of good behaviour, these countries are effectively precluded from taking on additional debt anyhow—removing the main benefit of financial integration even if one assumes that capital flows will revive soon.

Many of them are engaged in highly costly self-insurance efforts, which would not be necessary if there were reduced financial openness. For example, a common strategy is to build up foreign reserves as insurance against reversals in capital flows. However, this entails exchanging low-yielding U.S. Treasury securities for high-cost debt—a boon for the U.S. Treasury but a rotten deal for the home economy.[22]

The heterotopia for Brazil and the many other countries in a similar situation would be one in which they can choose their own economic policies without interference from the IMF and the U.S. Treasury. But of course, the IMF and the U.S. Treasury have this capacity precisely because this heterotopia is currently forestalled; indeed, this heterotopia has to be obviated as a condition of the IMF and the U.S. Treasury having the ability to constrain Brazil's economic policies so that even a left-wing Brazilian president has to toe the line laid down by the IMF, the U.S. Treasury, and their ancillary institutions. So how can this heterotopia, now virtual but not yet actual, be brought to the point of actualization?

I have suggested that what is needed to establish a heterotopia as an actuality for less-developed countries like Brazil is an economic strategy based on a piecemeal and ad hoc delinking from the global market, where a country which perceives itself not to be a beneficiary in the current economic dispensation is given the latitude to examine one by one the linkages it has with economically and politically privileged countries, and then to sever those linkages which are not to its advantage or which function to its detriment. These linkages are then "subtracted" from the sum total of that country's connections with other economic entities, so that gradually (but sometimes perhaps quite rapidly) the heterotopian situation is attained, at least in principle. In this heterotopian situation the country in question will have reached a point where it has been able to disconnect itself from the powers which prevent it from achieving its own "autocentric" economic development. Heterotopia is achieved when a country like Burkina Faso or Papua New Guinea can take practical steps to bring about its own autocentric development, and this kind of development is not therefore the exclusive preserve of the wealthy OECD nations. In fact, it is these wealthy nations which collude actively in a state of affairs that prevents this already real heterotopia from being achieved in actuality. This heterotopia will come about in the poorer countries only when impediments to its realization are subtracted from the components of an actually existing capitalism.

Class struggle is the pivot of the previous versions of the delinking strategy, and thus of any attempt to bring about a heterotopia for disadvantaged countries. This emancipatory project has as its focal point the reconstitution of an alternative class in the peripheral countries whose heterotopia is, ultimately, the avoidance of the recompradorization of the country in question.[23] Class struggle is thus the ineliminable basis of heterotopia. Only through such struggles, and they are likely to be protracted, can radically new kinds of communal and collective institutions be created. The regnant capitalist regimes of accumulation all presuppose a fundamental division in political and economic decision making between classes with more direct and more immediate access to the levers of such decision making and classes whose level of access is either diminished or even nonexistent (with disparities in income levels pretty much reflecting this ability or inability to secure access to the loci of power and authority). There can be no genuine democracy as long as moneyed elites in nearly every country on the planet are able to tilt their political and economic systems in favor of those able to purchase power and authority.

Many forms of militancy will be needed to counter the Leviathan of global capitalism and to establish this heterotopia as an actuality, but we know in outline what is required if life is to be better for the ordinary citizens of Mali, Honduras, Fiji, India, Indonesia, Mozambique, El Salvador, Haiti, Iraq, Somalia, Yemen, East Timor, Ethiopia, Myanmar, Sierra Leone, Liberia, Bangladesh, Rwanda, and so on. At the same time it has to be acknowledged that there is no ready-made model of democratic socialism that can be trotted out with a proverbial snap of the fingers, and a great deal remains to be done in the way of experimentation and self-interrogation.

Heterotopia versus Utopia . . . Again

But how is this characterization of heterotopia really different from utopia? Is it not positively a utopian state of affairs when countries like Mali and Haiti can hope, realistically, to feed their people by (hopefully) delinking their economies from countries at the economic center, that is, the wealthy nations who belong actively to a system that prevents such LDCs from promoting what would otherwise be an autocentric development? Are we merely splitting terminological hairs by insisting that a sought-after transformation of this kind is "nicely" heterotopian and not "unacceptably" utopian? What really is the difference between these two titles or forms of words for what seems very much like the same mode of emancipation, beyond a kind of semantic shadowboxing?

The utopian, as I pointed out at the beginning of this chapter, is premised on a relatively clear contrast between a drastically flawed situation and its negation that culminates in a perfect or completely transformed condition ("another country") that for its proponents is appropriately to be designated as "utopia." Dialectical negation is thus the basic enabling mechanism for the creation of utopia. By contrast, heterotopia does not rely on dialectical negation for its coming into being; a heterotopia already exists because it had already to be warded off in order for an existing state of affairs to be what it is. To actualize the virtuality that is heterotopia there need not be a recourse to dialectical negation. What is required is something quite different, namely, an operation of a piecemeal, but still conceivably protracted, subtraction, that is, a subtraction of all those linkages to the global market which serve systemically to disadvantage a poor country. This operation is not to be confused or conflated with a shallow reformism capable of being sanctioned by the existing neoliberal order; while many heterotopias can undoubtedly be merely reformist in this sense, the more significant ones aren't. After all, a scenario that enables a Chad or a Yemen to pursue an autocentric development would be truly revolutionary in the current setting, since it would require a wholesale transformation of existing economic knowledge and any policy prescriptions derived from such knowledge. At present countries are marginalized and censured when they give the slightest hint of not conforming to the prevailing neoliberal consensus, as Malaysia was when it decided to regulate capital flows during the Asian economic crisis of 1997–98 in the face of the conventional wisdom trumpeted by the IMF and the U.S. Treasury.[24]

A heterotopia that allowed countries to follow the example set by Malaysia would be a momentous development, but it would not be utopian. One indication that it is not utopian is the fact that heterotopias of the kind envisaged here can be linked to each other to form a more encompassing set, a heterotopia of heterotopias, so to speak. Thus a heterotopia in which countries can pursue economic policies not constrained by the neoliberal consensus could be coupled to a heterotopia which pursued policies of sustainable development or which treated economic refugees and immigrants more justly. In each case it would be up to a particular group of countries and economic agents to form the heterotopia in question, and it is conceivable that a country or transnational institution serving the cause of one heterotopic formation would not be able or willing to facilitate another, adjacent heterotopic formation. In each case, it would take a certain set of political arrangements, buttressed by the appropriate institutions, to adhere to a particular heterotopic formation. Without these, there would be no heterotopia of type X, though this would not in itself preclude the emergence of heterotopia type Y or Z, given other, somewhat different arrangements and institutions.

The centrality of political arrangements and institutions when it comes to constituting heterotopia point to a feature of heterotopia that Foucault tended to overlook in his admittedly brief and sometimes gnomic essay on the subject, namely, that heterotopias come to be actualized only when they are effectively mobilized by agents who act more or less strategically. Thus some actualized heterotopias are the direct and sometimes immediate outcome of large-scale popular mobilizations along the lines of the mass protests that resulted in the overthrow of Ferdinand Marcos, the shah of Iran, and Slobodan Milosevic. Others are actualized when antagonisms which had previously been muted or neutralized are suddenly exacerbated or brought into the open, such as the American civil rights struggles in the 1960s and the struggles for independence in the postwar period in Asia and Africa. Still others come about when certain limits in the formation of a consensus are recognized, and it becomes clear that the existing system can't form a new consensus to deal with an emerging social or political problem. This seems to be the case with the Bush administration's so-called war on terror, with its constant appeals to a "state of exception" that a liberal consensus will probably not be able to accommodate, as civil liberties are increasingly eroded, normal administrative procedures suspended in such areas as immigration and law enforcement, unilateralism overwhelmingly defines foreign policy, and the U.S. government keeps the populace in a constant state of anxiety over "security threats" in order to frighten people into supporting the "firm and resolute" George W. Bush and his administration. Liberalism as an ideology has an incredible elasticity, but it remains to be seen if it can be stretched to include the so-called war on terror and its palpable manipulation by the post-9/11 American national security state. Here is an opportunity for the actualization of heterotopia if the liberal consensus fails, though this opportunity could also lead to something much worse, as xenophobic and authoritarian proclivities are given more room to manifest themselves by this American national security state.

Such concerns notwithstanding, there is still a fundamental difference between a conceivable utopia and the heterotopia that can potentially be actualized in the current conjuncture. Utopia is a "better country" no doubt, but it is much easier to conceptualize this better country than to identify the complexities of the systems that have to be modified or replaced if the project of liberation is to be brought to fruition. The notion of a reverse causation allows the proponent of heterotopia to focus on the precise mechanisms that have to be put in place if heterotopia is to be actuated. There is a world, real but not yet actual, in which there is no George W. Bush presidency (or rather, in which there would be no possibility of making him president again in 2004),[25] no American national security state, no specious "war on terror," no illegal preemptive wars. In this respect the issue where heterotopia is concerned has overwhelmingly to do with the realization of a quite specific political project, one whose lineaments are contingent upon the historically and politically determinate circumstances that prevail at this time and place.

This political project will pivot on countering the powerful pressures exerted by a certain state of capitalism and will respond to the requirements of this singular conjuncture by seeking to orchestrate the forces needed to actuate the countervailing powers associated with heterotopia. The principle behind this orchestration is class struggle, to the extent that the ruling powers forestalling the actuation of heterotopia operate on the need to maintain existing economic and social inequalities and a globally polarized development, and in so doing creating a worldwide class of the dispossessed and disadvantaged. (It is important to stress that this class is not to be confined to the industrial proletariat.) The greatest challenge for the proponents of heterotopia is the mobilization of this international class. Those most dispossessed have the greatest stake in doing away with the murderous and brutal powers that rule over us, but it has also to be acknowledged that extreme privation often cheats people of the very resources required for reaching even the threshold of political mobilization.

This points to a political project inaugurated primarily in the countries of the South, whose masses often experience levels of insecurity unthinkable to those who make speeches about national security in the United States and Britain. What can be done in the West and North? Here there is an interesting contrast between the countries of old Europe and the United States. A great deal can be done, and needs to be done, in the United States and elsewhere. To mention a single example: until very recently in the United States it was considered unpatriotic to criticize George W. Bush in public without mincing one's words. Who would say without mincing words in an editorial in the *New York Times* or the *Washington Post*, let alone the *Wall Street Journal*, that in truth George W. Bush is a child of privilege, an intellectual mediocrity with a sketchy record in the Texas Air National Guard during the Vietnam War and a failed business career afterward, who for nearly eight years postured as the "top gun" enforcer of the global order? People would fall down laughing if it were suggested to them in Britain, Australia, France, Spain,

Germany, and Italy that it was unpatriotic to criticize Tony Blair, Gordon Brown, John Howard, Jacques Chirac, Nicolas Sarkozy, José-Maria Aznar, Gerhard Schroeder, or Silvio Berlusconi. Many American heterotopias exist, some only potentially, of course, but one of them certainly involves the cessation of such mindless patriotic blathering. In America, to deride a George W. Bush (at the start of his presidency as opposed to its sunset, when the proverbial rats were starting to flee the sinking ship) in the way that the lecherous Berlusconi has always been mocked in Italy—that could have been an American heterotopia (with no Italian equivalent, of course).[26]

Heterotopia is inextricably bound up with the creation of a range of truth-effects that usher into the realm of actuality what is already real, albeit as a virtuality. There are many enabling conditions for the crossing of this threshold between the virtual and the actual, but one of the primary conditions for this movement is a desire, organized with sufficient force and coherence, for the making of this transition. Using the notion of an incompossibility invoked earlier, we can say that the world desired by proponents of the project of liberation—a heterotopia, or maybe even a heterotopia of heterotopias—is one that is incompossible with regard to the (now) actual world, since the actual world is the world in which vast numbers of human beings go hungry and lack most of life's basic necessities while having absolutely no recourse to a just solution for these problems. To desire this heterotopia is perforce to desire all that conduces to the supplanting of this now actual world; it is to desire to remove all the conditions that sustain this actual world and serve in the end only to ensure that the heterotopian world is kept at bay. To want heterotopia is to want a certain kind of causality with regard to the world. (As an aside, we may note that perhaps it was Spinoza who first systematized this insight.) It is this axiom, more than any other, that separates the notion of heterotopia from most kinds of utopia. If I could summarize all this in my own pidgin English, I'd say "Heterotopia good; utopia not totally bad, but not as good as heterotopia." Paradoxically, this probably captures the same insight expressed in what Slavoj Žižek has called (mistakenly) one of the great Bushisms. To quote former vice president Dan Quayle (whose saying it really was), "The future will be better tomorrow."

CHAPTER 12

Prospects for the New Political Subject and Liberation

In this chapter I focus on the question of the steps that need to be taken if a policy of delinking on the part of the countries of the South is to be implemented. I also deal with the question of the new forms of subjectivity that conceivably will have to be devised if this policy of delinking, and its supervening project of liberation, are going to stand a chance of being achieved. The proposals I advance here will be somewhat schematic, but I hope that the previous chapters have identified the theoretical grounds for the claims set out in this final chapter.

Using Michael Mann's well-known typology for classifying the primary forms or modes of power, namely, the economic, political, military, and ideological, the rest of this chapter considers the desiderata or requirements for a project of liberation with a decided emphasis on the needs of the citizens of the world's poor countries.

Where *economic* power is concerned, I have argued that the countries of the South have little alternative but to espouse a finely calibrated delinking strategy if their economic situation is not to become even more parlous than it is today. With regard to such a delinking strategy, the LDCs will do no economic harm to themselves if they conduct a fundamental but judicious reassessment of their economic linkages with the advanced industrial nations and the international economic institutions (such as the World Bank, IMF, and WTO) that in the main operate at the behest of the wealthy countries. Each linkage should be scrutinized, and if it is seen to be disadvantageous to the poor country in question, it should be dispensed with. The corollary is that the linkages which confer advantages on the less wealthy country are to be retained. This policy of a judicious and piecemeal assessment of what works in a poor country's economic interests is not to be confused with the wholesale autarky practiced by Albania during the regime of Enver Hoxha (1908–85), a confusion that is seldom avoided by those who criticize Samir Amin and other advocates of delinking for wanting a "pie in the sky" economic isolation in an age of global integration. The rationale for such a strategy is obvious and completely rational: If something costs your people more than it benefits them, and if there is little or no prospect that these costs will be ameliorated, why continue to make your people suffer in order to pay, and continue to pay, for it?

As Dani Rodrik points out, countries that buck conventional economic wisdom (such as the Washington consensus) on such measures as restrictions on the movement of capital face an immediate howl of protest from those who subscribe to this wisdom, but once that economy does well despite its repudiation of the supposed wisdom, capital quickly flows back to it. Capitalists are very scrupulous about making money, but they are often not scrupulous when scruples get seriously in the way of making money. The example cited by Rodrik is Malaysia, which was heavily criticized for going against the advice of the international financial institutions by imposing capital controls when the East Asian financial crisis started to spread across the region from Thailand in 1997, but which had no problem attracting back this international capital when it became clear that Malaysia had weathered the crisis better than its neighbors who had fallen in line with what economic orthodoxy had enjoined. The options here therefore amount to the proverbial no-brainer: fall in line with the orthodoxy enjoined by the Washington consensus and crash, and foreign capital will flee the shores of your country, or try something different (to wit, capital controls), and if you succeed the foreign money will soon come back, and if these capital control measures do not succeed, the money had in any case already fled your markets through the now well-known "contagion effect." Poor countries, according to Rodrik, should therefore have no qualms about imposing restrictions on capital movements if this will secure them against destabilizing flows of capital.[1]

The United States may be the sole superpower left, but it does not follow from this that the world is also becoming less complex from a geopolitical standpoint. Far from it, this American primacy is perfectly compatible with an increased complexity in the socioeconomic and political domains, and America's superiority in military power does not necessarily translate into lasting configurations of economic, ideological, and political power.[2]

Especially important for the poor countries has to be an industrialization of agriculture, though this has to be an industrialization conducted not in terms of the requirements of the export-based agribusiness promoted by the advanced industrial countries as an economic panacea, but one subserving the economic needs of the LDCs themselves. This industrialization of agriculture, if undertaken properly, will allow the LDCs to move beyond subsistence agriculture, and with these agricultural surpluses, industrialization can begin to occur. The members of these societies can then move beyond finding ways of feeding themselves at a subsistence level and seek ways of producing industrial surpluses to benefit their own people, and not necessarily for export to the high-income countries.

Where *military* power is concerned, a major curtailment of America's military power will help not only its poorer citizens (though there can certainly be no guarantee here, given the vagaries of the American electoral system), but will also aid any area of the world that can potentially benefit from a world system that allows power to be dispersed in a more ramified way. The swiftest way of accomplishing this objective is to do away with the U.S. dollar as the world's reserve currency (or at any rate to have another currency, such as the euro, serve as a competitor alternative to the U.S. dollar). Some would argue that there are other sound economic reasons for retaining the U.S. dollar as the world's primary reserve currency, and that these reasons are sufficient to outweigh any perceived need to diminish American military power by reducing America's capacity to finance its wars by using the dollar's supremacy to borrow easily from external sources. It is widely accepted that the United States basically subsidizes its military by having other countries hold their reserves in U.S. Treasury bills; once they can hold these reserves in euros or the yen or yuan (in whatever combination), the United States will not be able to finance its military expenditures by the simple expedient of manipulating interest rates. The UN report *World Economic Situation and Prospects 2006* is well aware of the perilous situation that lies ahead once other countries start to diversify their reserve holdings:

> Despite low interest rates worldwide and ample liquidity in global financial markets [this was before the 2008 bank liquidity crisis], there are strong reasons to be concerned about the sustainability of the global imbalances. The current account deficit of the United States continues to increase at a rapid pace. The concomitant rise in the United States net foreign liability position could eventually erode the willingness of foreign investors to buy dollar-denominated assets. This could lead to a precipitous fall in the value of the

United States dollar and an abrupt and disorderly adjustment of the global imbalances.[3]

The rest of the world should hold the United States accountable for the military impact of its geopolitical decisions by making any willingness to buy dollarized assets contingent on U.S. compliance with international environmental treaties, international judicial accords and weapons conventions, and the basic tenets of international law regarding the use of torture in the interrogation of those labeled "terrorists" who are currently detained without due process. The rationale for this step is not to create global economic chaos, but to show, in a principled and considered way, that the willingness of the rest of the world to buy dollarized assets will from now on depend on the readiness of the United States and its allies to act in accord with the principles of international law (as opposed to paying mere lip service to international law).[4]

This makes sense for those wanting a world heedful of the needs of its poorest and most beleaguered citizens, not only from the point of view of political strategy, but also economically, since most of the rest of the world is in danger of getting a raw deal every time the United States manipulates its interest rates to subsidize its current account deficits (and its military expenditures), and more generally its levels of domestic consumption.

More important, however, the ability of the United States to use its weaponry to pummel an enemy into fairly prompt submission does not translate into a similar ability to negotiate the many gradations between military force and political capability. As the occupations of Iraq and Afghanistan have revealed, the sheer exercise of American military power does not in and of itself culminate in a "mission accomplished." The capacity to deal with insurrections and insurgencies, to police rather than to bombard, to bring about local political transitions, to set up protocols that facilitate the transition from conquest to reconstruction, all of these require the deployment of a political power whose subtlety vastly exceeds the compass of brute "shock and awe" military force.[5]

Politically, and this is the complement of its indisputable military supremacy, the United States has the advantage of being able to set or influence in decisive ways the rules by which the international system functions. This capacity is reflected in a propensity toward unilateralism, as opposed to seeking multilateral accords, when dealing with contentious international issues. The unwillingness to accommodate the countries of the United Nations (except in situations where this suits the immediate and obvious convenience of the United States) and the scorn heaped by the Bush administration on treaties regarding environmental protection, weapons limitations, and the jurisdiction of international courts signify a profound aversion on the part of the United States to act in concert with other nations except when this is to its immediate convenience or advantage. The poor people of the world could benefit immeasurably from a geopolitical system with several nuclei, so that no one nucleus of power could assert its unqualified ascendancy over the others. But how is the American imperial juggernaut to be slowed down? No matter how little one sympathizes with the motivations and aspirations of some of its associated ideological movements, Michael Mann is right to say that to this point the only concerted opposition to American imperial ambitions has come from the Muslim world, which, in addition to the self-inflicted wounds afflicting many of its polities, is having to bear the traumatic burden of opposing the first empire of the twenty-first century, while the Tony Blairs, John Howards, Silvio Berlusconis, and Nicolas Sarkozys of this world comport themselves as supplicants on bended knees, and its Gordon Browns and Vladimir Putins duck and weave their way around the proverbial eight-hundred-pound gorilla so as not to be pummeled by it into immediate and abject submission.[6]

The fundamental point to be grasped here is that the United States and its cronies (and their proconsular auxiliaries such as the IMF and World Bank) have no right whatsoever to determine the future of Iraq or sub-Saharan Africa, or indeed any other part of the world. This nonnegotiable principle has to be enshrined in any framework for a more just and equitable, and thus truly alternative political order for the poor countries of the world. This alternative political order can begin to take shape only if these poor countries are able to carve out a space of refusal for themselves, where their destinies will no longer be governed by diktats derived from neoliberalism, with its blind attachment to market fundamentalism, and from American neoconservatism, with its self-serving American exceptionalism and bellicosity.[7] Only in such a radically different space where a "high-intensity democracy" is likely to flourish can the LDCs reclaim their own development and improve the lives of their ordinary citizens.

The interesting question here, of course, is the connection between the LDCs' need for a "thicker" democracy and the scarcely deniable absence of such a democracy in the United States and the United Kingdom. There will come a time when the LDCs may see that having a democracy that is more substantial than the attenuated, because merely "representational," democracy espoused by the richer countries of the North and West is somehow inextricably connected with the movement to a high-intensity democracy in the North and West itself. In other words, there has to be a movement toward a fuller version of democracy in the rich countries as a concomitant to the sought-after transformations in the (poor) countries of the South and East. Wherever it needs to happen, real democracy must always begin at home.

The fundamental shift that has to take place involves a supersession of the prevalent "thin" forms of democracy. (What *really* happens to American democracy when one has the good or ill fortune to be represented by crooks like Tom DeLay, Ted Stevens, or Randy "Duke" Cunningham; or by skilled, or somewhat less skilled, opportunists like Newt Gingrich, John Edwards, Arnold Schwarzenegger, John McCain, Joe Lieberman, and Bill and Hillary Clinton; or by the senescent Strom Thurmond, who left the U.S. Senate at the age of one hundred in 2003, by which time he was clearly unable to distinguish the U.S. Capitol from the Parthenon; or by Elizabeth Dole and the late Jesse Helms, or indeed a huckster like the former Texas senator Phil Gramm; as well as by countless mediocrities, though the list would almost certainly have to begin with George W. Bush, Dan Quayle, and Sarah Palin?) The only alternative to this constricted and thin-boned version of democracy, with its built-in propensity for sound-bite sloganeering by political hacks or demagogues prepared to say whatever it takes to gain office, and even for the stealing of elections, as happened in Florida in 2000, is a democracy that requires an inherently greater degree of participation on the part of those who are effectively disenfranchised by the existing "low-intensity" democracies.[8]

But the poor countries cannot wait for their wealthy counterparts to become more democratic before they themselves espouse a thicker version of democracy; the economies of Burkina Faso and East Timor simply cannot afford to wait while Americans debate the merits of Sarah Palin as a 2012 presidential candidate. The delinking strategy advocated in this book is designed to allow the poor countries the opportunity to create this alternative space of refusal by themselves and on their own terms, initially by creating conditions which enable the LDCs at least to begin to establish their own circuits of accumulation. This process has to be accompanied by a state construction geared to providing administrative and other resources essential for the well-being of all citizens and not just the ruling elite and its partners. The current form of imperialism is, in Mann's apt phrase, an "ostracizing imperialism," inasmuch as the structure of exploitation enjoined by this imperialism is highly selective; many countries are excluded from the global economic system simply because they do not meet the minimum conditions for exploitation, so that a Macau or a Tunisia qualify for "investment" (the euphemism for exploitation, given the fact that profits from such investment will almost certainly be repatriated), but a Mali or a Haiti do not.[9]

These economically disenfranchised countries desperately need to have access to their own regime of accumulation since their current situation leaves them completely excluded from any kind of productive accumulation and production. (Admittedly, the Macaus and Tunisias are inserted in a capitalist regime of accumulation, but in so doing have to sacrifice their people to the demands of this unrelenting capitalist accumulation process, and so they too have a dire need for an alternative regime of accumulation favoring a globalized economic democracy.) More will be said later about the conception of participatory democracy favored by the argument being advanced here.

Ideologically, the LDCs will have to find ways of enhancing their ideological resources since these are now tilted very much in the directions favored by the United States and its allies. The American message of "individual freedom, material abundance, and democracy" may still resonate in many parts of the world, but its appeal has been declining, and precipitously so in the Muslim world. America's peremptory instructions for a "global governance" matching the stark unilateralism it has espoused since September 11 has caused it to be viewed with greatly increased suspicion in many parts of the world. The core of this unilateralism is the doctrine of a "permeable sovereignty," which allows the United States and its partners to intervene with a missionary zeal (by invoking the ideals of "human rights" and "democracy") in the state structures of other countries, precisely in order to align, or realign, these structures so that they are in harmony with American self-interest.[10]

This American ideology is certainly being contested, and the primary impetus for this contestation is provided by nationalism, and Muslim nationalism in particular. The insistence on an inviolable sovereignty that lies at the core of any nationalism is clearly reflected in the attempts of the Muslim nationalisms to posit themselves as a "countersovereignty" to America's global hegemony. Not that these countersovereignties necessarily involve a viable state formation, since the American occupations have transformed Iraq and Afghanistan into failed states and the long-suffering Palestinians constitute a nation that is yet to become a state.[11]

The poor countries, who urgently need something richer and more substantial than the American version of individual freedom, (thin) democracy, and material abundance (based as it is on the need to maintain concerted and systemic inequalities that cannot be reconciled with the requirements of justice), even if only to provide their citizens with basic necessities, clearly have to enhance their state capacities so that these can further the creation of an alternative, fairer and more democratic global order. The nation-state is not going to be abolished by globalization, though its functions, and the arrays of strategies associated with these functions, have undoubtedly changed and will continue to be transformed in the years to come. Only by creating this more equitable and democratic political order, with its active and well-informed citizens and progressive domestic social movements, will it be possible to show, in concrete terms, the colossal mistake involved in conflating this hoped-for equitable and democratic order with what is deemed desirable, or indeed simply "unavoidable," by the bared fangs of American militarism countersigned by its governing elite, the Bush administration's prating about "freedom" and "democracy" notwithstanding.[12]

This enhancement of LDC state capacities is premised on a revived and revolutionized nationalism which eschews the calamitous ethnically and religiously based nationalisms that have prevailed up to now. Leaving behind these flawed nationalisms that have been in place since the eighteenth century and pressing forward to launch this new civic nationalism will pose stiff challenges for the LDCs, especially since the distractions afforded by demagogic appeals to religious and ethnic differences are a constant temptation for governing elites faced by citizens desperate for the simple necessities that make life tolerable.[13] We long for a universalism that will take us beyond the vicious particularities of the endlessly contending nationalisms, but the only universalism we have today is the one provided by capitalism. There may be a productive and harmonious universal that lies on the other side of capitalism, but for now the only large-scale formation able to disrupt the tidal wave of global capitalism is the political nationality of the nation-state, and the urgent project confronting us is to construct this political nationality along the lines of a civic nationalism. The current capitalist regime of accumulation consigns entire nations and regions (and I am not referring here only to the poorest economies of the South) and social groups and communities (the rust belt, unproductive smokestack industries, uncompetitive hill farms, low-skill sectors, etc.) to an economically sterile redundancy. To achieve a less inequitable world, social arrangements will have to emphasize the well-being of entire societies; this will almost certainly require relating production and consumption, despite all the obstacles and complexities, to more general and more extended interests than is currently permitted by existing capitalist arrangements.

This civic and secular nationalism will in turn have to employ an important distinction, made by Samir Amin, between the state apparatus and the nation. The overwhelming tendency has been for a country's state apparatus to be appropriated by its ruling elite or national bourgeoisie. In the case of the LDCs this has invariably led to a recompradorization, since the national bourgeoisie has always favored alliances with international capital as long as these alliances have left the state apparatus in their hands. The construction of a project of national liberation, however, involves not only delinking along the lines outlined in the previous chapters (and this in order to avert recompradorization), but also the formation of a popular national alliance among the people.[14] The construction of a broad national popular alliance, functioning independently of the state system, will provide the impetus for the adoption of a different kind of allocation strategy, one premised on a selective delinking involving several policy elements intended to reverse the processes of recompradorization that have so far afflicted the LDCs. "Financial openness" along the lines specified in the Washington consensus that governs the thinking of the IMF, World Bank, WTO, and OECD has been shown to be of no benefit to the LDCs; to the contrary, financial openness has tended to favor the forces of recompradorization and the accompanying economic clientalism at the hands of the U.S.-led equity-based accumulation regime now dominating, but also troubling, the global economic system.

To forestall this dismal outcome a slate of policy initiatives favoring autocentric development for the LDCs must be espoused, including controls on capital movements, debt forgiveness, investment strategies designed to make the poorer LDCs less dependent on the production of primary commodities, the formation of regional blocs and alliances to pool resources and consolidate economic gains, and the taking of political steps that will ultimately result in the abolition of the IMF and the World Bank. All these policies will undoubtedly find immediate disfavor with Wall Street and the other stock markets of the world (though for the foreseeable future these entities will be fully occupied with their self-inflicted financial messes). But the obvious truth bears repeating: stock markets don't give a fig about improving the lives of the world's poor people.

A fundamental ingredient in the implementation of this autocentric growth regime will be the social and political mobilization of the appropriate classes and class fractions in the LDC in question. This mobilization will be undertaken with a view to transforming the state apparatus, especially in view of the fact that the state is the institutional assemblage that has ultimate control of the regime of accumulation and that there can indeed be no properly constituted regime of accumulation without the intervention of the state.

The goal of a "destatized" collective national liberation project is not an end in itself, since accomplishing this is intended to lead to a reconstitution of the state itself (as opposed to the abolition of the state, this being the fantasy of some antiglobalization movements). The current philosophy imposed by the Washington consensus requires making the reform and reconstitution of the state the primary focus of any economic and political reorganization in the LDCs, in the hope that this will lead to efficient economic development, alleged protection of the rights of the individual, and the upholding of democracy (alas, very low intensity democracy is what such reformers invariably have in mind).[15] The difficulty with this proposition is that it ignores the fact that in many LDCs the apparatuses of the state are much more likely to be commandeered by a small elite, and that in the current phase of capitalist development such elites (or oligarchies, as they are in many cases) perceive their economic interests to coincide with the imperatives of the Washington consensus. Without a radical transformation of the state project itself, therefore, it will not be possible for progressive social and political forces to create apparatuses (within the LDC in question) capable of functioning as plausible alternatives to existing forms of the capitalist state. This is an especially important consideration since the prevailing social and political forces are already likely to be subordinated to the interests of that LDC's elite, as well as to the overarching requirements of the Washington consensus itself.

There are no pregiven laws to shape or necessitate this outcome; only struggle, and failures always accompany successes in struggles, can do this. The only alternative is acceptance of the current finance-led, equity-based accumulation regime (neoliberalism), with its imperial American underpinning (neoconservatism). Worldwide economic polarization has been the only resultant of the primacy of this accumulation regime and its predecessors. For the poor people of the world this is hardly a satisfactory alternative.

Conclusion

At the time of writing this conclusion (April 2009), it is clear that capitalism is going through a phase involving major but not yet fully understood transformations associated with the current global liquidity crisis. In responding to this crisis, most of the economically advanced countries have at least nationalized a part of their major financial institutions, thereby controverting an essential tenet of the neoliberal orthodoxy that has prevailed since the collapse in the 1970s of the post–Second World War, Keynesian-New Deal capital-labor compact. It is too early to proclaim the demise of this neoliberal orthodoxy; it may have buried itself, or it may somehow find the wherewithal to achieve the economic equivalent of a fraught cardiac resuscitation. But for many informed observers, financialized globalization has reached a point of collapse from which there may not be a return to what is labeled "economic normality" in the business pages of the American daily newspapers. Unless "economic normality" is understood merely in terms of a restoration of CEO compensation to something like previous levels. There are clear signs that President Obama's "financial rescue package" is being milked for the purpose of this restoration. But, as I have said repeatedly in this book, the world's poor cannot wait for this American-led equity-based economic system to revive itself.

If a better world for the masses of human beings now trapped in conditions of crushing poverty is to be brought about—this of course being the basic goal of the project of liberation elaborated in these chapters—it is crucial that we ask whether liberal-democratic capitalism has within itself the resources needed to bring about this better world. If it does not, and capitalism has been given countless chances by its apologists (with the accompanying excuses and exculpations when the so far inevitable failures ensue), then the question has to arise whether this better world will begin to appear only when a range of decisive postcapitalist transformations needed to realize this better world can take place. If it is determined that these radical transformations are needed and that it is beyond the capacity of liberal-democratic capitalism to revive itself, then the question of a supersession of capitalism becomes urgent and perhaps even necessary. Very few today believe that a restoration of American prosperity is going to improve the lives of the abjectly poor in the United States and elsewhere. I argue that a historical and political point has been reached where there is now no alternative to this project of seeking a supersession of the capitalist order. Of course, there is no guarantee that this supersession can in fact be accomplished, just as there is no assurance that what may come after capitalism will be any better. But there is now virtually incontrovertible evidence that this capitalist system has failed most of the world. Something different can and needs to be tried, or the plight of the poor will in all likelihood become even more desperate. If the arguments advanced in this book have a measure of plausibility, then there is little alternative but for us to try to find, however hesitatingly, this different, and postcapitalist, way. But, as I have said at many points in the argument formulated here, there are no necessary laws which preordain this postcapitalist state of affairs. All routes to this better life for the world's poor people are going to be the object of struggle, protracted struggle, involving forms of social and political experimentation which may not always succeed.

In some parts of the world this struggle is already under way. For most of us in the wealthy countries, the question is whether we turn our back on this struggle or find even the smallest of small ways to register, in theory and practice, the fraught but powerful aspirations of the protagonists of this struggle. To be on the side of the seemingly chimerical hopes that the hopeless somehow find a way of holding fast to, or aligning ourselves with an economic system that repudiates these very hopes as a basic condition of its viability, this is the existential and systemic choice confronting those living in the wealthy countries (even as it can be acknowledged that the desperately poor also dwell in the very midst of the wealthy countries and are not confined to the countries of the Third and Fourth Worlds; after all, exploitation is everywhere, and so inevitably the exploited are also everywhere).

An increase in GNP does not abolish or ameliorate poverty; as we know all too well from the case of the United States and Britain, poverty is caused by the same mechanisms which create wealth for others. As much as the proponents of capitalism baulk at this "socialist" conclusion, given the capitalist character of these mechanisms, to be in favor of wealth creation is willy-nilly to be in favor of poverty creation. In capitalism these go hand in hand, though the "cunning of reason" peculiar to capitalism has so far been able to convince enough people that it is somehow a matter of pure accident when poverty accompanies capitalist wealth creation. I have argued for an alternative rationality whose core is the amelioration of global poverty, and thus for the supersession of the system of economic disenfranchisement and exploitation which has prevailed up to now.

NOTES

Introduction

1 There are as yet few detailed analyses of the crisis of 2008. However, I have found useful Wade, "Financial Regime Change?" Wade claims that the neoliberal paradigm which has prevailed since the 1970s has now received its quietus. Given what has transpired so far in the global economy in 2008 and 2009, it is difficult to disagree.

2 On this so-called Golden Age, see Glyn et al., "The Rise and Fall of the Golden Age," 39–125.

3 The grip of this "free market" ideology during the time of Reagan and Thatcher is displayed in the following passage from a column by the London *Guardian* journalist Peter Wilby: "In the mid-90s . . . I discussed with a senior New Labour adviser how a Blair government might change the country. The Thatcher governments had succeeded in doing so, we agreed, because so many policy proposals could be tested against a simple question: 'How does this create a market?' Civil servants, ministers, advisers and thinktanks all came to understand that if their ideas didn't create or enhance markets they were probably wasting their time." See Wilby, "Forget Raw Fish and Berries, It's Equality That Saves Lives," *The Guardian*, 28 October 2005.

4 See Mazier, Baslé, and Vidal, *When Economic Crises Endure*, xxii. The merger between neoliberalism and Keynesianism associated with OECD policies is also a key element of the "Third Way" espoused by Britain's New Labour government and Gerhard Schroeder's Social Democratic administration in Germany, as well as the succeeding Christian Democrat administration led by Germany's current chancellor, Angela Merkel.

5 On the blurring of the line between left and right, see Moschonas, *In the Name of Social Democracy*, xiii.

6 For commentary and analysis of the economic dimensions of the policies of Clinton and Blair, and their fundamental continuity with those of Reagan and

Thatcher, see Pollin, *Contours of Descent;* R. Brenner, *The Boom and the Bubble;* Baker, *The Conservative Nanny State* and *The United States Since 1980;* Duménil and Lévy, *Crise et sortie de crise.* See also Duménil and Lévy, "Costs and Benefits of Neoliberalism."

7 For a stinging critique of this ideology of human rights, see Badiou, *Ethics: An Understanding of Evil;* Žižek, "Against Human Rights." See also C. Foley, *The Thin Blue Line.*

8 On the current manifestation of the society of the spectacle, see Nairn, "At the G8."

9 See United Nations, *The Inequality Predicament: Report on the World Social Situation 2005:* "The global commitment to overcoming inequality, or redressing the imbalance between the wealthy and the poor, as clearly outlined at the 1995 World Summit for Social Development in Copenhagen and endorsed in the United Nations Millennium Declaration, is fading" (1). The *Report* goes on to say, "Eighty per cent of the world's gross domestic product belongs to the 1 billion people living in the developed world; the remaining 20 per cent is shared by the 5 billion people living in developing countries. Failure to address this inequality predicament will ensure that social justice and better living conditions for all people remain elusive, and that communities, countries and regions remain vulnerable to social, political and economic upheaval" (1). It is a central thesis of this book that the predicament of the world's dispossessed has to lie at the heart of any purported theory of liberation. Hopefully liberation will confront the likes of Rupert Murdoch, Donald Trump, T. Boone Pickens, Bernard Madoff, the Walton family, and others with the inevitability of a decisive transformation, but whatever happens, this hoped-for transformation for Murdoch, Trump, Pickens, Madoff, the Waltons, and their ilk will be qualitatively different from the changes that will matter for those living on less than one dollar a day. The comprehensive account of this global inequality is to be found in Milanovic, *Worlds Apart*, which shows that it is not only inequality between countries that has increased in the past two decades, but also inequality *within* countries. See also the country studies in Therborn, *Inequalities of the World.*

10 See Baker and Weisbrot, *Social Security;* BBC News, "Call for Sell-off of Royal Mail," at http://news.bbc.co.uk, accessed 14 May 2008. A wealth of available evidence discredits such calls for privatizations. A detailed analysis of the privatizations undertaken by the governments of Margaret Thatcher and John Major shows that they had virtually no impact in the longer term on British prices and overall productivity, while contributing to the widening of income gaps. For this analysis, see Florio, *The Great Divesture.*

11 Bacevich, *The Limits of Power*, provides a sober critique of this American exceptionalism.

12 Jacques Derrida is absolutely right to refer to the symbolism associated with 9/11 as the outcome of a "media-theatricalization." See his *Rogues*, xiii.

13 For a lucid overview of this transition from the Middle Ages to early Moder-

nity, see the summary article by Haakonssen, "Divine/Natural Law Theories in Ethics." See also the decisive account given in Macpherson, *The Political Theory of Possessive Individualism*, as well as Jonathan Israel's vastly erudite but also somewhat problematic two volumes, *Radical Enlightenment* and *Enlightenment Contested*.

14 Hume, "On the First Principles of Government," 16.

15 For useful discussion, see Hawthorn, *Enlightenment and Despair*, 23–29.

16 See Kant, *The Metaphysics of Morals*, 161–64. There is an ambiguity in Kant's definition of the will. On the one hand, as *Wille*, the will functions as a legislative faculty whose autonomy is the condition for issuing maxims in accord with a universal law; on the other, as *Willkür*, it is an executive faculty whose spontaneity or freedom is the condition of its adopting the autonomous decrees issued by *Wille*. For a useful untangling of this ambiguity, see Beck, "Kant's Two Conceptions of the Will," 38–49.

17 On the relation of Hobbes to the mechanist physical science of his time, see the fascinating account given in Shapin and Schaffer, *Leviathan and the Air-Pump*. For a more general overview, see Funkenstein, *Theology and the Scientific Imagination*. Hume's friend Adam Smith needs to be included in any detailed survey of the Zeitgeist of eighteenth-century mercantile capitalism. Jerrold Siegel rightly views Smith as the author of modern individualist "self-fashioning"; see *The Idea of the Self*, 139–67. On Adam Smith, see also Rothschild, *Economic Sentiments*.

18 There is a vast literature on this epochal transformation, and I have found especially useful Thom, *Republics, Nations, and Tribes*; A. D. Smith, *The Ethnic Origins of Nations* and *Chosen Peoples*; A. W. Marx, *Faith in Nation*; Löwy and Sayre, *Révolte et mélancolie*.

19 See Thom, *Republics, Nations, and Tribes*, 93, quoting in his own translation Anne-Louise-Germaine de Staël, *Des Circonstances actuelles qui peuvent terminer la Révolution et des principes qui doivent fonder la République en France*, 111–12.

20 The historical background to this period, and to its predecessors, is covered in Hobsbawm's superb trilogy *The Age of Revolution, 1789–1848*, *The Age of Capital: 1848–1875*, and *The Age of Empire: 1875–1914*. The era that follows is covered in Hobsbawm, *The Age of Extremes: A History of the World, 1914–91*. See also Bayly, *The Birth of the Modern World*.

21 For illuminating cross-country studies of the situation of Social Democratic parties since the 1980s, see Glyn, *Social Democracy in Neoliberal Times*.

22 Perhaps the only consolation to be derived from this dismal state of affairs is that it has inspired some of the most invigorating political polemics in decades. For the United States, see, for instance, Lazare, *The Velvet Coup;* T. Frank, *What's the Matter with Kansas?* For Britain, see Nairn, *Pariah* and *After Britain*. For France and Nicolas Sarkozy, see Badiou, *De quoi Sarkozy est-il le nom?* On market fundamentalism more generally, see Altvater, *The Future of the Market*. Leys, *Market-Driven Politics;* Glyn, *Capitalism Unleashed*.

23 McKibbin, "What Works Doesn't Work," 21. McKibbin invokes here the ideas of Robert Michels, who in *Ur Soziologie des Parteiwesens in der modernen Demokratie: Untersuchungen über die oligarchischen Tendenzen des Gruppenlebens*, published in 1911, argued that because of the need in modern industrial societies for rapid and complex decision making, political parties are increasingly managed by cadres of professional "experts" who, with power in their hands, would inexorably constitute themselves as an antidemocratic oligarchy.

24 On "low-intensity democracy," see Gills, Rocamora, and Wilson, "Low Intensity Democracy," 3–34. Significant here too is Jacques Rancière's notion of a "hatred for democracy," whereby supposedly liberal-democratic governments can get away with the mere profession of the trappings of democracy (while at the same time suspending *habeas corpus*, phone-tapping their citizens without legal oversight, making arbitrary arrests and deportations, etc.), as long as they find ways to convince their electorates that we as "democratic citizens" are somehow in the fortunate situation of living in a political order very different from those who are cruelly oppressed by the rulers of "evil" totalitarian regimes such as the ones in Cuba, Sudan, Iran, North Korea, Syria, or Venezuela. See Rancière, *Hatred of Democracy*.

25 McKibbin, "What Works Doesn't Work," 20.

26 The definitive work on "authoritarian populism" remains Stuart Hall's *The Hard Road to Renewal*. See also the essays by Hall, Critcher, Jefferson, Clark, and Robert in their *Policing the Crisis*. On political hypocrisy, see the historically researched and politically barbed volumes by David Runciman, *The Politics of Good Intentions* and *Political Hypocrisy*.

27 For some this claim about the decline of communal solidarity may resonate with the thesis advanced by Robert Putnam in his much publicized *Bowling Alone*. As critics have pointed out, Putnam's thesis is based on problematic conceptions of social capital and civic community. My argument is based instead on the documented segregative effects of significant and actual income disparity: rich and poor people don't live in the same neighborhoods, don't go to the same shops, don't have the same leisure activities, don't eat the same food, don't listen to the same music, don't go to the same schools, don't dress in the same way, don't go to the same places for their vacations (if indeed the poor can afford a vacation). The work of the late Pierre Bourdieu is pivotal on this issue of the fundamental spatial separation between those who are wealthy and those who are not. See, for instance, *Distinction*. For a more summary treatment, see Bourdieu's "The Aristocracy of Culture." Moreover, there is ample and consistent documentation correlating income levels and levels of political participation. See, for instance, U.S. Census Bureau, *Voter Turnout in 2006*: "The voting rate of citizens living in families with annual incomes of less than $20,000 (31 percent) was lower than those living in families with incomes of $50,000 or more (59 percent)."

28 The reference to "feeling" here has a theoretical import derived from Raymond Williams's well-known notion of a "structure of feeling." An example from popular culture may be apposite. When Mrs. Thatcher came to power and consolidated her grip on the British polity in 1979, the focal point of an initial popular cultural opposition to the Thatcherite *Gleichschaltuung* was lodged almost entirely in the punk rock movement. One thinks here of the Clash, Elvis Colstello, Sham 69, and Joy Division. Joy Division's album *Unknown Pleasures* represented an iconic repudiation, at the subliminal level, of anything that Mrs. Thatcher could ever have brought herself to avow as "pleasurable." The key theoretical text here is Jacques Attali, *Noise*, where it is argued that musical codes allow expressive possibilities that are in advance of what the regnant social codes are able to offer. As Attali put it, "What is noise to the old order is harmony to the new" (35). Interestingly, after the suicide of its lead singer, Ian Curtis, Joy Division became New Order.

29 Quoted in Dai Smith, *Raymond Williams*, 473. On the "long" revolution, see R. Williams, *The Long Revolution*. Some may argue that this tripartite division of the book's argument—(1) political economy I (the current system) → (2) subjectivity and the political → (3) political economy II (liberation)—is conceptually untidy. I have resisted the temptation to put the entire discussion of political economy into one large section, on the grounds that to do so would be to stack the discussion in favor of political economy from the outset, leaving the (for me) very important examination of the philosophy of the subject (and its crucial relation to the political) hanging on as a mere appendage to political economy.

Chapter 1. Thinking Subject and Citizen Subject

1 This understanding of the concept is based in part on Deleuze, "A Philosophical Concept . . . ," 94–95.

2 On reason as a legislative faculty, see Deleuze's lapidary explication in *Kant's Critical Philosophy*.

3 See Balibar, "Citizen Subject," 33–57. In another work, *Identité et différence*, Balibar goes on to argue that it is Locke and not Descartes who invents the modern concept of the self as that which the "you" or the "I" possesses.

4 For Descartes's letter to Mersenne, see his *Philosophical Essays and Correspondence*, 28; also in *Oeuvres de Descartes*, 1:145. Balibar refers to this letter on page 36 of "Citizen Subject." The great study of the king as the bodily representative of God's sovereignty is Kantorowicz's *The King's Two Bodies*.

5 The importance of the Augustinian tradition for Descartes is stressed in Menn, "The Intellectual Setting," 33–86, see especially 69. See also Menn, *Descartes and Augustine*, where Menn says that the Cartesian and Augustinian "doctrines of faith are the same; and naturally so, since Descartes' doctrine of faith is a conse-

quence of his adoption of the Augustinian doctrine of the free exercise of will in judgment" (333). See also Jolley, "The Reception of Descartes' Philosophy," 393–423.

6 According to Balibar, the notion of the transcendental subject arose from Kant's modification of the Cartesian *cogito*, with the Lockean self beginning a second tradition that circumvents Kant before ending up with William James and Bergson. See Balibar, "Je/moi/soi."

7 According to Kant, the monarch in an "age of Enlightenment" has authority only if he embodies the general will of the citizens: "Something which a people may not even impose upon itself can still less be imposed on it by a monarch; for his legislative authority depends precisely upon his uniting the collective will of the people in his own." See "An Answer to the Question 'What Is Enlightenment?'," 58.

8 For this, see Kant, "On the Common Saying: 'This May Be True in Theory but It Does Not Apply in Practice'," 77.

9 Kant, "Idea of a Universal History with a Cosmopolitan Purpose," 45–46.

10 Balibar, "Citizen Subject," 55. Balibar says a great deal more about the Cartesian and medieval theological *subjectus* than can be indicated here, rightly pointing out that a notion that had evolved over seventeen centuries from Roman times to the period of the European absolute monarchies is not easily encompassed in a single definition. He also rightly indicates that the supposed *novum* of the Citizen Subject has to be regarded with some skepticism, since under the aegis of bourgeois democracy this subject was always going to retain some traces of the old *subjectus*.

11 For Hegel's (early) view on the operation of "speculative" reason, see *The Difference between Fichte's and Schelling's System of Philosophy*, 88. For excellent commentary on this aspect of Hegel's relation to Kant, see Pinkard, *Hegel*, 160–67.

12 The essential correlation between Reason and the Absolute entails that every operation of consciousness, practical as much as theoretical, necessarily falls within the remit of the Absolute. The subject of thought then has to be the subject of morality and politics, and vice versa, a connection previously established by Kant when he moved from the First to the Second *Critique*, that is, from the subject's understanding to the subject's willing and acting.

13 On Kant and early German Romanticism, see Beiser, *The Fate of Reason*; *Enlightenment, Revolution, and Romanticism*; *German Idealism*; and *The Romantic Imperative*. See also Pinkard, *German Philosophy 1760–1860*.

14 There is an alternative philosophico-political tradition to the one just outlined here, which extends from Italian Renaissance humanism, with a particular focus on the Machiavelli of the *Discorsi*, to the tradition of English civic republicanism that J. G. A. Pocock and Quentin Skinner have done so much to define and analyze, James Harrington, John Milton, Henry Neville, and John Toland being the exemplary figures of this tradition. The English republican tradition in turn exerted a profound influence on the originating figures of American constitu-

tional thought, John Adams and Thomas Jefferson in particular. This strand of political thought placed far less emphasis on Enlightenment conceptions of the subject, though undeniably a deistic religious impulse runs through much of it, and this deism is of course one of the primary features of the Enlightenment. To bring the story up to date it has to be noted that Jeffersonian constitutional thought has been taken up by Antonio Negri, whose later writings can be said to reflect the influence of this tradition as much as they do that of marxism. For Skinner, see *Liberty before Liberalism* and his essays in Bock, Skinner, and Viroli, *Machiavelli and Republicanism*. For Pocock, see *Politics, Language, and Time* and *The Machiavellian Moment*. For Negri, see in particular *Insurgencies*, especially the first four essays. Also influential for Negri is Spinoza, who represents a Dutch strand of this civic republican tradition. For the relation of Spinoza's politics to his philosophy, see Israel, *Radical Enlightenment*.

15 Some would argue that there is no need to look too far for an alternative to the Citizen Subject that prevailed from Locke to Kant; the civic republican tradition mentioned in note 14 above is one obvious source for any sought-for replacement. The civic republican tradition does not underwrite the Enlightenment epistemology that proved to be insurmountably problematic for those seeking to uphold the fundamental tenets of this epistemology and its concomitant philosophico-theological subject. It would be premature for us to adjudicate in the apparent dispute between these two traditions, since there could be adequate grounds for upholding neither tradition (this in fact is the position taken in this book).

16 A case therefore exists for saying, where periodization is concerned, that the short twentieth century which began in 1918 really ended in 1968 or the early 1970s. For this view, see Negri, "The End of the Century," *The Politics of Subversion*, 61–74.

17 It is important to distinguish between the conditions of *possibility* that underlie the emergence and demise of the Citizen Subject (these having essentially to do with the historical and social conditions associated with capitalist development) and the conditions of *intelligibility* that underpin the philosophical rationales ("the knowledges") which sustain this subject. The two kinds of conditions function on different logical levels, and conditions of intelligibility serve a very different purpose than do conditions of possibility. We can follow Foucault in using the notion of the episteme to bridge the two sets of conditions, so that conditions of possibility allow an episteme to exist, and the existence of the episteme in turn enables discourses to be constructed which provide conditions of intelligibility for knowledges, and so forth. On this, see Deleuze, *Foucault*, 47–49.

18 On neoliberalism as a formation, see Harvey, *A Brief History of Neoliberalism*; Duménil and Lévy, *Crise et sortie de crise*; Chang, *Globalisation, Economic Development and the Role of the State*; Standing, *Beyond the New Paternalism*; Saad-Filho and Johnston, *Neoliberalism*; Boltanski and Chiapello, *The New Spirit of Capi-*

talism. On neoconservatism, see Dorrien, *Imperial Designs;* Norton, *Leo Strauss and the Politics of American Empire.*

19 George Monbiot himself made this point with a beautiful cynicism in an article which began thus: "If Jesus Christ were to return to earth and the beast that ascendeth out of the bottomless pit were to slay the greater part of mankind, the first thing the media would do would be to find out how the markets had reacted. The next would be to ring Sir Digby Jones, the head of the Confederation of British Industry, for a comment." See Monbiot, "Who Runs Britain?" The U.S. equivalent of the Confederation of British Industry would be the U.S. Chamber of Commerce, though the CBI, as the sole "trade union" of its CEOs and top industrial managers, has a position of influence in Britain that the Chamber of Commerce can achieve only in a dream world.

20 On proposals to outsource the IRS, see the article by Donald C. Alexander (a former IRS commissioner), "Hired Guns for the IRS," *New York Times,* 4 October 1995.

21 The hyperbole that possibly marks the "bake sale" example may be excused if one reads the careful analysis provided in Bacevich, *The New American Militarism.* Bacevich, a former U.S. Army colonel, is a Vietnam War veteran (whose son died in the Iraq war) who professes his "conservative Catholic inclinations" in the preface to *The New American Militarism.* Also relevant here is Bacevich's earlier *American Empire.* I have also benefited from reading Mann, *Incoherent Empire;* Singer, *Corporate Warriors;* Hirst, *War And Power in the 21st Century;* Shaw, *The New Western Way of War;* Harvey, *The New Imperialism.*

Chapter 2. A Marxist Concept of Liberation

1 At the level of the individual subject or consumer, the choice posed here seems relatively simple, inasmuch as reasoning about it involves an utterly basic counterfactual structure. Can the system as it is presently constituted deliver for me, my family, my village or city such things as affordable food and housing or medical benefits or an adequate retirement pension? If it can't, and if no amount of tinkering with the system in its present form can accomplish this, then the only alternative for those in need of such fundamental necessities is a quite radical reconstitution of the present order. The marxist tradition calls this novel reconstitution "revolution," and while not many individuals without adequate housing, health insurance, or pension plans, let alone food, would in all likelihood profess their adherence to those propositions given the name "marxism," their standpoint, once they are in the position of acknowledging that the system in its current form is able to do little or nothing for them, is perforce that of those who either acquiesce in their misery or who long, even in the face of despair, for some way out. Given the intractability of the existing order for those who benefit least from it, the way out for those in desperate and exigent need can only be what some of us call "revolution."

2 For an attempt to complicate and render more plausible this marxist developmental scheme, see Anderson, *Passages from Antiquity to Feudalism*, especially 18–46. For a more Weberian perspective on the transition from the end of the Roman Empire to the rise of European feudalism, see Mann, *The Sources of Social Power*, 374–99.

3 W. G. Runciman, "The 'Triumph' of Capitalism," 33–47.

4 This point about the mode of regulation's "regularizing" function is made by Bob Jessop in "The Social Embeddedness of the Economy." I am indebted to Jessop for my understanding of the capitalist mode of regulation. The question of the identities of political subjects as they function in the quest for liberation is taken up in the discussion of identity politics in chapter 6.

5 For example, the decision of many Americans to purchase their medicines online from Canadian pharmacies was highly instrumental in getting the Bush administration to join with American pharmaceutical manufacturers in introducing a nationwide prescription plan that quickly became notorious for its labyrinthine complexity and limited usefulness. What was a systemic constraint within the American system for getting affordable prescription medicines (high prices and limited choices due to the blatantly monopolistic conditions enjoyed by the pharmaceutical companies) became a strategic opportunity for those Americans with access to computers (as well as the Canadian pharmacies involved!). This in turn prompted the American pharmaceutical manufacturers to pressure the Bush administration to plug this loophole by introducing a prescription plan of its own that was more congruent with the interests of American drug companies than the alternative scenario of growing competition from Canadian pharmaceutical outlets able to undercut their American competitors. In this case, however, the taking up of this strategic opportunity by American consumers prompted a further systemic shift (the new prescription plan) on the part of the American pharmaceutical industry and its allies in the Bush administration, which yet again failed to serve the interests of those Americans in need of affordable prescription medicines.

6 On the dialectic of structure and agency, see Jessop, "Interpretive Sociology and the Dialectic of Structure and Agency."

7 For accounts of this lack of a necessary congruence between the means of production and the mode of societal regulation or domination, see W. G. Runciman, "The 'Triumph' of Capitalism"; Jessop, "Regulation Theory in Retrospect and Prospect"; Resnick and Wolff, *Class and History*. Runciman maintains that capitalism is an ensemble of practices in which ownership of the means of production can take several forms, ranging from individuals to the state. Runciman also believes that formally free labor can coexist alongside other work systems in capitalism. This conclusion is shared by Resnick and Wolff, using a very different theoretical framework. My account departs from Runciman's in three respects: (1) the notion of the mode of societal regulation (taken from Jessop) used in my rendering encompasses the two modes (coercion and persuasion) kept separate

by Runciman; (2) Runciman's pinpointing of markets and the quest for profits as defining features of capitalism does not emphasize capitalism's inherent propensity to realize profits precisely through the exploitation of wage labor (this being the cornerstone of Marx's theory of surplus value); and (3) Runciman accords centrality to a theory of social selection (indebted in a paradigmatic way to evolutionary biology) in singling out those practices responsible for instituting capitalism. Michael Mann's Weberian-inflected theory of social power distinguishes between economic, political, military, and ideological power, and the account of the mode of production and the mode of regulation developed here would, mutatis mutandis, place Mann's notions of political, military, and ideological power in the category of the mode of societal regulation, and his concept of economic power in that of the mode of (economic) production. For Mann's highly important work, see *The Sources of Social Power*: Vol. 1, *A History of Power from the Beginning to A.D. 1760*, and Vol. 2, *The Rise of the Classes and Nation-States, 1760–1914*.

8 The position delineated here on the mode of production and the mode of regulation is indebted to Jessop, "Post-Fordism and the State" and "Fordism and Post-Fordism." Jessop restricts his discussion to one version of capitalism in both these essays (viz., post-Fordism), but his account of capitalist regulation can easily be modified and generalized to provide the foundation for a general theory of capitalist development. Especially useful is his breakdown of the Ecole Régulation's notion of the mode of regulation into two distinct components: a "mode of societalization" and a "social mode of economic regulation." See also Jessop and Sum, *Beyond the Regulation Approach*.

9 For Lenin's remark, see Žižek, introduction to *Revolution at the Gates*, 11. It is noteworthy that many of Lenin's contemporaries took him to be more indebted, in his theory of revolution, to the writings of those who belonged to anarchist-inspired movements of rural insurgency than to the thought of Marx and Engels. On this, see the Palestinian marxist Tony Cliff's magisterial four-part biography, *Lenin*.

10 In *aRb*, if *a* is a theory (marxism, in this case) and *b* is the formation that is capitalism which stands in relation *R* to *a*, then while *a* is per definiens a theory, it is not clear at the same time what the ontological status of *b* is. While *b* is at the very least a set of material conditions and social relations, a distinction in principle needs to be made between a condition per se and the expressions or expressivities generated by that condition. More will be said about this in the next section.

11 On this, see Deleuze, "On the Superiority of Anglo-American Literature," in Deleuze and Parnet, *Dialogues*, 60.

12 This is why Slavoj Žižek has been right to insist in his various writings that it is both futile theoretically and unsatisfactory politically to seek to distinguish between "ideology" and some brute facticity represented by "economy." To be confronted by the concepts or expressivities of capitalism is to confront the

reality of capitalism (even if the "reality" overdetermines the expressivities in question), and vice versa.

13 It is possible to view this complexity in ways akin to Althusser's notion of an "overdetermined" relation between formations, and between formations and the points from which subject positions are constituted.

14 See Galbraith, *The New Industrial State*. For Veblen, see *Engineers and the Price System*.

15 See Aglietta, *A Theory of Capitalist Regulation*. See also Aglietta, "World Capitalism in the Eighties."

16 Certain forms of historical inquiry can do this just as well as ethnography, so there is no suggestion here that the study of the concrete forms of a particular embodiment of capitalism is the prerogative of the ethnographer and no one else. In *Truth and Truthfulness* Bernard Williams shows that even the description of historical and ethnographic particularities is suffused with traces or residues that are not contained within the described situation.

17 This understanding of the image and sign is derived from Gilles Deleuze: "The image itself is the system of the relationship between its elements, that is, a set of relationships of time from which the variable present only flows. . . . What is specific to the image . . . is to make perceptible, to make visible, relationships of time which cannot be seen in the represented object and do not allow themselves to be reduced to the present." See Deleuze, *Cinema 2: The Time-Image*, xii. Signs are "second-order" images that render these temporal relations visible in the "first-order" images that embody them (the first-order images being constituted intrinsically by the modalities of movement and time), through the intervention of a "third-order" image-sign that functions as the "interpretant" between the first- and second-order images (30). In other words, a sign functions as a packet of knowledge and affect regarding its object, but this knowledge and affect are "released" only through the intervention of the sign-image that is the interpretant, the latter increasing and adding new packets of knowledge and affect to the first-order image-sign. Images and signs are thus plastic, changeable assemblages.

18 The signs that compose an assemblage can be assigned to at least three levels or components of the assemblage. One set of signs will relate to the political subject's agency and practices; another will designate the forces, structures, and formations in which this agency and these practices are exercised; and a third will supply the particular context in which forces, structures, and formations are efficacious and the political subject's practices undertaken. Forces, structures, and formations (on the one hand) and agency and practices (on the other), along with the context in which both are manifested, together constitute an amalgam that is the social and political process in which social agents are inserted. This process is always stabilized and reduced in its complexity by social agents as a condition of their being able to act. The subject is thus always "in between" several social roles, statuses, names, identities, various affiliations and

disaffiliations, enfranchisements and disenfranchisements, and so forth, and the construction of this "in between" is the terrain in which the subject is produced ("subjectivization," as the jargon has it). This is also the terrain in which the project of liberation and equality finds its ground. Jacques Rancière has emphasized the centrality of this "in between" for a constitution of the political but says that the person who occupies this space of the "in between" is always the proletarian. This is an unnecessary circumscription: any social subject occupies this space by virtue of being a social subject. The proletarian, however, occupies this space under separate and specific auspices, in that he or she embodies an identification that subjects him or her to a constitutively inequitable structure, that is, a structure of exploitation that provides little or no benefit for the proletarian, at least in comparison to the advantages enjoyed by those who are beneficiaries of the capitalist system. See Rancière, "Politics, Identification, and Subjectivization," 63–70, and "The Cause of the Other."

19 Raymond Williams has constantly stressed the importance of local affiliations in the constitution of human subjectivity. See "Culture Is Ordinary," 3–18.

20 The presence of this structure of exploitation is a necessary but not in itself sufficient condition for the emergence and perpetuation of the condition that makes the capitalist subject what he or she is. As I pointed out earlier, a serf or a slave belongs to a structure of exploitation by virtue of being what he or she is, that is, an outcast who is wronged in fundamental ways. But historical or social circumstances alone would determine whether this serf or slave happened to belong to a precapitalist or capitalist structure of exploitation. Being a serf or a slave does not in itself specify how or why one is exploited, as much as it would provide a brutally clear awareness of the fact that one has been and is being wronged.

21 Liberation can also be the name of the extinction of that desire; the desire to end desire is treated in some religious traditions as the exemplary means of overcoming pain and suffering. For marxism this position is without warrant. Enjoining as it does the supersession of capitalism, marxism necessarily has to underwrite the desire for this supersession, and the desire to be released from all desire is simply not an option for the serious marxist.

22 Spinoza, *Ethics*, III, 9 scholium, p. 172.

23 Antonio Negri, in his great work *The Savage Anomaly*, has drawn attention to the centrality of this ontology of constitutive power for Spinoza's ethics of liberation.

24 On truth-effects, see Balibar, "The Infinite Contradiction," especially 162.

25 On this see Deleuze, "Doubts about the Imaginary," 65–66.

26 As contemporary newspaper accounts and the novels of Nadine Gordimer and J. M. Coetzee make very clear, there were many in white South Africa who placed themselves in positions where such truth-effects were simply not able to be manifested. There is a sense in which the Afrikaaner brute wholeheartedly in favor of apartheid is in a position of greater clarity with regard to such potential

truth-effects than the haplessly evasive, white South African "kind soul" who believed that blacks should of course be "treated well," but who thought at the same time that armed resistance was "bad" or "unnecessary," and that an appeal to the goodwill of H. F. Verwoerd, P. W. Botha, F. W. de Klerk, and other Afrikaaner leaders was all that was really needed to end apartheid, "given a bit of time," of course.

27 Badiou makes this point in "Philosophy and Politics," 29. Badiou clearly believes that a philosophy is necessary if the possible truth of this political standpoint is to emerge. He shares Plato's view that there has to be a necessary concatenation between philosophy and politics if justice is to find its place of actualization. Interestingly, a similar position is taken by the emphatically non-Platonist Deleuze, who insists that such things as rights are not created by "codes and pronouncements" but "by the philosophy of law." See Deleuze's essay "On Philosophy" in *Negotiations*, 153. The principle straddling the otherwise quite different positions of Badiou and Deleuze derives from the insight that politics cannot on its own transcend the disarray of partiality and interest (Badiou), and that political activity in the mainstream is typically constrained by having to be undertaken through the auspices of the apparatuses of the state (Deleuze). For the latter point, see Deleuze (with Parnet), "Many Politics," in Deleuze and Parnet, *Dialogues*, 124–47.

28 Admittedly, the pervasive nondecidability of quotidian reality comes about as a result of politics itself. In the age of integrated world capitalism, the state has the basic function of disaggregating and neutralizing the countervailing forces ranged against it, in this way placing the apparatuses of the state at the disposal of capitalist accumulation. Anyone who in 2009 doubts this is perhaps totally unaware of the massive government bailouts, in nearly every economically advanced country, of banks whose lending policies in recent years have been consistently reckless and intellectually discordant with any professed respect for "economic fundamentals" (I am referring here of course to the financial crisis of 2008 and 2009). The state's primary function, therefore, is to ensure this decisive continuity, with its concomitant undecidability, so that even those forces ranged against capital are somehow allowed to function in ways that augment capitalist accumulation. There is a confluence between the state and the social, in which the forms of opposition to capital are not effaced, but instead are used to intensify and extend the forms of social organization furthering capitalist accumulation. There is no better illustration of this phenomenon than the way the oil and coal-mining companies nowadays seek not to distance themselves from "green" causes, say, but instead project themselves as exemplary custodians of the environment, primarily in television commercials in which, to a backdrop of sunshine and chirping birds overlaid with soft new age music, disused oil fields or open-pit coal mines are shown to be planted with trees and blooming flowers. By rendering nondecidable the difference between a genuine stewardship of the environment and the lasting environmental despoliation that in fact

takes place when oil and coal extraction occurs, any opposition, potential or real, to the profit-taking activities of the American oil and coal companies is effectively neutralized or blunted. In the age of a cynical political reason, it is perhaps no surprise that the first President Bush should insist on calling himself an "environmentalist." The state is of course the principal architect of social arrangements designed to give the forces of nondecidability a freer rein. The American state is in effect the metacorporation of the corporations, as many left-leaning commentators have pointed out.

29 For this, see Badiou, "Philosophy and Politics," 29. See also Deleuze, "On Philosophy," in *Negotiations*, 153, where he asserts, "Jurisprudence . . . is the philosophy of law, and deals with singularities. . . . It advances by working out from singularities."

30 See Benjamin, "Theses on the Philosophy of History," 255–66.

31 In addition to the works of Taussig already mentioned, see Comaroff and Comaroff, *Of Revelation and Revolution*, and Jean Comaroff, *Body of Power, Spirit of Resistance*. See also the essays collected in Comaroff and Comaroff, *Modernity and Its Malcontents*.

32 This formulation and example is taken in slightly modified form from Bernard Williams, "Truth in Ethics."

33 See Negri, "Notes on the Evolution of the Thought of Louis Althusser," 54. Negri is discussing a line of reflection, involving revolutionary thought and practice, pursued by Althusser in the writings of the last few years of his life. My next few paragraphs are indebted to Negri. Benjamin's remark "Only for the sake of the hopeless are we given hope," though not mentioned by Althusser or Negri, also reflects this crux of liberation. For Benjamin, liberation can be expressed only in terms of what Adorno has called an "impossible possibility." See Adorno, "A Portrait of Walter Benjamin," 241.

34 As I pointed out earlier, Spinoza provides an exemplary formulation of this ontology of the desire for liberation in his *Ethics*.

35 For these terms, see Foucault, *The Order of Things*. Foucault's account of the three epistemes — classical, modern, and current — is being invoked here and in the following paragraphs. See also Rabinow, "Artificiality and Enlightenment," whose line of argument regarding Foucault is being followed very closely here.

36 See Deleuze, *Foucault*, 131.

37 See Deleuze, *Foucault*, 131.

38 For this image of Man as a drawing at the water's edge, see Foucault, *The Order of Things*, 387.

39 See Deleuze, *Foucault*, 132.

40 See Deleuze, *Foucault*, 132. The embedded quotation is from *The Order of Things*, 38.

41 See Mandel, "Karl Marx," 7.

1 On the Golden Age, see Kindleberger, "Why Did the Golden Age Last So Long?," and the somewhat *régulationniste* narrative provided in Glyn et al., "The Rise and Fall of the Golden Age." For accounts of the course taken by the advanced capitalist countries in the succeeding decades (the 1980s and 1990s), see Glyn, "The Costs of Stability" and "Global Imbalances"; Lipietz, "The Debt Problem"; Mazier et al., *When Economic Crises Endure;* Pollin, "Contemporary Economic Stagnation in World Historical Perspective" and *Contours of Descent.*

For accounts of the precise nature and causes of the crisis of the 1970s, associated by some with the demise of the Golden Age, see the *régulationniste* Lipietz, *Mirages and Miracles;* Mandel, *The Second Slump*, whose explanation is based on an application of "long-wave" theory; O'Connor, *Accumulation Crisis*, who views the crisis as one of a pervasive overproduction leading to an acute diminution of surplus value; and R. Brenner, *The Economics of Global Turbulence*, who rejects the Fordist/post-Fordist dichotomy, and indeed the whole notion of a Golden Age, in favor of an explanation in terms of a systemically debilitating competition between earlier and later developing national capitals. Ash Amin, "Post-Fordism," gives a lucid overview of the literature on the transition from the Golden Age to its successor.

2 Baker, Epstein, and Pollin, introduction, 1–34, see especially 16, explicitly link the onset of the Leaden Age in the mid-1970s with the emergence of globalization. Poulantzas, *Classes in Contemporary Capitalism*, links the emergence of a new imperial formation driven by American capital to the crisis experienced by the postwar system of accumulation.

3 Hirst and Thompson, *Globalization in Question*, are convinced that a "genuine" globalization occurs only if its associated processes involve the elimination of the state, and since the state has not ceased to exist and to be effective in international economic management, they conclude that there has not been a "true" globalization. The question of the role of the state in these transformations is obviously a crucial one, but *pace* Hirst and Thompson, it is somewhat implausible to presume that the elimination of the functions of the state has to be an absolutely necessary prerequisite for genuine globalization. For other skeptical arguments about the "openness" of the world economy, see Gordon, "The Global Economy," by now clearly dated, but still important as a relatively early but important statement of the skeptic's position. Gordon's data cover only up to 1984, and the world's economy has certainly become more "open" since then. The claim that the world economy prior to 1913 was just as integrated as its post-1970 counterpart is judiciously examined by Baker et al., introduction, 15. They conclude that while overall the levels of integration between the two economic dispensations are roughly similar, there are two very significant differences nonetheless: from 1950 to the present there has been a substantial rise

in the percentage of manufacturing exports on the part of the less developed economies (who were scarcely visible as economic forces prior to 1913), and, again unlike the earlier dispensation, there has been a massive growth of short-term capital movements in the current phase of capitalist accumulation. On the primacy of domestic national markets, see Mann, "Has Globalization Ended the Rise and Rise of the Nation-State?," who points out that 80 percent of world production is still for the domestic market. Mann's data are very likely to be out of date by 2008, but Glyn, in "Global Imbalances," 31, points out that based on OECD labor force statistics, such domestic economic activities as "wholesale and retail trade, community, personal and social services, utilities and construction together account for some 60 per cent of employment in the OECD as a whole, rather more in the U.S."

4 United Nations Development Programme, *Human Development Report 2005*, 116. Figures 4 and 5 are taken from the same publication. The calculations for figure 4 are taken from the United Nations Industrial Development Organization, *Industrial Development Report 2004*, and those for figure 5 are taken from the World Bank, *World Development Indicators 2005*.

5 United Nations Development Programme, *Human Development Report 2005*, 117.

6 The problem is that aggregate flows of trade and investment can tell us only part of the story. These flows have microeconomic effects, and until these effects are identified and analyzed, the fuller story is not likely to unfold. Thus in a more open economic environment of the kind said to be made possible by globalization, the possibility of a firm relocating to another country may make its workers opt for lower wages in the hope of maintaining overall employment levels, and the complete story can be told only by examining the effect of an investment flow on that country's demand curve for labor (since in some firms workers may still wish to sacrifice overall employment in order to safeguard their existing wage levels; the story of workers accepting job cuts in order to retain current wage levels is certainly one we read about nearly every week). Without looking at the demand curve for labor, we cannot tell whether workers in a particular sector are trading jobs for wages or wages for jobs. On the need to take such microeconomic considerations into account when examining the effects of global flows of trade and investment, see Bardhan, Bowles, and Wallerstein, introduction, 1–12.

7 Peck and Tickell, "Searching for a New Institutional Fix," 280–315, follow Altvater, "Fordist and post-Fordist International Division of Labor and Monetary Regimes," 21–45, in treating "post-Fordism" as a term employed in a purely negative sense to designate the end of a particular phase of capitalist development without the accompanying suggestion that a successor phase was already, or is soon to be, in place. According to Peck and Tickell, the ending of one such phase could be accompanied by a period in which several post-Fordist forms competed with each other for consolidation before one became dominant.

Hence their preference for the more neutral term *après-fordisme*, which carries no implication that the transition from an exhausted strand of capitalist development (Fordism) to another (post-Fordism) had already been accomplished.

8 The insight that a polarized world system is the condition for the emergence of any modern regime of capitalist accumulation lies at the heart of the writings of Samir Amin. See *Maldevelopment* and *Re-Reading the Postwar Period*.

9 The World Bank's *World Development Report* of 1997 espoused these neoliberal precepts in a chapter titled "Refocusing the Effectiveness of the State," whose basic premise is that "[the] state has much to do with whether countries adopt the institutional arrangements under which markets can flourish" (29). The clear presumption is that the "flourishing of markets" sets the primary agenda for a country's economic policy. This postulate lies at the heart of what Lipietz has called "liberal productivism," that is, the ideology which overturns the principle, crucial to any project of social emancipation, that technological progress is justified by social progress, in favor of the notion that technological progress is self-justifying and needs no other warrant. See Lipietz, "Post-Fordism and Democracy," 343–45, and "The Next Transformation," 112–40, especially 122–27.

The problem with Lipietz's characterization of neoliberalism is that it overlooks neoliberalism's part in supporting rent- and *rentier*-led economic activities (which have little or nothing to do with production per se). This is a critical oversight given the central role played by finance capital in the contemporary world economy (as pointed out in Dunford, "Towards a Post-Fordist Order?"). I shall deal with the vitally important relation of the state to financialized regimes of growth later in this chapter.

10 In four books, *The Capitalist State*, *State Theory*, *The Future of the Capitalist State*, and *State Power*, Jessop has provided the most sustained thinking in state theory undertaken from a marxist perspective since the late Nicos Poulantzas. Jessop's position, which merges insights taken from the Ecole Régulation and systems theory with a neo-Gramscian conception of hegemony, hinges crucially on the Fordism/post-Fordism dichotomy. Joachim Hirsch's position is very similar in its theoretical orientation, except that, more than Jessop, he emphasizes the causal centrality of the "denationalization" of capital that ensues from the crisis of Fordism. See Hirsch, "Nation-State, International Regulation, and the Question of Democracy," "Globalization of Capital, Nation-States and Democracy," and "Globalisation, Class and the Question of Democracy."

11 See Jessop, "Fordism and Post-Fordism," 47–52, and "Post-Fordism and the State," 251. Jessop also considers the emergence of new technologies to be another crucial factor in the rise of post-Fordism. See "Post-Fordism and the State," 258, and "Capitalism and Its Future." Interestingly, in "Post-Fordism and the State," Jessop considers the role of new technologies to be part of the movement to flexible specialization, whereas in "Capitalism and Its Future" he regards the appearance of new technologies as an independent (but still co-present) constituent of post-Fordism. It should also be noted that when refer-

ring to Fordism and post-Fordism, Jessop is careful to distinguish between the two strands, one "theoretical" and the other "practical," that are constitutive of each of them as structures: on the one hand, the "actually existing structural forms and dynamics," and on the other, "the presence of modes of calculation and strategies which aim to implement them" ("Post-Fordism and the State," 254). This distinction is analytically necessary because of the lag that can exist between the two levels. As Jessop points out, planners and economic agents can be engaged, often without evident intent, in implementing the rudiments of an emergent regime of accumulation (such as post-Fordism) even as its sometime-to-be replaced counterpart (Fordism in this case) is still active and dominant.

12 The caveat that Fordist-Taylorist production is not entirely displaced by post-Fordist flexible production is necessary because there is still a "peripheral" Fordism and Taylorism in the less-developed countries. For an attempt to analyze the first stages of this development, see Lipietz, "Towards Global Fordism?" This is because post-Fordism affords the possibility of recomposing Taylorist principles into a "neo-Taylorism" that can be inserted at selective points in the production process. On this, see Lipietz, *Towards a New Economic Order.*

For the counterargument that flexible specialization is not as generalized as many of its proponents take it to be, see Hirst and Zeitlin, "Flexible Specialization," 220–39. Jessop, however, is cautious enough to say that "flexibility alone is insufficient to define post-Fordism" ("Post-Fordism and the State," 258).

13 See Jessop, "Post-Fordism and the State," 258. The proposition that capitalist production regimes seek to overcome or bypass the alienation of the Fordist-Taylorist mass worker by moving to production systems relying on "after-Fordist" flexible labor practices and structures (and appropriately "socialized" workers and social subjects) is central to the thinking of other schools of marxism and not just the *régulationniste* Jessop. See, for instance, Negri, *Revolution Retrieved, The Politics of Subversion*, and "Twenty Theses on Marx."

14 See Jessop, "Post-Fordism and the State," 255, and "Capitalism and Its Future," 571.

15 Jessop is careful to stress that the emergence of the post-Fordist macroeconomy cannot "be reduced to effects of a crisis of Fordism" since other geopolitical factors played a key part in the unfolding of post-Fordism. The end of Fordism was succeeded by "often intense struggles between competing versions of capitalism," and these struggles were affected by such events as the end of the cold war, the onset of the Pacific Century, and the rise of multiculturalism, and not just by macroeconomic considerations ("Capitalism and Its Future," 573). Hirsch more than Jessop emphasizes the part played by the cold war in generating "global Fordism." See his "Globalization of Capital, Nation-States and Democracy," 39–40.

16 On "lean" production viewed from a perspective similar to that of the Ecole Régulation, see Hoogvelt and Yuasa, "Going Lean or Going Native?"

17 Jessop, "Restructuring the Welfare State," 54–76, and "The Transition to Post-Fordism and the Schumpeterian Workfare State," 13–37.

18 Jessop, "Post-Fordism and the State," 259–61.

19 Jessop, "Post-Fordism and the State," 260. The financial crisis of 2008, continuing into 2009, drives home Jessop's point that a "relatively stable" post-Fordist formation has yet to be realized.

20 Hirsch, "Nation-State," 276.

21 Jessop, "Post-Fordism and the State," 262.

22 Jessop argues that the post-Fordist state did not materialize directly from the crisis of Fordism. Rather, resources drawn from Fordist forms and principles were employed initially in an unsuccessful attempt to contain the crisis. Only when these failed did "transitional post-Fordist regimes" emerge. See "Post-Fordism and the State," 262.

23 Jessop, "Post-Fordism and the State," 264. See also Hirsch, "Globalization of Capital," 42.

24 Jessop, "Post-Fordism and the State," 266–71, suggests that there are in fact three Schumpeterian workfare state strategies. One, perhaps the most frequently acknowledged, is neoliberal and basically submits the state to the requirements of the private sector. The second is neocorporatism, which differs from its Fordist predecessor to the extent that it seeks to accommodate supply-side considerations and combine self-regulation with state regulation. The third is neostatism, which uses state apparatuses to orchestrate responses oriented to the supply side. In all cases the new international competitive environment that defines "after-Fordism" sets the terms for the implementation of these strategies. Jessop also says that these strategies can be combined, as they are in the European Union, for instance.

25 Jessop, "Post-Fordism and the State," 275. See also Lipietz, *Mirages and Miracles*, 25.

26 Jessop, "Capitalism and Its Future," 574–79.

27 Although, *pace* Jessop and Hirsch, the ability of the United States to head and direct this equity-based regime has, for the time being at any rate, put paid to notions of a "triadic" competition in which Germany and Japan are serious economic rivals of the United States. It is still early to tell whether the bursting of the housing market bubble, and its associated banking failures, has put paid to American leadership of the equity-based regime of accumulation. On the tendency of the Ecole Régulation to overestimate the potential of the Japanese and German models of capitalism to compete with their "Anglo-Saxon" counterparts, see Grahl and Teague, "The *Régulation* School, the Employment Relation and Financialization."

28 In his more recent work with Ngai-Ling Sum, Jessop does acknowledge the "Eurocentrism" of his earlier work. See Jessop and Sum, *Beyond the Regulation Approach*.

29 For this figure, see International Financial Services, London, *City Business Series*.

30 See Bhaduri, "Implications of Globalization for Macroeconomic Theory and Policy in Developing Countries," 152. See also Harris, "International Financial Markets and National Transmission Mechanisms," 199–212; Griffith-Jones and Stallings, "New Global Financial Trends," 143–73. A good summary of the changes that have taken place in global financial markets in the past two decades is in Helleiner, *States and the Reemergence of Global Finance*; Griffith-Jones, *Global Capital Flows*; Eatwell and Taylor, *Global Finance at Risk*; Obstfeld and Taylor, *Global Capital Markets*.

31 For these figures, see Drábek and Griffith-Jones, "Summary and Conclusions," 215.

32 Deutsches Bundesbank, *The Role of FDI in Emerging Market Economies*, 9.

33 Institute of International Finance, "Resilient Emerging Markets Attract Record Private Capital Flows," press release, 6 March 2008. This press release goes on to say that "direct investment into emerging economies is currently on an upswing with net inward FDI to total $286 billion this year, compared to an estimated $256 billion in 2007 and $167 billion above the 2006 volume."

34 Henwood, *Wall Street*, is still the most readable and informative account of many of these new financial instruments and the markets in which they operate. According to the *Manchester Guardian Weekly*, 9 November 1997, the United States had more than 2,800 mutual funds controlling over $4 trillion, with $220 billion being placed in them in 1996 alone (nearly double the 1995 total of $242 billion). At the time of the crash in October 1987 there were only 812 U.S. mutual funds managing a total of $242 billion. By 2003 pension funds constituted 40.7 percent of all U.S. equity assets, investment companies 22 percent, insurance companies 23.3 percent, bank and trust companies 11.7 percent, and foundations 2.4 percent. In the past twenty-five years investment companies and mutual funds have grown very rapidly (2.6 percent of assets in 1980 to 22 percent in 2003), followed by pension funds (32.6 percent in 1980 to 40.7 percent in 2003). In this period, bank and trust companies have declined significantly (38.8 percent of total assets in 1980 to 11.7 percent in 2003). For this information, see Conference Board, *Institutional Investment Report 2005*.

In 1994 two American pension funds alone, the Teachers' Insurance and Annuity Association–College Retirement Equities Fund (TIAA-CREF) and the California Public Employees Retirement System (CalPERS), had assets of $140 billion and $100 billion, respectively, and the largest pension fund in the United Kingdom, the Post Office and British Telecom Fund, had holdings of $35 billion. For these figures, see Minns, "The Social Ownership of Capital," 43. By December 2007, TIAA-CREF's assets had risen to $437 billion (see TIAA-CREF press release, www.tiaa-cref.org., accessed 18 May 2008); by March 2008, CalPERS holdings had risen to $242.4 billion (see CalPERS press release, www.calpers.ca.gov., accessed 18 May 2008). By January 2008, the total for worldwide pension fund assets in the major eleven markets had risen to $25 trillion (see Watson Wyatt's Global Pension Assets Study, www.watsonwyatt.com., accessed 18 May 2008).

On the "short-termism" of pension fund managers, see the detailed studies in Clark, *Pension Fund Capitalism*; Minns, *The Cold War in Welfare*; Blackburn, *Banking on Death*, and *Age Shock*.

35 Asian Development Bank, *Asian Development Outlook 1994*, 18. The Asian Bank welcomed the processes of liberalization that led to the surge in portfolio investment.

36 Singh, "Portfolio Equity Flows," 23, makes the point that in 1992 there were 6,700 companies quoted on the Indian stock market, compared with 7,014 companies in the United States, 1,874 in the United Kingdom, and 665 in Germany. In addition, the "average daily trading volume on the Bombay stock market has been about the same as that in London—about 45,000 trades a day."

37 See Asian Development Bank, *Asian Development Outlook 2004*, www.adb.org, accessed on 3 January 2005.

38 For a comprehensive overview of the effects of financial globalization on the emerging economies, see Prasad et al., *Effects of Financial Globalization on Developing Countries*, www.imf.org, accessed on 3 January 2005. The authors draw numerous conclusions from the data, but two stand out for our purposes: (1) increased financial integration is neither a necessary nor a sufficient condition for economic growth (India and China have impressive growth rates in spite of limited capital account liberalization, while Peru and Jordan have suffered economic decline in spite of being more open to capital flows); and (2) while developing countries do benefit in some ways from globalized financial integration, these benefits are more likely to be reaped by the advanced economies. The authors conclude that "the empirical evidence has not established a definitive proof that financial integration has enhanced growth for developing countries" (paragraph 114). This skepticism is reinforced in Rodríguez and Rodrik, "Trade Policy and Economic Growth."

39 Henwood, *Wall Street*, 16, provides a table which shows that in 1994 the United Kingdom, Japan, and the United States had shares of world stock market capitalization that totaled 8 percent, 24.5 percent, and 33.5 percent, respectively, while the share for the emerging world totaled a mere 12.7 percent: Malaysia had 1.3 percent, Taiwan 1.6 percent, Thailand 0.9 percent, the Philippines 0.4 percent, Korea 1.3 percent, and Indonesia 0.3 percent of world stock market capitalization that year (figures taken by Henwood from International Finance Corporation, *Emerging Stock Markets Factbook 1995*).

40 The United Nations High-Level Panel on Financing for Development, *Report*. The next few figures given in this paragraph are provided in the same *Report*.

41 Ibid. The next few figures given in this paragraph are provided in the same *Report*.

42 Roach, "Learning to Live with Globalization," Testimony before the Commit-

tee on Banking and Financial Services of the U.S. House of Representatives, 20 May 1999, cited in Pettis, *The Volatility Machine*, 46. Pettis's book remains the best guide for the institutional and other conditions which enable volatility-induced financial collapses to occur in the emerging countries.

43 The capacity of present-day stock markets to deviate from "fundamentals" for considerable periods of time is found not only in the stock exchanges of the emerging countries but also in the established stock markets of London and New York. On this, see Singh, "Portfolio Equity Flows and Stock Markets in Financial Liberalization," 24. See also the comprehensive overview in Desai, *Financial Crisis, Containment, and Contagion*.

44 For the notion of "fictitious capital," see Marx, *Capital*, vol. 3, part 5. Harris, "Alternative Perspectives on the Financial System," has invoked this notion to explain the highly autonomous character of present-day transnational capital markets. Eighty percent of all foreign transactions involve a round trip of a week or less, and most take place within a single day. See Tobin, "Prologue," xii.

45 See the various essays in Drábek and Griffith-Jones, *Managing Capital Flows in Turbulent Times*, which support the view of Mann, "Has Globalization Ended the Rise and Rise of the Nation-State?" (see note 3 above), and Weiss, *The Myth of the Powerless State*: states operating in a globalized economy still retain capacities which enable them to macromanage this or that element of globalization (in this case the problems associated with financial market fluctuations). States can also use these capacities to advance the course of globalization, and indeed globalization rarely advances without some degree of collusion on the part of the governments involved. See also the collection of essays in Weiss, *States in the Global Economy*. The evidence for state leadership of deregulation is carefully marshaled and analyzed in Vogel, *Freer Markets, More Rules*. On the state and globalization, see also Pettis, *The Volatility Machine*; Chang, *Globalisation, Economic Development and the Role of the State*; Calomiris, "Capital Flows, Financial Crises, and Public Policy"; Aybar and Lapavistas, "Financial System Design and the Post-Washington Consensus."

46 Larry Elliott, "Two Countries, One Booming, One Struggling: Which One Followed the Free-Trade Route?," *The Guardian*, 12 December 2005. See also Chang, *Bad Samaritans*.

47 Strictly speaking, this is not quite accurate, since Rosa Luxemburg, in *The Accumulation of Capital*, had already questioned Marx's formulations regarding this primitive accumulation when she came to the conclusion, in her theory of imperialism, that even "mature" phases of capitalism needed a precapitalist domain to serve as a base for the creation of surplus value.

48 Luxemburg, *The Accumulation of Capital*.

49 For this reason Luxemburg maintained that a precapitalist "space" would have to adjoin capitalist zones of accumulation to serve as the source of primordial demand, not just in the first phase of capitalist expansion but also in its "mature" stages.

50 See, for instance, Aglietta, "Le capitalisme de demain," 101, and "Shareholder Value and Corporate Governance"; Aglietta and Rebérioux, *Corporate Governance Adrift*; Boyer, "Le politique à l'ère de la mondialisation et de la finance," 13–75, and "Is a Finance-led Growth Regime a Viable Alternative to Fordism?"

51 Boyer, "Is a Finance-led Growth Regime a Viable Alternative to Fordism?," 112. The primacy of the central banks in the current system is demonstrated by the U.S. Federal Reserve's commanding role in responding to the current subprime crisis.

52 Aglietta, "Shareholder Value and Corporate Governance," 148, 150.

53 Boyer, "Is a Finance-led Growth Regime a Viable Alternative to Fordism?," 116. The notion of "shareholder value" developed from the 1980s onward is carefully explored in Fligstein, *The Architecture of Markets*, especially chapter 7. The institutional complement of this "unfettering" of the shareholder (now also encompassing the CEO executive stratum) is a new regime of "performance-oriented" surveillance for middle and lower-tier managers and workers using the latest information technology. See the fine, if somewhat chilling, account of these developments in Head, *The New Ruthless Economy*.

54 Boyer, "Is a Finance-led Growth Regime a Viable Alternative to Fordism?," 121. This fantasy of a benign (and of course completely depoliticized!) "synergy" between central bank policy, the performance of the financial markets, and the business plans of companies is very much behind the rationales provided by the Bush administration for its policy of "tax cuts for the rich." In his testimony to the U.S. House of Representatives in October 2008, Alan Greenspan (the previous head of the U.S. Federal Reserve) admitted his culpability in promoting this now discredited "synergy." On the pivotal role of advanced-country central banks in this new growth regime, see Orléan, *Le pouvoir de la finance*, 249–53; Pauly, *Who Elected the Bankers?*

55 In what follows I adhere closely to the overviews presented by Germain, *The International Organization of Credit*; Webb, *The Political Economy of Policy Coordination*; Pettis, *The Volatility Machine*; Grabel, "Ideology, Power, and the Rise of Independent Monetary Institutions in Emerging Economies," 25–52; Obstfeld and Taylor, *Global Capital Markets*; Harmes, "Institutional Investors and the Reproduction of Neoliberalism." Harmes is especially good on the shifts that have taken place in investment allocation criteria with the emergence of the new financial markets.

56 Germain, *International Organization of Credit*, 136.

57 Even those who write about international financial markets from a neoliberal perspective believe that there is a problem today with inadequately supervised markets. See, for example, Kapstein, *Governing the Global Economy*. The subprime credit crisis in the United States represents the latest pitfall for what is acknowledged to be a largely unregulated credit system.

58 It is important to note that the rise of instability is not necessarily to be equated

with a scaling down of international coordination. As Webb, *The Political Economy of Policy Coordination*, 252–59, points out, if anything there has been more coordination in the international economy since the 1970s, though it has not managed to provide levels of stability previously reached. Vogel, in *Freer Markets, More Rules*, also argues that deregulation "reform" has in fact been government-led.

59 Helleiner offers a good account of market deregulation by state and public monetary institutions. See *States and the Reemergence of Global Finance*, which stresses the preeminent role of the state in fostering the integration and deregulation of markets. See also Goodman and Pauly, "The Obsolescence of Capital Controls?," who use a more dialectical approach which views government policy leading to increased integration and mobility, and this new situation in turn leading private agents to press for even more deregulation.

60 As Webb puts it in *The Political Economy of Policy Coordination*, "Governments have preferred to take their chances with unpredictable burdens imposed by private markets responding to national policy differences, rather than coordinate in order to reduce the likelihood and magnitude of future international market pressures" (259–60).

61 Germain, *International Organization of Credit*, 161.

62 As mentioned earlier, the problem with the influential positions of Jessop and Hirsch is that they have not placed enough emphasis on the primacy of the equity-based growth regime; if anything, the weight of significance in their theoretical models is on the knowledge-based, information and communication technologies, and competition regimes, with little more than a glance being directed at financialization and its impact.

63 In fact labor and the holders of fixed assets are disproportionally subject to tax burdens since they lack the monetary mobility that is at the disposal of possessors of financial assets. It should be noted that the ability to use credit or money to synchronize the circuits of production and consumption is precisely what allows the United States to do what no other country can do: enjoy a respectable growth rate while having a negative savings rate and chronic external trade deficits. Basically, the United States is able to disconnect investment and savings (this connection being the theoretical heart of classical market theory) and to use income derived from financial asset holdings to subsidize investment and consumption (especially the latter). The growing perception now is that this disconnection is in fact the primary cause of the current financial crisis.

64 The relative freedom from path dependency of the structures associated with the acquisition of industrial capacity is the basic principle underlying the (now discredited) notion of the developmental state. Intrinsic to this notion is the formula that a single developmental trajectory of a hierarchical nature embraces all countries, and that development takes place when the less-developed countries move up this hierarchy by emulating their developed counterparts. (Theorists of underdevelopment or dependency maintain that subordination is the inevi-

table lot of the less-developed nations because the hierarchical character of the developmental trajectory virtually decrees that some nations remain economically disadvantaged precisely in order to furnish the advanced economies with resources needed for their own development.) On this developmental state, see the essays, both theoretical and based on case studies, in Woo-Cumings, *The Developmental State*.

Chapter 4. Uneven Development

1 Especially important here are the views of those who maintain that the important consideration in analyzing the functions of the state in economic development is the politics of the regimes, institutions, classes, and groupings that are inserted into this or that state process or state project, the state being anything but a static form or edifice that can be counterposed to "markets" or "multilateral institutions" or "transnational corporations." See, for instance, Cumings, "The Origins and Development of the Northeast Asian Political Economy," 44–83; Johnson, "Political Institutions and Economic Performance," 136–64; Deyo, *Beneath the Miracle*; Maxfield, *Governing Capital*; Woo, *Race to the Swift*; Reno, *Corruption and State Politics in Sierra Leone*; Mamdani, *Citizen and Subject*; Chang, "The Market, the State and Institutions in Economic Development," 41–60.

2 For useful general discussion of these two principles and their implications, see, inter alia, Escobar, *Encountering Development*; Larrain, *Theories of Development*; Leys, *The Rise and Fall of Development Theory*; Toye, *Dilemmas of Development*.

3 United Nations Development Programme, *Human Development Report 1997*.

4 The claim that the net worth of ten billionaires is 1.5 times the combined national income of the forty-eight least developed nations was the focus of the article by Larry Elliott and Victoria Brittain, "Seven Richest Could End World Poverty," *Manchester Guardian Weekly*, 22 June 1997. The United Nations Development Programme, *Human Development Report 1997*, estimated that the cost of its proposed $80 billion antipoverty program could be covered by the wealth of seven billionaires. The "structural adjustment" programs advocated by the International Monetary Fund and the World Bank for developing countries require the wholesale elimination of expenditure on education, health, and social services, and this in countries that may be experiencing a decrease in the years of average life expectancy.

5 United Nations Development Programme, *Human Development Report 2005*, 3. The HDI (Human Development Index) is a composite indicator encompassing three key aspects of human well-being: income, education, and health. As the *Human Development Report* puts it, "The HDI is a barometer for changes in human well-being and for comparing progress in different regions" (21). The next few statistical items in the main body of the text are taken from this report, and the pagination is cited in parentheses.

6 It is interesting to note that while the incidence of dollar-a-day poverty fell by 50 percent between 1990 and 2001, 90 percent of that decline took place between 1990 and 1996, with declines since the mid-1990s falling at one-fifth of the 1980–96 rate. See United Nations Development Programme, *Human Development Report 2005*, 34.

7 United Nations Development Programme, *Human Development Report 2005* defines a "stagnation period" as "a year in which a country's per capita income is lower than that of any time in the past two years and higher than at any time in the subsequent four years" (183 n. 43).

8 Thus in 1994 the GNP per capita in Rwanda and Mozambique was $80 and $90, respectively, and in the United States $25,800, Japan $34,630, and Switzerland $37,930. In 1994 average life expectancy at birth in Mozambique was 46 years (no figures were available for Rwanda), in the United States 77, Switzerland 78, and Japan 79. See the World Bank's *World Development Report 1996*, 188–89. In 2005 the GDP per capita in Rwanda and Mozambique was $1,206 and $1,242, respectively, and in the United States $41,890, Japan $31,267, and Switzerland $35,633. (The 1994 and 2005 figures have not been standardized for purchasing power parity and so are somewhat misleading, even if they convey an accurate enough picture of intercountry income disparities.) In the 2000–2005 period, average life expectancy at birth in Mozambique had declined to 44 years, while Rwanda's was 43.4; the United States, Switzerland, and Japan registered gains in life expectancy in comparison to 1993, achieving figures of 77.4, 80.7, and 81.9 years, respectively. See World Bank, *World Development Report 2006*, 292–93; United Nations Development Program, *Human Development Report 2007/2008*.

9 See Milanovic, *Worlds Apart*. In this incisive and detailed study, Milanovic defines these four categories (rich, contenders, Third World, Fourth World) by first stating that the dividing line between the rich and the contenders is determined by using the GDP per capita of the poorest WENAO country (i.e., countries of Western Europe, North America, and Oceania, excluding Turkey) as the demarcation point between rich countries and those just behind them (the contenders). Hence in 1960 and 1978 the poorest WENAO country was Portugal, with a GDP per capita of $3,205 and $7,993, respectively (these figures being adjusted to establish purchasing power parity, or PPP). In 2000 the poorest WENAO country was Greece, with a GDP per capita of $13,821 (adjusted for PPP). Countries above this demarcation point were classified as rich, and countries with a GDP no more than one-third below the least affluent WENAO country were termed "contenders." Contenders are "within striking distance [of] catching up and joining the rich." "Third World countries are those with a per capita GDP level within one-[third] and two-thirds of the least affluent WENAO country, and thus are not within "striking distance of the rich since their incomes would on average be only about one-half of the poorest WENAO country." Finally, Fourth World countries are those "very poor" countries whose

GDPs are less than a third of the per capita GDP of the least affluent WENAO country. See Milanovic, *Worlds Apart*, 61–62.

10 See Milanovic, *Worlds Apart*, 68–69.

11 These points are made by Ajit Singh, from whom these figures are taken, in "The Actual Crisis of the 1980s," 104–6. Singh also notes that virtually throughout the 1980s, a decade of economic recession, the Latin American and African countries made net resource transfers to the developed countries, rather than vice versa; in 1984–85 alone the Latin American and African countries transferred $40 billion and $5 billion, respectively, to the developed nations. In a paper published in 2000 Singh writes, "Developing countries need to attain a trend increase in their growth rates, possibly to their pre-1980 long-term rates of about 6 per cent per year . . . to achieve and maintain meaningful 'full employment' . . . with rising real wages and increasing standards of living" (*Global Economic Trends and Social Development*).

12 See "Income Inequality and Poverty Rising in Most OECD Countries," a summary of *Growing Unequal: Income Distribution and Poverty in OECD Countries*, www.oecd.org, accessed on 26 October 2008.

13 The claim that 1 percent of global income is all that is needed to eliminate poverty worldwide is perhaps unrealistic, given the complex causal relationship between economic factors and human capacities that has to be taken into account in any characterization of poverty. The United Nations Development Programme's 1996 *Human Development Report* tried to reflect this complexity by having two sets of indices of poverty, "income poverty" and "human poverty," but this only emphasized the difficulties involved in making plausible the claim that global poverty can be eliminated by expending 1 percent of the world's income.

The subsequent espousal by the *Human Development Report* of the Human Development Index, taking into account education and health as well as income in ascertaining the standard of living, is certainly a methodological advance on previous reports. But the 2005 *Report*'s claim that $300 billion, which "represents 1.6% of the income of the richest 10% of the world's population," will "[lift] 1 billion people living on less than $1 a day above the extreme poverty line threshold" (4) is implausible in the absence of specific proposals for achieving a rapid and irreversible transfer of wealth from the world's richest inhabitants. The 2005 *Report* goes on to recommend "achieving sustainable dynamic processes through which poor countries and poor people can produce their way out of extreme deprivation" (4). "Dynamic processes" in such statements is a typical example of international organization boilerplate prose; it means nothing unless the richest 10 percent of the world's population can actually be brought to the point of relinquishing 1.6 percent of their income, so the crucial question has to be the one of bringing about this desired state of affairs. Liberal-democratic appeals to good intentions (charity, voluntarism, etc.) have been issued in the

West for centuries to no real effect, and programs of significant and immediate economic redistribution are deemed invariably to be (too) "revolutionary," and thus unfeasible, in this postpolitical age. Precisely! For the very poorest, and those in solidarity with them, the alternative therefore is revolution, or nothing. The world's poorest people can only weep every time they see Bono or Bob Geldof or Sting appearing at the side of Tony Blair or George W. Bush, since such appearances give the impression that Blair and Bush are serious about the plight of the hungry and homeless. For a critique of Bono and Geldof and their fondness for photo ops with politicians who pay lip service to the needs of the poor, see Schlosberg, "The Day the Music Failed."

14 It is important that the question of East Asian economic success be broached because American apologists for neoliberalism such as Thomas Friedman are fond of citing the East Asian "tiger economies" as exemplars for poorer countries—as if there were one simple recipe for economic advancement that these countries have no alternative but to follow! There are numerous studies of the East Asian crisis, and I have benefited from reading the following: Jomo K. S., *Tigers in Trouble*; Michie and Grieve Smith, *Global Instability*; Akyüz, ed., *East Asian Development*; Pempel, *The Politics of the Asian Economic Crisis*; Noble and Ravenhill, *The Asian Financial Crisis and the Architecture of Global Finance*; Chang, Palma, and Whittaker, *Financial Liberalization and the Asian Crisis*; Stiglitz and Yusuf, *Rethinking the East Asian Miracle*; Jomo K. S., *After the Storm*; Chang, *The East Asian Development Experience*.

On these transformations I have consulted Griffith-Jones and Leape, *Capital Flows to Developing Countries*. A later version of this paper authored by Griffith-Jones is at www.gapresearch.org, accessed on 7 January 2006. References are to the latter paper. See also Harris, "International Financial Markets and National Transmission Mechanisms," 199–212; Sen, "On Financial Fragility and Its Global Implications," 35–59. A good summary of the changes that have taken place in the global financial architecture of the past two decades is in Griffith-Jones, "Regulatory Implications of Global Financial Markets," 174–97. The institutional basis of these shifts is discussed in Woods, *The Political Economy of Globalization*. More recently, there is a mine of data and information in the historically inflected overviews given in Obstfeld and Taylor, *Global Capital Markets*; Andrews, Hennings, and Pauly, *Governing the World's Money*. A useful conspectus of the global financial architecture is in Michie, *The Handbook of Globalisation*.

15 Griffith-Jones, *Capital Flows to Developing Countries*, 2.

16 Institute of International Finance, www.iif.com, accessed 6 January 2005. The projected figures for 2005 are expected to be near those of 2004.

17 Institute of International Finance, www.iif.com, accessed 20 May 2008.

18 On this investment growth, see tables 2 and 3 in chapter 3.

19 The capacity of present-day stock markets to deviate from "fundamentals" for considerable periods is found not only in the stock exchanges of the emerging

countries but also in the established stock markets of London and New York. See Singh, "Portfolio Equity Flows," 24. See also Aglietta, "Financial Fragility, Crises, and the Stakes of Prudential Control," 293–301.

20 On "fictitious capital," see Marx, *Capital*, vol. 3, part 5; Harris, "Alternative Perspectives on the Financial System"; Tobin, "Prologue," xii.

21 Khan, "Recent Developments in International Financial Markets," 52. Khan is now a senior official with the IMF. Granted that there is no consensus on the effects created in host country financial markets by rises in foreign interest rates, there is also no consensus on the specific impact of foreign portfolio investment on domestic country exchange rates, especially expected exchange rates. Empirical work is still being done here. One study that shows a correlation between the inflow and outflow of portfolio investment in and out of Mexico and the behavior of U.S. interest rates is Grabel, "Marketing the Third World," 1761–76. The often highly complex transaction mechanisms for these new markets have not been around for very long, and information on them is still incomplete, though becoming less scarce. But Mohsin Khan's advice was hopelessly inadequate from the beginning. The LDCs can try to be "prudent" and "implement sound structural policies" but still not attract foreign investment or reduce their poverty levels. A more productive assessment than Khan's of the potential problems posed by transnational portfolio capital of this kind is given in Devlin, Ffrench-Davis, and Griffith-Jones, "Surges in Capital Flows and Development," 225–60. See also Weeks, "The Essence and Appearance of Globalization," 50–74; Palley, "International Finance and Global Deflation," 97–110.

22 See Griffith-Jones and Stallings, "New Global Financial Trends," 164. The option of borrowing from foreign banks to deal with an LDC's internal economic exigencies has now been virtually eliminated by the bank liquidity crisis in the OECD countries. If HICs are facing a seemingly unprecedented crisis, the plight of the poorer countries is, given the balance of probabilities, more likely to be devastating.

23 For these figures, see Tobin, "Prologue," xvi. According to the World Bank, in 1990 there were 232 emerging market funds throughout the world, with net assets totaling $13.7 billion. By mid-1995 these had increased nearly sixfold, with estimated net assets of about $123 billion. See World Bank, *World Debt Tables*, 20. For the 2005 figure, see Merrill Lynch and Capgemini, *World Wealth Report 2005*.

24 In 1995 Malaysia had a services account deficit of $6.7 billion (20 billion ringgit), due mainly to foreign companies repatriating profits from their investments. See *Far Eastern Economic Review*, 12 December 1997, 65. The propensity for "fast money" to gravitate toward property development and speculation is borne out by the fact that in Kuala Lumpur, the capital of Malaysia, the volume of newly constructed office space in 1997 alone exceeded the volume for the whole of the preceding ten years, and the supply of retail space in 1998 represented a rise of

140 percent from 1995 levels. See *Far Eastern Economic Review*, 15 May 1997, 86.

25 On the inconsistent triad or "trilemma" of capital mobility, stable exchange rates, and monetary policy independence, see B. J. Cohen, "Phoenix Risen"; Obstfeld and Taylor, *Global Capital Markets*, 29–31. On the thesis that in principle capital mobility disposes governments to seek a multilateral cooperative framework for monetary and fiscal policy adjustments, see Andrews, "Capital Mobility and State Autonomy"; Andrews and Willett, "Financial Interdependence and the State." There is an ample literature indicating that, globalization notwithstanding, national governments do have room to make macroeconomic policy changes that stabilize overseas capital flows. See, inter alia, Harris, "Financial Markets and the Real Economy," 60–72; Goodman and Pauly, "The Obsolescence of Capital Controls?" Goodman and Pauly make the argument that there need not be a separation between (longer term) foreign direct investment and (short-term) portfolio capital since the political arrangements devised to deal with the latter will have implications for the former (81).

26 Andrews and Willett, "Financial Interdependence and the State," 487, make the relevant point that the United States can pursue fiscal policies that cause significant fluctuations in the dollar, whereas the course taken by the dollar on international currency markets rarely affects U.S. fiscal policy. At the time of this writing the U.S. dollar has reached historical lows against the euro, and yet nothing has changed significantly in U.S. macroeconomic policy in response. Few other countries enjoy the luxury of being able to overlook to such a degree the impact of fiscal policy on their currencies, and vice versa. The greater economic flexibility afforded wealthy countries such as the United States was noted sixty years ago by Albert Hirschman in *National Power and the Structure of International Trade*. For the problems small states encounter when international markets are able to constrain domestic economic policy, see Katzenstein, *Small States in World Markets*.

27 There were of course other factors at work in the Mexican collapse, not least the vast amounts of foreign equity capital that flowed into Mexico in the 1990s. Between 1992 and 1994 the average annual capital inflow rate was 8 percent of GDP (as opposed to 5 percent of GDP during the previous peak in 1977–81). The share price index in the Mexican stock market rose from 250 in 1989 to 2,500 in 1994, even though its average annual GDP growth rate between 1990 and 1994 was only 2.5 percent, and even though Mexico's current account deficit in 1993 was $20 billion, representing 6 percent of GDP (it rose to 9 percent of GDP in 1994). On the matter of high interest rates, it should be acknowledged that the Bundesbank was also pursuing a policy of high interest rates in the early 1990s. After the collapse, Mexico's real GDP fell by 7 percent in 1995, and that in Argentina by 5 percent through a "knock-on" effect. For this, see Singh, "Portfolio Equity Flows," 26. The similarities between Mexico and Argentina and some of the East Asian countries a few years later are easy to see.

28 The dot-com boom of the late 1990s ended very quickly, and the United States started to go into recession in 2001. The U.S. expansion that has taken place since 2003 has now petered out with the current financial crisis, so dependent was this expansion on a housing market boom that collapsed precipitously. Japan is only now emerging, albeit fitfully and very slowly, from a decade and a half of recession, and the Western European nations still face high levels of unemployment and relatively low growth rates.

29 These "market-friendly" injunctions are contained in the World Bank's influential *World Development Report* published in 1991 (see especially 5). The United Nations Development Programme, *Human Development Report 1997*, after chronicling the widening gap between wealthier and poorer countries (a gap that has a great deal to do with the inhospitability poorer countries experience "systemically" at the hand of international trade regimes that use "free trade" and "open markets" as shibboleths), still brings itself to commend the market as a solution to the plight of the poor: "Market competition offers an important way in which people, especially poor people, can escape economic domination by exploitative government, big landlords and big retailers" (102).

30 For the World Bank's assessment of East Asia's economic success, see its publication *The East Asian Miracle*. Robert Wade provides a fascinating account of the ways this report was gerrymandered to fit the terms of the Bank's neoliberal ideology in "Japan, the World Bank, and the Art of Paradigm Maintenance." The Bank's *World Development Report 1997* backtracks on its earlier and sheerly ideological hostility to the state, but tries to show that state intervention, whose effectiveness in some cases the Bank now grudgingly acknowledges, is nonetheless compatible with "market friendliness." As Lance Taylor noted in "Editorial: The Revival of the Liberal Creed," there have been other recent changes in the World Bank's policy disposition: the already noted "recognition of the importance of at least functional public intervention" and "the need to provide supporting revenues; realization that controls on external capital movements and prudential regulation can help contain financial fragility; abandonment of the doctrine that raising the local interest rate will stimulate saving and thereby growth; initiatives to roll over or forgive the bulk of official debt owed by the poorest economies." At the same time, Taylor rightly believes that the World Bank is still some way short of adopting policies that fully support the economic advancement of lower-income countries. A very similar assessment is to be found in Singh, "Openness and the Market Friendly Approach to Development," who provides trenchant criticism of the Total Factor Productivity model that underlies the World Bank's approach to developing countries. This model, says Singh, unrealistically assumes "full employment of resources and perfect competition, none of which obtain in the real world. Moreover, it is a wholly supply-side model which ignores altogether the role of demand-factors" (1813). The problem with Singh's argument, however, is his belief that the institutional basis for the Japanese model of economic growth was replicated by Taiwan and

South Korea, with Indonesia and Malaysia possibly following close behind. The latter part of this claim will appear wildly implausible to anyone with firsthand experience of the corruption-ridden bureaucracies of Indonesia and Malaysia.

31 For Arrighi, see *The Long Twentieth Century* and "Workers of the World at Century's End." Though Arrighi is careful to acknowledge that "it is not at all clear whether the emergent Japanese leadership can actually translate into a fifth systemic cycle of accumulation" (335), I shall argue below that it is possible that the emerging or next system of accumulation may not be one that can be understood in terms of a national hegemony that makes intelligible or plausible the notion of a leadership exercised in these terms by Japan or China or anyone else. The view that the rise of the East Asian nations has started to put an end to U.S. economic supremacy is complemented in some quarters by the conviction that their emergence as economic powers also effectively discredits dependency theory, which maintains that nations outside the capitalist core, such as the East Asian economies, find it structurally difficult if not impossible to leave behind their initial "peripheral" or "semiperipheral" developmental situations. For such a view, see Doner, "Limits of State Strength," 398; Hawes and Liu, "Explaining the Dynamics of the Southeast Asian Political Economy," 630. More recently, Arrighi has championed China as the successor of the American economic hegemony. See his *Adam Smith in Beijing*. Arrighi's argument is detailed and sophisticated and can be responded to only in a similarly detailed way. Suffice it to say that while he seems to be right in his assessment of the unraveling of America's hegemony, China will not really become the next global economic hegemon until it is able to command financial markets and their accompanying instruments in the ways the U.S. and Western Europe have at their disposal.

32 See International Monetary Fund, *Global Financial Stability Report*.

33 See OECD, "Total Assets of Private Pension Funds within OECD Countries (2001)," www.oecd.org, accessed on 7 January 2006.

34 In this connection Lance Taylor has noted that "[half] the people and two-thirds of the countries in the world lack full control over their own economic policy. Expatriate 'experts' managed by industrial country nationals and based in Washington DC regulate their macroeconomics, investment projects, and social spending" ("Editorial," 145).

35 On this, see Fishlow, "Economic Development in the 1990s," 1826. Fishlow makes the point that the World Bank has consistently ignored the issue of income distribution, emphasizing instead the question of higher productivity. I am indebted to his account in the rest of this paragraph.

36 Thus, according to UNCTAD's *World Investment Directory 2004*, in Latin America and the Caribbean "[FDI] flows were down by 4% in 2003 and an overall 55% between 1999 and 2003." The same report does say, however, that this decline shows signs of bottoming out. This note of optimism perhaps reflects the fact that in 2004 developing country GDP grew by the record figure of 6.6 percent, a trend that had begun in 2003. But at the same time, net capital flows to devel-

oping countries reached 4.5 percent of their GDP, still some way below the high figure of over 6 percent attained in the mid-1990s. See World Bank, *Global Development Finance 2005*, http://siteresources.worldbank.org, accessed on 9 January 2006.

37 To quote the World Bank, "Net FDI inflows [to sub-Saharan Africa] amounted to $11 billion in 2004, compared to portfolio equity inflows of $3.5 billion and private debt inflows of under $2 billion. Oil producing countries, notably Angola and Nigeria, along with the largest economy in the region, South Africa, accounted for 36 percent of the FDI inflows to the region, below the average of 53 percent over the previous seven years. All of the portfolio equity flows and most of the private debt flows are concentrated in South Africa." See World Bank, *Global Development Finance 2005*, http://siteresources.worldbank.org, accessed on 9 January 2006.

38 Akyüz and Gore, "The Investment-Profits Nexus in East Asian Industrialization," emphasize the importance in East Asian growth of overall capital accumulation and the role of government in speeding it up. Many analysts, including those at the World Bank, have tended to stress the importance of resource allocation for East Asian industrialization at the expense of the interactions between profits and investment. I don't want to generalize the East Asian model, but the importance of profits and investment for growth highlighted by Akyüz and Gore puts in even plainer relief the predicament of many LDCs, who simply do not have the resources to invest in growth. For Samir Amin, see his *Capitalism in the Age of Globalization*. In my characterizations of uneven development and the "theorizations" of it provided by marxists, I have had Amin's pioneering work most in mind, though I have tried to remain aware of the differences between him and other members of this tradition.

39 Kozul-Wright, "Mind the Gaps," 58.

40 Kozul-Wright, "Mind the Gaps," 59. Kozul-Wright's argument is supported by Wade, "Financial Regime Change?," who shows that China's rise accounts overwhelmingly for what many regard (mistakenly!) as *overall* LDC economic advancement since the 1980s, and moreover that China's economic success is not due to the "open market" shibboleths underwritten by the neoliberal consensus, but rather by a government-driven and strictly regulated development policy. The state, and not markets, has been the driver of China's economic growth.

41 It is precisely for this reason that Ernesto Laclau regarded dependency theory as a deviation from marxism. According to Laclau, dependency theory eschews analysis of the mode of production and the relations of production (for Laclau the heart of marxism) in favor of the analysis of the system of exchange between nations. See his "Feudalism and Capitalism in Latin America."

42 See Arrighi, "Hegemony Unravelling: Part 2," 87.

43 Arrighi, "Financial Expansions in World Historical Perspective," 155; see also Arrighi, "Hegemony Unravelling: Part 2," 86. I take this description of his posi-

tion from Arrighi's somewhat heated response to a review of his book by Robert Pollin. See Pollin, "Contemporary Economic Stagnation in World Historical Perspective." I don't mean to adjudicate in this exchange, and merely use part of Arrighi's response because it contains an excellent summary of the position he sets out in *The Long Twentieth Century*.

44 Arrighi, "Financial Expansions," 157. See also Arrighi and Silver, *Chaos and Governance in the Modern World System*.

45 Arrighi, "Financial Expansions," 157. Pollin agrees with Arrighi on this point (that all financial expansions are succeeded by their material counterparts) in "Contemporary Economic Stagnation," 115–17.

46 That no such Hegelian *Weltgeist* is at work in Arrighi's architectonic is clear from his insistence that "sustained financial expansions materialize only when the enhanced liquidity preference of capitalist agencies is matched by adequate 'demand' conditions" ("Financial Expansions," 156). For Arrighi these "demand" conditions arise only when there is interstate competition for mobile capital, and in each phase a new round of interstate competition and a new set of "imperialist practices" is introduced. See "Hegemony Unravelling: Part 2," 90. The gist of my position, however, is that the current regime of accumulation makes financial expansion possible without the promptings of interstate competition (a notion Arrighi gets from Weber) since (1) the overwhelming majority of states are in no position structurally to join this competition even at the most rudimentary level, and (2) the new kinds of capital come in a bewildering number of forms (which are often hybridized) and move at such velocities that states cannot "compete" for them in the old ways. Even the World Bank, for all its enthusiasm in fostering what it takes to be competitive trade and markets, can do no more than enjoin LDCs who are anxious to attract such capital to "keep exchange rates favorable" and have "sound macroeconomic fundamentals." Though well meant, such prefectural advice is simply gratuitous and akin to the injunction that pupils should give it a go when competing in the school three-legged race. But the World Bank's vapidity in this context is profoundly symptomatic; as the preceding discussion has shown, there is virtually nothing that most undeveloped countries can do at present to create "adequate 'demand' conditions" for mobile portfolio capital. Warren Buffett does not stay up at night pondering over a possible lucrative investment opportunity that Berkshire Hathaway (his investment company) could exploit in East Timor or Mali. And yet, until the current financial collapse, this has been an era of prodigious expansion of financial capital.

47 Arrighi considers roughly similar scenarios in his epilogue to *The Long Twentieth Century* when he outlines three possible outcomes that may transpire in the event of a supersession of the U.S. regime of accumulation (354–55). First, the United States may use its military and political power to retain the surplus capital that would otherwise go to a new center of accumulation, in which case

it would become "a truly global world empire." Second, East Asian capital may supersede the American regime, but since the new regime would not have the military and global political power of its predecessor, "the underlying layer of the market economy would revert to some kind of anarchic order." Third, capitalist history may be terminated by the growing violence that its various orders have spawned in the past six hundred years. The argument broached in the final part of this chapter poses an alternative to these three scenarios. I maintain that a polynucleated, multispatial regime of global capitalist accumulation now prevails, one premised on different and sometimes quite radical degrees of separation between Marx's two primary forms of capital, namely, productive capital and finance (or financial) capital. The term "finance capital" does not occur in Marx's oeuvre, but chapter 27 of volume 3 of *Capital* ("The Role of Credit in Capitalist Production") was the basis of the fuller elaboration of the concept in Hilferding's *Finanzkapital*. Marx did suggest that there were two ways of extending the means of credit available to industrial capital that correspond in brief outline to Hilferding's two notions of productive capital and finance capital.

48 There is a problem in mapping the distinctions made in this chapter onto Arrighi's distinction between the "material phase" $M \to C$ and the "financial phase" $C \to M^1$ of a systemic cycle of accumulation. Pollin suggests that Arrighi's renditions of Marx's formulas are problematic because they "obscure the logic operating in both phases," namely, that more money (profits) must ensue at the end of each of these processes. This may be so. In this chapter, however, the distinction between "productive capital" and "financial capital" refers not so much to two alternating phases as to two different spatial configurations or logics for the organization of capital. Consequently, "productive capital" and "financial capital" do not map easily onto (Arrighi's) $M \to C$ and $C \to M^1$, respectively, and I use "productive capital" and "financial capital" rather than his formulas in giving my account. In "Hegemony Unravelling: Part 1" and "Hegemony Unravelling: Part 2" Arrighi borrows David Harvey's notion of a "spatial fix" to talk about the forms of reorganization created by new phases of accumulation, but this emphasis on spatiality is still compatible with his axiomatic presumption that distinct phases of accumulation succeed each other epochally (i.e., temporally).

49 Helleiner, "The World of Money," 295. The volume of transactions on foreign exchange markets more than quadrupled between 1986 and 1992, and the daily total reported gross turnover rose from $932 billion in April 1989 to $1,354 billion in April 1992, a rise of 35 percent. For these figures, see Eichengreen, *International Monetary Arrangements for the 21st Century*, 61. Eichengreen also notes that the volume of net daily foreign exchange transactions now exceeds the total official reserves of all IMF member countries combined (64). The IMF had 178 member nations in December 1993 (Eichengreen's time of writing).

50 For these figures, see the speech by U.S. Securities and Exchange Commissioner Roel C. Campos on 13 June 2005, www.sec.gov, accessed on 9 January 2006.

51 On this, see Germain, *The International Organization of Credit*, 161.

52 The importance of path dependency is recognized in Pollin, "Contemporary Economic Stagnation," 117.

53 Pollin, "Contemporary Economic Stagnation," 116. This question is posed because it is important for Arrighi and Pollin, though, as will be seen, it is not necessary for us to answer it if we think of the relation between financial capital and productive capital in terms other than those of alternation or succession.

54 Arrighi, *The Long Twentieth Century*, 348.

55 On American Airlines, see Harmes, "Institutional Investors," 112; for Fannie Mae and Freddie Mac, see Henwood, *Wall Street*, 91. Henwood's book is a remarkable source of information for anyone interested in the myriad new and different ways in which the current capital recycling mechanism works.

56 The details are given in my unpublished paper "The 1997–8 East Asian Financial Crisis."

57 See Arrighi, *The Long Twentieth Century*, 325–56, for his assessment of East Asia's economic advance, made prior to the collapse in 1997 of the region's economies. Arrighi is right to emphasize the importance of "cheap-labor seeking investment" in promoting regional growth, but account also needs to be taken of the path-dependent structural sensitivity of the industrial policies of the Southeast Asian governments to what was happening in Northeast Asia in the mid-1980s. On this structural sensitivity, see Jomo K. S. et al., *Southeast Asia's Misunderstood Miracle*, 160.

58 Dani Rodrik has rightly called this U.S. "accomplishment" a "financial confidence game," and says that it amounts to "a boon for the U.S. Treasury but a rotten deal for the home economy." See "Why Financial Markets Misbehave," 190.

59 I take the term "investor aristocracy" from Harmes, "Institutional Investors," 114, where it is used to designate those workers who may have belonged to a "labor aristocracy" in the days of the Keynesian and New Deal economic dispensation, but who (in considerably smaller numbers) are now transformed into investors by the succeeding phase of accumulation. It is important to note that an effective state formation is a prerequisite for the United States successfully to channel into the fiscal system tax revenues harvested from stock exchange speculation. The role of the state as the forcing house par excellence for securing tax revenues has been stressed by Max Weber and Michael Mann. For Mann, see "The Autonomous Power of the State," 109–36. See also Hobson, *The Wealth of States*, especially 252–53. Marxists need to engage more strenuously with this neo-Weberian approach to the state system if they are to analyze satisfactorily the ensemble of substructures that make up the FCSR.

60 See especially Samir Amin, *Delinking*; Diaz-Alejandro, "Delinking North and South," 72–121.

Chapter 5. Delinking

1 For a powerful critique of the way such international organizations as the World Bank systematically exclude any consideration of the class-based nature of the allocation of surpluses in capitalist regimes, see Wolff, "World Bank/Class Blindness," 172–83. "Class" here is understood as a particular kind of social structure needed to organize and allocate surpluses. Harriss, *Depoliticizing Development*, shows how the World Bank's newfound interest in the notion of "social capital," an emphasis associated with Joseph Stiglitz's previous tenure as its chief economist, serves to efface the effects of class divisions in the poor countries.

2 The magnitude of the North-South polarization is reflected in the fact that the so-called three Northern blocs (the United States, Europe, and Japan and East Asia) between them account for over 80 percent of world production, trade, and finance and over 95 percent of global research and development. On this see Mann, "The First Failed Empire of the Twenty-First Century," 58.

3 Anyone who thinks that the poor nations benefit from such compliance need only look at the fate of the privatization of Tanzania's water supply, imposed by the World Bank as a condition of debt forgiveness. The Tanzanian government subsequently cancelled the privatization contract in 2005 because of the British-German consortium's poor performance. Numerous such privatizations have been imposed on Third World countries as a part of structural adjustment programs. On the Tanzania water supply case, see Vidal, "Flagship Water Privatisation Fails in Tanzania," *The Guardian*, 25 May 2005. On the narrow technocratic criteria used by the World Bank to assess development projects, see Pincus, "State Simplification and Institutional Building."

4 In this account, "exploitation" refers to the appropriation of a society's surplus product by a particular class or social group. As Marx argued, every society, if it is to grow, needs to produce more than is required merely for that society to reproduce itself; the appropriation of this surplus, which typically is created by every productive force in that society, by one class or social group therefore involves the exploitation (by that appropriating class or group) of the other classes and groups whose productive efforts were an inextricable part of the processes by which that society's surpluses are generated. On this see Foley, "The Value of Money, the Value of Labor Power, and the Marxian Transformation Problem."

5 Taylor, "Economic Openness," 91–147. Those inclined to be sanguine about the way LDCs are treated by the World Bank and IMF can find in press reports numerous examples of how these organizations "advise" the poorest LDCs, such as Sierra Leone after the end of its recent civil war. According to a report in *The Guardian*:

> Even before Sierra Leone's 11-year civil war ended in February 2002, the aid advisers from Washington and London had arrived in the capital of Freetown with their prescriptions for development and tackling poverty.
> Their solution to the problems of the second poorest country in the world

was to privatise virtually the entire country, including, most controversially, the national water utility.

See David Pallister, "Developing World Confused by UK Aid Guidelines," *The Guardian*, 24 September 2005.

6 Weisbrot, Baker, and Rosnik, "The Scorecard on Development," 45–46.

7 Taylor, "The Rocky Road to Reform," 141. Taylor has analyzed several results from the adoption of the prescriptions enshrined in the Washington consensus and concludes that they have been only barely successful as a reform package, not infrequently providing a combination of "high interest rates, stagflation, deregulation and financial crashes." This leads him to suggest that LDCs would be better off not underwriting capital markets and choosing instead state-provided credit channeled through development banks or made available directly by the government. Taylor concludes that "the Bretton Woods institutions . . . remain impervious to the fact that the invisible hand plus a minimal government (especially in its fiscal, regulatory and investment roles) do *not* necessarily act together to support sustainable economic growth" (96). See also Taylor, "External Liberalization, Economic Performance, and Distribution in Latin America and Elsewhere," 166–96. Support for this position is given in the country studies in Armijo, *Financial Globalization and Democracy in Emerging Markets*.

8 Uki Goñi, "Argentina's Unorthodox Rehab," *The Guardian*, 10 January 2006.

9 For proposals regarding a "new regionalism" that would involve dismantling the World Bank and the IMF, see S. Amin, "Regionalization in Response to Polarizing Globalization," 54–84.

10 Rudra, *Globalization and the Race to the Bottom in Developing Countries*, has argued on the basis of empirical studies that while globalization has indeed promoted a "race to the bottom" on the part of the LDCs, the "losers" in the LDCs are not the poor (who have never benefited from LDC domestic institutions), but the LDC middle classes, who are vulnerable to the opening of LDC domestic institutions to the forces of globalization.

11 On this point and for these ratios, see S. Amin, "The Conditions for an Alternative Global System Based on Social and International Justice."

12 S. Amin, "The Conditions for an Alternative Global System."

13 The root of this very powerful fantasy is actually an axiom in neoclassical economics now widely discredited outside the domain of neoclassicism, but which is still entrenched in the thinking of the Washington consensus, namely, the assumption that the "rational" expectations of self-interested market actors can be "adjusted" by market forces provided those forces are not "distorted" by governments or other agencies with an interest in market manipulation. On this axiom and its role in LDC economies, see Grabel, "The Political Economy of 'Policy Credibility'"; Shaikh, "The Economic Mythology of Neoliberalism," 41–49. For all his reluctance to move to a policy position that not only repudiates the Washington consensus (which he already has) but also regards some form of postcapitalism as the only real way beyond this consensus (which he has

not), Joseph Stiglitz, then chief economist at the World Bank, did begin to see that this axiom is not really tenable when one begins to grasp the modus operandi of actually existing capitalism. On Stiglitz, see his collection of speeches and lectures, with a commentary by Chang, in Chang, *Joseph Stiglitz and the World Bank*. On the World Bank's problematic instrumentality with regard to LDC macroeconomic policy, see Pincus and Winters, *Reinventing the World Bank*. As Chang points out in his *Kicking Away the Ladder*, 2–3, hardly any of the developed countries now propping up the Washington consensus themselves espoused the nakedly laissez-faire policies they now advocate for LDCs during their own developmental phases in the eighteenth and nineteenth centuries. See also the detailed country studies in Hobson, *The Wealth of States;* Hobson and Weiss, *States and Economic Development;* Berger and Dore, *National Diversity and Global Capitalism*. A move beyond the Washington consensus emerged under Stiglitz's intellectual leadership at the World Bank, but this "post–Washington consensus" quickly came under fire for focusing too much on market imperfections while studiously ignoring questions of power, and thus for adhering to the very liberal capitalism responsible in the first place for the Third World's lack of development. For this critique of the "post–Washington consensus," see Fine, Lapavitsas, and Pincus, *Development Policy in the Twenty-First Century*. See also Fine, "New Growth Theory," 201–17.

14 This elucidation of Baran and Sweezy is taken from Patnaik, "A Saint and A Sage." See also Baran and Sweezy, *Monopoly Capital;* Sweezy, *The Theory of Capitalist Development*.

15 The problem here is that capitalism needs to treat labor as a full-fledged commodity, yet this is impossible. Commodities are fully intersubstitutable, and while labor-substituting technology can be introduced, and is being introduced all the time, in this way substituting for workers, in the end there can be no substitution capable of creating a completely workerless environment. Even if machines did all the work, certain information inputs at least would have to be made by workers or manager-workers, such as the decision whether to install machines of type X or type Y.

16 To quote Marx, "A fall in the profit rate, and accelerating accumulation, are simply different expressions of the same process, in so far as both express the development of productivity . . . there is an acceleration of accumulation, as far as its mass is concerned, even though the rate of this accumulation falls with the rate of profit" (*Capital*, 3:349). There was a severe decline in profitability in the capitalist centers between 1970 and 1990, when the profit rate in the G7 countries was on average about 40 percent lower than for the period 1950–70, while in 1990 it was 45 percent below the peak reached in 1965. On this, see R. Brenner, *The Economics of Global Turbulence*, 186, figure 11. There is an endless debate among marxists as to the plausibility of Marx's theory of the falling rate of profit; one such debate is whether the "underconsumptionist" view (e.g., Baran and Sweezy) is right or whether the "overaccumulationist" view (e.g., Robert

Brenner) is more persuasive. For obvious reasons I cannot delve into the details of these debates. Suffice to say that the empirical evidence is firmly on the side of some kind of declining profitability thesis (here Marx was therefore right), as much as we may debate the nature of the precise mechanisms responsible for this decline. My position is that there is a fundamental spatial division between structures of accumulation which enables both these theories to operate in tandem: the countries in the South generally suffer from underconsumption, while those in the North tend to encounter overcapacity and overproduction, and in both instances the rate of profit is driven down. Hence the frequent exhortation made by economic policymakers in Washington and London that the Asian economies should save less and consume more! It should also be noted that this theory was extended by Rosa Luxemburg into an account of imperialism; according to Luxemburg, capitalism has to counter the falling rate of profit by seeking new zones of accumulation, and these are perforce located outside the developed capitalist centers. On spatial divisions and their impact on accumulation, see R. Brenner, Jessop, Jones, and MacLeod, *State/Space*. On weak effective demand in the LDCs, see the empirically detailed studies used in Taylor, "External Liberalization," 192–93, which lead him to conclude that even when trade regimes were liberalized, "trade . . . held back or added weakly to effective demand" (192).

17 See R. Brenner, *The Economics of Global Turbulence* and *The Boom and the Bubble*. The page references cited in the text in the following paragraphs are to *The Economics of Global Turbulence*.

18 As Michael Parenti points out, the aim here is for firms, with the ready collusion of governments, to ensure that "the costs are socialized; the profits are privatized." See his "Government by Giveaway," to which this paragraph is indebted. For socialism, since costs are socialized, profits have likewise to be socially owned and distributed. On the impact of the British Conservative government privatizations, see Florio, *The Great Divesture*, who concludes that these privatizations had little long-term impact on prices and productivity but contributed to a widening of income disparities.

19 United Nations, *World Economic Situation and Prospects 2006*, www.un.org/esa, accessed on 4 February 2006.

20 United Nations, *World Economic Situation and Prospects 2008*, www.un.org/esa, accessed on 21 May 2008. The financial crisis worsened rapidly toward the end of 2008, so clearly this projection of growth for 2009 may need to be revised in the light of recent events.

21 Even the judicious Branko Milanovic comes to the conclusion that the only way to deal with the increasingly entrenched global plutocracy is for there to be a move toward redistribution. See his *Worlds Apart*, 157–63.

22 For these proposals, see S. Amin, "The Conditions for an Alternative Global System."

23 The interest in removing the causes of poverty is not a new one, nor is it con-

fined to marxist and neo-marxist thinkers. As Gareth Stedman Jones points out in his invaluable *An End to Poverty?*, this debate goes back to the late eighteenth century, when it engaged Thomas Paine, Condorcet, and others. See also Thompson, *The Politics of Inequality*, which shows that a strong egalitarian strain existed in the thought of the founding fathers of the Republic which has since been extirpated.

Chapter 6. The Politics of Identity

1 The true picture regarding working-class consciousness in the postwar period is much more complicated than the one provided in my cursory sketch. Michael Mann's pioneering *Consciousness and Action among the Western Working Class*, based on surveys in Britain, France, Italy, and the United States, shows that working-class consciousness in these countries is marked by a profound "dualism," so that "co-existing with a normally passive sense of alienation is an experience of (largely economic) interdependence with the employer at a factual, if not a normative, level. Surges of class consciousness are continually undercut by economism, and capitalism survives" (68). Mann confirms the picture given in this text, and goes on to say that "those who are most alienated and most desperate are those who are least confident of their ability to change their situation. Those who are most confident in their own power and clearest in their intentions feel least embattled and disposed towards desperate remedies" (70).

2 The stultification of everyday life that accompanied the prosperity of the postwar years was mocked in the writings of the Beats in the United States (Ginsberg's *Howl* and Kerouac's *Dharma Bums* are exemplary in this regard). The inappropriately named Angry Young Men were a British parallel to the Beats, but the irreverence and contrariness that permeated such works as *Lucky Jim*, *Look Back in Anger*, and *Room at the Top* did not last long. By the time Mrs. Thatcher took office in 1979, the erstwhile Angry Young Men (Kingsley Amis, John Braine, John Osborne, and Philip Larkin) had become bibulous old reactionaries with an unstinting admiration for her policies. For the cultural context underlying the emergence of the Angry Young Men, see Alan Sinfield's excellent *Literature, Politics, and Culture in Postwar Britain*. For studies of the cultural context for Beat writing, see Minnen, van der Bent, and van Elteren, *Beat Culture*; Raskin, *American Scream*.

3 For two accounts, from rather different perspectives, that stress the considerable significance of Third World insurrectionary movements for left-wing activist groups in the West in the 1960s, see Elbaum, *Revolution in the Air*; K. Ross, *May '68 and Its Afterlives*.

4 The most notable recent attempt to delineate the significance of the new social movements for the quest for emancipation is probably Laclau and Mouffe, *Hegemony and Socialist Strategy*. See also their "Post-Marxism without Apologies"; Laclau, "Universalism, Particularism and the Question of Identity," 93–

108; Mouffe, "Democratic Politics and the Question of Identity," 33–45. For commentary, see Landry and MacLean, "Rereading Laclau and Mouffe"; Fisk, "Post-Marxism," 144–65. For an account which sees the crisis of the New Left as the ground for the emergence of the new social movements and its subsequent identity politics, see Farred, "Endgame Identity?"; Gilroy, "British Cultural Studies and the Pitfalls of Identity," 223–39.

5 See Palumbo-Liu, "Multiculturalism Now." See also his "Assumed Identities."

6 Palumbo-Liu regards Mead's *And Keep Your Powder Dry: An Anthropologist Looks at America* as the locus classicus of this endeavor. He is indebted to the discussion of Mead and Ruth Benedict in Shannon, *A World Made Safe for Differences*. Shannon argues that the American politics of identity arose not in the so-called countercultural 1960s, but two decades before, during the cold war.

7 See Palumbo-Liu, "Multiculturalism Now," 112–13, quoting Benedict, *The Chrysanthemum and the Sword*, 14–15.

8 Palumbo-Liu, "Multiculturalism Now," 115–16. See also Huntington, "The United States," 59–115; *The Clash of Civilizations and the Remaking of World Order*.

9 Homi Bhabha is the foremost thinker of the problems posed by this situation of a necessary negotiation between cultures, all of which are unavoidably partial by virtue of their embeddedness in the local. See *The Location of Culture* and "Culture's In-Between."

10 A qualification of "current" is needed here, because the need to engage in a negotiation between partial cultures is not confined to the past few decades, but was felt in bygone centuries. Linda Colley has made the point that a British identity had to be forged out of its Scottish, Welsh, and Irish elements in order to enable Protestant Britain to wage war with Catholic France and to enable Britain's imperial enterprises. See her *Britons: Forging the Nation, 1707–1837*. Her suggestion that facilitating Britain's imperial outreach is a motivating factor in this recourse to a British identity is borne out by Gananath Obeyeskere, who argues that British sailors exploring the Pacific in the eighteenth century had willy-nilly to resort to a conception of British identity in their attempts to make themselves understood, as "British," to the inhabitants of the islands. See Obeyeskere, "'British Cannibals,'" 7–31.

11 The suggestion here that a future collective liberation will almost certainly embody many disparate approaches and forms of action is in line with the late Iris Marion Young's persuasive argument that pluralism will be an unavoidable feature of a future transformed society. See her *Justice and the Politics of Difference*, chapter 6.

12 The foremost recent exponent of this argument is Walter Benn Michaels. See his "Political Science Fictions." Michaels's main point in this essay is that real antagonism arises only at the level of political or ideological difference, and not racial or cultural difference, and that here it is not "difference" but "sameness" that is germane. If one believes that one's ideological position is right or par-

takes of the truth, this is not because it happens to be different from someone else's, but because one believes it to be right or true for everyone. That is, one believes it to be the same for everyone. A contention between rival truths is thus more properly to be seen as fragmentation within the universal and not as a battle between particularisms. A similar point about the necessity of this "universalism of truth" is made by Alain Badiou in all his writings. Michaels's conclusion is that there is real politics only when there is "an indifference to difference" (662). His position is problematic insofar as he assumes that cultural or racial differences cannot be "real" political or ideological differences, whereas it is clear that there can be instances when racial or cultural differences are unavoidably political (apartheid South Africa would be a case in point). For a critique of Michaels along these lines, see M. B. Ross, "Commentary," especially 835–37.

13 I am certainly not suggesting that movements based on identity cannot be efficacious independently of anticapitalist struggles conducted under marxist auspices. As I indicated in chapter 2, this claim is not plausible when struggles occur in contexts marked by very diverse social relations, the range and plenitude of which cannot be encompassed within the remit of a single movement, however capacious and dynamic that movement is.

14 On thinking that the limits of capital are coextensive with those of the universe, see Deleuze and Guattari, *A Thousand Plateaus*, 23–24. The point that capital's supremacy is not unassailable is made by Slavoj Žižek in several of his works, but most notably in "Multiculturalism, or the Cultural Logic of Multinational Capitalism," especially 35.

15 For Gilroy, see "British Cultural Studies and the Pitfalls of Identity," 223–39, where he concludes that it is important "to dispose of the idea that identity is an absolute and to find the courage necessary to argue that identity formation—even body-coded ethnic and gender identity—is a chaotic process that can have no end. In this way, we may be able to make cultural identity a premise of political action rather than a substitute for it" (238). Gilroy contends that the theme of identity is already present when the question of class affiliation is posed, a proposition that is essential to E. P. Thompson's *The Making of the English Working Class* and Richard Hoggart's *The Uses of Literacy*. This adds an interesting complication for those who regard the concern with identity as a feature of a politics that succeeded one based on the institutions of class. Wendy Brown is less concerned to argue that identity politics is the successor of a previous class-based politics, and prefers instead to see this transformation in terms of the weakening or disappearance of a viable *critique* of capitalism. For Brown, see *States of Injury*, especially 59. See also Brown's "Wounded Attachments," 199–227.

16 Žižek in several of his works, but most notably in "Multiculturalism, or the Cultural Logic of Multinational Capitalism," especially 44.

17 Žižek, "Multiculturalism," 44; his emphasis.

18 Bobbitt, *The Shield of Achilles*, 750. Bobbitt's argument relies on a number of vast theses expressed with considerable magniloquence (e.g., "We are at the beginning of the sixth great revolution in strategic and constitutional affairs"; "The new age of indeterminacy into which we are now plunging") to conclude that the outmoded nation-state structure is not going to be able to deal with a whole range of geopolitical and cultural problems caused by an emerging conjuncture that will be dominated by "market states." See 213–42 for Bobbitt's account of the market-state. For a useful review of Bobbitt's book, to which I am much indebted, see David Runciman, "The Garden, the Park and the Meadow."

19 Bobbitt, *The Shield of Achilles*, 750–51; Bobbitt's italics. It should be pointed out that this is one of several scenarios countenanced by Bobbitt, though he does believe that this one is more likely to be realized than the others. What Bobbitt does in constructing this scenario is to intensify further tendencies that are already manifesting themselves demographically. For instance, the most recent U.S. census revealed that 53 percent of Californians do not identify themselves as white and that 40 percent of Californians speak a language other than English at home. The migration of "liberals" to states like Oregon and Vermont for cultural political reasons and Florida "snowbird" retirees with monocultural preferences to leave polyglot south Florida for less cosmopolitan Appalachian mountain towns in Georgia and North Carolina are phenomena that are in the process of being documented.

20 There is a slight but still significant difference between the operation of the "chain of equivalence" in the respective accounts provided by Žižek and Bobbitt. Žižek follows Laclau and Mouffe in taking the chain of equivalence to operate among progressive groups (women, blacks, workers, gays, and so forth), whereas in the "developmental picture of the State" constructed by Bobbitt this chain encompasses all identity-based groups. On the chain of equivalence in Laclau and Mouffe, see, in addition to their *Hegemony and Socialist Strategy*, Mouffe's "Feminism, Citizenship and Radical Democratic Politics," especially 372. Bobbitt, a professor of constitutional law and a former official on the National Security Council and other agencies (in both Republican and Democratic administrations), holds no brief for any kind of progressive politics, preferring instead to talk of the "importance of developing public goods—such as loyalty, civility, trust in authority, respect for family life, reverence for sacrifice, regard for privacy, admiration for political competence—that the market, unaided, is not well adapted to creating and maintaining" (814). Bobbitt is clearly a cold war liberal with the slightest of Third Way whiffs to some of his convictions, and his list of "virtues" would probably meet with approval from Dick Cheney and Donald Rumsfeld, but not perhaps Trotsky, Thomas Sankara, César Chávez, Mariategui, or Subcommandante Marcos (who today would probably want the invocation of such "public goods" to be tied in some way to a critique of the role of the United States as the principal architect of a baneful global order, a critique that is nowhere to be found in *The Shield of Achilles*). The argument of *The Shield*

of Achilles hinges on the thesis that states are constituted by the relationship that obtains between military power and strategy and the legal system, and for this reason Bobbitt cannot do real justice to notions of economic, political, and ideological power in the way that, say, Michael Mann does in *The Sources of Social Power*, volumes 1 and 2.

21 This point is made by Žižek and Wendy Brown. See Žižek, "Multiculturalism," 47; Brown, *States of Injury*, 64. Brown is likewise concerned with the problematic nature of the universal as it is invoked by a troubling version of the politics of identity.

22 All subsequent references to Nozick, *Anarchy, State, and Utopia* are cited in parentheses in the text. David Runciman has noted the affinity between Bobbitt and Nozick in "The Garden, the Park and the Meadow." Nozick subsequently moved to a version of liberalism inspired in part by Isaiah Berlin and repudiated his earlier libertarianism, preferring instead a position that acknowledged "multiple competing values." His earlier absolutist libertarianism was never more than a defense of one of these competing values, and this value could "sometimes be overridden or diminished in trade offs." For this repudiation, see Nozick's essay "The Zigzag of Politics," in *The Examined Life*, especially 292.

23 As David Runciman has correctly observed with regard to Nozick in "The Garden, the Park and the Meadow."

24 It is important to recognize a fundamental difference between Nozick and Bobbitt, their commonalities notwithstanding. Nozick's metautopia is derived conceptually from his doctrine of the minimal state, a doctrine he takes to be enjoined by the conception of the inviolability of individual rights he imputes to Kant (but which admittedly owes more to Nozick himself than to Kant). Nozick is simply not interested in the historical conditions that may or may not make such a "utopia of utopias" realizable. By contrast, Bobbitt is profoundly interested in historical processes, and in fact takes the market-state to be one of the outcomes of the "fifth great revolution in strategic and constitutional affairs," namely, "the Long War" that began in 1914 and ended with the settlement reached in Paris in 1990 that brought an official end to the cold war. Strictly speaking, Bobbitt's multicultural and decentralized market-state polity is not a utopia, if "utopia" is defined as the embodiment of an ideal state of affairs (however the content of this state of affairs is characterized). Where Bobbitt is concerned, this polity results from the "market in sovereignty" created by the weakening of the nation-state as the traditional repository of sovereignty. This polity in itself is not something that is necessarily desirable or undesirable from a philosophical standpoint, and Bobbitt does not pay attention to its philosophical underpinnings.

25 Bobbitt's decentralized federalism, in addition to showing that a multicultural politics will be a constitutive feature of the modus operandi of this system, also makes it clear that this multicultural politics is not likely to be in a position to distinguish in practically significant ways between progressive and reactionary

forms. In such a system, feminist, environmental protectionist, and gay and lesbian communities will exist alongside Southern Baptist fundamentalists and Alaskan wolf hunters in a relation of parity.

26 "We do not want a German Europe, but a European Germany," said Thomas Mann, implying that to be a "good German" is inextricably bound up with being a "good European." For a useful discussion of the implications of the quotation from Mann and other issues, see Risse and Englemann-Martin, "Identity Politics and European Integration," 287–316. Toward the end of his life, Raymond Williams took to referring to himself as a "Welsh European" in order to avoid having to designate himself as a Briton.

27 On religious identities, see Kastoryano, *Negotiating Identities*; and "Muslim Diaspora(s) in Western Europe."

28 This crisscrossing quality in identity constitution was dealt with in chapter 2.

29 See Herzfeld, "The European Self," 139–70. For Macpherson, see *The Political Theory of Possessive Individualism*. For Dumont, see *Homo Hierarchicus* and *Essays on Individualism*. One of the outcomes of this process, whereby the concept of a European identity came to be permeated by the dovetailing ideologies of an individualistic autonomy and colonial superiority, was the extrusion of non-Europeans (such as Muslims) from the conceptual fold of this identity. On this, see Asad, "Muslims and European Identity," 209–27. Herzfeld also makes the point that fields such as cultural anthropology can serve the useful function of identifying the effects exerted by this ideology of individualism in our analyses of nationalism and the role of the nation-state.

30 Herzfeld provides a list of anthropological texts and studies of nationalism which incorporate features of this troubling individualism in "The European Self." Of course the notion of identity is not confined to the individual and can be extended to groups and even nations, as indicated by the title of Fernand Braudel's magisterial *L'identité de la France*.

31 For such questions, see Herzfeld, "The European Self," 144. Herzfeld is of course speaking of an explicitly European identity in this essay, but his caveats about the invocation of a European identity can be generalized to cover any kind of identity.

32 The distinction between a *Grenze* and a *Schranke* is highly technical and not without its problems. For a discussion of the distinction and some of the problems involved, see Inwood, *A Hegel Dictionary*, 177–78.

33 An American colleague of mine, obviously fond of television, said that it was the telecasting for hours on end of these "sports," in which everything seemed to happen in an unending slow motion (and that was when something happened at all!), that gave him the greatest "culture shock" on his first visit to Britain. Incidentally, a similar sentiment in regard to cricket is expressed by Žižek, who calls it "a senselessly ritualized game, almost beyond the grasp of a Continental, in which the prescribed gestures (or, more precisely, the gestures established by an unwritten tradition), the way to throw a ball, for example, appear to be gro-

tesquely 'dysfunctional.'" See "Enjoy Your Nation as Yourself," 200–237, quotation from 280 n. 2.

34 On the essential derivability of individual from collective identities, see Caplan and Torpey, introduction to *Documenting Individual Identity*, 1–12, especially 3.

35 On the development of these citizenship rules and the history of these categories and collectivities, see the essays in part 3 of Caplan and Torpey, *Documenting Individual Identity*, 197–270. For a different approach to these questions, appealing to a logic of administration he calls "governmentality," see Foucault, "Governmentality," 87–104.

36 I discuss the nature and function of the state in the current regime of accumulation in chapter 11.

37 See Mann, *Consciousness and Action among the Western Working Class*, 12–13. The typology of forms of working-class consciousness provided by Mann is modified in my account to be more generally applicable to all forms of political struggle.

38 Mann, *Consciousness and Action among the Western Working Class*, 13.

39 Ibid.

Chapter 7. The Politics of Subjectivity

1 It would be more accurate to say that for Jacques Derrida this "place" of the subject is strictly speaking a "nonplace" positioned in a relationship of adjacency to the "place," in the chain of signification, from which the signifiers that constitute the subject are able to function. Or to put it in Heideggerian parlance: Derrida approaches the subject in terms of a poetics as opposed to a semiology.

2 Derrida, "Ethics and Politics Today," in *Negotiations*, 296.

3 Derrida, "Introduction: Desistance," 5.

4 Derrida, "To Arrive—at the Ends of the State," in *Rogues*, 143.

5 Though he never presents his thinking on the subject (or anything else for that matter) in the form of theses or arguments, Derrida nonetheless advocates a recasting or deconstruction of the "place" of the notion of the subject in "Eating Well," especially 272. In "To Unsense the Subjectile," he proposes that the notion of the subjectile (*le subjectile*) be substituted for that of the subject, the former connoting the elements of subjugation and projectability that are not present in the classical doctrine of the subject. To quote Derrida, "Subjectile, the word or the thing, can take the place of the subject or the object—being neither one nor the other" (61). As will be seen later, Derrida's account of justice and the ethics of responsibility views the place of this subjectile as its starting point.

6 Derrida, "Eating Well," 258.

7 For the English version of "La structure, le signe et le jeu dans le discourse des sciences humaines," see "Structure, Sign, and Play in the Discourse of the Human Sciences," in *Writing and Difference*, 278–93, especially 293.

8 Derrida, "The Ends of Man," in *Margins of Philosophy*, 111–36.

9 Derrida, "Eating Well," 261; emphasis and parentheses in original. This power to ask the question to which the subject is the answer is Derrida's rendering (which is not to be confused with anything like a straightforward appropriation) of Heidegger's *Dasein*. For insights into the relation between Derrida and Heidegger, I am indebted to Bennington and Derrida, *Jacques Derrida*, 274–81; D. Wood, *Thinking after Heidegger*, especially the essay "Heidegger after Derrida," 93–105.

10 Derrida states in "Eating Well" that not even Heidegger escaped the structure of a "transcendental analytic," and that no philosopher, and this again includes Heidegger, has been able to extricate philosophy from its grounding in an "anthropologism." This declaration and its ramifications are taken up and accentuated by Rapaport in *Later Derrida*, 97–137. For Derrida's own estimation of the relation of his thought to that of Heidegger's, see the essay "Différance" in *Margins of Philosophy*, 22–25, and *Positions*, 9–10. See also the fascinating essay by Derrida et al., "The Original Discussion of 'Différance,'" especially 86. Derrida's statement about Heidegger's failure to overcome the very anthropologism he criticized would be disputed by some of Heidegger's commentators, even if they happen not to engage directly with Derrida. See, for instance, Dastur, "The Critique of Anthropologism in Heidegger's Thought," 119–34.

11 Derrida's claims about the capacity of the animal to recognize the other qua other are likely to be controversial. Be that as it may, the argument regarding the parahuman and the singular that hinges on this claim can be detached from it and viewed in its own right.

12 This is a gloss on Derrida's construal of Heidegger's Dasein, which Derrida views as the power of a being to ask questions about itself. See "Eating Well," 160–61.

13 Derrida, "Eating Well," 271. The early Derridean text which recommends a decentering of the subject is "Structure, Sign, Play" (see note 7 above). But we should note Rapaport's salutary reminder that there is a fundamental difference between Heidegger and Derrida at this point. For Heidegger, unlike Derrida, the *who* which embodies this power to ask questions about itself is not to be identified with Dasein; as Heidegger sees it, the very capacity to ask such questions already makes the *who* into a social and psychological subject, and hence prevents it from being an appropriate manifestation of Dasein. For Derrida, on the other hand, and here the influence of Lévinas is perhaps more telling than that of Heidegger, this *who* is an alien element not to be incorporated into the nexus that makes it a psychological and social subject. See Rapaport, *Later Derrida*, 116–17. Rapaport's main argument is that there is an "earlier" and a "later" Derrida, the former espousing a deconstructed linguistic subject, the latter eschewing the linguistic turn and preferring the existential subject made well-known by Sartre and deconstructed in a "counter-existentialist existentialism" inaugurated by Lévinas, but developed by Bataille and Blanchot and taken up

by Derrida. Rapaport also suggests that Derrida oscillates between several philosophies of the subject (the humanist subject, the subject of writing, the subject of Dasein, the subject as the *who*, and so on) without according primacy to any one. My exposition in what follows is indebted to Rapaport's understanding of Derrida's positions, though I take issue with his reading of Derrida's subjectile. In fairness, however, it has to be noted that the problem with the subjectile is as much Derrida's as Rapaport's.

14 Both these positions are also present in Heidegger's writings. *Being and Time* straddles two senses of Dasein, one in which Dasein, because it possesses irreducibly the property of "mineness" (*Jemeinigkeit*), has always to be addressed by a personal pronoun ("I am," "you are"), and the other in which Dasein transcends the world. For the former, see *Being and Time*, 40; for the "transcendence of the Being of Dasein," see 33–34. In his later writings Heidegger stressed more the separation of Dasein from "Man," and maintained that its essential function is to serve as the "guardian" of being (which it does by "falling away" from itself). On this see Heidegger, *Gesamtausgabe*, 302. William J. Richardson suggests that in his later writings Heidegger stressed Dasein's grounding in "the primordial not that belongs to being," a grounding in negativity expressed through two images, that of the abyss (*Abgrund*) and that of the "nonground" (*Ungrund*), the former connoting "mystery" and the latter "subversive power." See Richardson, "Dasein and the Ground of Negativity," especially 50.

15 "Finis," in *Aporias*, 1–42, can be viewed as Derrida's unraveling (and simultaneous retention) of the key Heideggerian notion of a "being toward death."

16 Heidegger, *Being and Time*, 238–84. Heidegger takes this "voice of conscience" to be inextricably bound up with Dasein's "everyday self-interpretation." For valuable commentary, see Guest, "L'Origine de la Responsabilité"; Dastur, "The Call of Conscience," 87–98.

17 Heidegger, *Being and Time*, 285. The exemplary readings of this aspect of *Being and Time* are to be found in Dreyfus, *Being-in-the-World*; Haar, *Heidegger et l'essence de l'homme*.

18 Rapaport takes this mark of the subjectile, that is, its passing beyond the need to possess an essence, to be a primary feature defining the figure of the subaltern. For reasons outlined below (see note 20), I believe this claim to be quite problematic. For Rapaport's claim, see *Later Derrida*, 134–37.

19 It is for this reason that "Eating Well" takes seriously the possibility that animals can occupy the space of the subjectile.

20 At the same time it has to be stressed that the call of conscience is not a moral summons. As Michel Haar points out, this call is strictly "autoaffective" because it is addressed by Dasein to Dasein out of Dasein's thrownness, and does not correspond to an imperative issued by a deity or moral order that would stand in relation to Dasein as an exteriority. See Haar, *Heidegger*, 45–54.

21 Heidegger, *Being and Time*, 256; emphasis and ellipses in original; translation slightly altered.

22 Simon Critchley has made this criticism of Derrida, but it should also be directed at Heidegger. See Critchley's essays "Post-Deconstructive Subjectivity?" and "Deconstruction and Pragmatism: Is Derrida a Private Ironist or a Public Liberal?" in his collection *Ethics-Politics-Subjectivity*. One way of trying to neutralize an objection like Critchley's is to argue that Derrida is referring here to the political as such, that is, the *conditions* that make political acts and institutions possible, as opposed to politics as such, that is, the concrete activities and organizations that have their enabling conditions in the political as such. For a similar distinction, see Beardsworth, *Derrida and the Political*, ix. The focus on the political, as opposed to politics as such, enables us to appreciate Derrida's studied refusal to issue stipulations regarding this or that particular activity or political agenda, or to say that if one is a marxist, one would do such and such, or even if one were a marxist, one would *be* such and such. A certain metaphysics of the political has to be adhered to if one is to find such stipulations persuasive, and the whole point of deconstruction is to discredit a metaphysics of this kind.

Lévinas is exempt from this charge of voluntarism (which is not to suggest that his conception of the ethical is free of problems) because he uses the notion of an irreducible excess to serve, in effect even if not in intent, as a transcendental principle that is exterior to the ethical and the political, and which therefore relativizes both these domains. This transcendence, premised on the notion of an other infinitely different from all its others, is, however, the source of other difficulties. Derrida himself criticized Lévinas for resorting to the concept of infinity in this way, since the infinite always has a parasitic relation to the finite. See Derrida, "Violence et métaphysique," English version (revised) in *Writing and Difference*, 79–153. Derrida's use of "the political" as a quasi-transcendental may have apparent affinities with Lévinas's philosophic disposition for the transcendent, but differs from it because Derrida takes politics, in a very complicated way, to have lines of connection to particular active traditions, marxism being the tradition to which Derrida is in closest, though not necessarily unbroken, proximity as an "inheritor." On this inheritance, see Derrida, *Specters of Marx*, 54.

23 See Rapaport, *Later Derrida*, 124–25. Rapaport sees no problem with this and does not blink at the potentially problematic implications which stem from saying that the Derrida of "To Unsense the Subjectile" is speaking on behalf of the mute subjectile, who by virtue of this muteness is unavoidably subaltern. There is a glaringly obvious difficulty with this proposal, since having the philosopher speak on behalf of the subjectile, and there seems to be no alternative to this scenario in Rapaport's conception of the subjectile, effectively makes the philosopher the primary initiating force when it comes to undertaking any project of political transformation. At any rate, the onus for making this transformation, for giving it its initial impetus, will lie with the philosopher, who will be

in a position to name and authorize the desire of the mute subaltern. Rapaport thinks this is one way of resolving the problem identified by Gayatri Spivak in her classic essay "Can the Subaltern Speak?," that is, by having the philosopher speak on behalf of the ones who are rendered silent. But this is really no solution at all. The philosopher, or anyone else in a similar position, has to be able to hear the subaltern in the first place. Rapaport's error lies in presuming that having the intellectual resources and the inclination to fashion a theory of the subaltern (as he and Derrida undoubtedly have) is equivalent in some sense to having the ability to be heedful of the desire of the subaltern. Willingness (the domain of the ethical) cannot be conflated with ability or capability (the domain of the political) since someone can be willing and not able, or able and not willing.

24 As Richard Polt has noted, although there are only three footnote references to Kierkegaard in *Being and Time*, each of these comments favorably on the Danish philosopher widely regarded as the precursor of modern existentialism. See Polt, *Heidegger*, 166 n. 120. See also Dreyfus, *Being-in-the-World*, especially the appendix (cowritten with Jane Rubin) titled "Kierkegaard, Division II, and Later Heidegger," 284–340.

25 For this formulation regarding the "endurance of the aporia," see Derrida, *Aporias*, 16.

26 Derrida, *Aporias*, 16; emphasis in original. Subsequent quotations from *Aporias* are cited parenthetically in the text. See also Derrida, *Passions*, 5–35, and *The Gift of Death*.

27 Heidegger, *Being and Time*, 275–76. It is interesting that Derrida notes in *Aporias* that the structure of the "borderly edge" is expressed in a language that "does not fortuitously resemble that of negative theology" (19).

28 On the "unconditionality of the incalculable," see Derrida, "To Arrive—At the Ends of the State (and of War, and of World War)," in *Rogues*, 141–59.

29 This passage is quoted in *Aporias*, 20; emphasis in original. The original is in *The Other Heading*, 80–81. Derrida identifies three kinds of aporias: (1) an absolute impermeability of the borders between knowing and not knowing, (2) an excess of permeability between these borders, and (3) the antinomy which precludes the very notion of a passage across these borders (20–21). In each case, their differences notwithstanding, the outcome is a pervasive epistemological insufficiency.

30 The desire to analyze our situation without resorting to assumptions derived from philosophical anthropology, and ultimately theology, underlies Heidegger's recourse to the cumbersome apparatus that constitutes the "analytic of Dasein." Like Kierkegaard, Heidegger's ultimate goal is the critique of ontotheology, the theory of the intelligibility of the totality of being, premised on the existence of a highest being or its cognates. But this critique is not undertaken in the spirit of a skepticism directed at the highest being. Rather, Heidegger (and Derrida follows him here) undertakes this critique through an interrogation of

the immediately given, or that which is directly encountered in the everyday. On this, see Courtine, "Donner/Prendre," especially 28; Dastur, "The Critique of Anthropologism in Heidegger's Thought."

31 I am not sure that Derrida is entirely correct when he says that these concepts were not delineated by Heidegger because he regarded them as belonging to "derivative disciplines such as psychology or psychoanalysis, theology or metaphysics" (*Aporias*, 61). If the analytic of Dasein accords a primordiality (*Ursprünglichkeit*, perhaps Heidegger's favorite word!) to *Angst* as one of the "basic moods" that discloses Dasein's being to itself, then an equal emphasis is placed on *Enschlossenheit* (resoluteness), Heidegger's version of Nietzsche's creative transformation, which transfigures the past and opens up new possibilities of being. If there is anything like a decisive difference between Derrida and Heidegger (and there may be other, equally significant differences), it would reside in Derrida's unrelenting propensity to deconstruct all the places from which the philosopher speaks, and in so doing to bring philosophy into a relationship of adjacency to the promptings of a "new order of law and democracy to come" (this new law being for Derrida the law of an unconditional hospitality). Heidegger, by contrast, requires philosophy to be attuned only to the language of the ancient Greeks and his particular brand of philosophical German, since only these languages have, ostensibly, a special affinity for those rare and exceptional occasions when Being is disclosed. This criticism of Heidegger is trenchantly made in Bourdieu, *The Political Ontology of Martin Heidegger*. For Derrida on a "new order of law and democracy to come," see his essay "On Cosmopolitanism," in *On Cosmopolitanism and Forgiveness*, 23. It could be argued of course that the specific import of a work like *Being and Time* is at odds with this circumscription of the scope of philosophy, since the outcome of Heidegger's "destruction" of all previous Western humanisms (these having reduced the world to the projection of a human subject) is an expansion of Being's purview to include "everything," and that Heidegger's real failure lay in his inability to find a politics congruent with *Being and Time*'s occluded democratic principle. For this view of *Being and Time*'s fundamental, and radical, accomplishment, see Dastur, "The Critique of Anthropologism in Heidegger's Thought," 119; however, Dastur does not deal with the political implications of this line of thought. Derrida would probably not disagree with this assessment of *Being and Time*.

32 Geoffrey Bennington has modified and extended to philosophy Derrida's proposition that "there is no politics without an organization of the time and space of mourning" and argues that with the application of this doctrine of radical finitude there can also be no philosophy "without an organization of the time and space of mourning." See his "RIP," 1–17.

33 The death of the other can be named, however, and properly speaking is the only death that can be named. (I can experience the other's lack of presence, but never my own lack of presence, as much as I may dread, in a life that is always

too short, the onset of my own lack of "being-present" that is inevitable the moment I am born.)

34 For this claim, see Derrida, *Of Grammatology*, 158.

35 Lucien Goldman noted this connection between Derrida's account of différance and Marx's conception of the relation of theory to practice a long time ago (1968), when he said the following in the question-and-answer session that followed Derrida's lecture "Différance":

> If we try to situate Derrida's theories in relation to Marxist epistemology . . . we find a close kinship together . . . with a great terminological difference. I readily pay tribute to the linguistic resourcefulness of Derrida's employment of the words difference and *différance*, which seem to me to correspond fairly closely to Marxist concepts of theory and praxis (there is, in fact, no theory which does not bring along differences, nor is there a praxis which does not imply a *différance* in the attainability of the goal).
>
> In this perspective, to say that all theory is connected in a more or less mediated manner to praxis and derives from it, or indeed, to say that difference presupposes *différance*, do not appear to me to be . . . entirely different claims. For Marx, all knowledge . . . even sensible intuition, derives from praxis, which is a detour, an action in time, and implicitly, to use Derrida's terminology, *différance*.

See Derrida et al., "The Original Discussion of 'Différance'" (1968)," 90.

36 Différance is a quasi-transcendental, not a "pure" transcendental, because it lacks the stability that a true transcendental possesses, this stability being itself a condition of the transcendental's capacity to confer stability on the conceptual objects subsumed under it.

37 As Derrida puts it in his classic essay "Différance," "Such a play, *différance*, is . . . no longer simply a concept, but rather the possibility of a conceptuality, of a conceptual process and system in general" (*Margins of Philosophy*, 11).

38 Bennington, *Interrupting Derrida*, 16; emphasis in original.

39 Derrida's texts dealing with the theme of ethical and political responsibility tend to focus on the question of this negotiation with an inheritance, whose weight is displayed in ways that sometimes escape the purview of the one who is, however ambiguously, a recipient at the hands of this inheritance. *Specters of Marx* is the text in which Derrida's own inheritance is scrutinized for its presuppositions and unacknowledged dimensions.

40 For Derrida's assertion regarding justice, see "The Force of Law," 945.

41 Bennington especially has pressed home this point, and I follow his interpretation of Derrida in the next few paragraphs. See *Interrupting Derrida*, 25.

42 For these modalities, see Derrida, *Politics of Friendship*, 38.

43 Bennington, *Interrupting Derrida*, 27; emphasis in original. The internal quotation from Derrida is taken from *Politics of Friendship*, 68.

44 Derrida, *Politics of Friendship*, 68.

45 Derrida, *Politics of Friendship*, 68–69; emphasis in original.

46 The law of unlimited hospitality is stated thus by Derrida: "Let us say yes *to who or what turns up*, before any determination, before any anticipation, before any *identification*, whether or not it has to do with a foreigner, an immigrant, an invited guest, or an unexpected visitor, whether or not the new arrival is the citizen of another country, a human, animal, or divine creature, a living or dead thing, male or female" ("Step of Hospitality/No Hospitality," in Derrida and Dufourmantelle, *Of Hospitality*, 77; emphasis in original).

47 For this rejoinder to the objection posed by Simon Critchley, see Bennington, *Interrupting Derrida*, 200 n. 20. The gravamen of Bennington's reading of Derrida's distinction between the quasi-transcendental and the empirical is that Derrida makes this distinction precisely in order to permit a movement between the two poles, albeit a movement accordant with the logic of différance.

48 On the importance of the third party in my encounter with an other, see Derrida, "The Word of Welcome," in *Adieu: To Emmanuel Lévinas*. For valuable commentary on the relation of justice to ethics, see Bernasconi, "Justice without Ethics?"

49 This demand for self-reflexivity, when coupled with Derrida's relish for textual intricacy, influences much of the commentary on his writings, and so it is not uncommon for commentaries to begin with a declaration that professes to suspend commentary in the very course of undertaking it (e.g., "What is it to 'accompany Derrida' when writing on Derrida?"; "My dispatch is divided, without destination and without message"). For such a gesture, see Fynsk, "Derrida and Philosophy," 152, Leavey, "Destinerrance," 33. It is hard to imagine commentators on Deleuze or Badiou, say, anguishing in similar ways over the matter of "accompanying" these thinkers, or whether commentaries on Deleuze and Badiou can have a "destination" or convey a "message."

50 This demarcation between the two ways of undertaking a reflection on the political follows the position taken by Louis Althusser in *Machiavelli and Us*, 9. The next few paragraphs are deeply indebted to this book for its account of "conceptual practice."

51 See "Interview with Derrida," in Wood and Bernasconi, *Derrida and Différance*, 73. This interview was conducted by Catherine David of *Le nouvel observateur* and published in the issue of 9 September 1983.

52 The connection here is not only with the political and the ethical, but also with the religious, as Derrida's writings in the decade or so before his death made increasingly clear. Religion has not been dealt with in this chapter, and the reader is referred to the discussion of this subject in de Vries, "Derrida and Ethics," 172–92.

53 "Interview with Derrida," 73; emphasis in original.

54 It is a mistake therefore to charge Derrida with "quietism," "indifference to practical politics," and so on, as some of his more careless critics do, because of

this stress on undecidability and the "free play" of différance. The emphasis on the undecidable serves to banish teleology from history, and with this opening of history (teleology involving a foreclosure of possibility), historical change is aptly to be viewed as a concomitant of the operation of the undecidable. See Fenves, "Derrida and History," 271–95.

55 Bennington, *Interrupting Derrida*, 33; emphasis added.

56 For this conception of constitutive power and its antecedents in Spinoza, see Deleuze, *Spinoza*.

57 I use this Deleuzean understanding of singularity in chapter 10 to provide an account of the subject possessed by the collective desire for liberation.

58 Derrida, *Specters of Marx*, 169.

59 Derrida was taken to task for this "formalism" by Laclau in his review of *Specters of Marx*. See Laclau, "The Time Is Out of Joint." Stella Gaon valiantly attempts to extricate Derrida from the charge, leveled by Nancy Fraser, Gayatri Chakravorty Spivak, Kate Soper, Alex Callinicos, and others, that his steadfast preference for a "conditions of possibility" argument when dealing with the ethical and political effectively leaves him with nothing concrete to espouse but an anemic social liberalism. Gaon manages to show that the structure of promise identified by Derrida as an integral element of a marxist ontology of justice is precisely that, a necessary condition of this ontology of justice, without being able in the end to show us how Derrida will be able to identify the animating principles for the implementation of a marxist or marxisant project of liberation. See Gaon, "'Politicizing Deconstruction.'"

60 See Negri, "The Specter's Smile," 5–16.

61 I am referring here to Deleuze and Guattari's proposition, which serves as an axiom for the theoretical armature created by them in *Mille plateaux*, that "before being there is politics [*car avant l'être, il y a la politique*]." See *A Thousand Plateaus*, 249. There is a hiatus between the "actually" political and the "conceptually" political, and as much as Derrida is right to insist that there is an endless relay between the conceptual and the actual, his inability to move beyond a thinking immured in the formalism of an endlessly recycled "conditions of possibility" argument means that he cannot address adequately the situation of the dispossessed. The possible Derridean rejoinder, "But what is it to address the situation of the dispossessed?," has its place, but it has to be accompanied by the salutary realization that broaching this question can only be a conceptual prolepsis to the necessarily practical pursuit of liberation.

Chapter 8. The Politics of the Event

1 See Critchley, "Demanding Approval."

2 Bacevich, "Expanding War, Contracting Meaning."

3 See Badiou, "Afterword," 236.

4 On Earle's remark, see N. Cohen, "And Now the Trouble Really Begins."

5 For this equalitarian axiom, see Badiou, *L'Etre et l'événement*, 447; Badiou, *D'un désastre obscure*, 15.

6 On the "possibility of the impossible," see Badiou, *Ethics*, 39–42.

7 See Badiou, "Highly Speculative Reasoning on the Concept of Democracy," 28.

8 Thus, for Badiou, Paul is an exemplary militant because his "unprecedented gesture consists in subtracting truth from the communitarian grasp, be it that of a people, a city, an empire, a territory, or a social class" (*St. Paul*, 7).

9 Badiou, *Ethics*, 38.

10 Badiou, *Abrégé de métapolitique*, 156–67: "La politique de peut seulement penser comme pensée de tous."

11 For this principle, see Badiou, *La distance politique* (28 May 1998), 3, quoted in Hallward, "Badiou's Politics," paragraph 4. I am grateful to Hallward's article for some of my formulations.

12 Prathab Patnaik, in an article to which I am indebted for these reflections, mentions the advice given by the *Washington Post* when the Congress Party won the Indian general election. According to the *Post* (regarded in the United States as a liberal newspaper!), investors in India, and this would include foreign corporations, should have just as much say in Indian elections (purely by virtue of being investors) as individual Indian citizens, since the "stake" of investors in India was presumed to be just as considerable as the commitments of the individual citizens themselves. See Patnaik, "The Illusionism of Finance."

13 The affinity between this aspect of Badiou's thought and the work of Hardt and Negri is noted in Bosteels, "Logics of Antagonism."

14 Badiou, *Ethics*, 97–98; emphasis in original. See also *Abrégé de métapolitique*, 160, where Badiou's statement "Politics places the State at a distance" makes it explicit that the state is not annulled, but rather has its otherwise measureless power brought within the circumscription of politics. For Badiou's earlier circumscription of the part played by the state in politics, see *L'Etre et l'événement*, 258, where fidelity is depicted as a "counter-state" or "below-state."

15 Badiou, "Politics and Philosophy: An Interview with Alain Badiou," in *Ethics*, 105–6; emphases in original.

16 These injunctions to refrain from electoral voting and participating in party politics make sense only in specific political contexts. Thus in the United States, where both the Republican and Democratic Parties are parties of capital, with Wall Street and the corporations as their primary constituency, it matters little whether or not one takes part in the charade of American parliamentary politics. By contrast, say, if one of the nationalist parties in Scotland or Wales had a chance of displacing New Labour from power in their respective regional parliaments, then it would probably be a good idea to vote for Plaid Cymru or the Scottish Nationalist Party. Anything that contributes to the dismantling of the project of "Great Britain" is likely to enable a more productive form of politics in those countries.

17 Badiou, however, appears recently to have qualified his position on economics and its ancillary human sciences. Instead of dismissing these outright as mere "ideologies" designed to measure and uphold the status quo, he now seems to accept that there are areas of the human sciences that "touch upon the being of objects" (and thus avoid being merely ideological), to wit, "phonology in linguistics, the foundations of Marxist economics, perhaps a part of the anthropological theory of kinship, perhaps also a segment of psychoanalysis" ("Afterword," 234). He further acknowledges that *L'Etre et l'événement* did give the impression of a rigid demarcation between "pure conservation (situation, encyclopaedia) and becoming (inquiries, subjects, the generic)," and that he now sees the need for a more complex conceptualization of the modes by which change takes place in the world. This more refined conceptualization is set out in his recent *Logiques des mondes*, which arrived too late to be considered in detail in this chapter.

18 See note 16 above.

19 Badiou, "Afterword," 236. Subsequent references are cited parenthetically in the text.

20 Badiou, "The Ethics of Truths," 250; emphasis in original. Subsequent references are cited parenthetically in the text.

21 My analysis of Badiou's positions on truth owes a great deal to Bosteels, "Alain Badiou's Theory of the Subject," part I and part II. Bosteels's indispensable essays chart in fascinating detail the various changes that Badiou's views on truth have undergone in his numerous writings, concluding with an anticipation of the account of truth and subjectivization that Badiou was going to provide in *Logiques des mondes*. The account I give of the relation of truth to the event, while indebted to Bosteels, departs somewhat from the initial psychoanalytic context in which Badiou, and Bosteels following him, frame their formulations.

22 Thus if the car accident I had just outside Cambridge in September 1981 is the cause of my believing the statement "I must drive more cautiously," then I cannot remain indifferent to the event that is the car accident in which I was involved in September 1981. If I were indifferent to this event, then either I have another basis for assenting to this statement, or my believing this statement lacks any real basis, and I therefore have no adequate ground for choosing between "I must drive more cautiously" and "I have no need to drive more cautiously." A belief-causing event, once it is belief-causing, necessarily generates effects which can be termed its "truth-effects." This formulation needs further refinement, because it can be read as (1) *E* is the cause of my *coming to hold* the belief that *p*, and (2) *E* is the basis of my conviction that *p* is *true*. Where (1) is concerned, my relatively minor car accident could have triggered a deep-seated childhood fear (say) that, once aroused, simply shocks me into believing that I need to do something about my driving, whereas in (2) my accident causes me to revise and even falsify some of my previous somewhat self-deceiving beliefs about my driving (that I was a very cautious driver, that I drove within the limits

of my capability, etc.), in this way causing me to affirm the statement "I must drive more cautiously" as the resultant of this revision of my beliefs. Strictly speaking, *E* has truth-effects only in sense (2). However, if *E* shocks me into the conviction that I must drive more cautiously, then it need not be incompatible with (2), though of course both (1) and (2) can obtain without the other, even if there could be times when they may happen to obtain conjointly. *E* is a truth-event for Badiou more in sense (2), though given his alertness to the psychoanalytic core that subtends belief, it should not be concluded that he is indifferent to issues that surround sense (1).

23 There is a complexity here that cannot be ignored. "It is snowing in Manhattan" could be true in Manhattan, but it has no application to Burlington, Vermont, in terms of its presuppositions. (The utterer of the sentence "It is snowing in Manhattan" makes no reference to Burlington, and so, properly speaking, "It is snowing in Manhattan" is neither true nor false where Burlington is concerned.)

24 The example is mine, but I owe my understanding of Badiou to Hallward's excellent *Badiou: A Subject to Truth*, 135–39.

25 Badiou, "Vérité: Forçage et innomable," in Hallward, *Think Again*, 127; translation altered, emphasis in original. It is very likely that Badiou is adapting Lacan's notion of the "future anterior" or future perfect in his account of "forcing." The future anterior has a distinctive structure — "I was that which became who I am now so that I can become what I was not" — which begins from the premise that the truth is fundamentally incomplete. As this structure indicates, the truth unfolds when we become that which we were not, though what we are now is something that results from something that we had to become in order to be who we are now. According to this structure, one is always about to arrive or will have arrived at some later time. For this structure, see Lacan, "Logical Time and the Assertion of Anticipated Certainty." For explication, see Fink, *The Lacanian Subject*, 64–65.

26 Badiou, "Afterword," 235.

27 Here I summarize Badiou's argument in *L'Etre et l'événement*, 365–69. Peter Hallward notes that Badiou does not identify the subject with the investigations themselves; rather, the subject is realized only as he or she moves between terms, testing them and finding new ones to supplant those found inadequate. There is a profoundly aleatory quality to this movement, as the subject revises and modifies the modes of expression available to him or her in order to extend the implications of an event and to force new knowledges into being. See Hallward, *Badiou*, 141.

28 It has to be said from the outset that Badiou's espousal of the law of the excluded middle should not be read as an endorsement of the view that there is only one locus of truth or only one name for the truth. Badiou insists that truth has many loci from which it is sprung, and many names, but once a statement is a candi-

date for a truth-status, the principle of bivalence holds; that is, the statement is either true or false, and nothing else.

29 Desanti, "Some Remarks on the Intrinsic Ontology of Alain Badiou," 61. Subsequent references are cited parenthetically in the text.

30 To quote Desanti: "As I see it, the fact that Badiou takes up forcing is the price he has to pay for his decision to install himself from the outset with an intrinsic ontology" (63). A similar concern, albeit lodged from a different theoretical perspective, is expressed by Ernesto Laclau, who argues that Badiou's fundamental ontology is incapable of accommodating such notions as "overdetermination" or "analogy," which should have a place in any adequate conception of ontological possibility. See Laclau, "An Ethics of Militant Engagement," 136.

31 The unpublished manuscript in question is Badiou's "Topos, ou logiques de l'onto-logique. Un introduction pour philosophes, tome 1," dated 1993 in the bibliography of Hallward, *Badiou*. Hallward quotes the following passage from this manuscript: "Category theory is especially suited to the examination of 'dual' ontological situations, that is to say reversible correspondences, ambiguities of position, identities turned on their head, effects of symmetry and mirroring. In this sense its spontaneous philosophy is Deleuzian, and it narrows the gap between the symbolic and the imaginary as much as possible" (26). See Hallward, *Badiou*, 417 n. 22. I am deeply indebted to Hallward's exposition for the foregoing presentation of Badiou's use of category theory.

32 Hallward, *Badiou*, 307. Hallward refers here to the then unpublished text of Badiou's *Logiques des monde*, chapter 3, 10–12, and recapitulates Badiou's unavoidably technical discussion of category theory. Needless to say, my exposition here is greatly simplifying in comparison to the treatments of category theory provided by Badiou and Hallward. The reader wanting more than just a glimpse of the theory should consult *Badiou: A Subject to Truth*.

33 See *Badiou*, 308, where Hallward quotes from Badiou, "Topos, ou logiques de l'onto-logique. Un introduction pour philosophes, tome 1," 76.

34 For this claim, see *Badiou*, 308, where Hallward cites Badiou's *Court traité d'ontologie transitoire*, 134.

35 Hallward, *Badiou*, 52. For Badiou's early attempt to demarcate between these two conceptions of logic, see "La subversion infinitésimale."

36 With slight modifications this is the account given in Hallward, *Badiou*, 311. The difference between Badiou and Deleuze on ontology becomes clear at this point, since the latter is explicit in his repudiation of any ontology based on extensionality. For this, see Deleuze, *Difference and Repetition*. For a helpful comparison of their respective ontologies of mathematics, see D. W. Smith, "Badiou and Deleuze on the Ontology of Mathematics," 77–93.

37 Badiou has been taken to task for the "decisionism" that stems from the powerful focus he places on the sovereign act. See, for instance, Bensaïd, "Alain Badiou and the Miracle of the Event," 94–105.

38 For Badiou's attempt to bring these two ontological traditions together while maintaining the primacy of the Platonist tradition, see his *Court traité d'ontologie transitoire*.

39 In making this point I grant Desanti's assumption that the inhabitants of the territory in his fable need to be able to give an account of what lies beyond its borders if they are to be able to say something meaningful about the force that ostensibly repels them when they approach these borders.

40 The most important of these laws of classical set theory is the axiom of extensionality, that sets are the same if they have the same members or elements.

41 See Hallward, *Badiou*, 86. For Badiou's permitting of intensional objects in sets, see his "Topos, ou logiques de l'onto-logique. Un introduction pour philosophes," 42.

42 This formulation is indebted to Donald Davidson's well-known principle of charity, which holds that we have no alternative but to assume that other persons are to be reckoned right in their beliefs most of the time. The alternative would be to assume that someone could be wrong most of the time in his or her beliefs, and given that most other persons are rational beings like oneself, it would be a mistake to presume that one is a rational being who is right most of the time in one's beliefs, but that other persons are mistaken most of the time in their beliefs, despite being rational like oneself. Just as one would not presume that one's beliefs are overwhelmingly incoherent, so also one should make the presumption that the beliefs of others, as a generality, are not massively incoherent. For Davidson's principle of charity, see "Radical Interpretation."

43 This is true of any system of thought: as a regime of truth-effects it too cannot institute its own modes of existence, and it too can be prevented from realizing its truth-effects. On truth-effects, see Balibar, "The Infinite Contradiction," 162.

44 For this, see Badiou, *L'Etre et l'événement*, 257.

Chapter 9. The Religious Transcendent

1 The standard distinction between "transcendence" and "*the* transcendent" needs to be clarified at this point. "*The* transcendent" refers to a reality or force that lies in a realm that cannot be encompassed within the purview of worldly historical and social forces, while "transcendence" signifies any kind of exteriority to an existing state of affairs, and as such is not necessarily incompatible with "the immanent." In the latter case, there is nothing self-contradictory in affirming an "immanent transcendence," as long as "transcendence" is not understood as the equivalent of "*the* transcendent."

2 As Graham Ward correctly points out in his "Transcendence and Representation," especially 142.

3 On this need for a metaphysics of participation, see Milbank, Pickstock, and Ward, introduction to *Radical Orthodoxy*, 3–4.

4 For Badiou's suggestion that Paul's religious beliefs can effectively be discounted as "fable," see his *St. Paul*, 4–5.

5 This point needs to be qualified because it does not in itself amount to a critique of Badiou. It is not unacceptable to put to one side Paul's theological convictions if one is giving an account solely of his character as a militant, but his theological judgments cannot be overlooked if one is setting out to make sense of his discourse as a whole. The crucial point here is whether it is possible to determine the political import of Paul's discourse without taking its theological dimensions into account as well.

6 Cunningham, "Language," 64–65. Cunningham's position is developed in greater detail in his excellent *Genealogy of Nihilism*. See also Milbank, "Only Theology Overcomes Metaphysics," in his collection of essays *The Word Made Strange*, 36–52.

7 Leibniz, who made this doctrine the lynchpin of his philosophical system and who saw it as the expression of Christianity's philosophical core, is by virtue of this the great modern Christian philosopher. For aspects of commentary, see Riley, *Leibniz' Universal Jurisprudence*.

8 I am not talking of conversion in the empirical sense, involving such absurdities as forced baptism. Rather, conversion here refers to an ontological state of affairs in which all are somehow drawn into being adherents of the Christian mythos, whether consciously or implicitly.

9 It will be objected to univocity that, unlike Christianity's "good difference," it can legitimize only a "bad difference" since univocity has as its necessary concomitant immanentism, so that difference is cast entirely as phenomenality, in which case difference is negotiated only on the basis of the power of those who see things in *this* way and not *that*. According to these critics of immanence, in absolute immanence everything has to replicate the given (because ontologically this is all there is to replicate), and this then becomes the source of an unavoidable ontological violence. Univocity holds beings on the same plane through sheer and naked power, which then has perforce to destroy peaceability. I am indebted to John Milbank for many helpful discussions on this topic.

10 For Žižek's position, see *The Fragile Absolute*, *On Belief*, and *The Puppet and the Dwarf*. John Milbank arrives independently at a position similar to Žižek's when he says that "to achieve an adequate ontology . . . materialist socialism needs to invoke theology" ("Materialism and Transcendence," 7). Milbank diverges from Žižek (and Badiou) on the important question of the transcendent, which the marxist thinkers, with their "secularised *via negativa*," disavow. To quote Milbank, "The turn to the secularised *via negativa* however, because it does not admit any real transcendent superabundant plenitude within which religious performances might remotely participate, never recognises any degrees of more-or-less correct manifestation of the absolute, or any advance towards the absolute that is not equally and inversely a regression" (12).

11 Milbank, "Materialism and Transcendence," 14–16.

12 Howard Caygill has dealt brilliantly with this aspect of Kantian judgment in his *Art of Judgment*.

13 Gilles Deleuze has stated this problem perspicaciously: "Now we see Kant, at an age when great authors rarely have anything new to say, confronting a problem that will lead him to an extraordinary undertaking: if the faculties can thus enter into variable relationships in which each faculty is in turn regulated by one of the others, it must follow that, taken together, they are capable of free and unregulated relationships in which each faculty goes to its own limit, and yet in this way shows the possibility of its entering into an *indeterminate* [*quelconque*] harmony with the others" ("On Four Poetic Formulas That Might Summarize the Kantian Philosophy," *Essays Critical and Clinical*, 33–34; emphasis in original).

14 For a theological reading of this contemporary repristination of the sublime, see Milbank, "Sublimity," 211–34.

15 Deleuze, "On Four Poetic Formulas That Might Summarize the Kantian Philosophy," 34.

16 The basis for this new immanentist ontology is Spinoza's insight that the other is not a subject in the sense associated with Locke and Descartes, but is instead a mode whose expressivities are registered by other modes, each with its own specific kind of receptivity determined by the kind of mode that it is. For Spinoza's formulation, see his *Ethics*, especially part II, proposition 49 (pp. 156–57 of the Parkinson edition). For elaboration, see Deleuze, *Expressionism in Philosophy*; Howie, *Deleuze and Spinoza*.

17 This is the gist of Badiou's critique of Deleuze in his quite brilliant *Deleuze: The Clamor of Being*. John Milbank endorses this critique in "Materialism and Transcendence," 15–18. Conor Cunningham provides the first complete genealogy of this baneful trajectory from Deleuze back to Plotinus in his *Genealogy of Nihilism*. As I will shortly indicate, I disagree with this assessment of Deleuze.

18 Brian Massumi has correctly pointed out the fractal nature of Deleuze's conception of the object, which requires it to be understood in terms of the triptych of dimensions just mentioned. See *A User's Guide to "Capitalism and Schizophrenia,"* 35–38. I am indebted to Massumi's account.

19 Advocates of the *analogia entis*, John Milbank for instance, believe that the doctrine of analogy does not have to confront this problem because it avoids positing any kind of originary void. For Christian theology the source of the created order is the ineffable divine plenitude from which all things are engendered. The account just given of Deleuze's fractalized conception of the object shows that Deleuze too has a theory of the originary plenitude, except that in his case it is a rigorously immanent one.

20 For this definition of "potentiality," see Deleuze, *Spinoza*, 97.

21 See Milbank, "Materialism and Transcendence," 23–25.

22 See Massumi, *A User's Guide to "Capitalism and Schizophrenia,"* 57–58.

Chapter 10. Nomad Politics

1 There are significant affinities between the nomadology of Deleuze and Guattari and the theory of the multitude associated with Antonio Negri and Michael Hardt's *Empire*. See also their *Multitudes: War and Democracy in the Age of Empire*. These affinities hinge on their respective versions of autopoesis: nomadic formations and multitudes are said by Deleuze and Guattari and by Hardt and Negri to direct themselves according to their own powers and their own histories.

2 It should be pointed out that some of Alain Badiou's more recent work shows less emphasis on the exceptional event and more on the contribution of events, even of a quotidian variety, to the formation of subjectivity.

3 For an application of multitude theory to the events that led to Chávez's restoration as president of Venezuela, see Beasley-Murray, "It Happened on TV." For the Genoa G8 demonstrations, see Negri, "Italy's Postmodern Politics," 5.

4 See chapter 1 above.

5 See Deleuze, "Postscript on Societies of Control," *Negotiations*, 177–82.

6 See Deleuze, *The Fold: Leibniz and the Baroque*.

7 Like each of the plateaus in *A Thousand Plateaus*, the "Treatise on Nomadology" has a date attached to it, in this case 1227, the year in which Genghis Khan died. Deleuze and Guattari give no explanations for their choice of such dates, and one can only surmise that Genghis Khan's *Pax Mongolica* is for Deleuze and Guattari an emblematic instance of a countersovereignty to be posed against the sovereignty of the polis that Genghis Khan challenged from his movable base in the steppes. This much can be gleaned from pages 417–19 of *A Thousand Plateaus*.

8 Deleuze and Guattari, *A Thousand Plateaus*, 351–52; emphasis in original, translation slightly altered. Subsequent references are cited parenthetically in the text. The interior quotation is from Dumézil, *Mithra-Varuna*, 118–24, which deals with the difference between the bond and the contract.

9 It would be interesting to contrast Balibar's citizen subject with Deleuze and Guattari's subject of the state apparatus. The central premise of Balibar's argument, namely, that the *subjectus* of medieval polities had been supplanted by the post-Kantian *subjectum* or citizen subject, is not one that Deleuze and Guattari would readily accept. Balibar's cautionary note that under the remit of bourgeois democracy the citizen subject is always going to resemble in some important ways the *subjectus* of the dispensation that prevailed before the emergence of bourgeois democracy would be wholeheartedly assented to by Deleuze and Guattari. Where Deleuze and Guattari are concerned, however, the (current) era of a postpolitical politics, having jettisoned any substantive notion of sovereignty based on the principle of representation, can no longer provide the proper raison d'être for this bourgeois democratic subject.

10 Deleuze and Guattari, *Anti-Oedipus*, 4; emphasis in original.

11 It should be pointed out, though, that the state is understood by Deleuze and Guattari in two senses. In one sense the state is to be identified with the formations and apparatuses that constitute it. In another the state is, preeminently, a metaphysical conception, a machine of transcoding that (unlike the assemblages which embody it and which have to be constructed and positioned at this or that point in social space) "comes into the world fully formed and rises up at a single stroke, the unconditioned Urstaat" (*A Thousand Plateaus*, 437).

12 It follows from this that there is a sense in which consciousness (taken here to include all the ramified outreachings of desire) constitutes something like a domain of the virtual, and so precedes the "actuality" of social apparatuses and formations. The "thinking" of the state is a function of consciousness par excellence, and is therefore the product of this virtuality. Clearly this has significant implications for any simplistic claims about the primacy of the "actually" material in marxist thought and practice. The virtual, as Deleuze, following Bergson, has insisted, cuts across the division between the possible and the actual. "Before Being there is politics" (*A Thousand Plateaus*, 203), certainly, but inextricably bound up with politics is the thinking that is located in the realm of the virtual, and this thinking breaches the long-held distinctions between "thought" and "practice" and "materialism" and "idealism."

13 See Deleuze, *The Fold*, 130–37.

14 To quote Deleuze and Guattari: "There is no universal capitalism, there is no capitalism in itself; capitalism is at the crossroads of all kinds of formations, it is neocapitalism by nature" (*A Thousand Plateaus*, 20). In *Anti-Oedipus* Deleuze and Guattari indicate how capitalism is able to perform this integrative function: "Capitalism is in fact born of the encounter of two sorts of flows: the decoded flows of production in the form of money-capital, and the decoded flows of labor in the form of the 'free worker.' Hence, unlike previous social machines, the capitalist machine is incapable of providing a code that will apply to the whole of the social field. By substituting money for the very notion of a code, it has created an axiomatic of abstract quantities that keeps moving further and further in the direction of the deterritorialization of the socius" (33).

15 There have long been economic world-systems, of course, as Andre Gunder Frank, Christopher Chase-Dunn, Janet Abu-Lughod, and others have pointed out. My claim that capitalism in its current dispensation takes the form of a meta-accord is not about the world-system as such, but about its present manifestation, that is, how the meta-accord that is capital gets to establish a world-system with a fundamentally isomorphic structure, something that did not occur with previous world-systems.

16 The cynical would say that Jackson's morphing in the video is simply a recapitulation of the transformations that his own visage has undergone in recent times thanks to the ministrations of plastic surgeons.

17 Cage describes his work as "music without measurements, sound passing through circumstances" ("Diary: Emma Lake Music Workshop 1965," *A Year*

from Monday, 22). Slavoj Žižek has made a similar point about divergence and incompossibility when he says that many different sets can in principle be derived from the same collection. See *The Plague of Fantasies*.

18 Elsewhere Deleuze says that "the Anomalous is always at the frontier, on the borders of a band or multiplicity; it is part of the latter, but is already making it pass into another multiplicity, it makes it become, it traces a line-between" (Deleuze and Parnet, *Dialogues*, 42).

19 In an interview on Foucault and his work, Deleuze refers to this movement between outside and inside as something which involves "subjectless individuations" ("A Portrait of Foucault," *Negotiations*, 117). These "subjectless individuations" are a defining characteristic of the Anomalous. I am almost certainly going further than Deleuze and Guattari in my use of the Anomalous. They take this category to be a defining feature of the "line of flight," which is present wherever lines of flight are to be found. In the account given here, I take the Anomalous to be pervasively present in the epoch of the breakdown or dissolution of transcendental accords; that is, I view it as the operation of a currently regnant capitalist cultural logic. This, however, is entirely compatible with the positions set out in *Capitalisme et schizophrénie*. In *Dialogues*, Deleuze says, "The State can no longer . . . rely on the old forms like the police, armies, bureaucracies, collective installations, schools, families. . . . It is not surprising that all kinds of minority questions—linguistic, ethnic, regional, about sex, or youth—resurge not only as archaisms, but in up-to-date revolutionary forms which call once more into question in an entirely immanent manner both the global economy of the machine and the assemblages of national States. . . . Everything is played in uncertain games, 'front to front, back to back, back to front'" (147).

20 For his account of simulation, see Deleuze, *Différence et répétition*, 92–101, and *The Logic of Sense*. Deleuze's theory of simulation is complex, but its gist can be stated thus: if, contrary to Plato and the tradition of philosophy derived from him, there can be no primacy of a putative original over its copy, of a model over its representations, so that there can be no basis for differentiating between "good" original and "bad" copy, then everything is itself a "copy-original"; it is an "original" of itself, or rather its "origin" is a copy or "shadow" of itself. In the absence of any possibility of separating copies from ostensible originals, each thing, in simulation, is thus an absolute singularity. Everything is different from everything else, and this in turn is the basis of multiplicity. In this and the next few paragraphs I have taken several sentences from my "Reinventing a Physiology of Collective Liberation." It should be pointed out that a similar stress on the concept of a singularity is also to be found in Derrida's account of "political desire" in his *Politics of Friendship*, 20–27.

21 To quote Deleuze and Guattari:

> If Marx demonstrated the functioning of capitalism as an axiomatic, it was above all in the famous chapter on the tendency of the rate of profit to fall. Capitalism is indeed an axiomatic, because it has no laws but imma-

nent ones. It would like for us to believe that it confronts the limits of the Universe, the extreme limit of resources and energy. But all it confronts are its own limits (the periodic depreciation of existing capital); all it repels or displaces are its own limits (the formation of new capital, in new industries with a high rate of profit). This is the history of oil and nuclear power. And it does both at once: capitalism confronts its own limits and simultaneously displaces them, setting them down again farther along. (*A Thousand Plateaus*, 463)

22 In the process of removing the conditions that enable transcendental accords to maintain themselves, capitalism promotes a cultural logic that favors the description over the concept, and this cultural logic also contains within itself propensities that weaken or obviate the dichotomy between the individual and the collective, and thus creates the conditions for the emergence of a culture that, with the supersession of capitalist "nonbeing," will allow singularity potentially to become generalized as a cultural principle.

23 The sketchy account of singularity given here is taken from the much more substantial treatment in Agamben, *The Coming Community*.

24 A point well made in Lazare, *The Frozen Republic* and *The Velvet Coup*.

25 For discussion, see Jessop, "Capitalism and Its Future."

26 This formulation is owed to Jessop, "Capitalism and Its Future," 574–75.

27 Samir Amin has argued that only in this way can the system of a globalized economic polarization be neutralized and ultimately dismantled. See Amin, "Conditions for Re-launching Development," 73–84, and "For a Progressive and Democratic New World Order," 17–32.

28 S. Amin, "Conditions for Re-launching Development," 84.

29 S. Amin, *Delinking*, 136.

Chapter 11. Heterotopia

1 Finley, "Utopianism Ancient and Modern," 3. Sir M. I. Finley, born Moses Israel Finkelstein in New York in 1912, was associated with members of the Frankfurt school during its period of exile in the United States. Dismissed from his teaching post at Rutgers during the McCarthy era, he became a distinguished economic and social historian of the ancient world at Cambridge prior to his death in 1986.

2 Wilde, *The Soul of Man under Socialism*, 1089.

3 A caveat is necessary here. Finley makes a distinction between "static" (or "ascetic") and "dynamic" (or "want-satisfying") utopias, and suggests that premodern utopias were essentially static, in that they sought to attune the sensibilities of their protagonists to a world marked by seemingly ineluctable scarcities and limitations. According to Finley, it was only after the onset of modernity in general, and the Industrial Revolution in particular, that dynamic utopias came to be promulgated. He is careful to point out, however, that even after the Indus-

trial Revolution ascetic utopias existed alongside their modern counterparts. See "Utopianism Ancient and Modern," 12–14.

4 Foucault, "Of Other Spaces," 22. Subsequent references are cited parenthetically in the text.

5 Finley, "Utopianism Ancient and Modern," 12. It is interesting to contrast Finley's position with that of Deleuze and Guattari, who argue that the concept of utopia is problematic precisely because of its connection with history. Contrasting the event, which is pure becoming and thus outside history, with the state of affairs, which is historical, they contend that only the event is truly revolutionary, since utopia is "still subject to [history] and lodged within it as an ideal or motivation" (*What Is Philosophy?*, 110).

6 Foucault does not acknowledge the echoes of Bataille, Merleau-Ponty, and Lacan resonating in his delineation of heterotopia. There are of course important differences, especially with Lacan and Merleau-Ponty. Lacan uses the notion of the mirror stage primarily, though not exclusively, to adumbrate the logic of identification (with the Other), whereas Foucault, as we shall see, is concerned less (or indeed not at all) with the dynamic of inner identification and more with the topographical structure of a countervailing power. Merleau-Ponty's description of the "chiasm" which underlies *all* perceptual activity has an apparent bearing on Foucault's conception of what happens when one looks into a mirror: "As soon as I see, it is necessary that the vision (as is so well indicated by the double meaning of the word) be doubled with a complementary vision or with another vision: myself seen from without, such as another would see me, installed in the midst of the visible, occupied in considering it from a certain spot" (*The Visible and Invisible*, 134). Merleau-Ponty describes the necessary folding of this "outside" into any self-seeing. The big difference between Foucault and Merleau-Ponty resides in Foucault's rejection of anything that approximates a "philosophy of subjectivity," a philosophy integral to Merleau-Ponty's existential phenomenology. For this rejection, see Foucault, *The Order of Things*, xiv. For Bataille's concept of heterology, which he defines as "the science of the completely other" (*science de ce qui est tout autre*), see "The Use-Value of D. A. F. Sade (An Open Letter to My Comrades)," 91–102.

7 For a suggestive account, using a framework derived from Deleuze's philosophy, of how this constructivist conception of perception works, see Martin, "The Eye of the Outside," 18–28.

8 On Foucault's "constructivism," see Deleuze's interview on Foucault, "Breaking Things Open, Breaking Words Open," *Negotiations*, especially 91–93.

9 *Actuel* in French has the connotation of being present or current, or topical, and thus temporary, a sense not reflected in its English equivalent, whose semantic affinity is with "the real." Another semantic consideration to be borne in mind here is Foucault's propensity to gloss "the actual" in terms of Nietzsche's "untimeliness" (*Unzeitgemäss*), where it will have a meaning closer to "the non-actual," Foucault's terminology notwithstanding. On this see Deleuze, "Break-

ing Things Open," 86. Important here is Deleuze's "The Actual and the Virtual," in Deleuze and Parnet, *Dialogues*, 148–52. On the constitution of the world in terms of events and singularities, see Deleuze, *Différence et repetition*, 173–77. On the separation between states of affairs and events, see Deleuze, *The Logic of Sense*, 109–17. The key Foucauldian text is "The Thought from Outside," 9–58. There is a suggestive summary of Foucault's relation to Blanchot in Deleuze, "Life as a Work of Art," *Negotiations*, 94–101, especially 97.

10 Deleuze defines a singularity in the following way: "Far from being individual or personal, singularities preside over the genesis of individuals and persons; they are distributed in a 'potential' which admits neither Self nor I, but which produces them by actualizing or realizing itself, although the figures of this actualization do not at all resemble the realized potential. Only a theory of singular points is capable of transcending the synthesis of the person and the analysis of the individual as these are (or are made) in consciousness" (*The Logic of Sense*, 103). All references to this work will henceforth be cited in the main body of the text. I am indebted to *The Logic of Sense* for the next few paragraphs.

11 It is important to remember that the distinction between an individual and a singularity is central for Deleuze. According to him, individuality is the outcome of a process that relates actual ideas (e.g., *the political demonstration*), events (e.g., *my being present at this demonstration*), and sensations (e.g., *my growing excitement* while at this demonstration) to virtual intensities (e.g., *this excitement*) and Ideas (e.g., *the pure variation "to become excited" is becoming clearer as "to become apathetic" is receding into obscurity because their relation to "to become politically involved" is changed*), whereas singularity is this process of connection itself. An individuality is thus the outcome of the process of singularization. A helpful account of Deleuze's conception of the relation between a singularity and an individual is in James Williams, *Gilles Deleuze's "Difference and Repetition,"* 138–42.

12 Fundamental to this counterfactual structure is the condition that the state of affairs posited by the counterfactual in question does not currently obtain. Hence in the counterfactual "If having a top-class intellect were a condition for being president, George W. Bush would not be president," the antecedent of this conditional, to wit "Having a top-class intellect is a condition for being president," is one that does not obtain. It is of course possible for someone who is convinced that George W. Bush is an intellectual force to hold the opposing counterfactual, namely, "If having a top-class intellect were a condition for being president, George W. Bush would (still) be president (because I happen to regard him as a top-class intellect)."

13 See Funkenstein, *Theology and the Scientific Imagination*, 340–48. Funkenstein argues that a mechanistic philosophy, a resultant of this secularizing process, had to be in place in order for society to be conceived of as a machine that could be significantly modified and improved.

14 See Turner, *Dramas, Fields and Metaphors*.

15 The charge, often leveled by marxist or marxisant thinkers, that Foucault's thought is fundamentally depoliticized may have something to do with Foucault's emphasis on "micro-power" and "local strategies," this emphasis being integral to his characterization of heterotopia. The question of Foucault's relation to marxism is a complex one, but it centers primarily on what Foucault took to be marxism's one-sided and problematic emphasis on the ideological apparatuses of the state, leading it to deal inadequately with forms of power and resistance that fell outside the purview of these state apparatuses. In this Foucault was right, though it does not follow from this either that his supposedly Weberian conceptions of micro-power and local strategies were eo ipso adequate or that any resort to them by Foucault and his many followers is necessarily a mark of some kind of "depoliticization."

16 See Poincaré, *Les Methodes Nouvelles de la Mécanique Celeste*.

17 See Dasgupta, "The Economics of the Environment."

18 The notion of reverse causation is absolutely central for the "universal history" developed by Deleuze and Guattari in *A Thousand Plateaus*. For Deleuze and Guattari, as we have seen, the state has always existed, even in hunter-gatherer societies, because these "primal" peoples (*les primitives*) had to ward off the state apparatuses in order to be the kind of society they were. See especially page 341. Perhaps the most helpful treatment of Deleuze's conception of causality is De-Landa, *Intensive Science and Virtual Philosophy*, 117–31.

19 It has to be admitted that this is not how Foucault himself conceives of heterotopia, since by and large for Foucault heterotopias are spatially situated; that is, there has to be some "site" where the heterotopia is instantiated. But if this requirement is dispensed with, it is easy to see how the principle of reverse causation can be applied to heterotopia.

20 This of course overlooks the possibility that capitalism has always existed, in the sense that there has always been an accumulation of surpluses. Even hunter-gatherer societies needed surpluses to feed those who went out hunting and foraging, and were thus functionally capitalist. This is the argument of Deleuze and Guattari; see *A Thousand Plateaus*, 429–31.

21 Rodrik, "Why Financial Markets Misbehave," 189. For details of Brazil's economic situation around the time of Lula's election, see Rocha, "Neo-dependency in Brazil."

22 Ibid., 190.

23 See S. Amin, *Delinking*, 160.

24 On Malaysia's recalcitrance in respect to the neoliberal consensus, see Wade, "The Asian Crisis" and "The Asian Debt-and-Development Crisis of 1997–8." See also Wade and Veneroso, "The Gathering World Slump and the Battle over Capital Controls." Malaysia did recover more quickly from the crisis than did those countries which adhered to the consensus.

25 The logic of incompossibility adverted to earlier specifies that once Bush became president in the actual world it was not possible for him *not* to be president in

this particular world. Another world, real but not yet actuated, would have to be realized in order for him not to have been made president again in 2004.

26 On the buffoonish Berlusconi and the Italian media, see Ginsborg, *Silvio Berlusconi*. One also recalls here the satirical play "The Two-Headed Anomaly," written by the Italian Nobel laureate for literature Dario Fo, in which Berlusconi, known to be touchy about his height (he is 5 feet 5 inches tall without his platform shoes), is among other things portrayed as a puppet dwarf who received half of Vladimir Putin's brain after his own brain was severely injured in an attack by Chechnyan terrorists during his visit to Moscow. Putin, never doubting that his own brain was that of an extraordinary genius, decided he could easily function with half a brain, and donated the other half in a life-saving gesture to the now brain-dead Berlusconi. After his surgery Berlusconi senses he is Italian but has the disconcerting memories of the KGB colonel that Putin once was, and has developed a taste for vodka as opposed to fine Italian wine. Might a possible American heterotopia therefore include, as a very preliminary offering, someone who could perhaps be the American equivalent of Dario Fo?

Chapter 12. The New Political Subject

1 For Rodrik, see "Why Financial Markets Misbehave," 188–91.

2 The point that America's status as the sole superpower does not necessarily represent a simplification of power relationships in the direction of unipolarity is well made in Therborn, "Into the 21st Century," 89. For a similar view, see Mann, "Globalization and September 11."

3 See United Nations, *World Economic Situation and Prospects 2006*, www.un.org/esa, accessed on 5 February 2006.

4 Admittedly, this is a "weapon of the weak"; those who are perceived to be strong are in a position to ignore principles and conventions, while those who are weak have little option but to insist that such principles and conventions be observed. This adherence is strategic, however, insofar as those who espouse it will always be looking for a state of affairs in which they, who are consigned to a situation of subordination or subalternity, will no longer be subordinate (i.e., beholden in this case to the U.S. dollar as the international reserve currency).

5 This point is well made in Mann, "The First Failed Empire of the Twenty-First Century," 66, who points out that there is a gulf between "battlefield victory" and "imperial pacification" that the United States seems unable to bridge.

6 See Mann, "The First Failed Empire of the Twenty-First Century," 80.

7 This configuration of the G8 countries and the international financial organizations amounts to what Ignacio Ramonet has rightly called an unaccountable "planetary executive": "Over the past ten years, globalization, combined with a laxity on the part of politicians, has resulted in the surreptitious creation of a kind of planetary executive, consisting of four main actors: the International Monetary Fund, the World Bank, the Organisation for Economic Develop-

ment and Cooperation, and the WTO. Immune from democratic pressure, this informal power network runs our world and decides the fate of its inhabitants. And there is no counterpower—parliament, media, political parties—that can correct, alter or reject its decisions" ("A New Dawn," 1). Ramonet's account of this unaccountable planetary executive needs to be modified in at least one respect: the United States has to be added to his list of actors. Although the IMF, the World Bank, the OECD, and the WTO are rightly viewed as paranational formations in Ramonet's sense, the United States is the world's only truly supervening political and economic force: it is the guiding force behind these institutions, while also exercising its own version of an international executive power. The IMF, the World Bank, the OECD, and the WTO therefore complement and reinforce the U.S. government's policy objectives, but the United States is also a planetary executive in its own right. For a detailed account of how this unaccountable planetary executive works in the current world-system, see Leys, "Democracy," 57–67.

8 Thus the federal appeals judge and legal scholar Richard Posner characterizes the U.S. electoral system as an instrument explicitly designed to facilitate the orderly transition from one administration to another, and not some mysterious alchemy that converts the popular will into a (people's) government. As a judicial conservative, Posner has no objection to this "postpolitical" gutted electoral process, since for him wanting any alternative to it would be to succumb to romantic delusions. See his *Breaking the Deadlock*. Moreover, when, unreservedly, both the Republican and Democratic Parties are parties of capital, economic choices for voters cease to be meaningful. As my colleague Jerry Hough points out, "Both parties have structured their economic policy so as to try to maximize their support in the upper class of the population—the 25% of [the] population that makes above $75,000 a year in family income" (*Changing Party Coalitions*, 1).

9 For Mann on this "ostracizing imperialism," see his "Globalization and September 11," 53–56.

10 I take the notion of a "permeable sovereignty" from Gowan, "The New Liberal Cosmopolitanism," 60–65. See also Gowan, *The Global Gamble* and "US: UN." For a stirring critique of the appeal to human rights to justify wars against "fundamentalism," see Žižek, "Against Human Rights."

11 See Mann, "The First Failed Empire of the Twenty-First Century," 76–78, whose line of argument is taken up in these paragraphs.

12 On this conflation, see Blackburn, "The Imperial Presidency and the Revolutions of Modernity," 168–71. As I write Barack Obama has just won the 2008 presidential election, but I am inclined to the view that Obama will end up governing pretty much as a Clintonite centrist (albeit with one or two adjustments). Though matching Clinton's competence (definitely a considerable mercy given the course of American presidential politics from 2000 to 2008!), Obama is in all likelihood not going to do much more for the poor countries of the South

(and impoverished Americans) than Clinton did, especially given the currently unpropitious economic climate. The consensus so far on Obama's "financial rescue" package is that it is providing a windfall for those who caused the problem in the first place, as opposed to restructuring the banks themselves.

13 See Nairn, *Faces of Nationalism*, in which he makes the crucial point that "political nationality" and its concomitant "nationality politics" are unavoidable in the modern world, but need not be accompanied or tainted by ethnonationalism. Nairn believes the various ethnonationalisms to be a contingent historical phenomenon manifest from the mid-eighteenth century onward. These ethnonationalisms preempted otherwise more acceptable versions of political nationality (which he refers to as "civic nationalism") by endorsing irrational myths and atavistic conceptions of the *ethnos* ("chosen" peoples, "manifest destinies," etc.). Nairn derives the distinction between "civic nationalism" and "ethnic nationalism" from Ignatieff, *Blood and Belonging.* See also Nairn, "Breakwaters of 2000." Also very important here is Armstrong, *Nations before Nationalism.* Nairn's point is salutary because of the extremely common tendency to demonize the nation-state and nationalism.

14 See S. Amin, *Delinking*, 136.

15 Radical social and economic transformation occurs only when ruling elites find themselves compelled to take into account the interests of the less privileged while still trying to maintain their own privileges ("Whom do we invite to the negotiation table?"), or when they are placed in a social order that peremptorily withdraws their privileges ("Are we going to be exiled, are we going to be lined up against the wall by a firing squad, are our Swiss bank accounts going to be sequestered?"). The best detailed account of this attempt to establish a "democracy from below" is in E. J. Wood, *Forging Democracy from Below.* Wood's narrative shows that the impetus for a movement to democracy in many poor countries is provided by the country's impoverished classes, who insist on their inclusion in the prevailing political system.

BIBLIOGRAPHY

Adorno, Theodor W. "A Portrait of Walter Benjamin." *Prisms*, trans. Samuel Weber and Shierry Weber. Cambridge: MIT Press, 1981. Originally published as *Prismen* (Berlin: Suhrkamp, 1955).

Agamben, Giorgio. *The Coming Community*. Trans. Michael Hardt. Minneapolis: University of Minnesota Press, 1993.

Aglietta, Michel. "Capitalism at the Turn of the Century: Regulation Theory and the Challenge of Social Change." *New Left Review* 232 (old series, 1998), 41–90.

———. "Le capitalisme de demain." *Notes de la Fondation Saint-Simon*. Paris: 1998.

———. "Financial Fragility, Crises, and the Stakes of Prudential Control." *Governance, Equity, and Global Markets: The Annual Bank Conference on Development Economics—Europe*, ed. Joseph E. Stiglitz and Pierre-Alain Muet. Oxford: Oxford University Press, 1999.

———. "Shareholder Value and Corporate Governance: Some Tricky Questions." *Economy and Society* 29 (2000), 146–59.

———. *A Theory of Capitalist Regulation: The U.S. Experience*. New edition. Trans. David Fernbach. 1979; London: Verso, 2000. Originally published as *Régulation et crises du capitalisme* (Paris: Calmann-Lévy, 1976). New French edition (Paris: Odile Jacob, 1997).

———. "World Capitalism in the Eighties." *New Left Review* 136 (first series, 1982), 5–41.

Aglietta, Michel, and Antoine Rebérioux. *Corporate Governance Adrift: A Critique of Shareholder Value*. Cheltenham, United Kingdom: Edward Elgar, 2005.

Akyüz, Yilmaz. *East Asian Development: New Perspectives*. London: Frank Cass, 1999.

Akyüz, Yilmaz, and Charles Gore. "The Investment-Profits Nexus in East Asian Industrialization." *World Development* 24 (1996), 461–70.

Alfaro, Laura, Sebnem Kalemli-Ozcan, and Vadym Volosovych. "Why Doesn't Capital Flow from Rich to Poor Countries? An Empirical Investigation."

Working paper, November 2005. www.people.hbs.edu. Accessed on 6 January 2005.

Althusser, Louis. *For Marx.* Trans. Ben Brewster. London: Penguin Books, 1969. Originally published as *Pour Marx* (Paris: Maspéro, 1965).

———. *Lenin and Philosophy and Other Essays.* Trans. Ben Brewster. London: New Left Books, 1971. Originally published as *Lénine et la philosophie* (Paris: Maspéro, 1969).

———. *Machiavelli and Us.* Ed. François Matheron. Trans. Gregory Elliott. London: Verso, 1999. Originally published as *Solitude de Machiavel et autres textes.* Ed. Yves Sintomer (Paris: Presses Universitaires de France, 1998).

Altvater, Elmar. "Fordist and Post-Fordist International Division of Labor and Monetary Regimes." *Pathways to Industrialization and Regional Development,* ed. Michael Storper and Allen J. Scott. London: Routledge, 1992.

———. *The Future of the Market: An Essay on the Regulation and Nature after the Collapse of "Actually Existing Socialism."* Trans. Patrick Camiller. London: Verso, 1993. Originally published as *Die Zukunft des Markets: Ein Essay über die Regulation von Geld und Natur nach dem Scheitern des "real existierenden Sozialismus."* (Münster: Westfälisches Dampfboot, 1991).

Amin, Ash, ed. *Post-Fordism: A Reader.* Oxford: Blackwell, 1994.

Amin, Ash. "Post-Fordism: Models, Fantasies and of Transition." *Post-Fordism: A Reader,* ed. Ash Amin, Oxford: Blackwell, 1994.

Amin, Samir. *Accumulation on a World Scale: A Critique of the Theory of Underdevelopment.* Trans. Michael Wolfers. 2nd edition. New York: Monthly Review Press, 1974. Originally published as *L'accumulation à l'échelle mondiale* (Paris: Anthropos, 1970).

———. "*Accumulation on a World Scale*: Thirty Years Later." *Rethinking Marxism* 1 (1988), 54–75.

———. *Capitalism in the Age of Globalization: The Management of Contemporary Society.* Various translators. London: Zed Books, 1997.

———. "The Conditions for an Alternative Global System Based on Social and International Justice: Document for the World Social Forum, Mumbai 2004." http://business.guardian.co.uk. Accessed on 11 January 2006.

———. "Conditions for Re-launching Development." *Karl Polanyi: The Contemporary Significance of the Great Transformation,* ed. Kenneth McRobbie and Kari Polanyi. New York: Black Rose Books, 2000.

———. *Delinking: Towards a Polycentric World.* Trans. Michael Wolfers. London: Zed Books, 1990. Originally published as *La déconnexion* (Paris: La Découverte, 1985).

———. *Empire of Chaos.* Trans. W. H. Locke Anderson. New York: Monthly Review Press, 1992. Originally published as *L'Empire du chaos: La Nouvelle Mondialisation Capitaliste* (Paris: L'Hamarttan, 1991).

———. "For a Progressive and Democratic New World Order." *Globalization and the Dilemmas of the State in the South*, ed. Francis Adams, Satya Dev Gupta, and Kidane Mengisteab. London: Macmillan, 1999.

———. *Maldevelopment: Anatomy of a Global Failure.* Trans. Michael Wolfers. London: Zed Books, 1990.

———. "Regionalization in Response to Polarizing Globalization." *Globalism and the New Regionalism: Volume 1*, ed. Björn Hettne, András Inotai, and Osvaldo Sunkel. London: Macmillan, 1999.

———. *Re-Reading the Postwar Period: An Intellectual Itinerary.* Trans. Michael Wolfers. New York: Monthly Review Press, 1994. Originally published as *L'itinéraire intellectuel: Regards sur le demi-siecle 1945–90* (Paris: L'Hamarttan, 1993).

Anderson, Perry. *Considerations on Western Marxism.* London: New Left Books, 1976.

———. *Lineages of the Absolutist State.* London: New Left Books, 1974.

———. *Passages from Antiquity to Feudalism.* London: New Left Books, 1974.

———. "U.S. Elections: Testing Formula Two." *New Left Review* 8 (new series, 2001), 5–22.

———. *A Zone of Engagement.* London: Verso, 1992.

Andrews, David M. "Capital Mobility and State Autonomy: Toward a Structural Theory of International Monetary Relations." *International Studies Quarterly* 38 (1994), 193–218.

Andrews, David M., C. Randall Hennings, and Louis W. Pauly, eds. *Governing the World's Money.* Ithaca: Cornell University Press, 2002.

Andrews, David M., and Thomas D. Willett. "Financial Interdependence and the State: International Monetary Relations at Century's End." *International Organization* 51 (1997), 479–511.

Armijo, Leslie Elliott, ed. *Financial Globalization and Democracy in Emerging Markets.* London: Palgrave, 1999.

Armstrong, John. *Nations before Nationalism.* Chapel Hill: University of North Carolina Press, 1992.

Arrighi, Giovanni. *Adam Smith in Beijing: Lineages of the Twenty-First Century.* London: Verso, 2007.

———. "A Crisis of Hegemony." *Dynamics of Global Crisis*, ed. Samir Amin, Giovanni Arrighi, Andre Gunder Frank, and Immanuel Wallerstein. New York: Monthly Review Press, 1982.

———. "Financial Expansions in World Historical Perspective: A Reply to Robert Pollin." *New Left Review* 224 (old series, 1997), 154–59.

———. "Hegemony Unravelling: Part I." *New Left Review* 32 (new series, 2005), 23–80.

———. "Hegemony Unravelling: Part II." *New Left Review* 33 (new series, 2005), 83–116.

———. *The Long Twentieth Century: Money, Power, and the Origins of Our Times.* London: Verso, 1994.

———. "Workers of the World at Century's End." *Review of the Fernand Braudel Center* 19 (1996), 335–51.

Arrighi, Giovanni, Takeshi Hamashita, and Mark Selden. *The Resurgence of East Asia: 500, 150 and 50 Year Perspectives*. London: Routledge, 2003.

Arrighi, Giovanni, and Beverly J. Silver. *Chaos and Governance in the Modern World System*. Minneapolis: University of Minnesota Press, 1999.

Asad, Talal. "Muslims and European Identity: Can Europe Represent Islam?" *The Idea of Europe: From Antiquity to the European Union*, ed. Anthony Pagden. Cambridge: Cambridge University Press, 2002.

Asian Development Bank. *Asian Development Outlook 1994*. Oxford: Oxford University Press, 1994.

———. *Asian Development Outlook 2004*. www.adb.org. Accessed on 3 January 2005.

Attali, Jacques. *Noise: The Political Economy of Music*. Trans. Brian Massumi. Minneapolis: University of Minnesota Press, 1985. Originally published as *Bruits (Broché)* (Paris: Presses Universitaires de France, 1977).

Aybar, Sedat, and Costas Lapavistas. "Financial System Design and the Post-Washington Consensus." *Development Policy in the Twenty-First Century: Beyond the Post-Washington Consensus*, ed. Ben Fine, Costas Lapavistas, and Jonathan Pincus. London: Routledge.

Bacevich, Andrew J. *American Empire: The Realities and Consequences of U.S. Diplomacy*. Cambridge: Harvard University Press, 2002.

———. "Expanding War, Contracting Meaning: The Next President and the Global War on Terror." 2008. ww.commondreams.org. Accessed on 30 October 2008.

———. *The Limits of Power: The End of American Exceptionalism*. New York: Henry Holt, 2008.

———. *The New American Militarism: How Americans Are Seduced by War*. Oxford: Oxford University Press, 2005.

Badiou, Alain. *Abrégé de métapolitique*. Paris: Seuil, 1998.

———. "Afterword: Some Replies to a Demanding Friend." Trans. Alberto Toscano. *Think Again: Alain Badiou and the Future of Philosophy*, ed. Peter Hallward. London: Continuum, 2004.

———. *Court traité d'ontologie transitoire*. Paris: Seuil, 1998.

———. *Deleuze: The Clamor of Being*. Trans. Louise Burchill. Minneapolis: University of Minnesota Press, 1999. Originally published as *Deleuze* (Paris: Hachette, 1997).

———. *De quoi Sarkozy est-il le nom?* Paris: Nouvelles Editions Lignes, 2007.

———. *D'un désastre obscure (Droit, Etat, Politique)*. Paris: L'Aube, 1991.

———. *Ethics: An Understanding of Evil*. Trans. Peter Hallward. London: Verso, 2001. Originally published as *L'ethique: Essai sur la conscience du mal* (Paris: Hatier, 1993).

———. "The Ethics of Truths: Construction and Potency." Trans. Thelma Sowley. *Pli: The Warwick Journal of Philosophy* 12 (2001), 247–55.

———. *L'Etre et l'événement.* Paris: Seuil, 1988.

———. "Highly Speculative Reasoning on the Concept of Democracy." Trans. Jorge Jauregui. *lacanian ink* 16 (2000), 28–43.

———. *Logiques des mondes.* Paris: Seuil, 2006.

———. "Philosophy and Politics." *Radical Philosophy* 96 (1999), 29–32.

———. *St. Paul: The Foundation of Universalism.* Trans. Ray Brassier. Palo Alto: Stanford University Press, 2003. Originally published as *Saint Paul: La fondation de l'universalisme* (Paris: Presses Universitaires de France, 1997).

———. "La subversion infinitésimale." *Cahiers pour l'analyse* 9 (1968), 118–37.

Baker, Dean. *The Conservative Nanny State: How the Wealthy Use the Government to Stay Rich and Get Richer.* Washington: Center for Economic and Policy Research, 2006.

———. *The United States Since 1980.* Cambridge: Cambridge University Press, 2007.

Baker, Dean, Gerald Epstein, and Robert Pollin. Introduction to *Globalization and Progressive Economic Policy*, ed. Dean Baker, Gerald Epstein, and Robert Pollin. Cambridge: Cambridge University Press, 1998.

Baker, Dean, and Mark Weisbrot. *Social Security: The Phony Crisis.* Chicago: University of Chicago Press, 2001.

Balibar, Etienne. "Citizen Subject." *Who Comes after the Subject?*, ed. Eduardo Cadava, Peter Connor, and Jean-Luc Nancy. London: Routledge, 1991.

———. *Identité et différence.* Paris: Seuil, 1998.

———. "The Infinite Contradiction." Trans. Jean-Marc Poisson, with Jacques Lezra. *Yale French Studies* 88 (1995), 142–64.

———. "Je/moi/soi." *Vocabulaire européen des philosophies.* Paris: Seuil, 2001.

———. *Masses, Classes, Ideas: Studies on Politics and Philosophy before and after Marx.* Trans. James Swenson. London: Routledge, 1994.

———. "The Vacillation of Ideology." Trans. Andrew Ross and Constance Penley. *Marxism and the Interpretation of Culture*, ed. Cary Nelson and Lawrence Grossberg. Urbana: University of Illinois Press, 1988.

Bank of International Settlements. *Triennial Central Bank Survey of Foreign Exchange and Derivatives Market Activity 2004.* March 2005.

Baran, Paul A., and Paul M. Sweezy. *Monopoly Capital: An Essay on the American Economic and Social Order.* Harmondsworth, England: Penguin Books, 1966.

Bardhan, Pranab, Samuel Bowles, and Michael Wallerstein. Introduction to *Globalization and Egalitarian Redistribution*, ed. Pranab Bardhan, Samuel Bowles, and Michael Wallerstein. Princeton: Princeton University Press, 2006.

Bataille, Georges. "The Use-Value of D. A. F. Sade (An Open Letter to My Comrades)." *Visions of Excess: Selected Writings, 1927–1939*, ed. and intro. Allan Stoekl, trans. Allan Stoekl, with Carl R. Lovitts and Donald M. Leslie Jr. Minneapolis: University of Minnesota Press, 1985. Originally published as "La valeur d'usage de DAF Sade," *Oeuvres Complètes: II, Écrits posthumes, 1922–1940* (Paris: Gallimard, 1970).

Bayly, C. A. *The Birth of the Modern World, 1780–1914: Global Connections and Comparisons*. Oxford: Blackwell, 2004.

Beardsworth, Richard. *Derrida and the Political*. London: Routledge, 1996.

Beasley-Murray, Jon. "It Happened on TV." *London Review of Books* 24, no. 9 (2002), 6–7.

Beck, Lewis White. "Kant's Two Conceptions of the Will in Their Political Context." *Kant and Political Philosophy: The Contemporary Legacy*, ed. Ronald Beiner and William James Booth. New Haven: Yale University Press, 1993.

Beiser, Frederick C. *Enlightenment, Revolution, and Romanticism: The Genesis of Modern German Political Thought, 1790–1800*. Cambridge: Harvard University Press, 1992.

———. *The Fate of Reason: German Philosophy from Kant to Fichte*. Cambridge: Harvard University Press, 1987.

———. *German Idealism: The Struggle against Subjectivism, 1781–1801*. Cambridge: Harvard University Press, 2002.

———. *The Romantic Imperative: The Concept of Early German Romanticism*. Cambridge: Harvard University Press, 2003.

Benedict, Ruth. *The Chrysanthemum and the Sword*. Boston: Houghton Mifflin, 1946.

Benjamin, Walter. "Theses on the Philosophy of History." *Illuminations*. Trans. Harry Zohn. New York: Schocken Books, 1950.

Bennington, Geoffrey. *Interrupting Derrida*. London: Routledge, 2000.

———. "RIP." *Futures of Jacques Derrida*, ed. Richard Rand. Stanford: Stanford University Press, 2001.

Bennington, Geoffrey, and Jacques Derrida. *Jacques Derrida*. Trans. Geoffrey Bennington. Chicago: University of Chicago Press, 1993.

Bensaïd, Daniel. "Alain Badiou and the Miracle of the Event." Trans. Ray Brassier. *Think Again: Alain Badiou and the Future of Philosophy*, ed. Peter Hallward. London: Continuum, 2004.

Berger, Suzanne, and Ronald Dore, eds. *National Diversity and Global Capitalism*. Ithaca: Cornell University Press, 1995.

Bernasconi, Robert. "Justice without Ethics?" *Pli: Warwick Journal of Philosophy* 6 (1997), 58–69.

Bernstein, Jared, and Sylvia A. Allegretto. "Wages Picture." Economic Policy Institute, www.epi.org. Accessed on 20 January 2006.

Bhabha, Homi. "Culture's In-Between." *Questions of Cultural Identity*, ed. Stuart Hall and Paul du Gay. London: Sage, 1996.

———. *The Location of Culture*. London: Routledge, 1994.

Bhaduri, Amit. "Implications of Globalization for Macroeconomic Theory and Policy in Developing Countries." *Globalization and Progressive Economic Policy*, ed. Dean Baker, Gerald Epstein, and Robert Pollin. Cambridge: Cambridge University Press, 1998.

Blackburn, Robin. *Age Shock: How Finance Is Failing Us*. London: Verso, 2006.

————. *Banking on Death or Investing in Life: The History and Future of Pensions.* London: Verso, 2002.

————. "The Imperial Presidency and the Revolutions of Modernity." *Debating Cosmopolitics*, ed. Daniele Archibugi. London: Verso, 2003.

Blaney, David L. "Reconceptualizing Autonomy: The Difference Dependency Theory Makes." *Review of International Political Economy* 3 (1996), 459–97.

Bobbitt, Philip. *The Shield of Achilles: War, Peace, and the Course of History.* New York: Knopf, 2002.

Bock, Gisela, Quentin Skinner, and Maurizio Viroli, eds. *Machiavelli and Republicanism.* Cambridge: Cambridge University Press, 1990.

Boltanski, Luc, and Eve Chiapello. *The New Spirit of Capitalism.* Trans. Gregory Elliott. London: Verso, 2006. Originally published as *Le nouvelle esprit du capitalism* (Paris: Gallimard, 1999).

Bonefeld, Werner, Richard Gunn, and Kosmas Psychopedis, eds. *Open Marxism.* 2 vols. London: Pluto Press, 1992.

Bosteels, Bruno. "Alain Badiou's Theory of the Subject: Part I. The Recommencement of Dialectical Materialism?" *Pli: The Warwick Journal of Philosophy* 12 (2001), 200–229.

————. "Alain Badiou's Theory of the Subject: Part II. The Recommencement of Dialectical Materialism?" *Pli: The Warwick Journal of Philosophy* 13 (2002), 173–208.

————. "Logics of Antagonism: In the Margins of Alain Badiou's 'The Flux of the Party.'" *Polygraph* 15/16 (2004), 93–108.

Bourdieu, Pierre. "The Aristocracy of Culture." *Media, Culture and Society* 2 (1980), 225–54.

————. *Distinction: A Social Critique of the Judgment of Taste.* Trans. Richard Nice. London: Routledge, 1984. Originally published as *La distinction: Critique social du jugement* (Paris: Minuit, 1979).

————. *The Political Ontology of Martin Heidegger.* Trans. Peter Collier. Stanford: Stanford University Press, 1991. Originally published as *L'Ontologie politique de Martin Heidegger* (Paris: Minuit, 1988).

Boyer, Robert. "Is a Finance-led Growth Regime a Viable Alternative to Fordism? A Preliminary Analysis." *Economy and Society* 29 (2000), 111–45.

————. "Le politique à l'ère de la mondialisation et de la finance: Le point sur quelques recherches régulationnistes." *L'Année de la regulation no. 3.* Paris: La Découverte, 1999.

————. *The Regulation School: A Critical Introduction.* Trans. Craig Charney. New York: Columbia University Press, 1990. Originally published as *La Théorie de la Régulation* (Paris: Minuit, 1967).

Braudel, Fernand. *L'identité de la France.* Paris: Flammarion, 1986.

Brenner, Neil, Bob Jessop, Martin Jones, and Gordon MacLeod, eds. *State/Space: A Reader.* Oxford: Blackwell, 2003.

Brenner, Robert. *The Boom and the Bubble: The U.S. in the World Economy.* London: Verso, 2002.

———, ed. *The Economics of Global Turbulence.* Special issue of *New Left Review* 229 (first series, 1998).

Brown, Wendy. *States of Injury: Power and Freedom in Late Modernity.* Princeton: Princeton University Press, 1995.

———. "Wounded Attachments: Late Modern Oppositional Political Formations." *The Identity in Question*, ed. John Rajchman. London: Routledge, 1995.

Cadava, Eduardo, Peter Connor, and Jean-Luc Nancy, eds. *Who Comes after the Subject?* London: Routledge, 1991.

Cage, John. *A Year from Monday: New Lectures and Writings.* Middletown, Conn.: Wesleyan University Press, 1969.

Callaghy, Thomas, Ronald Kassimir, and Robert Latham, eds. *Intervention and Transnationalism in Africa: Global-Local Networks of Power.* Cambridge: Cambridge University Press, 2001.

Calomiris, Charles W. "Capital Flows, Financial Crises, and Public Policy." *Globalization: What's New*, ed. Michael W. Weinstein. New York: Columbia University Press, 2005.

Caplan, Jane, and John Torpey, eds. *Documenting Individual Identity: The Development of State Identities in the Modern World.* Princeton: Princeton University Press, 2001.

Caplan, Jane, and John Torpey. Introduction to *Documenting Individual Identity: The Development of State Identities in the Modern World.* Princeton: Princeton University Press, 2001.

Cardoso, Fernando Henrique. "Dependency and Development in Latin America." *New Left Review* 74 (first series, 1972), 83–95.

Cardoso, Fernando Henrique, and Enzo Faletto. *Dependency and Development in Latin America.* Trans. Marjorie Mattingly Urquidi. Berkeley: University of California Press, 1979. Originally published as *Dependencia y desarrollo en América Latina* (1969; Mexico City: Siglo Ventuino Editores, 1971).

Caygill, Howard. *Art of Judgment.* Oxford: Blackwell, 1989.

Central Intelligence Agency. *World Factbook 2004.* www.photius.com. Accessed on 19 January 2006.

Chang, Ha-Joon. *Bad Samaritans: The Myth of Free Trade and the Secret History of Capitalism.* New York: Bloomsbury Press, 2008.

———. *The East Asian Development Experience: The Miracle, the Crisis, and the Future.* London: Zed Books, 2006.

———. *Globalisation, Economic Development and the Role of the State.* London: Zed Books, 2003.

———, ed. *Joseph Stiglitz and the World Bank: The Rebel Within.* London: Anthem Press, 2001.

———. *Kicking Away the Ladder: Development Strategy in Historical Perspective.* London: Anthem Press, 2002.

———. "The Market, the State and Institutions in Economic Development." *Rethinking Development Economics*, ed. Ha-Joon Chang. London: Anthem Press, 2003.

Chang, Ha-Joon, Gabriel Palma, and Hugh D. Whittaker, eds., *Financial Liberalization and the Asian Crisis*. London: Palgrave Macmillan, 2001.

Clark, Gordon L. *Pension Fund Capitalism*. Oxford: Oxford University Press, 2000.

Clarke, Simon. "The Global Accumulation of Capital and the Periodisation of the Capitalist State Form." *Open Marxism*, vol. 1, ed. Werner Bonefeld, Richard Gunn, and Kosmas Psychopedis. London: Pluto Press, 1992.

Cliff, Tony. *Lenin*. London: Pluto Press, 2003.

Cohen, Benjamin J. "Phoenix Risen: The Resurrection of Global Finance." *World Politics* 48 (1996), 268–96.

Cohen, Nick. "And Now the Trouble Really Begins." *New Statesman* (London, 19 November 2001), http://newstatesman.co.uk.

Colley, Linda. *Britons: Forging the Nation, 1707–1837*. New Haven: Yale University Press, 1992.

Comaroff, Jean. *Body of Power, Spirit of Resistance: The Culture and History of a South African People*. Chicago: University of Chicago Press, 1985.

Comaroff, Jean, and John Comaroff, eds. *Modernity and Its Malcontents: Ritual and Power in Postcolonial Africa*. Chicago: University of Chicago Press, 1993.

Comaroff, Jean, and John Comaroff. *Of Revelation and Revolution*. 2 vols. Chicago: University of Chicago Press, 1991.

Conference Board. *Institutional Investment Report 2005: U.S. and International Trends*. www.conference-board.org. Accessed on 3 January 2006.

Courtine, Jean-François. "Donner/Prendre: La Main." *Heidegger Studies* 3/4 (1987–88), 25–40.

Critchley, Simon. "Demanding Approval: On the Ethics of Alain Badiou." *Radical Philosophy* 100 (2000), 16–27.

———. *Ethics-Politics-Subjectivity: Essays on Derrida, Levinas and Contemporary French Thought*. London: Verso, 1999.

Cumings, Bruce. "The Origins and Development of the Northeast Asian Political Economy: Industrial Sectors, Product Cycles, and Political Consequences." *The Political Economy of the New Asian Industrialism*, ed. Frederic Deyo. Ithaca: Cornell University Press, 1987.

Cunningham, Conor. *Genealogy of Nihilism: Philosophies of Nihilism and the Difference of Theology*. London: Routledge, 2002.

———. "Language: Wittgenstein after Theology." *Radical Orthodoxy: A New Theology*, ed. John Milbank, Catherine Pickstock, and Graham Ward. London: Routledge, 1999.

Dasgupta, Partha. "The Economics of the Environment." *Proceedings of the British Academy* 90 (1996), 165–221.

—————. *An Inquiry into Well-Being and Destitution.* Oxford: Oxford University Press, 1993.

Dastur, Françoise. "The Call of Conscience: The Most Intimate Alterity." *Heidegger and Practical Philosophy*, ed. François Raffoul and David Pettigrew. Albany: State University of New York Press, 2002.

—————. "The Critique of Anthropologism in Heidegger's Thought." *Appropriating Heidegger*, ed. James E. Faulconer and Mark A. Wrathall. Cambridge: Cambridge University Press, 2000.

Davidson, Donald. "Radical Interpretation." *Inquiries into Truth and Interpretation.* Oxford: Oxford University Press, 1984.

de Brunhoff, Suzanne. "Fictitious Capital." *The New Palgrave Marxian Economics*, ed. John Eatwell, Murray Milgate, and Peter Newman. London, Palgrave 1990.

DeLanda, Manuel. *Intensive Science and Virtual Philosophy.* London: Continuum, 2002.

Deleuze, Gilles. *Cinema 1: The Movement-Image.* Trans. Hugh Tomlinson and Barbara Habberjam. Minneapolis: University of Minnesota Press, 1986. Originally published as *Cinéma I: L'image-mouvement* (Paris: Minuit, 1983).

—————. *Cinema 2: The Time-Image.* Trans. Hugh Tomlinson and Robert Galeta. Minneapolis: University of Minnesota Press, 1989. Originally published as *Cinéma II: L'image-temps* (Paris: Minuit, 1993).

—————. *Desert Islands and Other Texts.* Ed. David Lapoujade. Trans. Michael Taormina. New York: Semiotext(e), 2004. Originally published as *L'île deserte et autres texts: Textes et entretiens 1953–1974* (Paris: Minuit, 2002).

—————. *Deux régimes de fous: Textes et entretiens 1975–1995.* Paris: Minuit, 2003.

—————. *Difference and Repetition.* Trans. Paul Patton. New York: Columbia University Press, 1994. Originally published as *Différence et répétition* (Paris: Minuit, 1968).

—————. "Doubts about the Imaginary." *Negotiations, 1972–1990.* Trans. Martin Joughin, 62–67. New York, Columbia.

—————. *Essays Critical and Clinical.* Trans. Daniel W. Smith and Michael A. Greco. Minneapolis: University of Minnesota Press, 1997. Originally published as *Critique et clinique* (Paris: Minuit, 1993).

—————. *Expressionism in Philosophy: Spinoza.* Trans. Martin Joughin. New York: Zone Books, 1990. Originally published as *Spinoza et le problems de l'expression* (Paris: Minuit, 1968).

—————. *The Fold: Leibniz and the Baroque.* Trans. Tom Conley. Minnesota: University of Minnesota Press, 1993. Originally published as *Le Pli: Leibniz et le baroque* (Paris: Minuit, 1988).

—————. *Foucault.* Trans. Séan Hand. Minneapolis: University of Minnesota Press, 1988. Originally published as *Foucault* (Paris: Minuit, 1986).

—————. *Kant's Critical Philosophy: The Doctrine of the Faculties.* Trans. Hugh Tomlinson and Barbara Habberjam. Minneapolis: University of Minnesota Press, 1984.

Originally published as *La Philosophie Critique de Kant* (Paris: Presses Universitaires de France, 1963).

———. *The Logic of Sense.* Trans. Mark Lester. Ed. Constantin V. Boundas. New York: Columbia University Press, 1990. Originally published as *Logique du sens* (Paris: Minuit, 1969).

———. *Negotiations, 1972–1990.* Trans. Martin Joughin. New York, Columbia University Press, 1995. Originally published as *Pourparlers* (Paris: Minuit, 1990).

———. "A Philosophical Concept. . . ." *Who Comes after the Subject?*, ed. Eduardo Cadava, Peter Connor, and Jean-Luc Nancy. London: Routledge, 1991.

———. *Pure Immanence: Essays on a Life.* Trans. Anne Boyman. New York: MIT Press, 2001.

———. *Spinoza: Practical Philosophy.* Trans. Robert Hurley. San Francisco: City Lights Books, 1988. Originally published as *Spinoza, philosophie pratique*, revised edition (Paris: Minuit, 1981).

Deleuze, Gilles, and Félix Guattari. *Anti-Oedipus: Capitalism and Schizophrenia.* Trans. Robert Hurley, Mark Seem, and Helen R. Lane. Minneapolis: University of Minnesota Press, 1983. Originally published as *L'anti-Oedipe*, vol. 1 of *Capitalisme et schizophrénie* (Paris: Minuit, 1977).

———. *A Thousand Plateaus: Capitalism and Schizophrenia.* Trans. Brian Massumi. Minneapolis: University of Minnesota Press, 1987. Originally published as *Mille plateaux*, vol. 2 of *Capitalisme et schizophrénie* (Paris: Minuit, 1980).

———. *What Is Philosophy?* Trans. Hugh Tomlinson and Graham Burchell. New York: Columbia University Press, 1994. Originally published as *Qu'est ce que la philosophie?* (Paris: Minuit, 1993).

Deleuze, Gilles, and Claire Parnet. *Dialogues.* Trans. Hugh Tomlinson and Barbara Habberjam. New York: Columbia University Press, 1987. Originally published as *Dialogues* (1977; Paris: Flammarion, 1996).

Derrida, Jacques. *Adieu: To Emmanuel Lévinas.* Trans. Pascale-Anne Brault and Michael B. Naas. Stanford: Stanford University Press, 1999. Originally published as *Adieu á Emmanuel Lévinas* (Paris: Galilée, 1997).

———. *Aporias: Finis and Awaiting (at) the Arrival.* Trans. Thomas Dutoit. Stanford: Stanford University Press, 1993. Originally published as *Apories: Mourir s'attendre aux "limites de la vérité"* (Paris: Galilée, 1993).

———. "'Eating Well,' or the Calculation of the Subject." *Points . . . Interviews, 1974–1994.* Ed. Elisabeth Weber. Trans. Peter Connor and Avitall Ronnell. Stanford: Stanford University Press, 1995.

———. "The Force of Law: The 'Mystical Foundation' of Authority." Trans. Mary Quaintance, with the original French text. *Cardozo Law Review* 11 (1990), 920–1045. Published in French as *Force de loi* (Paris: Galilée, 1994).

———. *The Gift of Death.* Trans. David Wills. Chicago: University of Chicago Press, 1995. Originally published as *Donner la mort: L'ethique du don*, by Jacques Derrida et al. (Paris: Métailié-Transition, 1992). A later French edition of *Donner la mort* (Paris: Galilée, 1999) has a revised concluding section.

————. "Interview with Derrida." *Derrida and Différance*, ed. David Wood and Robert Bernasconi. Evanston, Ill.: Northwestern University Press, 1988.

————. "Introduction: Desistance." *Typography: Mimesis, Philosophy, Politics*, by Philippe Lacoue-Labarthe. Ed. Christopher Fynsk. Cambridge: Harvard University Press, 1989.

————. *Margins of Philosophy*. Trans. Alan Bass. Chicago: University of Chicago Press, 1992. Originally published as *Marges de la philosophie* (Paris: Minuit, 1972).

————. *Negotiations: Interventions and Interviews, 1971–2001*. Ed. and trans. Elizabeth Rottenberg. Stanford: Stanford University Press, 2002.

————. *Of Grammatology*. Trans. Gayatri Chakravorty Spivak. Baltimore: Johns Hopkins University Press, 1976. Originally published as *De la Grammatologie* (Paris: Minuit, 1967).

————. *On Cosmopolitanism and Forgiveness*. Trans. Mark Dooley and Michael Collins Hughes. London: Routledge, 2001. The essay "On Cosmopolitanism" in this volume originally published as *Cosmopolites de tous les pays, encore un effort!* (Paris: Galilée, 1997).

————. *The Other Heading: Reflections on Today's Europe*. Trans. Pascale-Anne Brault and Michael B. Naas. Bloomington: Indiana University Press, 1992. Originally published as *L'autre cap suivi de "La démocratie ajournée"* (Paris: Minuit, 1991).

————. *Passions*. Trans. David Wood. *Derrida: A Critical Reader*, ed. David Wood. Oxford: Blackwell, 1992.

————. *Politics of Friendship*. Trans. George Collins. London: Verso, 1997. Originally published as *Politiques de l'amitié* (Paris: Galilée, 1994). The French edition has an appendix on Heidegger.

————. *Positions*. Trans. Alan Bass. Chicago: University of Chicago Press, 1981. Originally published as *Positions* (Paris: Minuit, 1972).

————. *Rogues: Two Essays on Reason*. Trans. Pascale-Anne Brault and Michael Naas. Stanford: Stanford University Press, 2005.

————. *Specters of Marx: The State of the Debt, the Work of Mourning and the New International*. Trans. Peggy Kamuf. London: Routledge, 1994. Originally published as *Spectres de Marx: L'Etat de la dette, le travail du deuil et la nouvelle Internationale* (Paris: Galilée, 1993).

————. "To Unsense the Subjectile." *The Secret Art of Antonin Artaud*, by Jacques Derrida and Paule Thévenin. Trans. Mary Ann Caws. Cambridge: MIT Press, 1998. Originally published as "Forcener le subjectile." *Antonin Artaud: Dessins et Portraits*, by Paule Thévenin and Jacques Derrida (Paris: Gallimard, 1986).

————. *Writing and Difference*. Trans. Alan Bass. London: Routledge, 1978. Originally published as *L'Ecriture et la différence* (Paris: Seuil, 1967).

Derrida, Jacques, and Anne Dufourmantelle. *Of Hospitality: Anne Dufourmantelle Invites Jacques Derrida to Respond*. Trans. Rachel Bowlby. Stanford: Stanford University Press, 2000. Originally published as *De l'hospitalité: Anne Dufourmantelle invite Jacques Derrida à répondre* (Paris: Calmann-Lévy, 1997).

Derrida, Jacques, et al. "The Original Discussion of 'Différance' (1968)." *Derrida and Différance*, ed. David Wood and Robert Bernasconi. Evanston, Ill.: Northwestern University Press, 1988. Originally published in the *Bulletin de la Societé Française de Philosophie* 62 (1968).

Desai, Padma. *Financial Crisis, Containment, and Contagion: From Asia to Argentina.* Princeton: Princeton University Press, 2003.

Desanti, Jean-Toussaint. "Some Remarks on the Intrinsic Ontology of Alain Badiou." Trans. Ray Brassier. *Think Again: Alain Badiou and the Future of Philosophy*, ed. Peter Hallward. London: Continuum, 2004. Originally published as "Quelques remarques à propos de l'ontologie intrinsèque d'Alain Badiou." *Les tempes moderne* 526 (1990), 61–71.

Descartes, René. *Oeuvres de Descartes.* Paris: J. Vrin, 1996.

———. *Philosophical Essays and Correspondence.* Ed. Roger Ariew. Indianapolis: Hackett, 2000.

Deutsche Bundesbank. *The Role of FDI in Emerging Market Economies Compared to Other Forms of Financing: Past Developments and Implications for Financial Stability of Emerging Market Economies.* Frankfurt, 2003. www.bis.org. Accessed on 2 January 2006.

Devlin, Robert, Ricardo Ffrench-Davis, and Stephany Griffith-Jones. "Surges in Capital Flows and Development: An Overview of Policy Issues." *Coping with Capital Surges: The Return of Finance to Latin America*, ed. Ricardo Ffrench-Davis and Stephany Griffith-Jones. Boulder, Colo.: Lynne Rienner, 1995.

Deyo, Frederic. *Beneath the Miracle: Labor Subordination in the New Asian Industrialism.* Berkeley: University of California Press, 1989.

———, ed. *The Political Economy of the New Asian Industrialism.* Ithaca: Cornell University Press, 1987.

Diaz-Alejandro, Carlos. "Delinking North and South: Unshackled or Unhinged?" *Trade, Development and the World Economy: Selected Essays of Carlos F. Diaz-Alejandro,* ed. Andres Velasco. Oxford: Blackwell, 1988.

Doner, Richard F. "Limits of State Strength: Towards an Institutional View of Economic Development." *World Politics* 44 (1992), 398–431.

Dore, Ronald. *Flexible Rigidities: Industrial Policy and Structural Adjustment in the Japanese Economy, 1970–1980.* London: Athlone Press, 1987.

Dorrien, Gary. *Imperial Designs: Neoconservatism and the New Pax Americana.* London: Routledge, 2004.

Drábek, Zdenek, and Stephany Griffith-Jones, eds. *Managing Capital Flows in Turbulent Times: The Experience of Europe's Emerging Market Economies in Global Perspective.* Armonk, N.Y.: M. E. Sharpe, 1999.

Drábek, Zdenek, and Stephany Griffith-Jones. "Summary and Conclusions: Managing Capital Flows in Central and Eastern Europe." *Managing Capital Flows in Turbulent Times: The Experience of Europe's Emerging Market Economies in Global Perspective,* ed. Zdenek Drábek and Stephany Griffith-Jones. Armonk, N.Y.: M. E. Sharpe, 1999.

Dreyfus, Hubert L. *Being-in-the-World: A Commentary on Heidegger's Being and Time, Division I*. Cambridge: MIT Press, 1991.

Duménil, Gérard, and Dominique Lévy. "Costs and Benefits of Neoliberalism: A Class Analysis." *Review of International Political Economy* 8 (2001), 578–607.

Duménil, Gérard, and Dominique Lévy. *Crise et sortie de crise: Ordre et désordres néolibéraux*. Paris: Presses Universitaires de France, 2000.

Duménil, Gérard, and Dominique Lévy. "Neoliberal Income Trends: Wealth, Class and Ownership in the USA." *New Left Review* 30 (new series, 2004), 105–33.

Duménil, Gérard, and Dominique Lévy. "Periodizing Capitalism: Technology, Institutions and Relations of Production." *Phases of Capitalist Development: Booms, Crises and Globalizations*, ed. Robert Albritton, Makoto Itoh, Richard Westra, and Alan Zuege. New York: Palgrave, 2001.

Dumézil, Georges. *Mithra-Varuna*. Paris: Gallimard, 1948.

Dumont, Louis. *Essays on Individualism: Modern Ideology in Anthropological Perspective*. Chicago: University of Chicago Press, 1986. Originally published as *Essais sur l'individualisme: Une perspective anthropologique sur l'idéologie moderne* (Paris: Editions du Seuil, 1983).

———. *Homo Hierarchicus: An Essay on the Caste System*. Trans. Mark Sainsbury, Louis Dumont, and Basia Gulati. Revised edition. Chicago: University of Chicago Press, 1980. Originally published as *Homo hierarchicus, essai sur le système des castes* (Paris: Gallimard, 1967).

Dunford, Mick. "Towards a Post-Fordist Order?" *Review of International Political Economy* 2 (1995) 185–96.

Eatwell, John, and Lance Taylor. *Global Finance at Risk: The Case for International Regulation*. New York: New Press, 2000.

Eichengreen, Barry. *International Monetary Arrangements for the 21st Century*. Washington: Brookings Institution, 1994.

Elbaum, Max. *Revolution in the Air: Sixties Radicals Turn to Lenin, Mao and Che*. London: Verso, 2002.

Elwell, Craig K. "Global Capital Market Integration: Implications for U.S. Economic Performance." *Congressional Research Service Reports*. 12 January 2001. www.ncseonline.org. Accessed on 31 December 2005.

Escobar, Arturo. *Encountering Development: The Making and Unmaking of the Third World*. Princeton: Princeton University Press, 1995.

Farred, Grant. "Endgame Identity? Mapping the New Left Roots of Identity Politics." *New Literary History* 31 (2000), 627–48.

Federal Reserve Bank of New York. *The Basics of Foreign Trade and Exchange: Foreign Currency Exchange*. www.ny.frb.org. Accessed on 31 December 2005.

Fenves, Peter. "Derrida and History: Some Questions Derrida Pursues in His Early Writings." *Jacques Derrida and the Humanities: A Critical Reader*, ed. Tom Cohen. Cambridge: Cambridge University Press, 2001.

Fine, Ben. "New Growth Theory." *Rethinking Development Economics*, ed. Ha-Joon Chang. London: Anthem Press, 2003.

Fine, Ben, Costas Lapavitsas, and Jonathan Pincus, eds. *Development Policy in the Twenty-First Century: Beyond the Post-Washington Consensus.* London: Routledge, 2001.

Fink, Bruce. *The Lacanian Subject: Between Language and Jouissance.* Princeton: Princeton University Press, 1996.

Finley, M. I. "Utopianism Ancient and Modern." *The Critical Spirit: Essays in Honor of Herbert Marcuse*, ed. Kurt H. Wolff and Barrington Moore Jr. Boston: Beacon Press, 1967.

Fishlow, Albert. "Economic Development in the 1990s." *World Development* 22 (1994).

Fisk, Milton. "Post-Marxism: Laclau and Mouffe on Essentialism." *Radical Philosophy: Tradition, Counter-Tradition,* ed. Roger S. Gottlieb. Philadelphia: Temple University Press, 1993.

Fligstein, Neil. *The Architecture of Markets: An Economic Sociology of Twenty-First-Century Capitalist Societies.* Princeton: Princeton University Press, 2001.

Florio, Massimo. *The Great Divesture: Evaluating the Welfare Impact of the British Privatizations 1979–1997.* Cambridge: MIT Press, 2004.

Foley, Conor. *The Thin Blue Line: How Humanitarianism Went to War.* London: Verso, 2008.

Foley, Duncan. "The Value of Money, the Value of Labor Power, and the Marxian Transformation Problem." *Review of Radical Political Economics* 14 (1982), 37–47.

Foucault, Michel. *Ethics (Subjectivity and Truth).* In *The Essential Works of Foucault 1954–1984, Volume 1.* Ed. Paul Rabinow, trans. Robert J. Hurley. New York: New Press, 1994. Originally published as *Dits et écrits, 1954–1988* (Paris: Gallimard, 1994).

———. "Governmentality." *The Foucault Effect: Studies in Governmentality*, ed. and trans. Graham Burchell. Chicago: University of Chicago Press, 1991.

———. "Of Other Spaces." Trans. Jay Miskowiec. *Diacritics* 16 (1986), 22–27. Originally published as "Des espaces autres," *Architecture-Mouvement-Continuité* 5 (1984), 46–49, and reprinted in *Dits et écrits* (Paris: Gallimard, 1994), 4:752–62.

———. *The Order of Things: An Archaeology of the Human Sciences.* Unidentified collective translation. New York: Pantheon Books, 1971. Originally published as *Les mots et choses: Une archéologie des sciences humaines* (Paris: Gallimard, 1966).

———. "The Thought from Outside." *Foucault/Blanchot*, by Maurice Blanchot and Michel Foucault. Trans. Brian Massumi. New York: Zone Books, 1987.

Frank, André Gunder. *Capitalism and Underdevelopment in Latin America: Historical Studies of Chile and Brazil.* Revised edition. Harmondsworth, England: Penguin, 1971.

———. "The Development of Underdevelopment." *Monthly Review* 18 (1966), 17–31.

Frank, Thomas. *What's the Matter with Kansas? How Conservatives Won the Heart of America*. New York: Metropolitan Books, 2004.

Funkenstein, Amos. *Theology and the Scientific Imagination from the Middle Ages to the Seventeenth Century*. Princeton: Princeton University Press, 1986.

Fynsk, Christopher. "Derrida and Philosophy: Acts of Engagement." *Jacques Derrida and the Humanities: A Critical Reader*, ed. Tom Cohen. Cambridge: Cambridge University Press, 2001.

Galbraith, John Kenneth. *The New Industrial State*. 3rd edition, revised. Boston: Houghton-Mifflin, 1978.

Gaon, Stella. "'Politicizing Deconstruction': On Not Treating *Specters of Marx*." *Rethinking Marxism* 11 (1999), 38–48.

Germain, Randall. *The International Organization of Credit: States and Finance in the World-Economy*. Cambridge: Cambridge University Press, 1997.

Gills, Barry, Joel Rocamora, and Richard Wilson. "Low Intensity Democracy." *Low Intensity Democracy: Political Power in the New World Order*, ed. Barry Gills, Joel Rocamora, and Richard Wilson. London: Pluto Press, 1993.

Gilroy, Paul. "British Cultural Studies and the Pitfalls of Identity." *Black British Cultural Studies: A Reader*, ed. Houston A. Baker, Manthia Diawara, and Ruth H. Lindeborg. Chicago: University of Chicago Press, 1996.

Ginsborg, Paul. *Silvio Berlusconi: Television, Power and Patrimony*. London: Verso, 2005.

Glyn, Andrew. *Capitalism Unleashed: Finance, Globalization, and Welfare*. Oxford: Oxford University Press, 2007.

———. "The Costs of Stability: The Advanced Capitalist Countries in the 1980s." *New Left Review* 195 (first series, 1992), 71–95.

———. "Global Imbalances." *New Left Review* 34 (new series, 2005), 5–37.

———. "Marxist Economics." *The New Palgrave Marxian Economics*, ed. John Eatwell, Murray Milgate, and Peter Newman. New York: Norton, 1990.

———, ed. *Social Democracy in Neoliberal Times: The Left and Economic Policy Since 1980*. Oxford: Oxford University Press, 2001.

Glyn, Andrew, and V. Bhaskar, eds. *The North, the South, and the Environment: Ecological Constraints and the Global Economy*. New York: St. Martin's Press, 1995.

Glyn, Andrew, Alan Hughes, Alain Lipietz, and Ajit Singh. "The Rise and Fall of the Golden Age." *The Golden Age of Capitalism: Reinterpreting the Postwar Experience*, ed. Stephen A. Marglin and Juliet B. Schor. Oxford: Oxford University Press, 1990.

Goodman, John B., and Louis Pauly. "The Obsolescence of Capital Controls? Economic Management in an Age of Global Markets." *World Politics* 46 (1993), 50–82.

Gordon, David M. "The Global Economy: New Edifice or Crumbling Foundations?" *New Left Review* 168 (old series, 1988), 24–64.

Görg, Christoph, and Joachim Hirsch. "Is International Democracy Possible?" *Review of International Political Economy* 5 (1998), 585–615.

Gowan, Peter. *The Global Gamble: Washington's Faustian Bid for World Dominance.* London: Verso, 1999.

———. "The New Liberal Cosmopolitanism." *Debating Cosmopolitics*, ed. Daniele Archibugi. London: Verso, 2003.

———. "US: UN." *New Left Review* 24 (new series, 2003), 5–28.

Grabel, Ilene. "Ideology, Power, and the Rise of Independent Monetary Institutions in Emerging Economies." *Monetary Orders: Ambiguous Orders, Ubiquitous Politics,* ed. Jonathan Kirshner. Ithaca: Cornell University Press, 2003.

———. "Marketing the Third World: The Contradictions of Portfolio Investment in the Global Economy." *World Development* 24 (1996), 1761–76.

———. "The Political Economy of 'Policy Credibility': The New-Classical Economics and the Remaking of Emerging Economies." *Cambridge Journal of Economics* 24 (2000), 1–19.

Grahl, John, and Paul Teague. "The *Régulation* School, the Employment Relation and Financialization." *Economy and Society* 29 (2000), 160–78.

Griffith-Jones, Stephany. *Capital Flows to Developing Countries: Does the Emperor Have Clothes?* www.gapresearch.org. Accessed on 7 January 2006.

———. "Capital Flows to Latin America: Lessons for Central and Eastern Europe." *Managing Capital Flows in Turbulent Times: The Experience of Europe's Emerging Market Economies in Global Perspective*, ed. Zdenek Drábek and Stephany Griffith-Jones. Armonk, N.Y.: M. E. Sharpe, 1999.

———. *Global Capital Flows: Should They Be Regulated?* New York: St. Martin's Press, 1998.

———. "Regulatory Implications of Global Financial Markets." *Financial Fragility, Debt and Economic Reforms*, ed. Sunanda Sen. New York: St. Martin's Press, 1996.

Griffith-Jones, Stephany, and Jonathan Leape. *Capital Flows to Developing Countries: Does the Emperor Have Clothes?* Working Paper 89, Queen Elizabeth House, Oxford University, 2002. www.qeh.ox.ac.uk. Accessed on 31 December 2005.

Griffith-Jones, Stephany, and Barbara Stallings. "New Global Financial Trends: Implications for Development." *Global Change, Regional Response: The New International Context of Development*, ed. Barbara Stallings. Cambridge: Cambridge University Press, 1995.

Guest, Gérard. "L'Origine de la Responsabilité ou De la 'Voix de la Conscience' a la Penseé de la 'Promesse.'" *Heidegger Studies* 8 (1992), 29–62.

Haakonssen, Knud. "Divine/Natural Law Theories in Ethics." *The Cambridge History of Seventeenth Century Philosophy, Vol. 2*, ed. Daniel Garber and Michael Ayers. Cambridge: Cambridge University Press, 1998.

Haar, Michel. *Heidegger et l'essence de l'homme.* Grenoble: Millon, 1990.

Hall, Stuart. *The Hard Road to Renewal: Thatcherism and the Crisis of the Left.* London: Verso, 1988.

Hall, Stuart, Charles Critcher, Tony Jefferson, John Clark, and Brian Robert. *Polic-*

ing the Crisis: Mugging, the State and Law and Order. London: Palgrave Macmillan, 1978.

Hallward, Peter. *Badiou: A Subject to Truth.* Minneapolis: University of Minnesota
Press, 2003.

———. "Badiou's Politics: Equality and Justice." *Culture Machine*, 2000, http://
culturemachine.tees.ac.uk. Accessed on 2 November 2003.

———, ed. *Think Again: Alain Badiou and the Future of Philosophy.* London: Continuum, 2004.

Hansen, Thomas Blom, and Finn Steputat, eds. *Sovereign Bodies: Citizens, Migrants,
and States in the Postcolonial World.* Princeton: Princeton University Press,
2005.

Hardt, Michael, and Antonio Negri. *Empire.* Cambridge: Harvard University Press,
2000.

Hardt, Michael, and Antonio Negri. *Multitudes: War and Democracy in the Age of
Empire.* New York: Penguin, 2004.

Harmes, Adam. "Institutional Investors and the Reproduction of Neoliberalism."
Review of International Political Economy 5 (1998), 92–121.

———. "Mass Investment Culture." *New Left Review* 9 (second series, 2001), 103–
24.

Harris, Laurence. "Alternative Perspectives on the Financial System." *New Perspectives on the Financial System*, ed. Laurence Harris, Jerry Coakley, Martin Croas-
dale, and Trevor Evans. London: Croom Helm, 1988.

———. "Financial Markets and the Real Economy." *Financial Fragility, Debt and
Economic Reforms*, ed. Sunanda Sen. New York: St. Martin's Press, 1996.

———. "International Financial Markets and National Transmission Mechanisms."
Managing the Global Economy, ed. Jonathan Michie and John Grieve Smith.
Oxford: Oxford University Press, 1995.

Harriss, John. *Depoliticizing Development: The World Bank and Social Capital.* London: Anthem Press, 2001.

Harvey, David. *A Brief History of Neoliberalism.* Oxford: Oxford University Press,
2005.

———. *The New Imperialism.* Oxford: Oxford University Press, 2003.

Hawes, Gary, and Hong Liu. "Explaining the Dynamics of the Southeast Asian Political Economy: State, Society, and the Search for Economic Growth." *World
Politics* 45 (1993), 627–60.

Hawthorn, Geoffrey. *Enlightenment and Despair: A History of Social Theory.* 2nd ed.
Cambridge: Cambridge University Press, 1987.

Head, David. *The New Ruthless Economy: Work and Power in the Digital Age.* Oxford:
Oxford University Press, 2003.

Hegel, G. W. F. *The Difference between Fichte's and Schelling's System of Philosophy.*
Trans. Horton S. Harris and Walter Cerf. Albany: State University of New
York Press, 1977.

Heidegger, Martin. *Being and Time.* Trans. Joan Stambaugh. Albany: State University of New York Press, 1996. Originally published as *Sein und Zeit*, in *Jahrbuch für Phänomenologie und phänomenologsiche Forschung* 3 (spring 1927).

———. *Gesamtausgabe*. Vol. 65: *Beiträge zur Philosophie [Vom Ereignis]*. Frankfurt: Klostermann, 1989.

Helleiner, Eric. *States and the Reemergence of Global Finance: From Bretton Woods to the 1990s*. Ithaca: Cornell University Press, 1994.

———. "The World of Money: The Political Economy of International Capital Mobility." *Policy Sciences* 27 (1994).

Henwood, Doug. *Wall Street*. London: Verso, 1997.

Herzfeld, Michael. "The European Self: Rethinking an Attitude." *The Idea of Europe: From Antiquity to the European Union*, ed. Anthony Pagden. Cambridge: Cambridge University Press, 2002.

Hirsch, Joachim. "Globalisation, Class and the Question of Democracy." *Socialist Register 1999*, ed. Leo Panitch and Colin Leys. New York: Monthly Review Press, 1999.

———. "Globalization of Capital, Nation-States and Democracy." *Studies in Political Economy* 54 (1997), 39–58.

———. "Nation-State, International Regulation, and the Question of Democracy." *Review of International Political Economy* 2 (1995), 267–84.

Hirschman, Albert. *National Power and the Structure of International Trade*. Berkeley: University of California Press, 1945.

Hirst, Paul. *War and Power in the 21st Century: The State, Military Conflict and the International System*. Oxford: Polity Press, 2001.

Hirst, Paul, and Grahame Thompson. *Globalization in Question*. Oxford: Polity Press, 1986.

Hirst, Paul, and Jonathan Zeitlin. "Flexible Specialization: Theory and Evidence in the Analysis of Industrial Change." *Contemporary Capitalism: The Embeddedness of Institutions*, ed. J. R. Hollingsworth and Robert Boyer. Cambridge: Cambridge University Press, 1997.

Hobsbawm, Eric. *The Age of Capital: 1848–1875*. London: Weidenfeld and Nicolson, 1978.

———. *The Age of Empire: 1875–1914*. New York: Pantheon, 1987.

———. *The Age of Extremes: A History of the World, 1914–91*. New York: Pantheon, 1994.

———. *The Age of Revolution, 1789–1848*. New York: New American Library, 1962.

Hobson, John M. *The Wealth of States: A Comparative Sociology of International Economic and Political Change*. Cambridge: Cambridge University Press, 1997.

Hobson, John M., and Linda Weiss, eds. *States and Economic Development*: *A Comparative and Historical Analysis*. Cambridge, England: Polity Press, 1995.

Hoggart, Richard. *The Uses of Literacy: Aspects of Working Class Life*. London: Chatto and Windus, 1957.

Hoogvelt, Anke, and Masae Yuasa. "Going Lean or Going Native? The Social Regulation of 'Lean' Production Systems." *Review of International Political Economy* 1 (1994), 281–303.

Hough, Jerry F. *Changing Party Coalitions: The Mystery of the Red State–Blue State Alignment.* New York: Algora Press, 2006.

Howie, Gillian. *Deleuze and Spinoza: An Aura of Expressionism.* London: Palgrave, 2002.

Hume, David. "On the First Principles of Government." *Political Essays.* Ed. Knud Haakonssen. Cambridge: Cambridge University Press, 1994. Originally published in a posthumous edition in 1777.

Huntington, Samuel. *The Clash of Civilizations and the Remaking of World Order.* New York: Simon and Schuster, 1996.

———. "The United States." *The Crisis of Democracy: Report on the Governability of Democracies to the Trilateral Commission*, ed. Michel J. Crozier, Samuel Huntington, and Joji Watanuki. New York: New York University Press, 1975.

Ignatieff, Michael. *Blood and Belonging: Journeys into the New Nationalism.* New York: Penguin Books, 1994.

Institute of International Finance. "Resilient Emerging Markets Attract Record Private Capital Flows." Press release, 6 March 2008. www.iif.com. Accessed on 18 May 2008.

International Financial Services, London. *City Business Series: Foreign Exchange October 2004.* www.ifsl.org.uk. Accessed on 31 December, 2005.

International Monetary Fund. *Global Financial Stability Report: Market Developments and Issues.* April 2004. www.imf.org. Accessed on 7 January 2006.

———. *Private Market Financing for Developing Countries.* Washington, D.C.: IMF, 1995.

———. *World Economic Outlook*, September 2002. http://imf.org. Accessed on 18 September, 2008.

Inwood, Michael. *A Hegel Dictionary.* Oxford: Blackwell, 1992.

Israel, Jonathan I. *Enlightenment Contested: Philosophy, Modernity, and the Emancipation of Man 1670–1752.* Oxford: Oxford University Press, 2006.

———. *Radical Enlightenment: Philosophy and the Making of Modernity 1650–1750.* Oxford: Oxford University Press, 2001.

Jay, Martin. *The Dialectical Imagination: A History of the Frankfurt School 1923–50.* London: Heinemann, 1973.

Jessop, Bob. "Capitalism and Its Future: Remarks on Regulation, Government and Governance." *Review of International Political Economy* 4 (1997), 561–81.

———. *The Capitalist State: Marxist Theories and Methods.* Oxford: Blackwell 1982.

———. "Changing Forms and Functions of the State in an Era of Globalization and Regionalization." *The Political Economy of Diversity: Evolutionary Perspectives on Economic Order and Disorder*, ed. Robert Delorme and Kurt Dopfer. Brookfield, Vt.: Edward Elgar, 1994.

———. "Fordism and Post-Fordism: A Critical Reformulation." *Pathways to Indus-*

trialization and Regional Development, ed. Michael Storper and Allen J. Scott. London: Routledge, 1992.

———. *The Future of the Capitalist State*. Cambridge, England: Polity Press, 2002.

———. "Interpretive Sociology and the Dialectic of Structure and Agency." *Theory, Culture and Society* 13 (1996), 119–28.

———. "Narrating the Future of the National Economy and the National State: Remarks on Remapping Regulation and Reinventing Governance." *State/Culture: State-formation after the Cultural Turn*, ed. George Steinmetz. Ithaca: Cornell University Press, 1999.

———. "Post-Fordism and the State." *Post-Fordism: A Reader*, ed. Ash Amin. Oxford: Blackwell, 1994.

———. "Regulation Theory in Retrospect and Prospect." *Economy and Society* 19 (1990), 153–216.

———. "Restructuring the Welfare State, Re-orienting Welfare Strategies, Re-Visioning the Welfare Society." *What Constitutes a Good Society?*, ed. B. Greve. New York: St. Martin's Press, 2000.

———. "The Social Embeddedness of the Economy and Its Implications for Economic Governance." *Economy and Society: Money, Capitalism and Transition*, ed. Fikret Adaman and Pat Devine. Montreal: Black Rose Books, 2002.

———. *State Power: A Strategic-Relational Approach*. Cambridge: Polity Press, 2007.

———. *State Theory: Putting Capitalist States in Their Place*. Cambridge, England: Polity Press, 1990.

———. "The Transition to Post-Fordism and the Schumpeterian Workfare State." *Towards a Post-Fordist Welfare State?*, ed. Roger Burrows and Brian Loader. London: Routledge, 1994.

———. "What Follows Fordism? On the Periodization of Capitalism and Its Regulation." *Phases of Capitalist Development: Booms, Crises, and Globalizations*, ed. Robert Albritton, Makoto Itoh, Richard Westra, and Alan Zuege. New York: Palgrave, 2001.

Jessop, Bob, and Ngai-Ling Sum. *Beyond the Regulation Approach: Putting Capitalist Economies in Their Place*, Cheltenham, England: Edward Elgar, 2006.

Johnson, Chalmers. "Political Institutions and Economic Performance: The Government-Business Relationship in Japan, South Korea, and Taiwan." *The Political Economy of the New Asian Industrialism*, ed. Frederic Deyo. Ithaca: Cornell University Press, 1987.

Jolley, Nicholas. "The Reception of Descartes' Philosophy." *The Cambridge Companion to Descartes*, ed. John Cottingham. Cambridge: Cambridge University Press, 1992.

Jomo K. S. [Jomo Kwame Sundaram], ed. *After the Storm: Crisis, Recovery and Sustaining Development in Four Asian Economies*. Singapore: University of Singapore Press, 2004.

————, ed. *Tigers in Trouble: Financial Governance, Liberalisation and Crises in East Asia*. London: Zed Books, 1998.

Jomo, K. S. [Jomo Kwame Sundaram], et al. *Southeast Asia's Misunderstood Miracle: Industrial Policy and Economic Development in Thailand, Malaysia, and Indonesia*. Boulder, Colo.: Westview Press, 1997.

Jones, Gareth Stedman. *An End to Poverty? A Historical Debate*. New York: Columbia University Press, 2004.

Kant, Immanuel. "An Answer to the Question 'What Is Enlightenment?'" *Kant: Political Writings*. Ed. Hans Reiss. Trans. H. B. Nisbet. 2nd edition. Cambridge: Cambridge University Press, 1991. Originally published as "Beantwortung der Frage: Was ist Aufklärung?," *Berlinische Monatsschrift* 4 (11 November 1784), 385–411.

————. "Idea of a Universal History with a Cosmopolitan Purpose." *Kant: Political Writings*. Ed. Hans Reiss. Trans. H. B. Nisbet. 2nd edition. Cambridge: Cambridge University Press, 1991. Originally published as "Idee ze einer allgemeinen Geschichte in weltbürgerlicher Absicht," *Berlinische Monatsschrift* 4 (12 December 1784), 481–94.

————. *The Metaphysics of Morals*. *Kant: Political Writings*. Ed. Hans Reiss. Trans. H. B. Nisbet. 2nd edition. Cambridge: Cambridge University Press, 1991. Originally published as *Die Metaphysik der Sitten* (Königsberg: Friedrich Nicolovius, 1797).

————. "On the Common Saying: 'This May Be True in Theory but It Does Not Apply in Practice.'" *Kant: Political Writings*. Ed. Hans Reiss. Trans. H. B. Nisbet. 2nd edition. Cambridge: Cambridge University Press, 1991. Originally published as "Das mag in der Theorie richtig sein, taugt aber nicht für die Praxis," *Berlinische Monatsschrift* 22 (September 1793), 201–84.

Kantorowicz, Ernst. *The King's Two Bodies: A Study In Mediaeval Political Theology*. Princeton: Princeton University Press, 1957.

Kapstein, Ethan. *Governing the Global Economy: International Finance and the State*. Cambridge: Harvard University Press, 1994.

Kastoryano, Riva. "Muslim Diaspora(s) in Western Europe." *South Atlantic Quarterly* 98 (1999), 191–202.

————. *Negotiating Identities: States and Immigrants in France and Germany*. Trans. Barbara Harshav. Princeton: Princeton University Press, 2002. Originally published as *La France, l'Allemagne et leurs immigrés: Négocier l'identité* (Paris: Armand Colin, 1997).

Katzenstein, Peter J. *Small States in World Markets*. Princeton: Princeton University Press, 1985.

Khan, Mohsin S. "Recent Developments in International Financial Markets." *Asian Development Review* 13 (1995).

Kindleberger, Charles P. "Why Did the Golden Age Last So Long?" *The World Economy and National Finance in Historical Perspective*. Ann Arbor: University of Michigan Press, 1995.

Kozul-Wright, Richard. "Mind the Gaps: Economic Openness and Uneven Development." *Growth Divergences: Explaining Differences in Economic Performance*, ed. José Antonio Ocampo, Jomo K. S., and Rob Vos. London: Zed Books, 2007.

Kozul-Wright, Richard, and Paul Rayment. *The Resistible Rise of Market Fundamentalism: The Struggle for Economic Development in a Global Economy.* London: Zed Press, 2008.

Lacan, Jacques. "The Function and Field of Speech and Language in Psychoanalysis." *Écrits: A Selection*. Trans. Alan Sheridan. London: Tavistock, 1977. Originally published as "Fonction et champ de la parole et du langue en psychanalyse," *Écrits* (Paris: Seuil, 1966).

———. "Logical Time and the Assertion of Anticipated Certainty." *Newspaper of the Freudian Field* 2 (1988), 4–22.

Laclau, Ernesto. "An Ethics of Militant Engagement." *Think Again: Alain Badiou and the Future of Philosophy*, ed. Peter Hallward. London: Continuum, 2004.

———. "Feudalism and Capitalism in Latin America." *New Left Review* 67 (1971), 19–38.

———. "The Time Is Out of Joint." *diacritics* 25 (1995), 86–96.

———. "Universalism, Particularism and the Question of Identity." *The Identity in Question*, ed. John Rajchman. London: Routledge, 1995.

Laclau, Ernesto, and Chantal Mouffe. *Hegemony and Socialist Strategy: Towards a Radical Democratic Politics.* Trans. Winston Moore and Paul Cammack. London: Verso, 1985.

Laclau, Ernesto, and Chantal Mouffe. "Post-Marxism without Apologies." *New Left Review* 166 (first series, 1987), 79–106.

Landry, Donna, and Gerald MacLean. "Rereading Laclau and Mouffe." *Rethinking Marxism* 4 (1991), 41–60.

Larrain, Jorge. *Theories of Development: Capitalism, Colonialism and Dependency.* Cambridge, England: Polity Press, 1989.

Lash, Scott, and John Urry. *The End of Organized Capitalism.* Cambridge, England: Polity Press, 1987.

Lazare, Daniel. *The Frozen Republic: How the Constitution Is Paralyzing Democracy.* New York: Harcourt Brace, 1996.

———. *The Velvet Coup: The Constitution, the Supreme Court, and the Decline of American Democracy.* London: Verso, 2001.

Leavey, John P., Jr. "Destinerrance: The Apotropocalyptics of Translation." *Deconstruction and Philosophy: The Texts of Jacques Derrida*, ed. John Sallis. Chicago: University of Chicago Press, 1987.

Leborgne, Danièle, and Alain Lipietz. "Conceptual Fallacies and Open Questions on Post-Fordism." *Pathways to Industrialization and Regional Development*, ed. Michael Storper and Allen J. Scott. London: Routledge, 1992.

Leys, Colin. "Democracy." *Against G8*, ed. Gill Hubbard and David Miller. London: Pluto Press, 2005.

———. *Market-Driven Politics: Neoliberal Democracy and the Public Interest*. London: Verso, 2001.

———. *The Rise and Fall of Development Theory*. Bloomington: Indiana University Press, 1996.

Lipietz, Alain. "Behind the Crisis: The Exhaustion of a Regime of Accumulation. A 'Regulation School' Perspective on Some French Empirical Works." *Review of Radical Political Economics* 18 (1986), 13–32.

———. "The Debt Problem, European Integration and the New Phase of the World Crisis." *New Left Review* 178 (old series, 1989), 37–50.

———. *Mirages and Miracles: The Crisis of Global Fordism*. London: Verso, 1987.

———. "New Tendencies in the International Division of Labor: Regimes of Accumulation and Modes of Regulation." Trans. Kipham Kan and Allen Scott. *Production, Work, Territory: The Geographical Anatomy of Industrial Capitalism*, ed. Allen J. Scott and Michael Storper. London: Allen and Unwin, 1986.

———. "The Next Transformation." *The Milano Papers: Essays in Societal Alternatives*, ed. M. Cangiani. New York: Black Rose Books, 1997.

———. "Post-Fordism and Democracy." *Post-Fordism: A Reader*, ed. Ash Amin. Oxford: Blackwell, 1994.

———. *Towards a New Economic Order: Postfordism, Ecology and Democracy*. Trans. Malcolm Slater. New York: Oxford University Press, 1992.

———. "Towards Global Fordism?" *New Left Review* 132 (first series, 1982), 33–47, 48–59.

Löwy, Michael, and Robert Sayre. *Révolte et mélancolie: Le romantisme à contre-courant de la modernité*. Paris: Payot, 1992.

Luxemburg, Rosa. *The Accumulation of Capital*. Trans. Agnes Schwarzschild. New York: Monthly Review Press, 1951.

Macpherson, C. B. *The Political Theory of Possessive Individualism: From Hobbes to Locke*. Oxford: Clarendon Press, 1962.

Mamdani, Mahmood. *Citizen and Subject: Contemporary Africa and the Legacy of Late Colonialism*. Princeton: Princeton University Press, 1996.

Mandel, Ernest. "Karl Marx." *The New Palgrave Marxian Economics*, ed. John Eatwell, Murray Milgate, and Peter Newman. New York: Norton, 1987.

———. *The Second Slump: A Marxist Analysis of Recession in the Seventies*. Trans. Jon Rothschild. London: New Left Books, 1980.

Mann, Michael. "The Autonomous Power of the State: Its Origins, Mechanisms, and Results." *States in History*, ed. John A. Hall. Oxford: Blackwell, 1986.

———. *Consciousness and Action among the Western Working Class*. London: Macmillan, 1973.

———. "The First Failed Empire of the Twenty-First Century." *American Power in the 21st Century*, ed. David Held and Mathias Koenig-Archibugi. Cambridge, England: Polity Press, 2004.

———. "Globalization and September 11." *New Left Review* 12 (new series, 2001), 51–72.

———. "Has Globalization Ended the Rise and Rise of the Nation-State?" *Review of International Political Economy* 4 (1997), 472–96.

———. *Incoherent Empire.* London: Verso, 2003.

———. *The Sources of Social Power:* Vol. 1, *A History of Power from the Beginning to A.D. 1760.* Cambridge: Cambridge University Press, 1986.

———. *The Sources of Social Power:* Vol. 2, *The Rise of the Classes and Nation-States, 1760–1914.* Cambridge: Cambridge University Press, 1993.

Marglin, Stephen A., and Juliet B. Schor, eds. *The Golden Age of Capitalism: Reinterpreting the Postwar Experience.* Oxford: Oxford University Press, 1990.

Martin, Jean-Clet. "The Eye of the Outside." Trans. Tom Gibson and Anthony Uhlmann. *Deleuze: A Critical Reader*, ed. Paul Patton. Oxford: Blackwell, 1996.

Marx, Anthony W. *Faith in Nation: Exclusionary Origins of Nationalism.* Oxford: Oxford University Press, 2003.

Marx, Karl. *Capital.* Vol. 1. Trans. Ben Fowkes. New York: Vintage Books, 1977.

———. *Capital.* Vol. 3. Trans. David Fernbach. New York: Vintage Books, 1981.

———. *Capital.* Vol. 3. Trans. S. Moore and E. Aveling. New York: International Publishers, 1967.

Massumi, Brian. *A User's Guide to "Capitalism and Schizophrenia": Deviations from Deleuze and Guattari.* Cambridge: MIT Press, 1992.

Maxfield, Sylvia. *Governing Capital: International Finance and Mexican Politics.* Ithaca: Cornell University Press, 1990.

Mazier, Jacques, Maurice Baslé, and Jean-François Vidal. *When Economic Crises Endure.* Trans. Myriam Rosen. London: M. E. Sharpe, 1999. Originally published as *Quand les crises durent*, 2nd edition (1984; Paris: Economica, 1993).

McKibbin, Ross. "What Works Doesn't Work." *London Review of Books* 30 (11 September 2008), 20–22.

Mead, Margaret. *And Keep Your Powder Dry: An Anthropologist Looks at America.* New York: William Morrow, 1942.

Menn, Stephen. *Descartes and Augustine.* Cambridge: Cambridge University Press, 1998.

———. "The Intellectual Setting." *The Cambridge History of Seventeenth-Century Philosophy*, ed. Daniel Garber and Michael Ayers. Cambridge: Cambridge University Press, 1998.

Merleau-Ponty, Maurice. *The Visible and Invisible.* Ed. Claude Lefort. Trans. Alphonso Lingis. Evanston, Ill.: Northwestern University Press, 1968.

Merrill Lynch and Capgemini, Inc. *World Wealth Report 2005.* www.us.capgemini.com. Accessed on 7 January 2006.

Michaels, Walter Benn. "Political Science Fictions." *New Literary History* 31 (2000), 649–64.

Michie, Jonathan, ed. *The Handbook of Globalisation.* Cheltenham, England: Edward Elgar, 2003.

Michie, Jonathan, and John Grieve Smith, eds. *Global Instability: The Political Economy of World Economic Governance.* London: Routledge, 1999.

Michie, Jonathan, and John Grieve Smith, eds. *Managing the Global Economy.* Oxford: Oxford University Press, 1995.

Milanovic, Branko. *Worlds Apart: Measuring International and Global Inequality.* Princeton: Princeton University Press, 2005.

Milbank, John. "Materialism and Transcendence." Unpublished manuscript, 2001.

———. "Sublimity: The Modern Transcendent." *Transcendence: Philosophy, Literature, and Theology Approach the Beyond*, ed. Regina Schwartz. London: Routledge, 2004.

———. *The Word Made Strange: Theology, Language, Culture.* Oxford: Blackwell, 1997.

Milbank, John, Catherine Pickstock, and Graham Ward, eds. *Radical Orthodoxy: A New Theology.* London: Routledge, 1999.

Minnen, Cornelis, Jaap van der Bent, and Mel van Elteren, eds., *Beat Culture: The 1950's and Beyond.* Amsterdam: VU University Press, 1999.

Minns, Richard. *The Cold War in Welfare: Stock Markets versus Pensions.* London: Verso, 2001.

———. "The Social Ownership of Capital." *New Left Review* 219 (old series, 1996), 42–61.

Monbiot, George. "Who Runs Britain?" ZNet, www.zmag.org. Accessed on 23 December 2005.

Moschonas, Gerassimos. *In the Name of Social Democracy: The Great Transformation, 1945 to the Present.* Trans. Gregory Elliott. London: Verso, 2002.

Mouffe, Chantal. "Democratic Politics and the Question of Identity." *The Identity in Question*, ed. John Rajchman. London: Routledge, 1995.

———. "Feminism, Citizenship and Radical Democratic Politics." *Feminists Theorize the Political*, ed. Judith Butler and Joan W. Scott. London: Routledge, 1992.

Nairn, Tom. *After Britain: New Labour and the Return of Scotland.* Cambridge, England: Granta, 2000.

———. "At the G8." *London Review of Books* 27, no. 15 (2005), 19–20.

———. "Breakwaters of 2000: From Ethnic to Civic Nationalism." *New Left Review* 215 (old series, 1995), 91–109.

———. *Faces of Nationalism: Janus Revisited.* London: Verso, 1997.

———. *Pariah: Misfortunes of the British Kingdom.* London: Verso, 2002.

Negri, Antonio. *Insurgencies: Constituent Power and the Modern State.* Trans. Maurizia Boscagli. Minneapolis: University of Minnesota Press, 1999. Originally published as *Il potere constituente: Saggio sulle alternative del moderno* (Carnago: SugarCo, 1992).

———. "Italy's Postmodern Politics." *Le Monde Diplomatique*, English edition, August 2002.

———. "Notes on the Evolution of the Thought of Louis Althusser." Trans. Olga Vasile. *Postmodern Materialism and the Future of Marxist Theory: Essays in the Althusserian Tradition*, ed. Antonio Callari and David F. Ruccio. Hanover, N.H.: Wesleyan University Press, 1996.

———. *The Politics of Subversion: A Manifesto for the Twenty-First Century.* Trans. James Newell. Cambridge, England: Polity Press, 1989. Originally published in 1986.

———. *Revolution Retrieved: Selected Writings on Marx, Keynes, Capitalist Crisis and New Social Subjects (1967–83).* London: Red Notes, 1988.

———. *The Savage Anomaly: The Power of Spinoza's Metaphysics and Politics.* Trans. Michael Hardt. Minneapolis: University of Minnesota Press, 1988. Originally published as *L'anomalia selvaggia: Daggio su potere e Potenza in Baruch Spinoza* (Milan: Feltrinelli, 1981).

———. "The Specter's Smile." *Ghostly Demarcations: A Symposium on Jacques Derrida's "Specters of Marx,"* ed. Michael Sprinker London: Verso, 1999.

———. "Twenty Theses on Marx: Interpretation of the Class Situation Today." Trans. Michael Hardt. *Marxism beyond Marxism*, ed. Saree Makdisi, Cesare Casarino, and Rebecca E. Karl. London: Routledge, 1996.

Nissanke, Machiko. "Revenue Potential of the Currency Transaction Tax for Development Finance: A Critical Appraisal." *World Institute for Development Economics Research*, December 2003. www.currencytax.org. Accessed on 31 December 2005.

Noble, Greg, and John Ravenhill, eds., *The Asian Financial Crisis and the Architecture of Global Finance.* Cambridge: Cambridge University Press, 2000.

Norton, Anne. *Leo Strauss and the Politics of American Empire.* New Haven: Yale University Press, 2004.

Nozick, Robert. *Anarchy, State, and Utopia.* Oxford: Blackwell, 1974.

———. *The Examined Life: Philosophical Meditations.* New York: Simon and Schuster, 1989.

Obeyeskere, Gananath. "'British Cannibals': Contemplation of an Event in the Death and Resurrection of James Cook, Explorer." *Identities*, ed. Kwame Anthony Appiah and Henry Louis Gates Jr. Chicago: University of Chicago Press, 1995.

Obstfeld, Maurice, and Alan M. Taylor. *Global Capital Markets: Integration, Crisis, and Growth.* Cambridge: Cambridge University Press, 2004.

O'Connor, James. *Accumulation Crisis.* Oxford: Blackwell, 1984.

OECD (Organization for Economic Cooperation and Development). "Total Assets of Private Pension Funds within OECD Countries (2001)." www.oecd.org. Accessed on 7 January 2006.

Ong, Aihwa. *Spirits of Resistance and Capitalist Discipline: Factory Women in Malaysia.* Albany: State University of New York Press, 1987.

Orléan, André. *Le pouvoir de la finance.* Paris: Odile Jacob, 1999.

Pagden, Anthony, ed. *The Idea of Europe: From Antiquity to the European Union.* Cambridge: Cambridge University Press, 2002.

Palley, Thomas I. "International Finance and Global Deflation: There Is an Alternative." *Managing the Global Economy*, ed. Jonathan Michie and John Grieve Smith. Oxford: Oxford University Press, 1995.

Palma, Gabriel. "Dependency and Development." *Dependency Theory: A Critical Reassessment*, ed. Dudley Seers. London: Frances Pinter, 1981.

Palumbo-Liu, David. "Assumed Identities." *New Literary History* 31 (2000), 765–80.

———. "Multiculturalism Now: National Identity, and Difference before and after September 11th." *boundary 2* 29 (2002), 109–27.

Parenti, Michael. "Government by Giveaway." *ZNet Daily Commentary*. www.zmag.org. Accessed on 14 January 2006.

Patnaik, Prabhat. "The Illusionism of Finance." *International Development Economics Association*, 2005. www.networkideas.org. Accessed on 25 March 2005.

———. "A Saint and a Sage: Paul Marlor Sweezy (1910–2004)," International Development Economics Associates. www.ideaswebsite.org. Accessed on 11 January 2006.

Pauly, Louis W. *Who Elected the Bankers? Surveillance and Control in the World Economy*. Ithaca: Cornell University Press, 1999.

Peck, Jamie, and Adam Tickell. "Searching for a New Institutional Fix: The After-Fordist Crisis and the Global-Local Disorder." *Post-Fordism: A Reader*, ed. Ash Amin. Oxford: Blackwell, 1994.

Pempel, T. J., ed. *The Politics of the Asian Economic Crisis*. Ithaca: Cornell University Press, 1999.

Pettis, Michael. *The Volatility Machine: Emerging Economies and the Threat of Financial Collapse*. Oxford: Oxford University Press, 2001.

Phillips, Adam. "Malingering: Review of Peter Barham, *Forgotten Lunatics of the Great War*." *London Review of Books* 27, no. 5 (2005), 20–21.

Pieterse, Jan Nederveen. "The Development of Development Theory: Towards Global Criticism." *Review of International Political Economy* 3 (1996), 541–64.

———. "Dilemmas of Development Discourse: The Crisis of Developmentalism and the Comparative Method." *Development and Change* 22 (1991), 5–29.

Pincus, Jonathan R. "State Simplification and Institutional Building in a World Bank–Financed Development Project." *Reinventing the World Bank*, ed. Jonathan R. Pincus and Jeffrey A. Winters. Ithaca: Cornell University Press, 2002.

Pincus, Jonathan R., and Jeffrey A. Winters, eds. *Reinventing the World Bank*. Ithaca: Cornell University Press, 2002.

Pinkard, Terry. *German Philosophy 1760–1860: The Legacy of Idealism*. Cambridge: Cambridge University Press, 2002.

———. *Hegel: A Biography*. Cambridge: Cambridge University Press, 2000.

Piore, Michael, and Charles Sabel. *The Second Industrial Divide: Possibilities for Prosperity*. New York: Basic Books, 1984.

Pocock, J. G. A. *The Machiavellian Moment: Florentine Political Thought and the Atlantic Republican Tradition*. Princeton: Princeton University Press, 1975.

———. *Politics, Language, and Time: Essays on Political Thought and History*. Chicago: University of Chicago Press, 1960.

Poincaré, Henri. *Les Methodes Nouvelles de la Mécanique Celeste*. Paris: Gauthier-Villars, 1892.

Pollin, Robert. "Contemporary Economic Stagnation in World Historical Perspective." *New Left Review* 219 (old series, 1996), 109–18.

———. *Contours of Descent: U.S. Economic Fractures and the Landscape of Global Austerity*. London: Verso, 2003.

Polt, Richard. *Heidegger: An Introduction*. Ithaca: Cornell University Press, 1999.

Posner, Richard. *Breaking the Deadlock: The 2000 Election, the Constitution and the Courts*. Princeton: Princeton University Press, 2001.

Poulantzas, Nicos. *Classes in Contemporary Capitalism*. London: Verso, 1975.

Prasad, Eswar, Kenneth Rogoff, Shang-Jin Wei, and M. Ayhan Kose. *Effects of Financial Globalization on Developing Countries: Some Empirical Evidence*. International Monetary Fund Paper, March 17, 2003. www.imf.org. Accessed on 3 January 2005.

Pryor, Frederic L. *The Future of U.S. Capitalism*. Cambridge: Cambridge University Press, 2002.

Putnam, Robert D. *Bowling Alone: The Decline and Revival of American Community*. New York: Simon and Schuster, 2001.

Rabinow, Paul. "Artificiality and Enlightenment: From Sociobiology to Biosociality." *Incorporations: Zone 6*, ed. Jonathan Crary and Sanford Kwinter. New York: Zone Books, 1992.

Rajchman, John, ed. *The Subject in Question*. London: Routledge, 1995.

Ramonet, Ignacio. "A New Dawn." *Le monde diplomatique*, English edition, January 2000.

Rancière, Jacques. "The Cause of the Other." Trans. David Macey. *Parallax* 7 (1998), 25–34.

———. *Hatred of Democracy*. Trans. Steve Corcoran. London: Verso, 2007. Originally published as *La Haine de la démocratie* (Paris: La Fabrique, 2005).

———. "Politics, Identification, and Subjectivization." *The Subject in Question*, ed. John Rajchman. London: Routledge, 1995.

Rapaport, Herman. *Later Derrida: Reading the Recent Work*. London: Routledge, 2003.

Raskin, Jonah. *American Scream: Allen Ginsberg's "Howl" and the Making of the Beat Generation*. Berkeley: University of California Press, 2004.

Reno, William. *Corruption and State Politics in Sierra Leone*. Cambridge: Cambridge University Press, 1995.

Resnick, Stephen A., and Richard D. Wolff. *Class and History: Capitalism and Communism in the USSR*. London: Routledge, 2002.

Retort [Iain Boal, T. J. Clark, Joseph Matthews, and Michael Watts]. *Afflicted Powers: Capital and Spectacle in an Age of War*. London: Verso, 2005.

Richardson, William J. "Dasein and the Ground of Negativity: A Note on the Fourth Movement in the *Beiträge*-Symphony." *Heidegger Studies* 9 (1992), 35–52.

Riley, Patrick. *Leibniz' Universal Jurisprudence: Justice as the Charity of the Wise.* Cambridge: Harvard University Press, 1996.

Risse, Thomas, and Daniella Englemann-Martin. "Identity Politics and European Integration: The Case of Germany." *The Idea of Europe: From Antiquity to the European Union*, ed. Anthony Pagden. Cambridge: Cambridge University Press, 2002.

Rocha, Geisa Maria. "Neo-dependency in Brazil." *New Left Review*, no. 216 (second series, 2002), 5–33.

Rodríguez, Francisco, and Dani Rodrik. "Trade Policy and Economic Growth: A Skeptic's Guide to the Cross-National Evidence." *NBER Macroeconomics Annual 2000*, ed. Ben S. Bernanke and Kenneth Rogoff. Cambridge: MIT Press, 2001.

Rodrik, Dani. "Why Financial Markets Misbehave." *Real Economic Outlook, the Legacy of Globalization: Debt and Deflation*, ed. Ann Pettifor. London: Palgrave, 2003.

Rose, Nikolas. "Governing Cities, Governing Citizens." *Democracy, Citizenship and the Global City*, ed. Engin F. Isin. London: Routledge, 2000.

———. *Powers of Freedom: Reframing Political Thought.* Cambridge: Cambridge University Press, 1999.

Ross, Kristin. *May '68 and Its Afterlives.* Chicago: University of Chicago Press, 2002.

Ross, Marlon B. "Commentary: Pleasuring Identity, or the Delicious Politics of Belonging." *New Literary History* 31 (2000), 827–50.

Rothschild, Emma. *Economic Sentiments: Adam Smith, Condorcet, and the Enlightenment.* Cambridge: Harvard University Press, 2001.

Rowthorn, Bob, and Ha-Joon Chang. "Public Ownership and the Theory of the State." *The Political Economy of Privatization*, ed. Thomas Clarke and Christos Pitelis. London: Routledge, 1993.

Rudra, Nita. *Globalization and the Race to the Bottom in Developing Countries: Who Really Gets Hurt?* Cambridge: Cambridge University Press, 2008.

Runciman, David. "The Garden, the Park and the Meadow." *London Review of Books* 24, no. 11 (2002), 7–11.

———. *Political Hypocrisy: The Mask of Power, from Hobbes to Orwell and Beyond.* Princeton: Princeton University Press, 2008.

———. *The Politics of Good Intentions: History, Fear and Hypocrisy in the New World Order.* Princeton: Princeton University Press, 2006.

Runciman, W. G. "The 'Triumph' of Capitalism as a Topic in the Theory of Social Selection." *New Left Review* 210 (first series, 1995), 33–47.

Saad-Filho, Alfredo, and Deborah Johnston, eds. *Neoliberalism: A Critical Reader.* London: Pluto Press, 2005.

Santos, Bonaventura de Sousa. *Democratizing Democracy: Beyond the Liberal Democratic Canon.* London: Verso, 2005.

Sassen, Saskia. *The Global City: New York, London, Tokyo.* Princeton: Princeton University Press, 1991.

———. *The Mobility of Capital and Labor: A Study in International Investment and Labor Flow*. Cambridge: Cambridge University Press, 1988.

Sassoon, Donald. "Fin-de-Siècle Socialism: The United, Modest Left." *New Left Review* 227 (first series, 1998), 88–96.

Sayer, Andrew, and Richard Walker. *The New Social Economy: Reworking the Division of Labor*. Oxford: Blackwell, 1992.

———. *One Hundred Years of Socialism: The West European Left in the Twentieth Century*. New York: New Press, 1996.

Schlosberg, Justin. "The Day the Music Failed: A Reflection on 6 Months after the Live 8 Concerts, the Broken Promises and Bob's Unusual Silence." Common Dreams Newscenter. www.commondreams.org. Accessed on 5 January 2006.

Scott, James C. *Weapons of the Weak: Everyday Forms of Peasant Resistance*. New Haven: Yale University Press, 1985.

Sen, Sunanda. "On Financial Fragility and Its Global Implications." *Financial Fragility, Debt and Economic Reforms*, ed. Sunanda Sen. New York: St. Martin's Press, 1996.

Shaikh, Anwar. "The Economic Mythology of Neoliberalism." *Neoliberalism: A Critical Reader*, ed. Alfredo Saad-Filho and Deborah Johnston. London: Pluto Press, 2005.

———. "Organic Composition of Capital." *The New Palgrave Marxian Economics*, ed. John Eatwell, Murray Milgate, and Peter Newman. New York: Norton, 1990.

Shannon, Christopher. *A World Made Safe for Differences: Cold War Intellectuals and the Politics of Identity*. Lanham, Md.: Rowman and Littlefield, 2000.

Shapin, Steven, and Simon Schaffer. *Leviathan and the Air-Pump: Hobbes, Boyle, and the Experimental Life*. Princeton: Princeton University Press, 1985.

Shaw, Martin. *The New Western Way of War: Risk-Transfer War and Its Crisis in Iraq*. Oxford: Polity Press, 2005.

Siegel, Jerrold. *The Idea of the Self: Thought and Experience in Western Europe Since the Seventeenth Century*. Cambridge: Cambridge University Press, 2005.

Sinfield, Alan. *Literature, Politics, and Culture in Postwar Britain*. Berkeley: University of California Press, 1989.

Singer, P. W. *Corporate Warriors: The Rise of the Privatized Military Industry*. Ithaca: Cornell University Press, 2003.

Singh, Ajit. "The Actual Crisis of the 1980s: An Alternative Policy Perspective for the Future." *New Directions in Development Economics*, ed. Amitava Krishna Dutt and Kenneth P. Jameson. Aldershot, England: Edward Elgar, 1992.

———. *Global Economic Trends and Social Development*. United Nations Research Institute for Social Development Research Paper. Geneva, June 2000. www.unrisd.org. Accessed on 4 January, 2006.

———. "Openness and the Market Friendly Approach to Development: Learning the Right Lessons from Development Experience." *World Development* 22 (1994), 1811–23.

———. "Portfolio Equity Flows and Stock Markets in Financial Liberalization." *Development* 40 (1997), 22–29.

Skinner, Quentin. *Liberty before Liberalism*. Cambridge: Cambridge University Press, 1998.

Smith, Anthony D. *Chosen Peoples: Sacred Sources of National Identity*. Oxford: Oxford University Press, 2003.

———. *The Ethnic Origins of Nations*. Oxford: Blackwell, 1986.

Smith, Dai. *Raymond Williams: A Warrior's Tale*. London: Parthian, 2008.

Smith, Daniel W. "Badiou and Deleuze on the Ontology of Mathematics." *Think Again: Alain Badiou and the Future of Philosophy*, ed. Peter Hallward. London: Continuum, 2004.

Spinoza, Benedict de. *Ethics*. Ed. and trans. G. H. R Parkinson. Oxford: Oxford University Press, 2000.

Standing, Guy. *Beyond the New Paternalism: Basic Security as Equality*. London: Verso, 2002.

Stiglitz, Joseph E., and Shahid Yusuf, eds., *Rethinking the East Asian Miracle*. Oxford: Oxford University Press, 2001.

Surin, Kenneth. "'The Continued Relevance of Marxism' as a Question: Some Questions." *Polygraph* 6/7 (1993), 39–71.

———. "On Producing the Concept of a Global Culture." *Nations, Cultures, and Identities*, ed. V. Y Mudimbe. Durham, N.C.: Duke University Press, 1997.

———. "Reinventing a Physiology of Collective Liberation: Going 'Beyond Marx' in the Marxism(s) of Negri, Guattari, and Deleuze." *Rethinking Marxism* 7 (1994), 9–27.

Sweezy, Paul M. *The Theory of Capitalist Development: Principles of Marxian Political Economy*. New York: Monthly Review Press, 1956.

Taussig, Michael. *The Devil and Commodity Fetishism in South America*. Chapel Hill: University of North Carolina Press, 1980.

———. *Shamanism, Colonialism and the Wild Man: A Study in Terror and Healing*. Chicago: University of Chicago Press, 1987.

Taylor, Lance. "Economic Openness: Problems to the Century's End." *Economic Liberalization: No Panacea (The Experiences of Latin America and Asia)*, ed. Tariq Banuri. Oxford: Oxford University Press, 1991.

———. "Editorial: The Revival of the Liberal Creed—The IMF and the World Bank in a Globalized Economy." *World Development* 25 (1997), 145–52.

———. "External Liberalization, Economic Performance, and Distribution in Latin America and Elsewhere." *Inequality, Growth, and Poverty in an Era of Liberalization and Globalization*, ed. Giovanni Andrea Cornia. Oxford: Oxford University Press, 2004.

———. "The Rocky Road to Reform: Trade, Industrial, Financial and Agricultural Strategies." *State, Market and Civil Organizations: New Theories, New Practices and Their Implications for Rural Development*, ed. Alain de Janvry, Samir Radwan, Elisabeth Sadoulet, and Erik Thorbecke. Basingstoke, England: Macmillan, 1995.

Therborn, Göran, ed. *Inequalities of the World: New Theoretical Frameworks, Multiple Empirical Approaches.* London: Verso, 2006.

———. "Into the 21st Century: The Parameters of Global Politics." *New Left Review* 10 (2001), 87–110.

Théret, Bruno. "Theoretical Problems in International Comparisons: Toward a Reciprocal Improvement of Societal Approach and Régulation Theory by Methodic Structuralism." *Association Recherche et Régulation.* 2000. http://web .upmfgrenoble.fr. Accessed on 22 January 2006.

Thom, Martin. *Republics, Nations, and Tribes.* London: Verso, 1995.

Thompson, E. P. *The Making of the English Working Class.* Harmondsworth: Penguin Books, 1991.

Thompson, Michael J. *The Politics of Inequality: A Political History of the Idea of Economic Inequality in America.* New York: Columbia University Press, 2007.

Tobin, James. "Prologue." *The Tobin Tax: Coping with Financial Volatility*, ed. Mahbub ul Haq, Inge Kaul, and Isabelle Grunberg. Oxford: Oxford University Press, 1996.

Toye, John. *Dilemmas of Development: Reflections of the Counter-Revolution in Development Economics.* 2nd edition. Oxford: Blackwell, 1993.

Turner, Victor. *Dramas, Fields and Metaphors.* Ithaca: Cornell University Press, 1974.

United Nations. *The Inequality Predicament: Report on the World Social Situation 2005.* New York: United Nations Department of Social and Economic Affairs, 2005.

———. *World Economic Situation and Prospects 2004.* www.un.org. Accessed on 2 January 2006.

———. *World Economic Situation and Prospects 2006.* www.un.org. Accessed on 4 February 2006.

———. *World Economic Situation and Prospects 2008*, www.un.org.esa. Accessed on 21 May 2008.

United Nations Conference on Trade and Development. *2004, Development and Globalization: Facts and Figures.* Geneva: UNCTAD, 2004.

———. *World Investment Directory 2004.* June 2004. www.unctadxi.org. Accessed on 9 January 2006.

United Nations Development Programme. *Human Development Report 1997.* Oxford: Oxford University Press, 1997.

———. *Human Development Report 2005.* Oxford: Oxford University Press, published for UNDP, 2005.

———. *Human Development Report 2007/2008.* London: Palgrave Macmillan, published for UNDP, 2007.

United Nations High-Level Panel on Financing for Development. *Report.* United Nations Department of Public Information, DPI/2171/B/Rev.2. June 2001. www.un.org. Accessed on 3 January 2006.

United Nations Industrial Development Organization. *Industrial Development Report 2004: Industrialization, Environment, and the Millennium Development Goals in Sub-Saharan Africa: The New Frontier in the Fight against Poverty.* Vienna: UNIDO, 2004.

U.S. Census Bureau. "Voter Turnout in 2006." News release, July 2008. www.census.gov. Accessed August 2008.

Veblen, Thorstein. *Engineers and the Price System.* New Brunswick, N.J.: Transaction Books, 1983. Originally published 1921.

Vogel, Steven K. *Freer Markets, More Rules: Regulatory Reform in Advanced Industrial Countries.* Ithaca: Cornell University Press, 1996.

Vries, Hent de. "Derrida and Ethics: Hospitable Thought." *Jacques Derrida and the Humanities: A Critical Reader*, ed. Tom Cohen. Cambridge: Cambridge University Press, 2001.

Wade, Robert. "The Asian Crisis: The High Debt Model versus the Wall Street–Treasury–IMF Complex." *New Left Review*, no. 228 (first series, 1998), 3–23.

———. "The Asian Debt-and-Development Crisis of 1997–8: Causes and Consequences." *World Development* 26 (1998), 1535–53.

———. "Financial Regime Change?" *New Left Review* 53 (2008), 5–21.

———. "Japan, the World Bank, and the Art of Paradigm Maintenance: *The East Asian Miracle* in Political Perspective."

Wade, Robert, and Frank Veneroso. "The Gathering World Slump and the Battle over Capital Controls." *New Left Review*, no. 231 (first series, 1998), 13–42.

Ward, Graham. "Transcendence and Representation." *Transcendence: Philosophy, Literature, and Theology Approach the Beyond*, ed. Regina Schwartz. London: Routledge, 2004.

Webb, Michael C. *The Political Economy of Policy Coordination: International Adjustment Since 1945.* Ithaca: Cornell University Press, 1995.

Weeks, John. "The Essence and Appearance of Globalization: The Rise of Financial Capital." *Globalization and the Dilemmas of the State in the South*, ed. Francis Adams, Satya Dev Gupta, and Kidane Mengisteab. London: Macmillan, 1999.

Weisbrot, Mark, Dean Baker, and David Rosnik. "The Scorecard on Development: 25 Years of Diminished Progress." *Flat World, Big Gaps: Economic Liberalization, Globalization, Poverty and Inequality*, ed. Jomo K. S., with Jacques Baudot. London: Zed Books, 2007.

Weiss, Linda. *The Myth of the Powerless State.* Ithaca: Cornell University Press. 1998.

———, ed. *States in the Global Economy: Bringing Domestic Institutions Back In.* Cambridge: Cambridge University Press, 2003.

Wilde, Oscar. *The Soul of Man under Socialism. Complete Works of Oscar Wilde.* Ed. J. B. Foreman. New edition. London: Collins, 1966.

Williams, Bernard. *Truth and Truthfulness: An Essay in Genealogy.* Princeton: Princeton University Press, 2002.

———. "Truth in Ethics." *Ratio* 8 (1995), 227–42.

Williams, James. *Gilles Deleuze's "Difference and Repetition": A Critical Introduction and Guide*. Edinburgh: Edinburgh University Press, 2003.

Williams, Raymond. "Culture Is Ordinary." *Resources of Hope*. London: Verso, 1989.

———. *The Long Revolution*. New York: Columbia University Press, 1961.

Wolff, Richard. "World Bank/Class Blindness." *World Bank Literature*, ed. Amitava Kumar. Minneapolis: University of Minnesota Press, 2003.

Woo, Jung-en [Meredith Woo-Cumings]. *Race to the Swift: State and Finance in Korean Industrialization*. New York: Columbia University Press, 1991.

Woo-Cumings, Meredith, ed. *The Developmental State*. Ithaca: Cornell University Press, 1999.

Wood, David. *Thinking after Heidegger*. Cambridge, England: Polity Press, 2002.

Wood, David, and Robert Bernasconi, eds. *Derrida and Différance*. Evanston, Ill.: Northwestern University Press, 1988.

Wood, Elisabeth Jean. *Forging Democracy from Below: Insurgent Transitions in South Africa and El Salvador*. Cambridge: Cambridge University Press, 2000.

Woods, Ngaire, ed. *The Political Economy of Globalization*. London: Palgrave Macmillan, 2000.

World Bank. *The East Asian Miracle: Economic Growth and Public Policy*.

———. *Global Development Finance 2005*. http://siteresources.worldbank.org. Accessed on 9 January 2006.

———. *World Debt Tables: External Finance for Developing Countries*. Washington: World Bank, 1996.

———. *World Development Indicators 2005*. Washington: World Bank, 2005.

———. *World Development Report: The Challenge of Development*. Oxford: Oxford University Press, 1991.

———. *World Development Report 1996*. Oxford: Oxford University Press, 1996.

———. *World Development Report 1997*. Oxford: Oxford University Press, 1997.

———. *World Development Report 2006*. Oxford: Oxford University Press, 2006.

Young, Iris Marion. *Justice and the Politics of Difference*. Princeton: Princeton University Press, 1990.

Žižek, Slavoj. "Against Human Rights." *New Left Review* 34 (new series, 2005), 115–31.

———. "Enjoy Your Nation as Yourself." *Tarrying with the Negative: Kant, Hegel, and the Critique of Ideology*. Durham: Duke University Press, 1993.

———. *For They Know Not What They Do: Enjoyment as a Political Factor*. London: Verso, 1991.

———. *The Fragile Absolute—Or Why Is the Christian Legacy Worth Fighting For?* London: Verso, 2000.

———. "Multiculturalism, or the Cultural Logic of Multinational Capitalism." *New Left Review* 225 (first series, 1997), 28–51.

———. *On Belief*. London: Routledge, 2001.

———. *The Plague of Fantasies*. London: Verso, 1997.

———. *The Puppet and the Dwarf: The Perverse Core of Christianity*. Cambridge: MIT Press, 2003.

———, ed. *Revolution at the Gates: Selected Writings of Lenin from 1917*. London: Verso, 2002.

———. *The Ticklish Subject: The Absent Centre of Political Ontology*. London: Verso, 1999.

———. "The Undergrowth of Enjoyment: How Popular Culture Can Serve as an Introduction to Lacan." *The Žižek Reader*. Ed. Elizabeth Wright and Edmond Wright. Oxford: Blackwell, 1999.

Bernasconi, Robert, 352 n. 48

Bhabha, Homi, 157, 158, 340 n. 9

Blackburn, Robin, 369 n. 12

Blair, Tony, 3–5, 9, 10, 31, 199, 243, 270, 299 n. 6, 325 n. 13, 343 nn. 24–25

Blanchot, Maurice, 346 n. 13, 365 n. 9

Bobbitt, Philip, 151–56, 342 nn. 18–20

Bonaparte, Napoleon, 224

Bosteels, Bruno, 354 n. 13, 355 n. 21

Bourdieu, Pierre, 302 n. 27, 350 n. 31

Boyer, Robert, 76, 88, 90, 321 n. 50, 321 n. 51, 321 n. 53, 321 n. 54

Braudel, Fernand, 344 n. 30

Brenner, Robert, 133–34, 313 n. 1, 337 nn. 16–17

Brown, Gordon, 9

Brown, Wendy, 150, 341 n. 15, 343 n. 21

Buffett, Warren, 332 n. 46

Burma, 225

Bush, George W., 3, 5, 10, 31, 159, 193, 194, 197, 198, 199, 212, 214–16, 225, 243, 259, 269–72, 276, 282–83, 289, 292, 307 n. 5, 321 n. 54, 325 n. 13, 366 n. 12, 367 n. 25

Cage, John, 255, 362 n. 17

Capital: controls on movement; 86, 107, 286, 320 n. 45, 328 n. 25; "fictitious," 85, 91, 105, 320 n. 44; limits of, 149–50; as meta-accord of accords, 243–44, 252–53; mobility of, 85, 88–90, 105–8, 320 n. 44, 332 n. 46; postwar compromise with labor, 8–9, 72, 75, 141–42, 295; social, 302 n. 27, 335 n. 1

Capitalism: developmentalist conception of, 36, 69–70; industrial, 8, 116–23; mercantile, 6–8; modernization and, 30, 69–70; modes of production of, 36, 53; new mutations of, 65, 116–23, 150, 202, 276–78; postwar "Golden Age" of, 2–3, 9, 13,

65–66, 69–70, 95, 108, 122, 141, 313 n. 1; supersession of, 12, 16, 35, 54, 135, 276, 310 n. 21, 336 n. 13 (see also Revolution); system of regulation, 36–40, 53, 141. See also Globalization

Caygill, Howard, 359 n. 12

Chang, Ha-Joon, 86, 320 n. 46, 336 n. 13

China, 115, 330 n. 31, 331 n. 40

Christianity, 7, 62; and theology, 226–40

Clinton, William Jefferson, 3–5, 10, 299 n. 6

Cohen, Benjamin J., 328 n. 25

Cohen, Paul, 213, 219

Colley, Linda, 340 n. 10

Comaroff, Jean, 58, 312 n. 31

Comaroff, John, 58, 312 n. 31

Communism: Soviet, 1, 14–16, 29, 72; still to come, 275 (see also Revolution)

Conceptual practice, 188, 191, 193–96, 352 n. 50

Critchley, Simon, 186, 197, 348 n. 22, 352 n. 47, 353 n. 1

Cuba, 128

Cunningham, Conor, 229, 359 n. 6

Dasgupta, Partha, 275, 367 n. 17

Dastur, Françoise, 350 n. 31

Davidson, Donald, 358 n. 42

Debord, Guy, 4

DeLanda, Manuel, 367 n. 18

Deleuze, Gilles, 21, 42, 45, 61–62, 192, 195, 211, 227, 229, 231, 235–40, 241–61, 303 n. 2, 305 n. 17, 308 n. 11, 310 n. 25, 312 n. 29, 312 n. 36, 312 n. 37, 312 n. 39, 312 n. 40, 341 n. 14, 352 n. 49, 357 n. 31, 357 n. 36, 359 n. 13, 360 n. 15, 360 nn. 17–20, 361 n. 1, 361 nn. 5–10, 362 nn. 11–14, 363 nn. 18–21, 365 n. 5, 365 nn. 7–9, 367 n. 18, 367 n. 20

Foucault, Michel (*continued*)
  on governmentality, 42, 345 n. 35,
    363 n. 19, 365 n. 6, 365 n. 8, 365 n. 9,
    367 n. 15, 367 n. 19
French Revolution, 223–24
Freud, Sigmund, 26, 30, 61, 245
Friedman, Thomas L., 326 n. 14
Funkenstein, Amos, 366 n. 13

Galbraith, John Kenneth, 48–49, 309
  n. 14
Gaon, Stella, 353 n. 59
Germain, Randall, 89, 321 nn. 55–56,
  322 n. 61, 334 n. 51
Gilroy, Paul, 150, 339 n. 4, 341 n. 15
Globalization, 27–28, 65–68, 71, 73–93,
  96, 102–3, 118, 141, 151, 286, 292, 313
  n. 2, 313 n. 3, 314 n. 6, 319 n. 38, 328
  n. 25, 336 n. 10, 368 n. 7
Glyn, Andrew, 313 n. 3
Goldman, Lucien, 351 n. 35
Gowan, Peter, 369 n. 10
Greenspan, Alan, 94, 321 n. 54
Griffith-Jones, Stephany, 103, 326 nn.
  14–15
Guantánamo, 215–16
Guattari, Félix, 42, 195, 231, 241–61,
  341 n. 14, 353 n. 61, 361 n. 1, 361 nn.
  7–10, 362 n. 11, 362 n. 12, 362 n. 14,
  363 n. 19, 363 n. 21, 365 n. 5, 367
  n. 18, 367 n. 20
Gummer, John Selwyn, 4

Haakonssen, Knud, 300 n. 13
Haar, Michel, 347 n. 20
Hall, Stuart, 157
Hallward, Peter, 214–19, 354 n. 12, 356
  n. 24, 356 n. 27, 357 nn. 31–36, 358
  n. 41
Hardt, Michael, 29, 42, 203, 354 n. 13,
  361 n. 1
Harmes, Adam, 321 n. 55, 334 n. 55,
  334 n. 59

Harriss, John, 335 n. 1
Harvey, David, 333 n. 48
Hegel, G. W. F., 21–22, 26, 62, 117,
  157–61, 168, 172, 202, 207, 250, 256,
  304 n. 12, 332 n. 46
Heidegger, Martin, 23, 26, 56, 166, 169,
  171–79, 185–86, 188, 190, 345 n. 1,
  346 n. 9, 346 n. 10, 346 n. 12, 346
  n. 13, 347 nn. 14–17, 347 nn. 20–21,
  348 n. 22, 349 n. 24, 349 n. 27, 349
  n. 30, 350 n. 31
Helleiner, Eric, 322 n. 59, 333 n. 49
Henwood, Douglas, 318 n. 34, 319
  n. 39, 334 n. 55
Herzfeld, Michael, 157, 344 nn. 29–31
Heterotopia, 155, 265–84
Hirsch, Joachim, 71, 74–76, 315 n. 10,
  316 n. 16, 317 n. 20, 317 n. 23, 322
  n. 62
Hirst, Paul, 313 n. 3
Hobbes, Thomas, 6, 21, 172, 242, 256
Hobson, John M., 336 n. 13
Hough, Jerry, 369 n. 8
Hume, David, 7, 21, 231, 301 n. 14
Huntington, Samuel T., 145, 147, 340
  n. 8

Identity: American, 143–45; British,
  146; politics of, 147–64, 201, 242
Immanence, 226–40
India, 115, 354 n. 12
Indonesia, 122
Institute of International Finance
  (IIF), 79, 104, 326 nn. 16–17
International Financial Services (London), 318 n. 29
International Monetary Fund (IMF),
  70, 103, 107–8, 114, 123, 127, 128,
  129, 136, 278, 281, 285, 289, 323 n. 4,
  327 n. 21, 330 n. 32, 335 n. 5, 368 n. 7;
  dismantling of, 293, 336 n. 9
International trade, 66–69, 76–94, 114,
  314 n. 6

Inwood, Michael, 344 n. 32
Israel, Jonathan I., 300 n. 13, 304 n. 14

James, William, 304 n. 6
Jameson, Fredric, 42–43
Japan, 109, 116, 120, 329 n. 28, 329
  n. 30; share of global foreign ex-
  change market, 78
Jefferson, Thomas, 304 n. 14
Jessop, Bob, 38–39, 70–76, 307 n. 4,
  n. 6, n. 7, 308 n. 8, 315 nn. 10–11, 316
  nn. 12–15, 317 nn. 17–28, 322 n. 62,
  364 nn. 25–26
Jones, Gareth Stedman, 338 n. 23
Joy Division, 303 n. 28

Kant, Immanuel, 7, 21–27, 61, 202,
  233–37, 301 n. 16, 304 nn. 6–13, 305
  n. 15, 343 n. 24, 361 n. 9
Kantorowicz, Ernst, 23, 303 n. 4
Kastoryano, Riva, 344 n. 27
Keynesianism, 3, 71, 72–73, 75, 108,
  135, 142–43, 146, 296, 334 n. 59
Khan, Mohsin S., 105, 327 n. 21
Kierkegaard, Søren, 174, 195, 349
  n. 24, n. 30
Klein, Naomi, 30
Kindleberger, Charles P., 313 n. 1
Kozul-Wright, Richard, 114–15, 331
  nn. 39–40

Lacan, Jacques, 47, 166, 267, 356 n. 25,
  365 n. 6
Laclau, Ernesto, 153, 331 n. 41, 339 n. 4,
  342 n. 20, 353 n. 59, 357 n. 3
Lautréamont (Isidore Lucien
  Ducasse), 254–55
Leibniz, G. W., 21, 23, 217–19, 225,
  243, 254, 269, 359 n. 7
Lenin, Vladimir Illich, 41, 56, 197
Lévinas, Emmanuel, 167, 173, 187, 346
  n. 13, 348 n. 22
Leys, Colin, 368 n. 7

Liberation movements: new social
  movements, 143, 155; Third World,
  143, 339 n. 3
Life-world, 51–53, 57, 60, 141–42, 147,
  163, 193, 194–96
Lincoln, Abraham, 193
Lipietz, Alain, 315 n. 9, 316 n. 12
Locke, John, 6, 21–23, 303 n. 3, 305
  n. 15
Luxemburg, Rosa, 46, 87, 91, 320 nn.
  47–49, 337 n. 16

Macmillan, Harold, 142
Macpherson, C. B., 157, 300 n. 13, 344
  n. 29
Major, John, 135, 300 n. 10
Malaysia, 122, 252–53, 281, 327 n. 24,
  329 n. 30, 367 n. 24
Mandel, Ernest, 63, 312 n. 41
Mandela, Nelson, 55–56, 188
Mann, Michael, 74, 163–64, 286, 289,
  290, 307–8 n. 7, 313 n. 3, 320 n. 45,
  334 n. 59, 335 n. 2, 339 n. 1, 342 n. 20,
  345 nn. 37–39, 368 n. 1, 368 n. 5, 368
  n. 6, 369 n. 9, 369 n. 11
Mann, Thomas, 344 n. 26
Market: fundamentalism and dogma
  of, 9, 31–32, 289, 301 n. 22, 329
  n. 29; "openness," 84–87, 89, 108,
  114–15, 126, 129–32, 293, 329 nn.
  29–30, 331 n. 40
Marx, Karl, 26, 30, 41–43, 61, 63, 85,
  87, 105, 116–23, 132, 133, 249, 257,
  307 n. 7, 308 n. 9, 320 n. 44, 320
  n. 46, 332 n. 47, 335 n. 4, 337 n. 16,
  351 n. 35
Massumi, Brian, 240, 360 n. 18, 360
  n. 22
Materialism: historical, 63–64; political, 41–43, 50, 55–60, 63–64
Mazier, Jacques, 3, 299 n. 4
McKibbin, Ross, 10–11, 302 n. 23, 302
  n. 25

Rawls, John, 242
Reagan, Ronald, 1–4, 10, 70, 72, 108, 142–43, 160, 235, 258, 299 n. 6
Reason, 22–27, 61, 175, 233, 235–37, 250, 311 n. 28
Regulation School (Ecole Régulation), 76, 77, 87, 313 n. 1, 315 n. 10, 316 n. 13, 316 n. 16
Revolution, 147, 189, 191, 200, 203, 225, 234, 237, 260, 275, 325 n. 13; definition of, 16–17, 306 n. 1; French, 223–24; as opposed to insurrection or rebellion, 16
Richardson, William J., 347 n. 14
Roach, Stephen, 84–85, 319 n. 42
Robinson, Joan, 47, 66
Rodrik, Dani, 86, 278–79, 286, 334 n. 58, 367 nn. 21–22, 368 n. 1
Romanticism, 8, 25
Rousseau, Jean-Jacques, 7, 172, 202, 242, 256
Rudra, Nita, 336 n. 10
Runciman, David, 342 n. 18, 343 nn. 22–23
Runciman, W. G., 39, 307 n. 3, 307 n. 7

Said, Edward, 157
Sarkozy, Nicolas, 3–5
Sartre, Jean-Paul, 166, 224, 346 n. 13
Schizoanalysis, 241–61
Schmitt, Carl, 56, 186, 202
Schumpeter, Joseph, 71, 72–73, 75–76
Scott, James C., 52
Sierra Leone, 335 n. 6
Singh, Ajit, 81, 104, 319 n. 36, 320 n. 43, 325 n. 11, 326 n. 19, 328 n. 27, 329 n. 30
Singularity, 56, 169, 170, 172–76, 179–87, 189–93, 197, 201, 231, 236, 256–58, 268–69, 312 n. 29, 353 n. 57, 363 n. 20, 365 nn. 10–11
Smith, Adam, 134

Smith, Anthony D., 160
Smith, Daniel W., 357 n. 36
Social democracy, 1–6, 14, 143, 301 n. 21
Society of control, 28, 242–45
South Korea, 107
Sovereignty: divine, 22–23, 27; political, 6–8, 11, 24, 27–31, 34, 65, 74, 152, 172, 202, 236, 256, 258–61, 291, 343 n. 24, 361 n. 7
Spectacle, society of, 9
Spinoza, Baruch, 6, 42, 45, 54, 63, 192, 211, 227, 229, 230, 236–38, 284, 304 n. 14, 310 nn. 22–23, 312 n. 34, 353 n. 56
Spivak, Gayatri Chakravorty, 157, 348 n. 23
Staël, Anne-Louise-Germaine de (Madame de), 8, 301 n. 19
Stalin, Joseph, 41
State: capacities, functions, and projects, 69–76, 89, 163, 172, 201–2, 206, 225, 236, 241–61, 292, 315 n. 9, 322 n. 59, 323 n. 1, 354 n. 14, 362 n. 11; capitalist, 1–8, 65–76, 205–6, 240; globalization and, 69–76, 89, 313 n. 3, 321 n. 58, 322 n. 59; "hollowing-out" of, 70–77, 243; ideological apparatuses of, 2–6, 71–72, 75, 142, 152; nation-state, 8–9, 69, 71, 74, 151–52, 292, 343 n. 24, 344 n. 29; workfare-state, 71–72, 75
Stiglitz, Joseph, 335 n. 1, 336 n. 13
Struggle: class-based, 13, 141–44, 150, 163–64, 279–80, 283; economic and social, 17, 34–35, 40, 53, 240, 242, 261, 294, 296; gender-focused, 39, 147, 277; race-focused, 147, 277
Subject: Badiou on the, 200–201; citizen, 6–9, 25–34, 40, 65, 304 n. 10, 305 n. 17, 361 n. 9; consumer, 31; Derrida on the, 165–94; political

KENNETH SURIN is Chair of the Program in Literature and a professor of religion and critical theory at Duke University.

Parts of this book appeared previously in the following:

"'The Continued Relevance of Marxism' as a Question: Some Questions," *Polygraph*, no. 6/7 (1993), 39–71; "'Reinventing a Physiology of Collective Liberation': Going 'Beyond Marx' in the Marxism(s) of Negri, Guattari, and Deleuze," *Rethinking MARXISM* 7 (1994), 9–27; "On Producing the Concept of a Global Culture," *Nations, Cultures, and Identities*, ed. V. Y. Mudimbe (Durham, N.C.: Duke University Press, 1997), 199–219; "The Epochality of Deleuzean Thought," *Theory, Culture, and Society* 14 (1997), 9–21; "Liberation," *Critical Terms for Religious Study*, ed. Mark C. Taylor (Chicago: University of Chicago Press, 1998), 173–85; "Standing Schumpeter on His Head: Robert Brenner's *Economics of Global Turbulence*," *Comparative Studies of South Asia, Africa and the Middle East* 19 (1999), 53–60; "Afterthoughts on Diaspora," *South Atlantic Quarterly* 98 (1999), 275–325; "'A Question of an Axiomatics of Desires': The Deleuzean Imagination of Geoliterature," *Deleuze and Literature*, ed. Ian Buchanan and John Marks (Edinburgh: Edinburgh University Press, 2000), 167–93; "'*Délire* Is World-historical': Political Knowledge in *Capitalism and Schizophrenia*," *Polygraph* 14 (2001), 129–41; "'Now Everything Must Be Reinvented': Negri and Revolution," *The Philosophy of Antonio Negri*, ed. Timothy Murphy and Mustapha Abdul-Karim (London: Pluto Press, 2005), 205–42; "World Ordering," *South Atlantic Quarterly* 104 (2005), 185–97; "Control Societies and the Managed Citizen," *Junctures* 8 (2007), 11–25; "1000 Political Subjects," *Deleuze and the Social World*, ed. Adrian Parr and Ian Buchanan (Edinburgh: Edinburgh University Press, 2006), 57–78; "Rewriting the Ontological Script of Liberation: On the Question of Finding a New Kind of Political Subject," *Ontology in Practice*, ed. John Milbank, Slavoj Žižek, and Creston Davis (Durham, N.C.: Duke University Press, 2005), 240–66; "Hostage to an Unaccountable Planetary Executive: The Flawed 'Washington Consensus' and Two *World Bank Reports*," *World Bank Literature*, ed. Amitava Kumar (Minneapolis: University of Minnesota Press, 2002), 238–57.

Library of Congress Cataloging-in-Publication Data
Surin, Kenneth
Freedom not yet : liberation and the next world order / Kenneth Surin.
p. cm. — (New slant)
Includes bibliographical references and index.
ISBN 978-0-8223-4617-3 (cloth : alk. paper)
ISBN 978-0-8223-4631-9 (pbk. : alk. paper)
1. Philosophy, Marxist. 2. Marxian economics. 3. Communism and society.
4. Socialism and society. I. Title. II. Series: New slant.
B809.8.S865 2009
335.4—dc22   2009030107